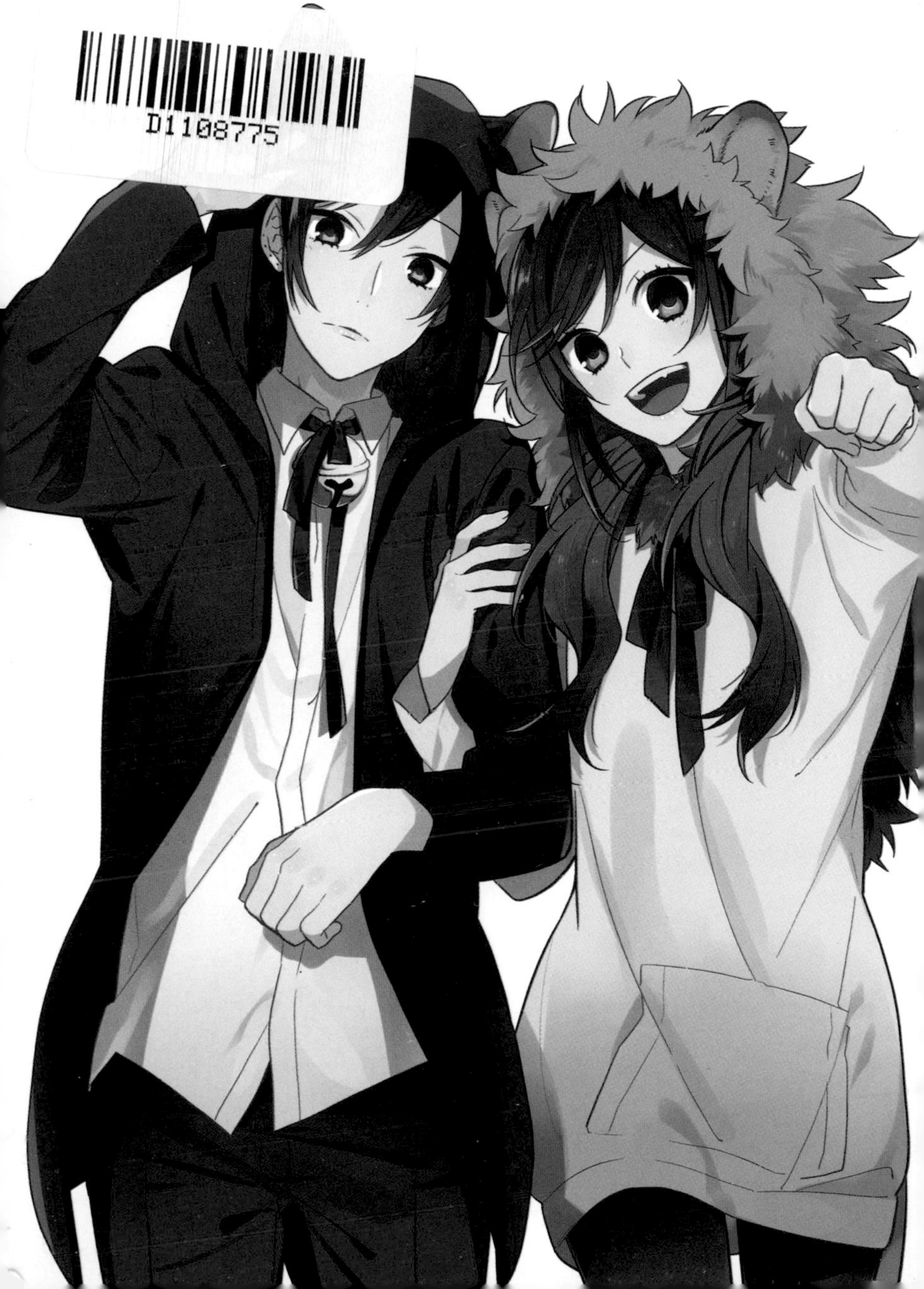

HORIMIYA

HORI-SAN AND MIYAMURA-KUN

HORIMIYA

HERO × DAISUKE HAGIWARA

06

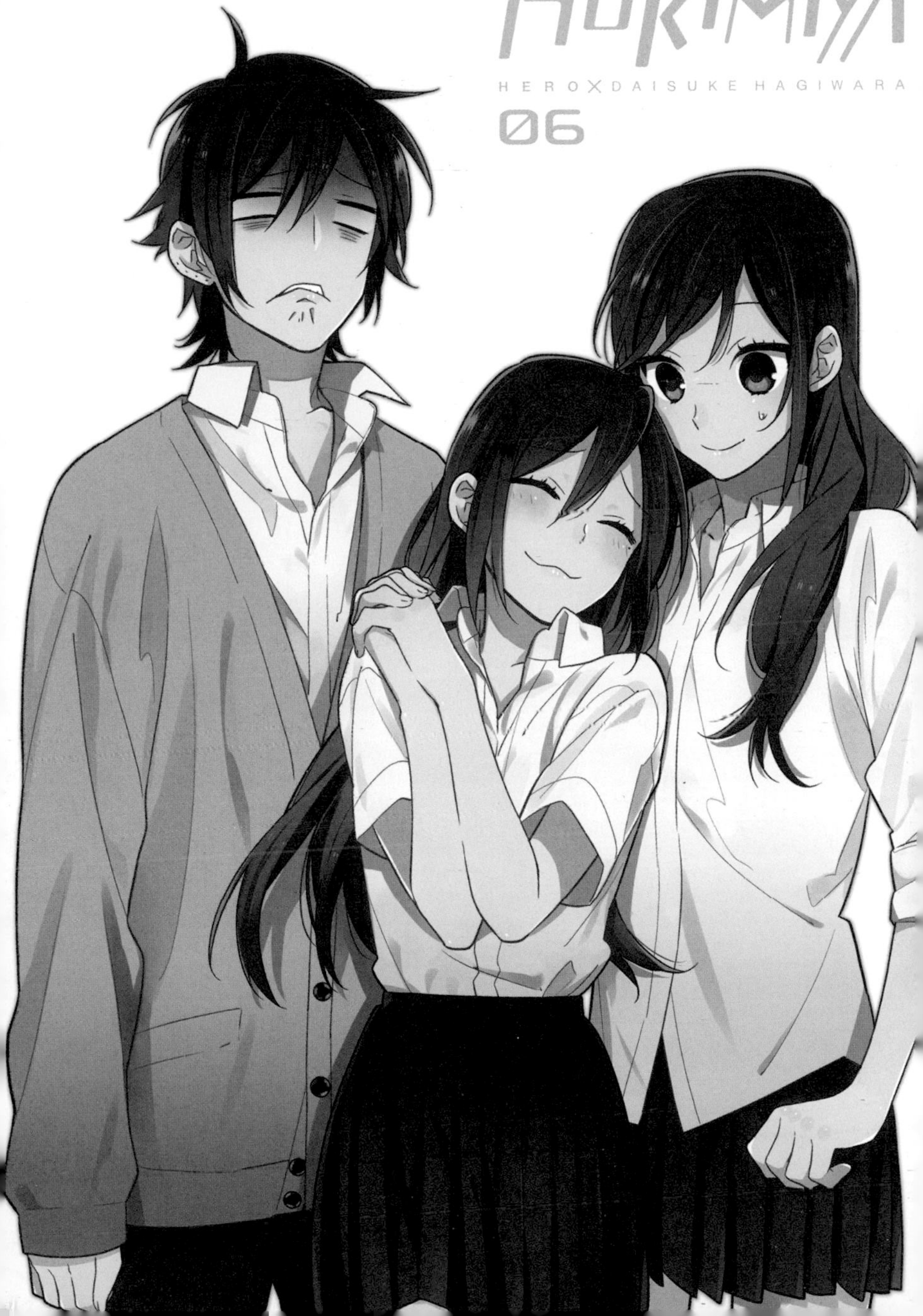

HORI-san and
MIYAMURA-kun

HORIMIYA

06

C O N T E N T S ★

page·35	5
page·36	29
page·37	53
page·38	85
page·39	107
page·40	121
page·41	141
page·42	155

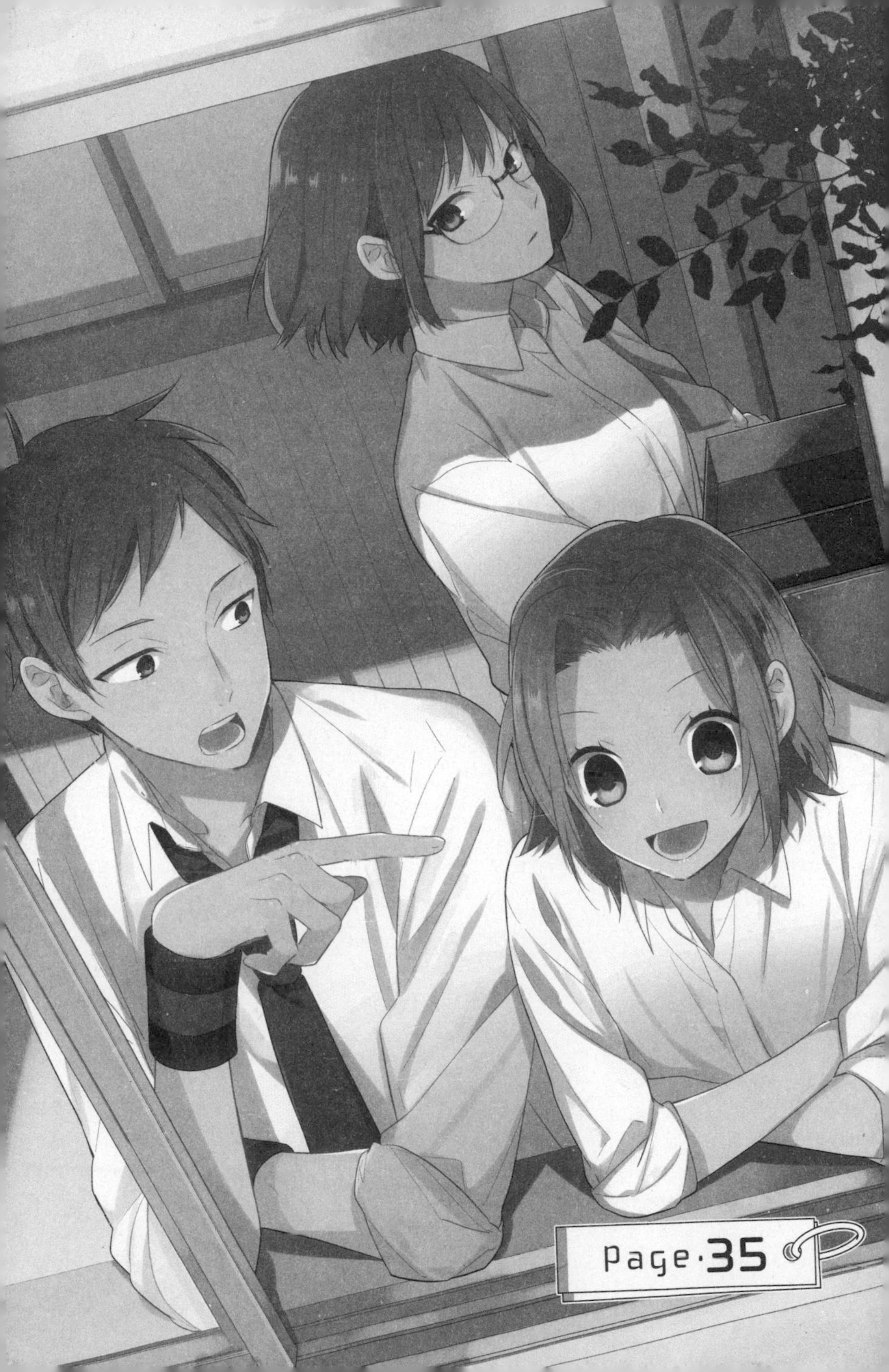
Page·35

HORIMIYA

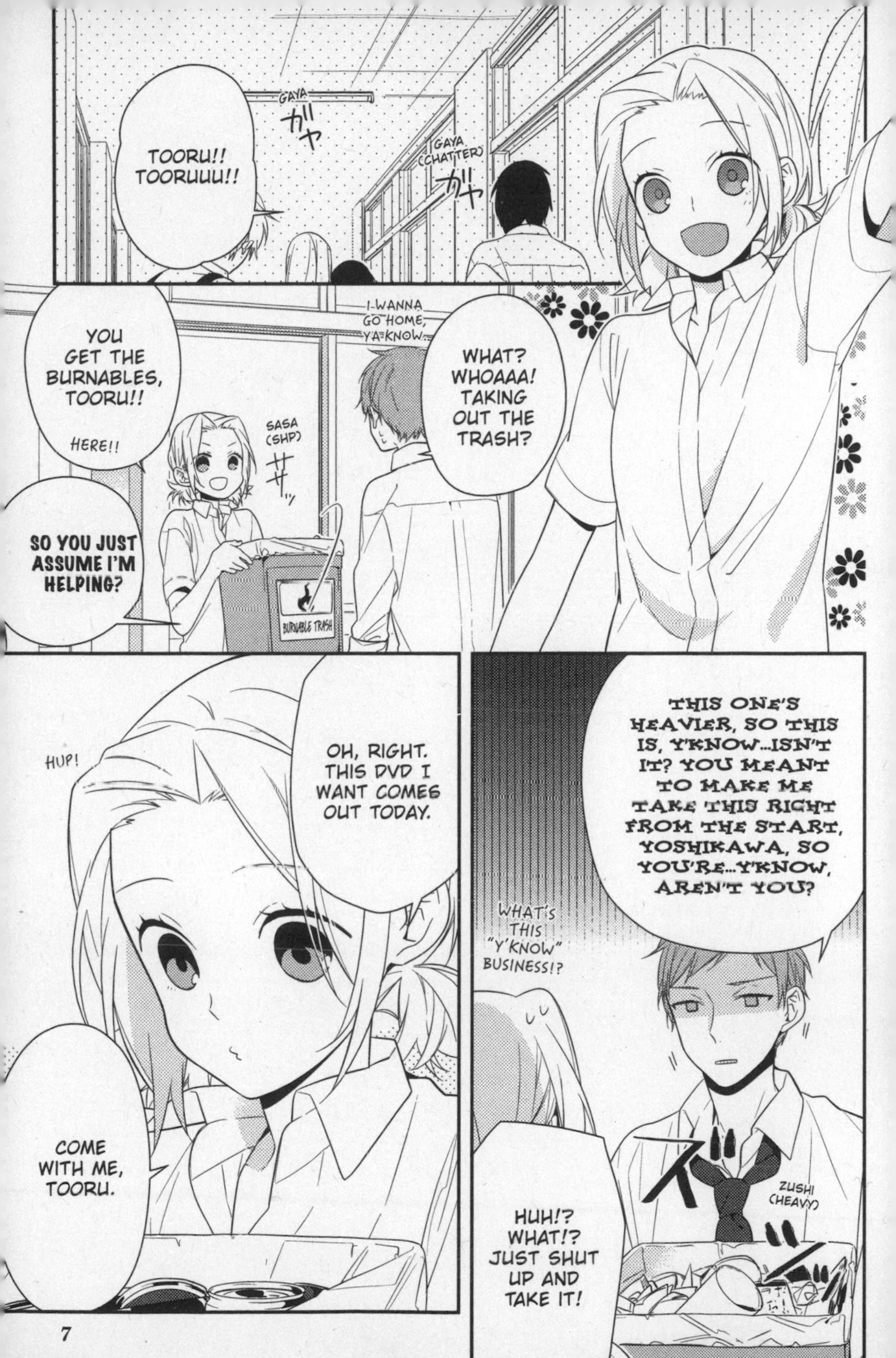
GAYA
GAYA (CHATTER)
TOORU!! TOORUUU!!
I-WANNA GO HOME, YA-KNOW...
WHAT? WHOAAA! TAKING OUT THE TRASH?
SASA (SHP)
YOU GET THE BURNABLES, TOORU!!
HERE!!
SO YOU JUST ASSUME I'M HELPING?
BURNABLE TRASH
THIS ONE'S HEAVIER, SO THIS IS, Y'KNOW...ISN'T IT? YOU MEANT TO MAKE ME TAKE THIS RIGHT FROM THE START, YOSHIKAWA, SO YOU'RE...Y'KNOW, AREN'T YOU?
WHAT'S THIS "Y'KNOW" BUSINESS!?
ZUSHI (HEAVY)
HUH!? WHAT!? JUST SHUT UP AND TAKE IT!
OH, RIGHT. THIS DVD I WANT COMES OUT TODAY.
HUP!
COME WITH ME, TOORU.

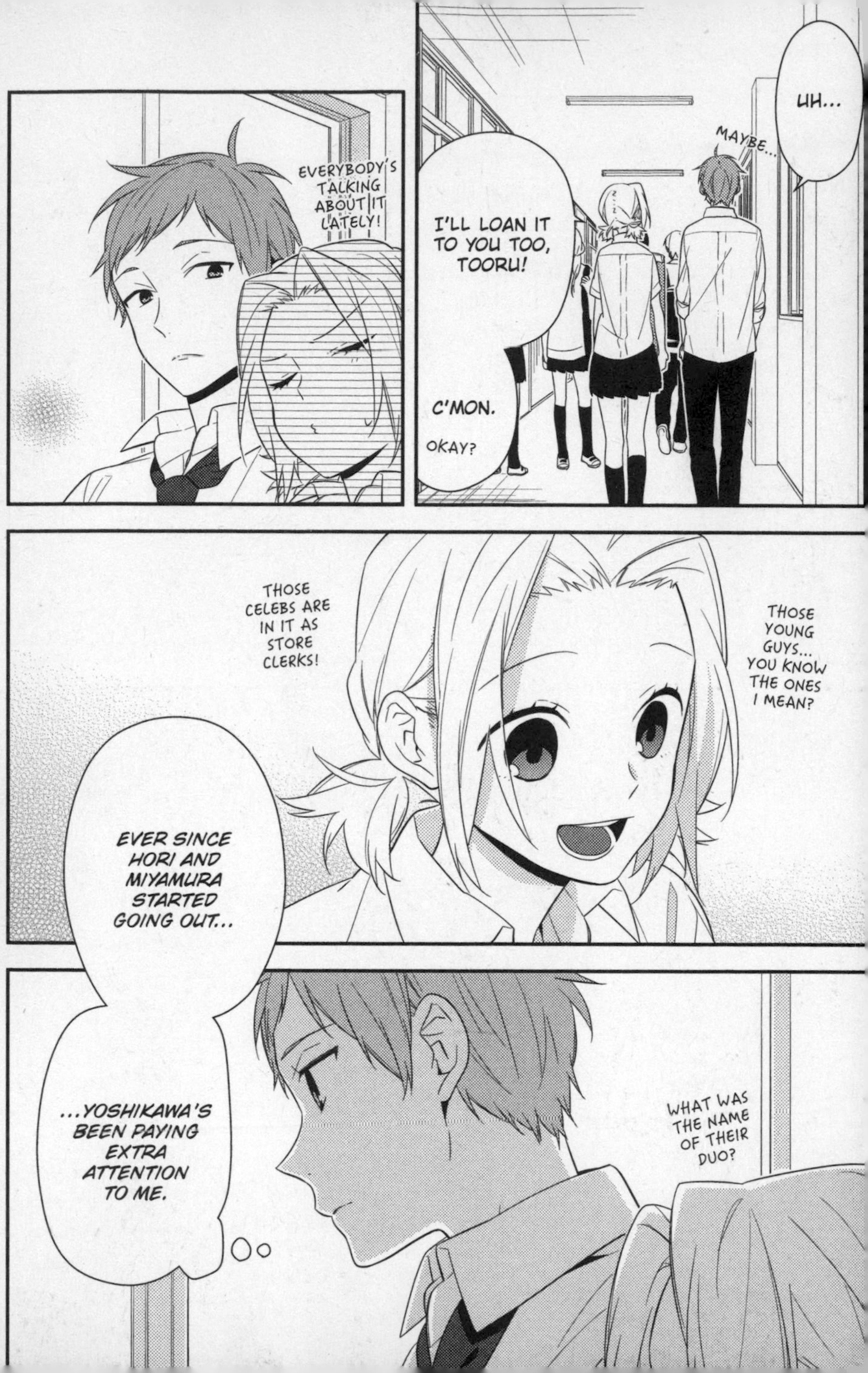
UH...
MAYBE...
I'LL LOAN IT TO YOU TOO, TOORU!
C'MON.
OKAY?
EVERYBODY'S TALKING ABOUT IT LATELY!
THOSE YOUNG GUYS... YOU KNOW THE ONES I MEAN?
THOSE CELEBS ARE IN IT AS STORE CLERKS!
EVER SINCE HORI AND MIYAMURA STARTED GOING OUT...
...YOSHIKAWA'S BEEN PAYING EXTRA ATTENTION TO ME.
WHAT WAS THE NAME OF THEIR DUO?

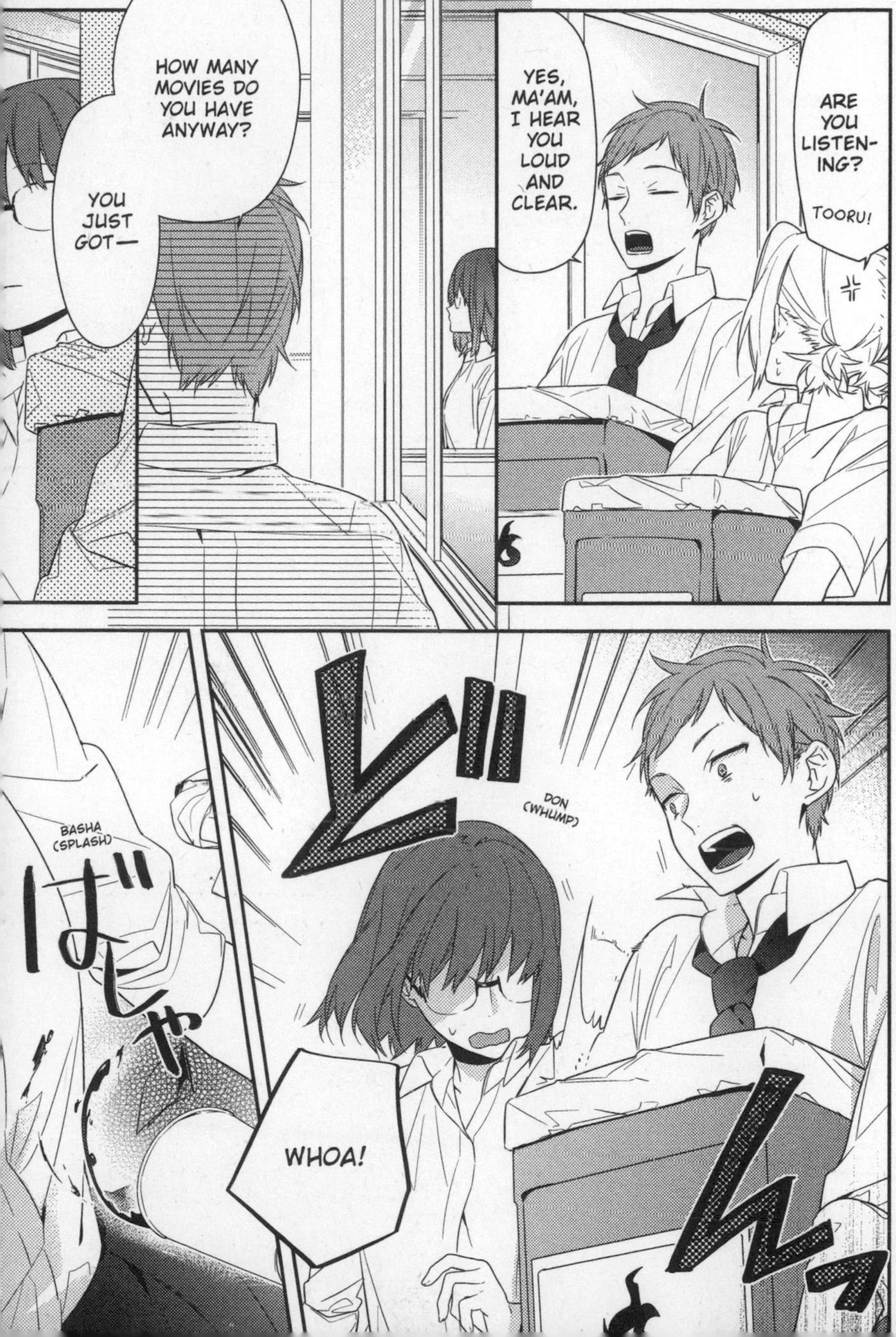
ARE YOU LISTENING-ING?
TOORU!
YES, MA'AM, I HEAR YOU LOUD AND CLEAR.
HOW MANY MOVIES DO YOU HAVE ANYWAY?
YOU JUST GOT—
DON (WHUMP)
BASHA (SPLASH)
WHOA!

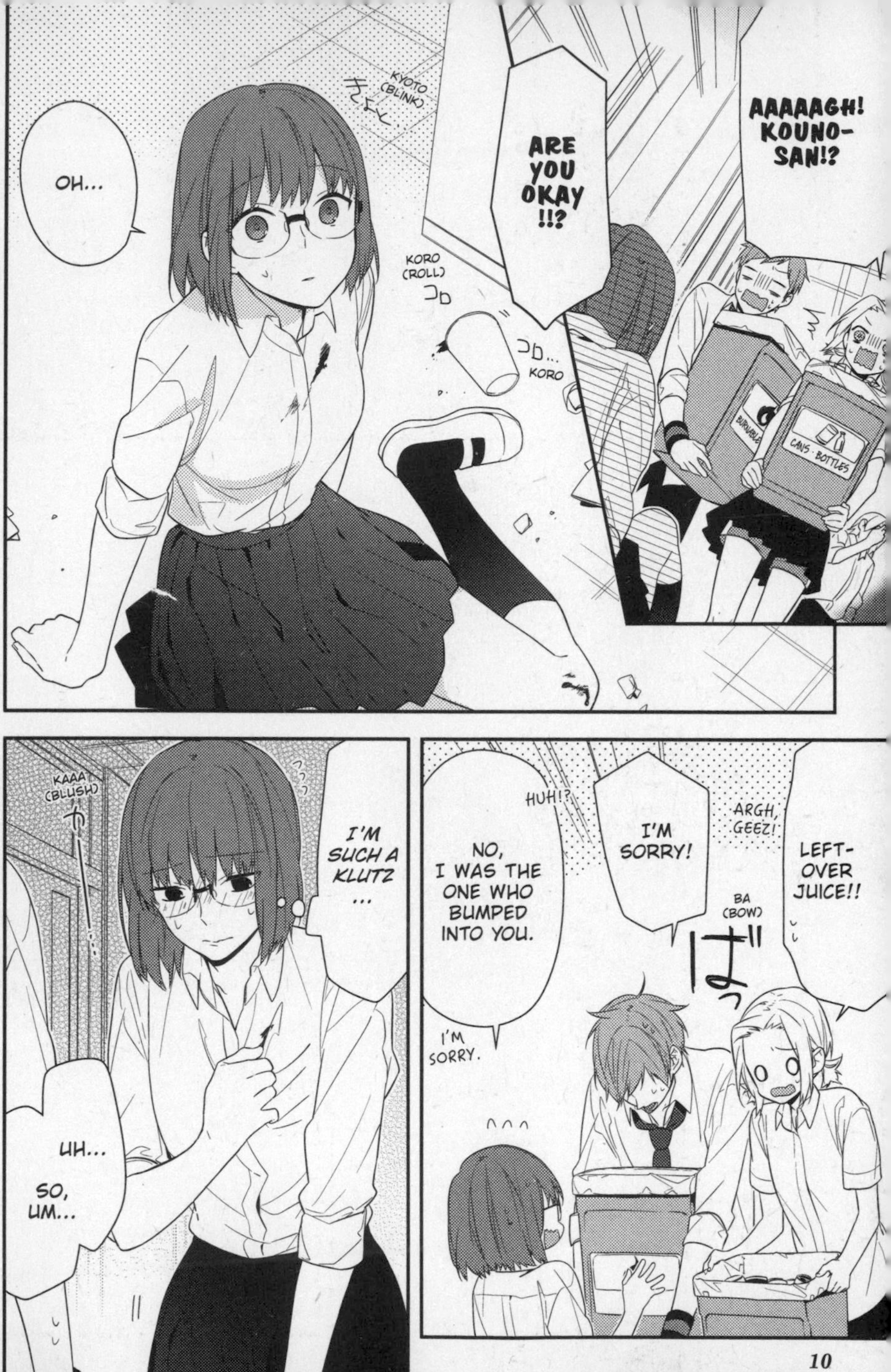

AAAAAGH! KOUNO-SAN!?
ARE YOU OKAY!!?
KYOTO (BLINK)
OH...
KORO (ROLL)
KORO
LEFT-OVER JUICE!!
ARGH, GEEZ!
BA (BOW)
I'M SORRY!
HUH!?
NO, I WAS THE ONE WHO BUMPED INTO YOU.
I'M SORRY.
I'M SUCH A KLUTZ...
KAAA (BLUSH)
UH...
SO, UM...
BURNABLE
CANS · BOTTLES

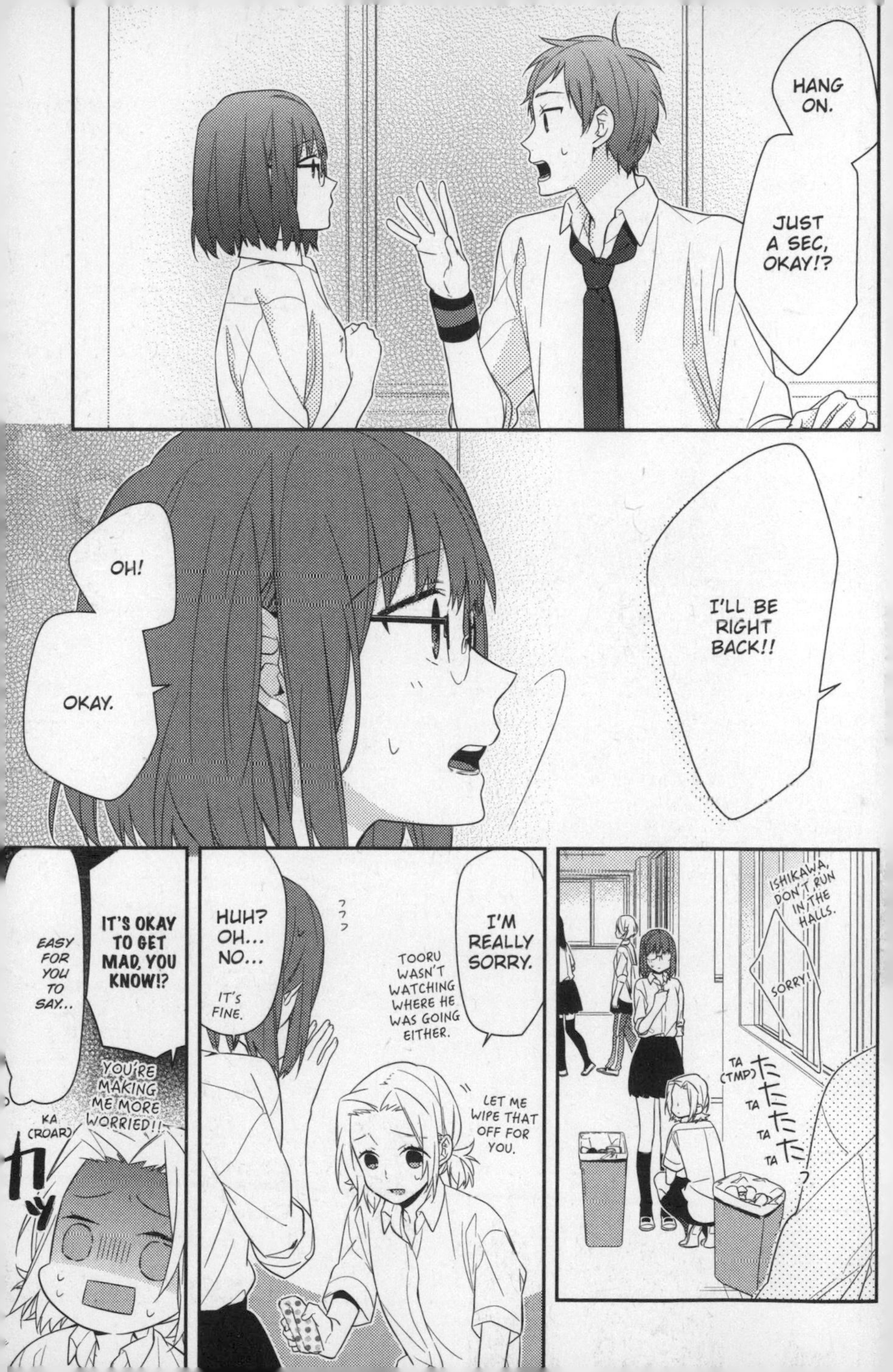

HANG ON.
JUST A SEC, OKAY!?
I'LL BE RIGHT BACK!!
OH!
OKAY.
ISHIKAWA, DON'T RUN IN THE HALLS.
SORRY!
TA (TMP) TA TA TA
I'M REALLY SORRY.
TOORU WASN'T WATCHING WHERE HE WAS GOING EITHER.
HUH? OH... NO...
IT'S FINE.
LET ME WIPE THAT OFF FOR YOU.
IT'S OKAY TO GET MAD, YOU KNOW!?
EASY FOR YOU TO SAY...
YOU'RE MAKING ME MORE WORRIED!!
KA (ROAR)

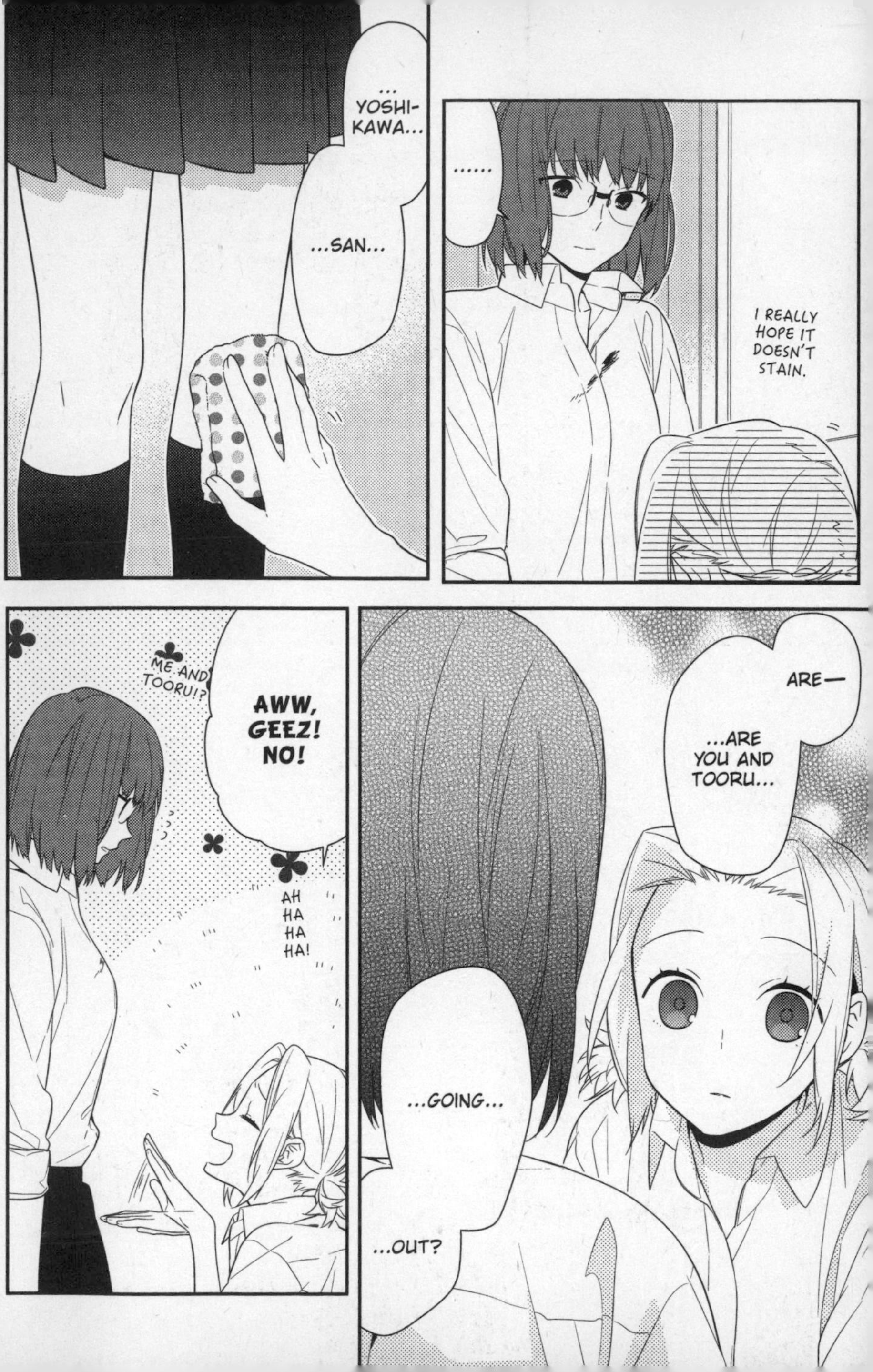
......
I REALLY HOPE IT DOESN'T STAIN.
... YOSHI-KAWA...
...SAN...
ARE—
...ARE YOU AND TOORU...
...GOING...
...OUT?
AWW, GEEZ! NO!
ME AND TOORU!?
AH HA HA HA!

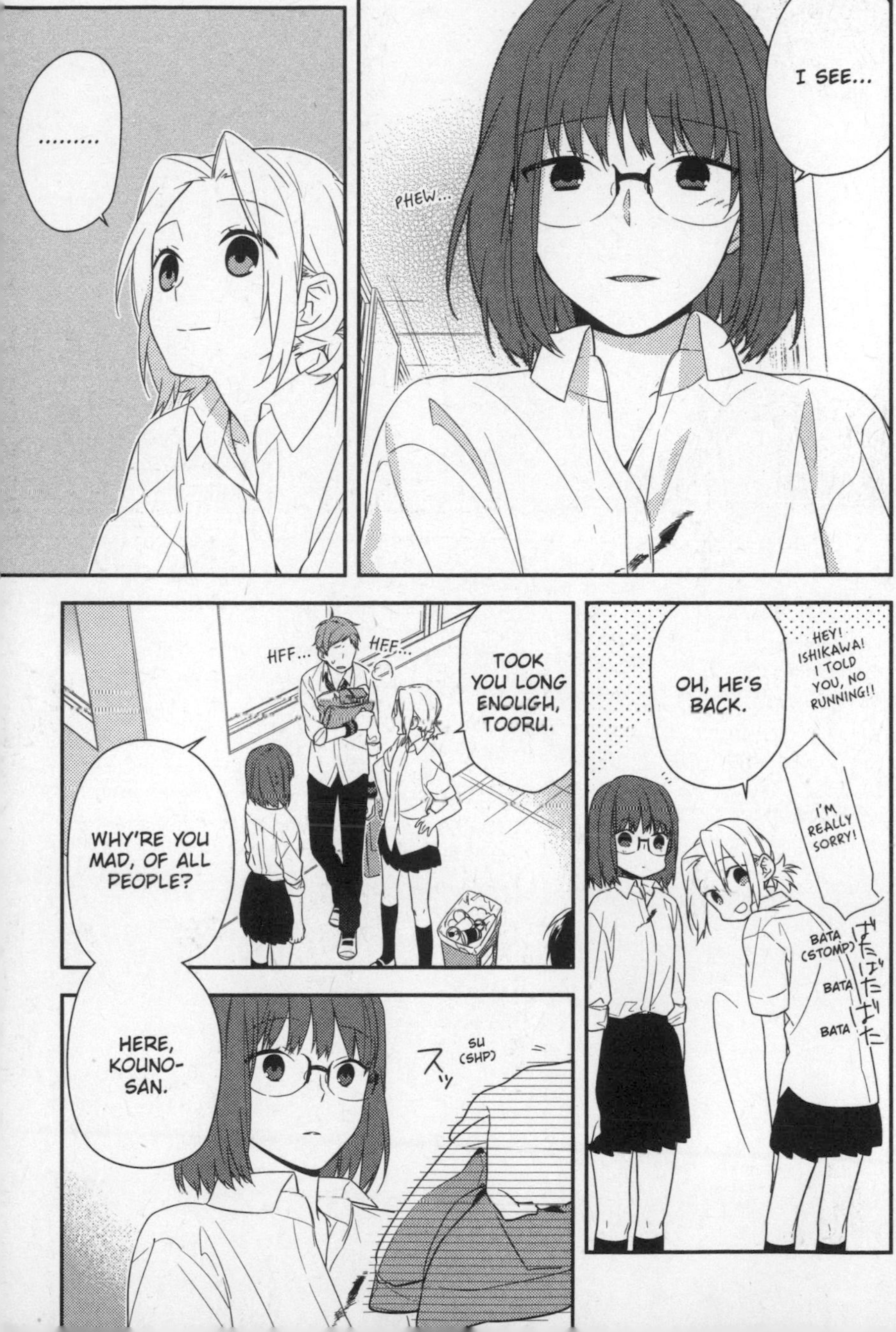
I SEE...
PHEW...
....
HEY! ISHIKAWA! I TOLD YOU, NO RUNNING!!
OH, HE'S BACK.
I'M REALLY SORRY!
ばたばたばた
BATA (STOMP)
BATA
BATA
TOOK YOU LONG ENOUGH, TOORU.
HFF... HFF...
WHY'RE YOU MAD, OF ALL PEOPLE?
スッ
SU (SHP)
HERE, KOUNO-SAN.

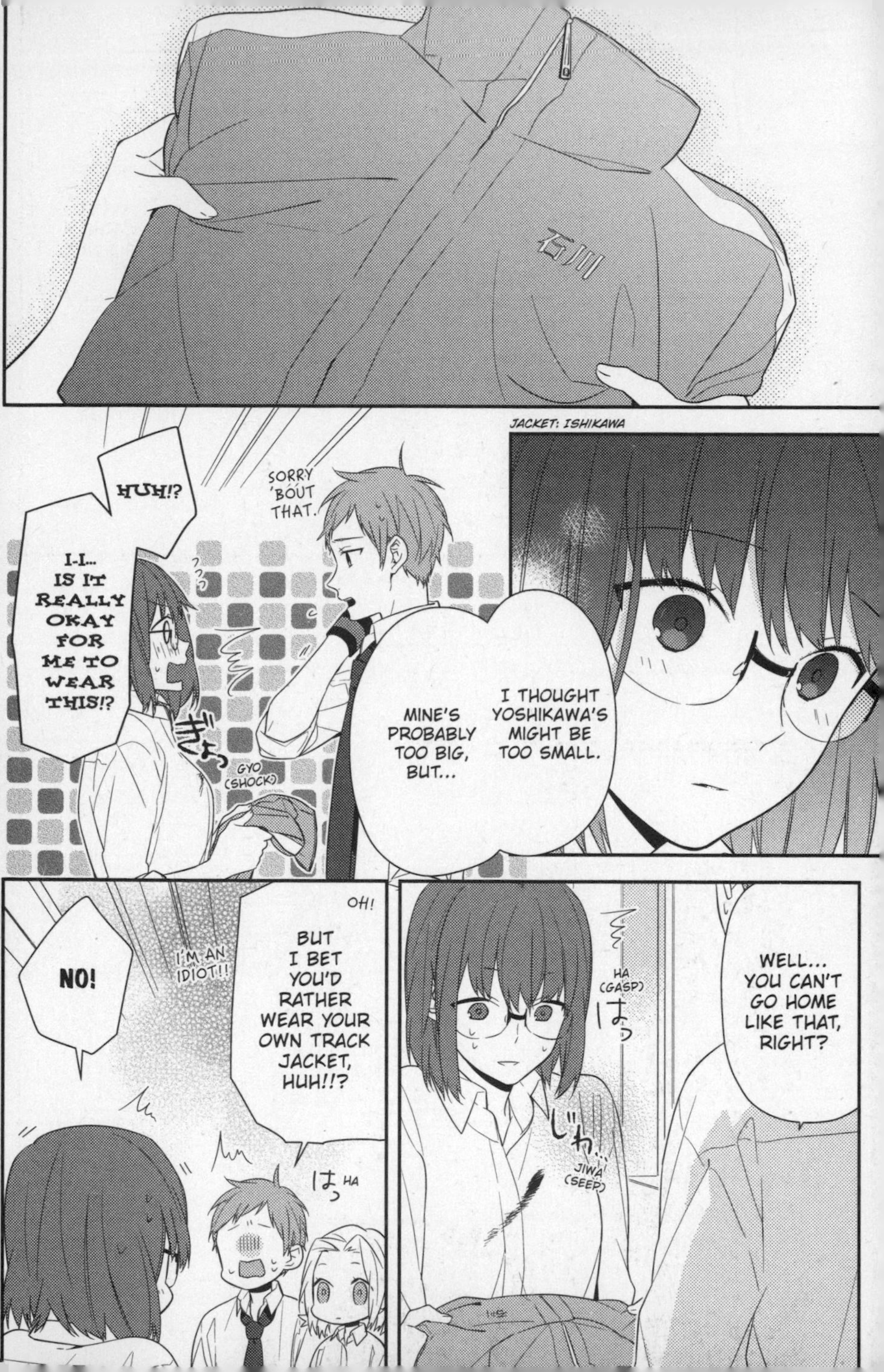
石川
JACKET: ISHIKAWA
I THOUGHT YOSHIKAWA'S MIGHT BE TOO SMALL.
MINE'S PROBABLY TOO BIG, BUT...
SORRY 'BOUT THAT.
HUH!?
I-I... IS IT REALLY OKAY FOR ME TO WEAR THIS!?
ぎょっ
GYO (SHOCK)
WELL... YOU CAN'T GO HOME LIKE THAT, RIGHT?
HA (GASP)
はっ
じわ…
JIWA (SEEP)
OH!
BUT I BET YOU'D RATHER WEAR YOUR OWN TRACK JACKET, HUH!!?
I'M AN IDIOT!!
NO!
はっ HA

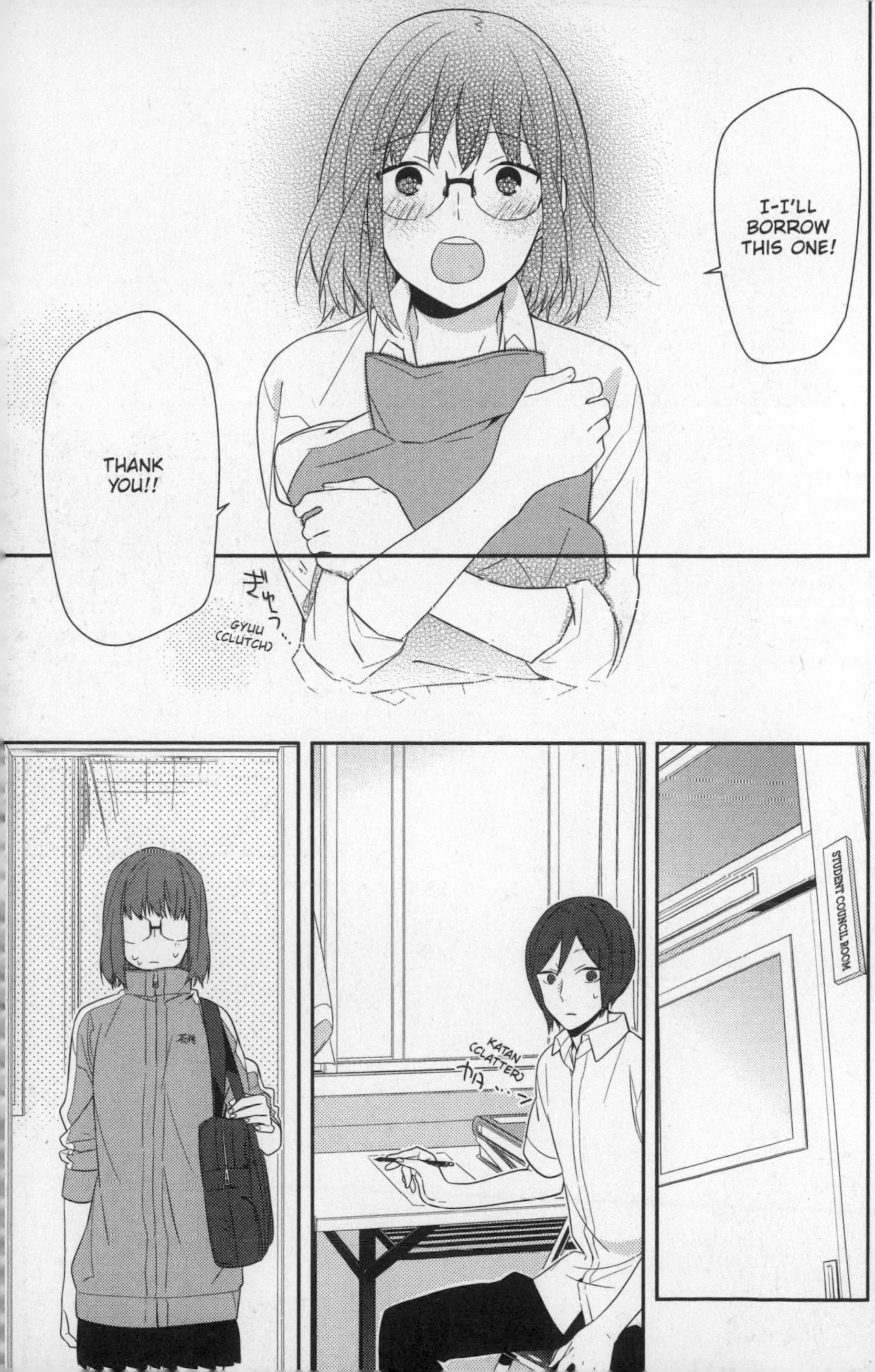
I-I'LL BORROW THIS ONE!
THANK YOU!!
ぎゅっ
GYUU (CLUTCH)
STUDENT COUNCIL ROOM
KATAN (CLATTER)
カタ…

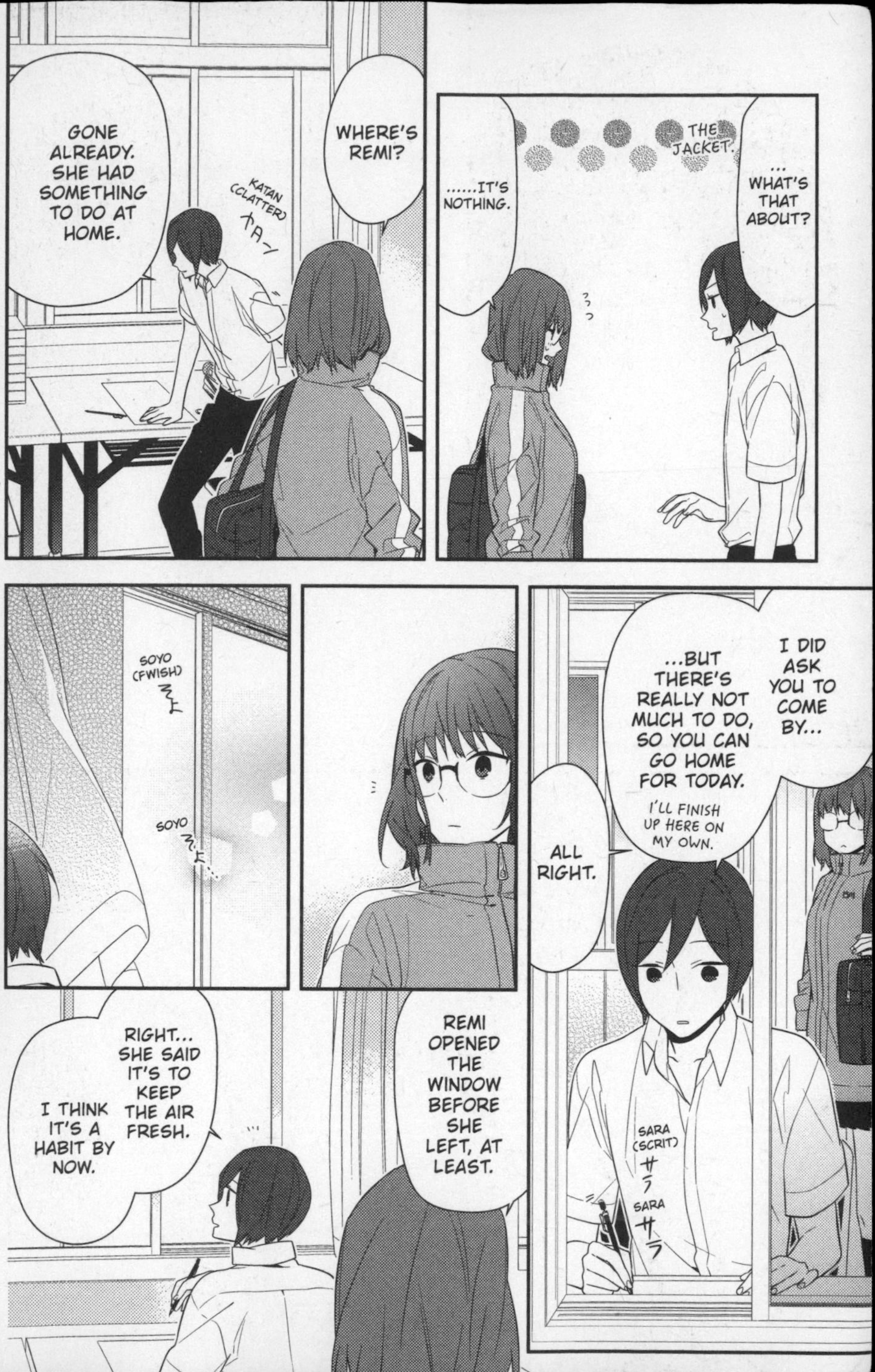
...WHAT'S THAT ABOUT?
THE JACKET.
......IT'S NOTHING.
WHERE'S REMI?
GONE ALREADY. SHE HAD SOMETHING TO DO AT HOME.
KATAN (CLATTER)
I DID ASK YOU TO COME BY...
...BUT THERE'S REALLY NOT MUCH TO DO, SO YOU CAN GO HOME FOR TODAY.
I'LL FINISH UP HERE ON MY OWN.
ALL RIGHT.
SARA (SCRIT)
サラ
SARA
サラ
SOYO (FWISH)
SOYO
REMI OPENED THE WINDOW BEFORE SHE LEFT, AT LEAST.
RIGHT... SHE SAID IT'S TO KEEP THE AIR FRESH.
I THINK IT'S A HABIT BY NOW.

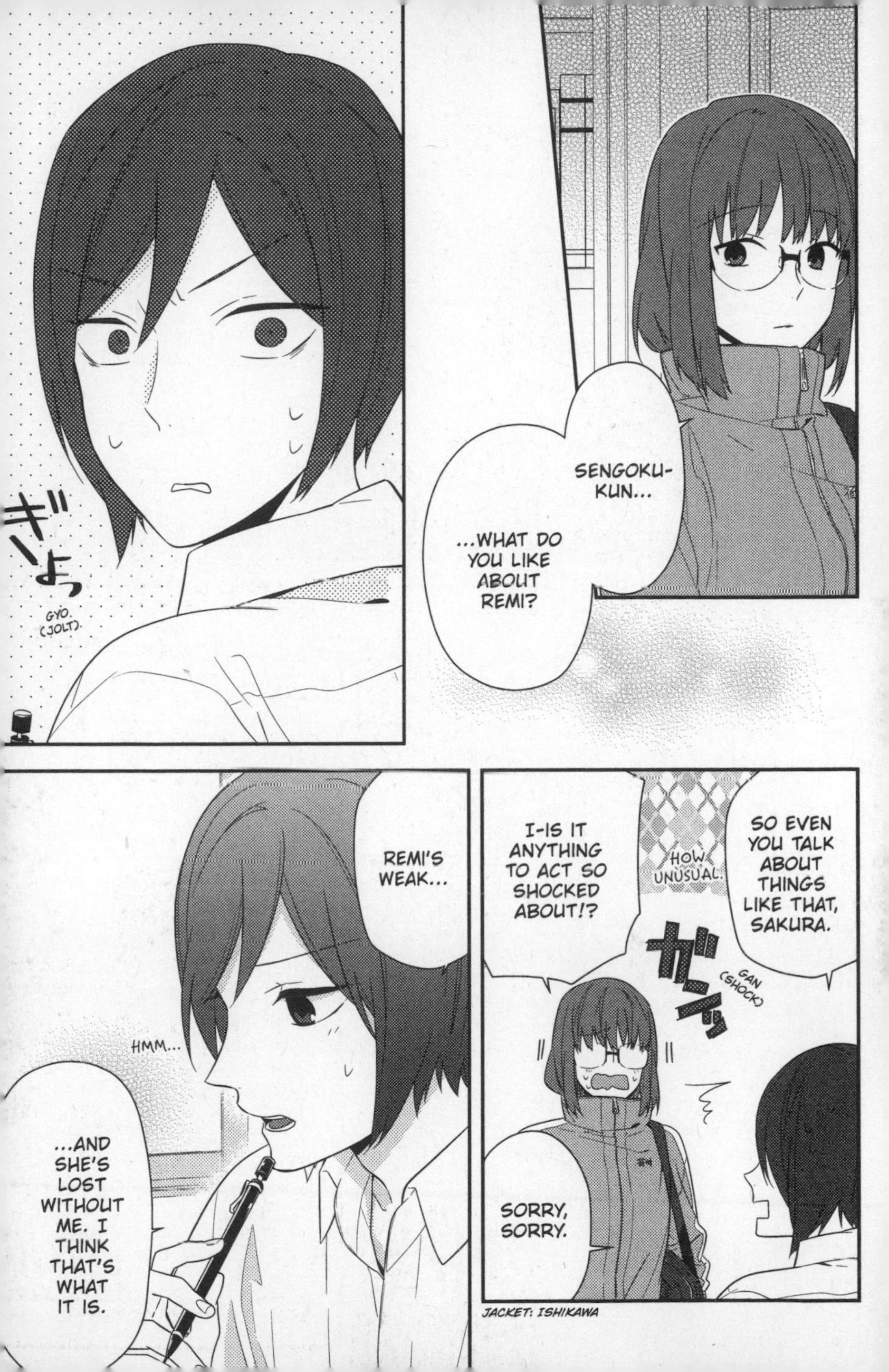
SENGOKU-KUN...
...WHAT DO YOU LIKE ABOUT REMI?
ギョッ
GYO. (JOLT).
SO EVEN YOU TALK ABOUT THINGS LIKE THAT, SAKURA.
HOW UNUSUAL.
I-IS IT ANYTHING TO ACT SO SHOCKED ABOUT!?
ガーン
GAN (SHOCK)
SORRY, SORRY.
JACKET: ISHIKAWA
REMI'S WEAK...
HMM...
...AND SHE'S LOST WITHOUT ME. I THINK THAT'S WHAT IT IS.

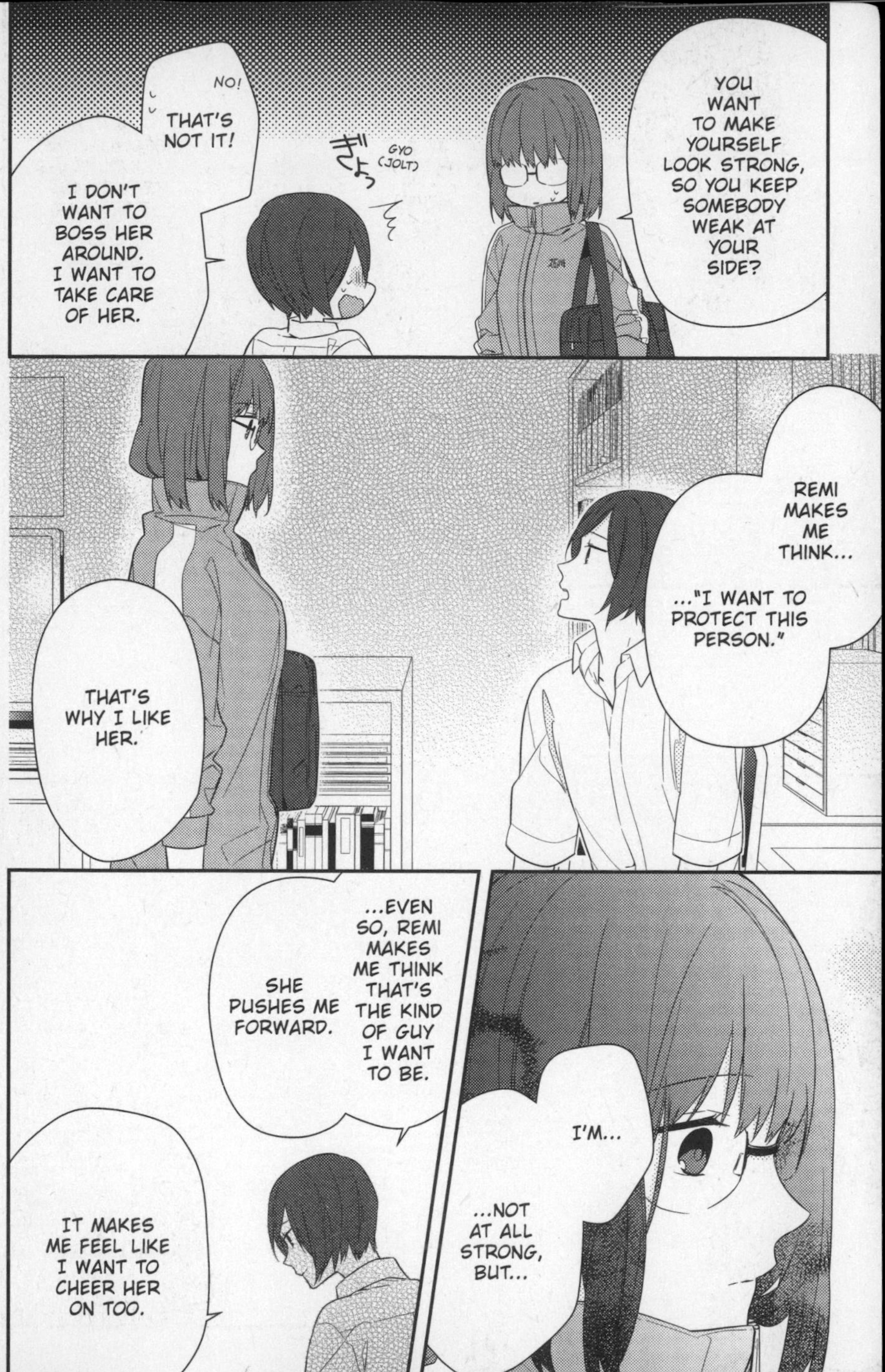
YOU WANT TO MAKE YOURSELF LOOK STRONG, SO YOU KEEP SOMEBODY WEAK AT YOUR SIDE?
ぎょっ
GYO (JOLT)
NO! THAT'S NOT IT!
I DON'T WANT TO BOSS HER AROUND. I WANT TO TAKE CARE OF HER.
REMI MAKES ME THINK...
..."I WANT TO PROTECT THIS PERSON."
THAT'S WHY I LIKE HER.
I'M...
...NOT AT ALL STRONG, BUT...
...EVEN SO, REMI MAKES ME THINK THAT'S THE KIND OF GUY I WANT TO BE.
SHE PUSHES ME FORWARD.
IT MAKES ME FEEL LIKE I WANT TO CHEER HER ON TOO.

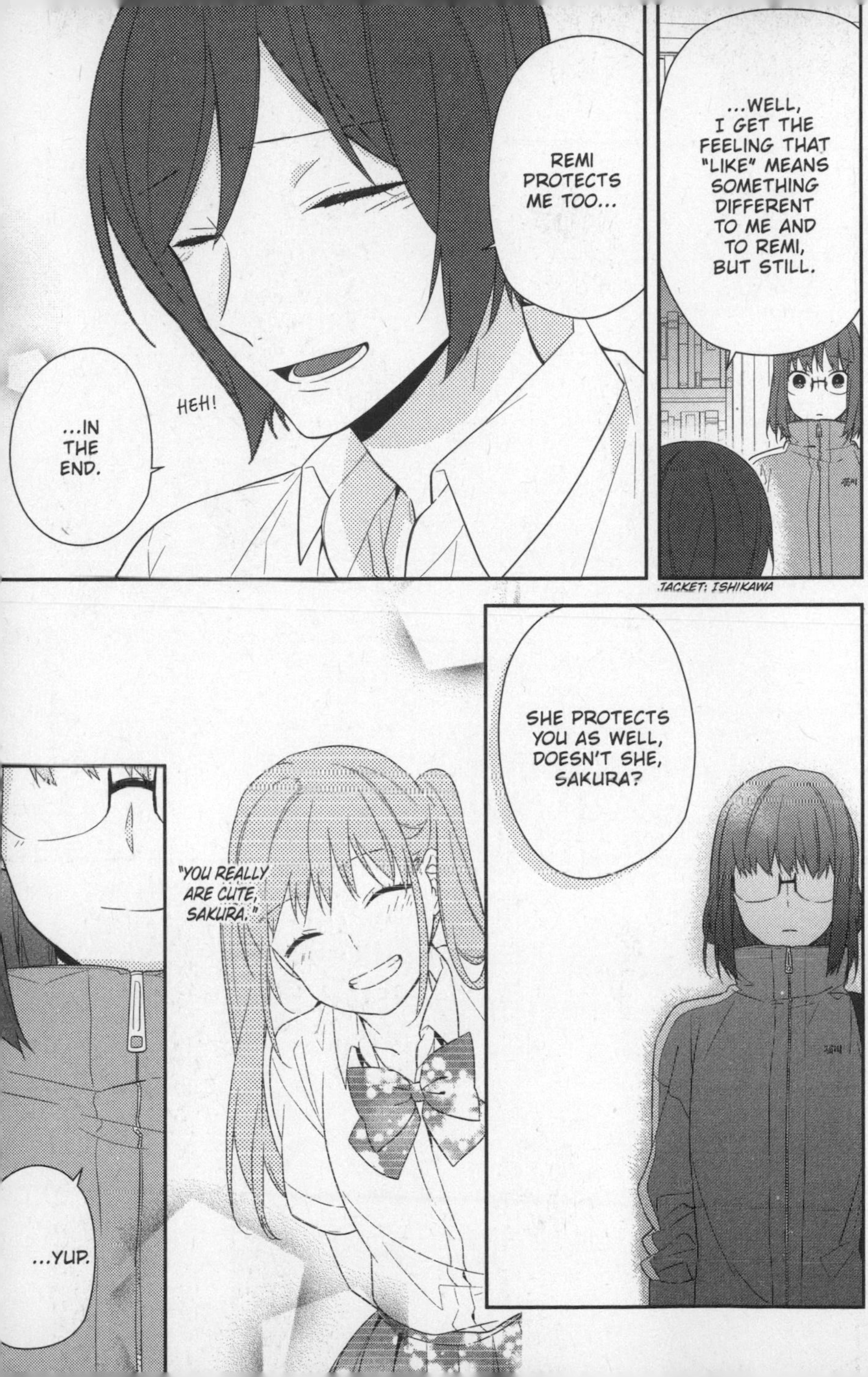
...WELL, I GET THE FEELING THAT "LIKE" MEANS SOMETHING DIFFERENT TO ME AND TO REMI, BUT STILL.
JACKET: ISHIKAWA
REMI PROTECTS ME TOO...
HEH!
...IN THE END.
SHE PROTECTS YOU AS WELL, DOESN'T SHE, SAKURA?
"YOU REALLY ARE CUTE, SAKURA."
...YUP.

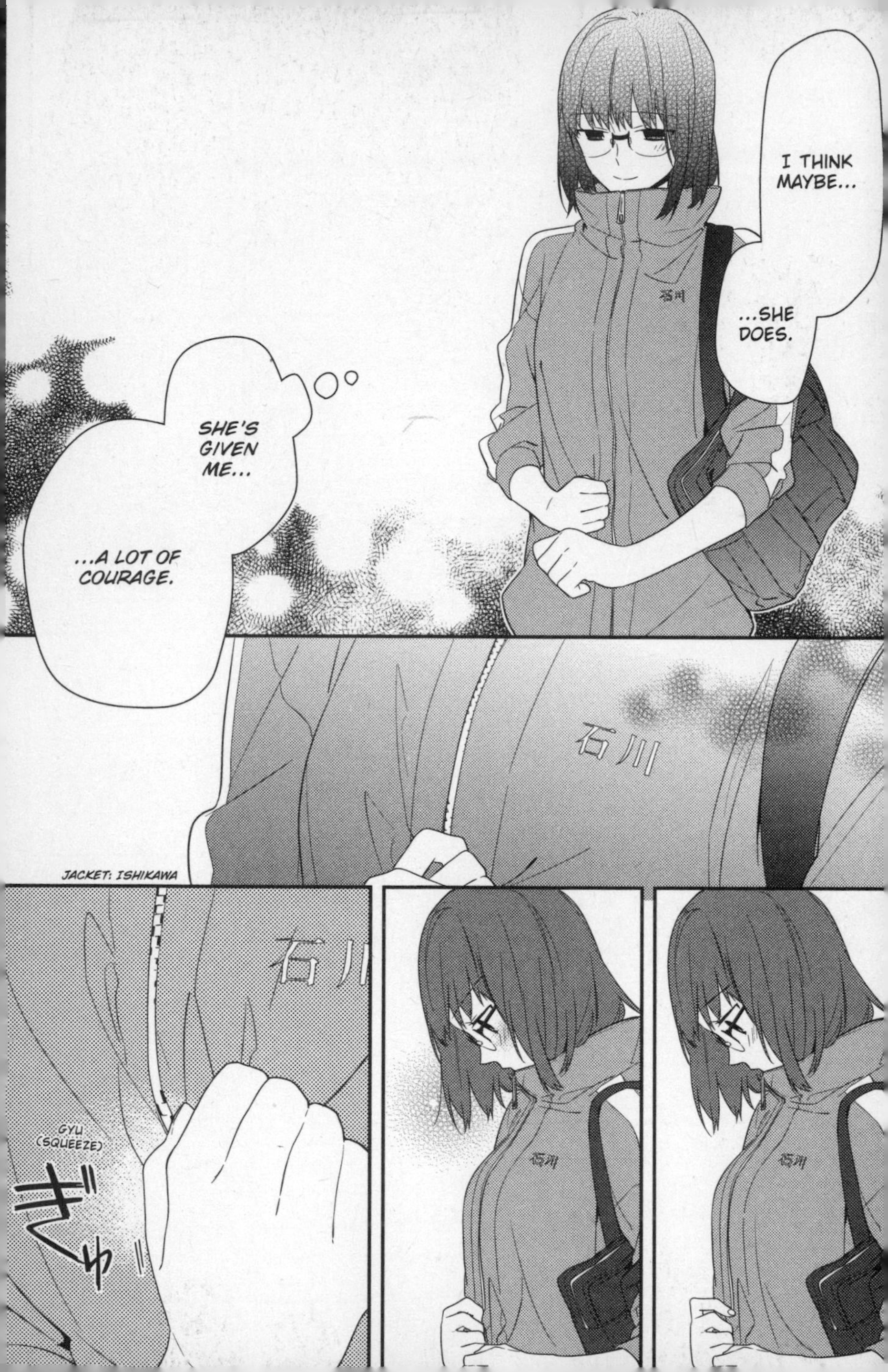
I THINK MAYBE...
...SHE DOES.
SHE'S GIVEN ME...
...A LOT OF COURAGE.
石川
JACKET: ISHIKAWA
石川
GYU (SQUEEZE)
ぎゅ

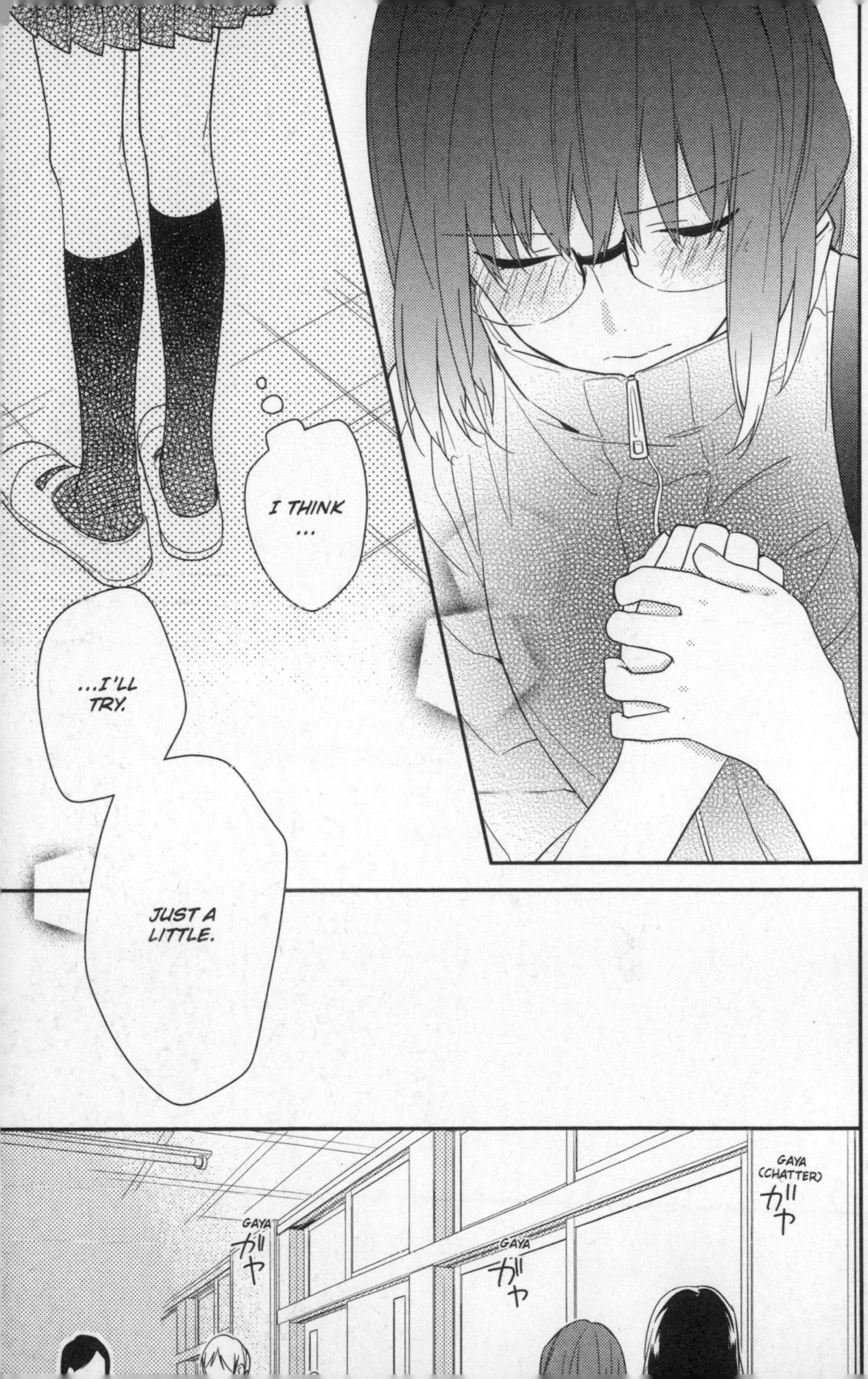
I THINK ...
...I'LL TRY.
JUST A LITTLE.
GAYA (CHATTER)
ガヤ
GAYA
ガヤ
GAYA
ガヤ

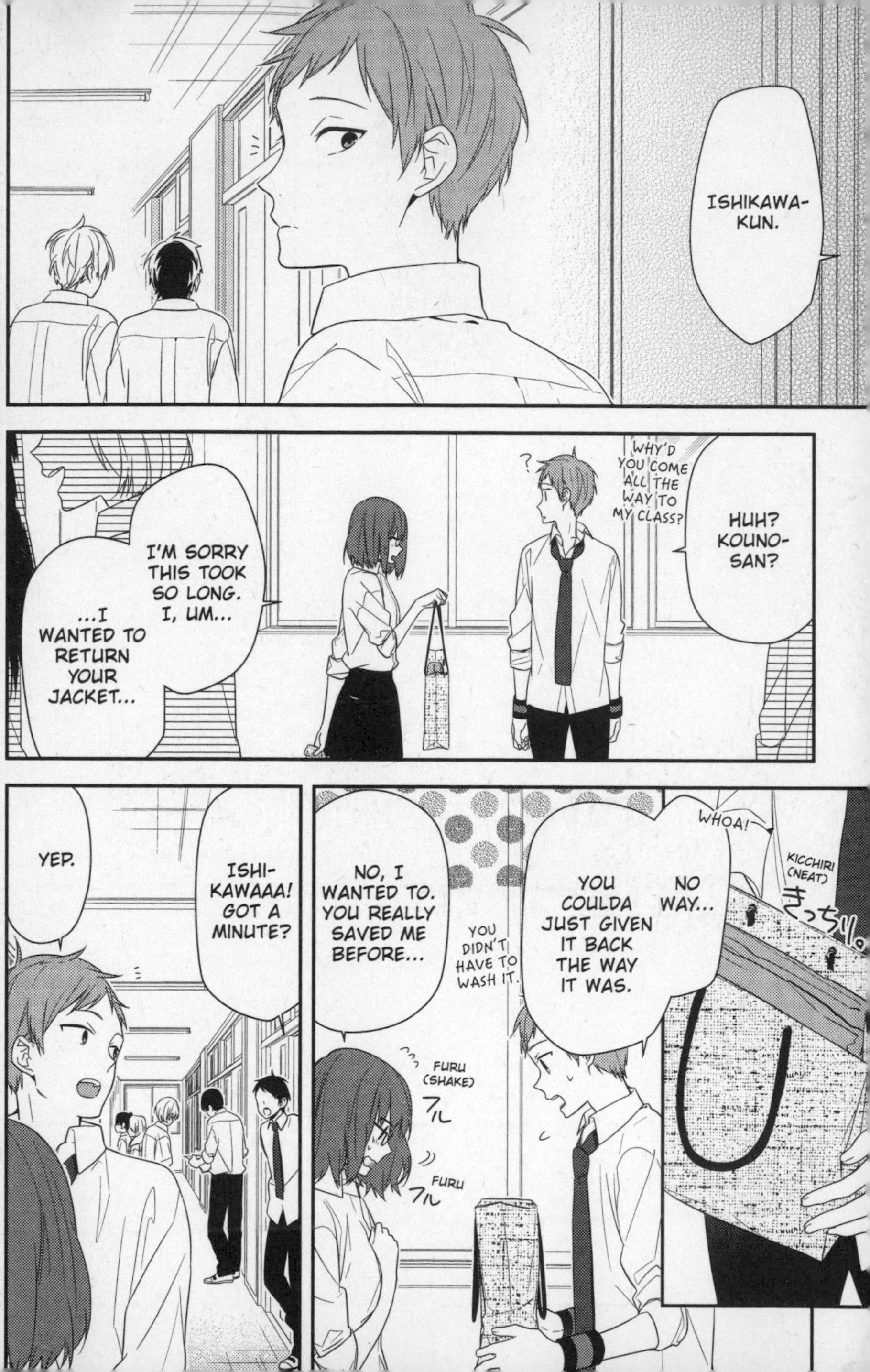
ISHIKAWA-KUN.
HUH? KOUNO-SAN?
WHY'D YOU COME ALL THE WAY TO MY CLASS?
I'M SORRY THIS TOOK SO LONG. I, UM...
...I WANTED TO RETURN YOUR JACKET...
WHOA!
KICCHIRI (NEAT)
きっちり。
NO WAY...
YOU COULDA JUST GIVEN IT BACK THE WAY IT WAS.
YOU DIDN'T HAVE TO WASH IT.
NO, I WANTED TO. YOU REALLY SAVED ME BEFORE...
FURU (SHAKE)
フル
FURU
フル
ISHI-KAWAAA! GOT A MINUTE?
YEP.

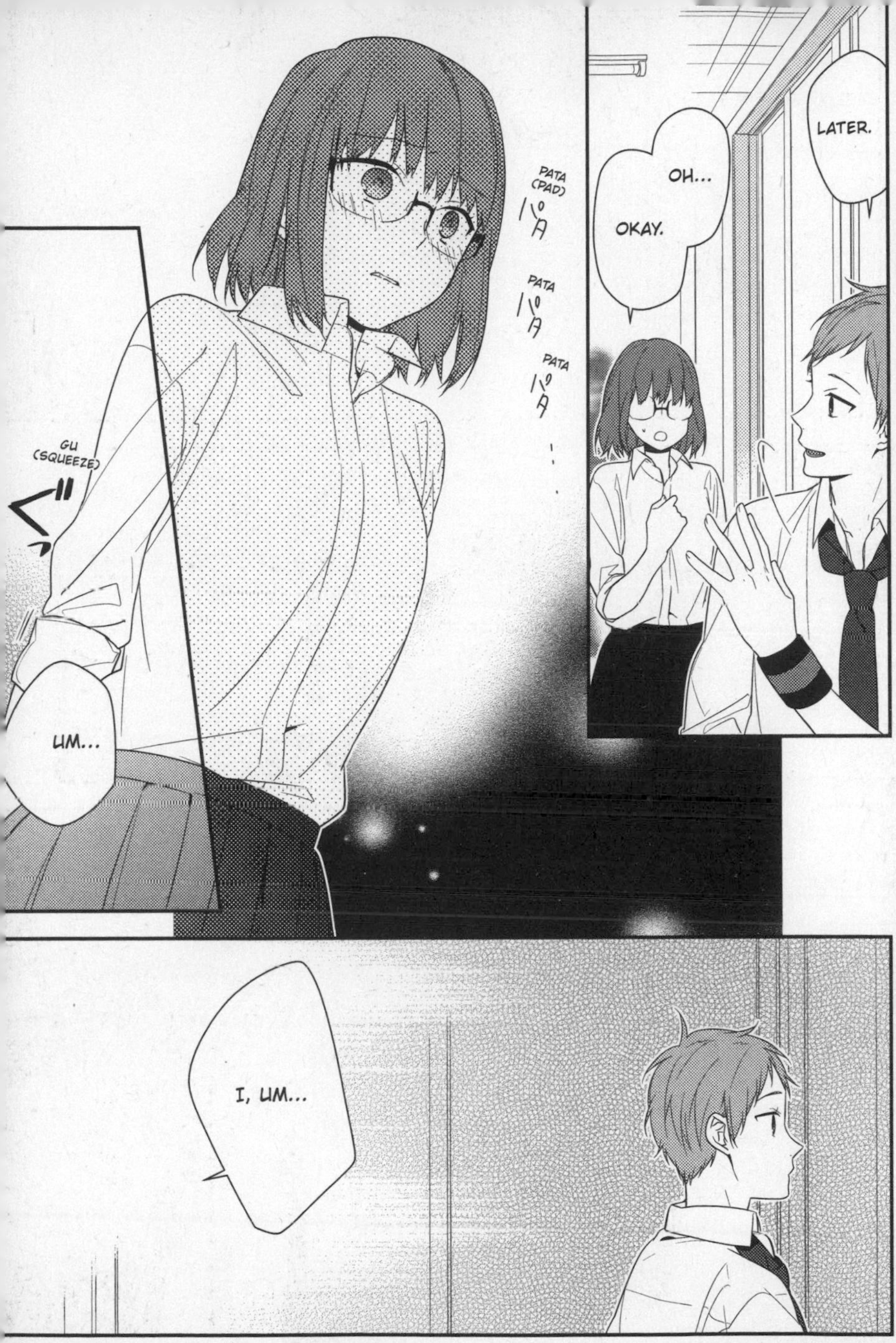
LATER.
OH...
OKAY.
PATA (PAD)
パタ
PATA
パタ
PATA
パタ
GU (SQUEEZE)
ぐっ
UM...
I, UM...

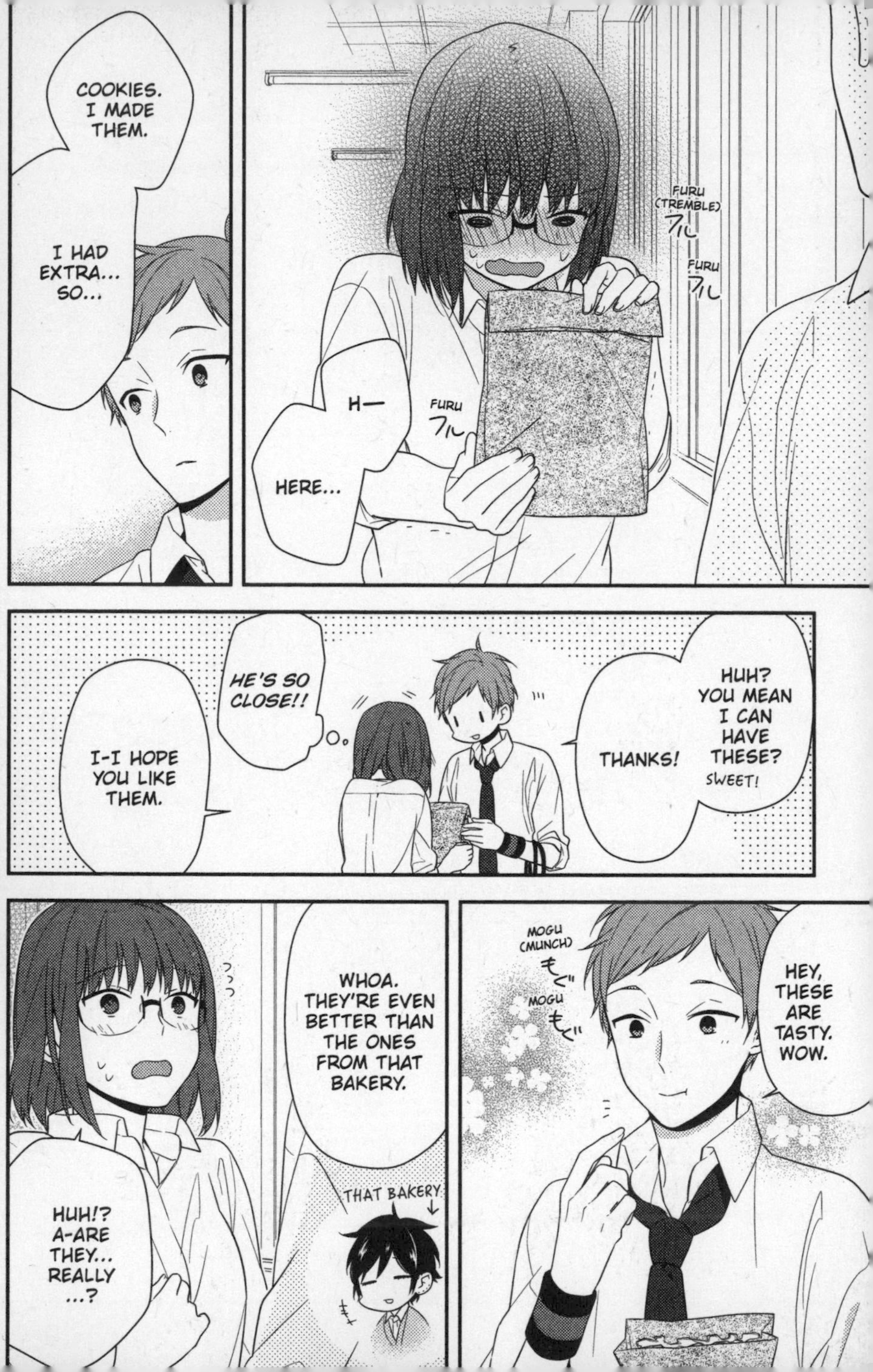
FURU (TREMBLE) フル
FURU フル
FURU フル
H—
HERE...
COOKIES. I MADE THEM.
I HAD EXTRA... SO...
HUH? YOU MEAN I CAN HAVE THESE?
SWEET!
THANKS!
HE'S SO CLOSE!!
I-I HOPE YOU LIKE THEM.
HEY, THESE ARE TASTY. WOW.
MOGU (MUNCH) もぐ
MOGU もぐ
WHOA. THEY'RE EVEN BETTER THAN THE ONES FROM THAT BAKERY.
THAT BAKERY ↓
HUH!? A-ARE THEY... REALLY ...?

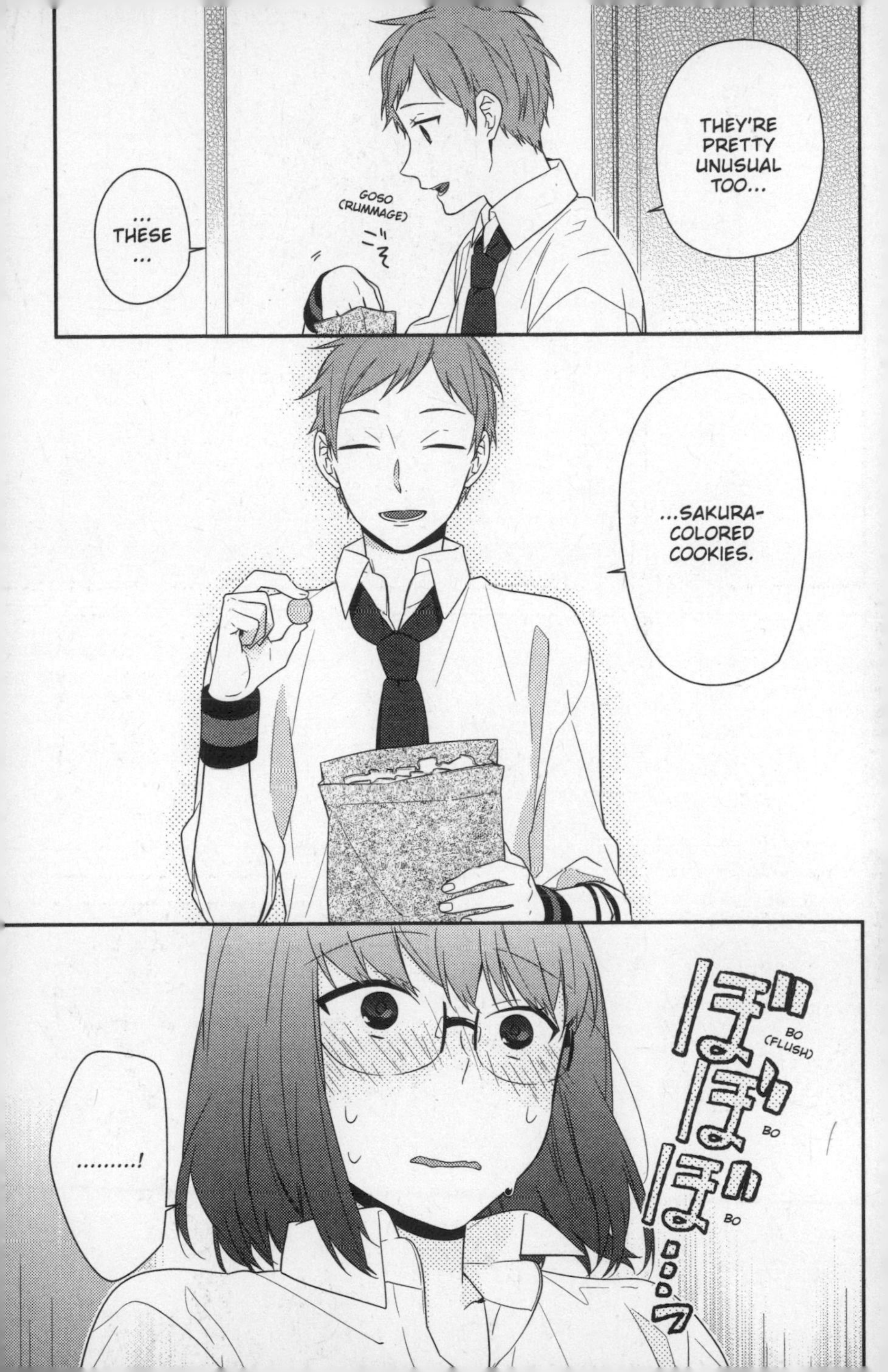
THEY'RE PRETTY UNUSUAL TOO...
GOSO (RUMMAGE)
ごそ
... THESE ...
...SAKURA-COLORED COOKIES.
ぼぼぼっ
BO (FLUSH)
BO
BO
.........!

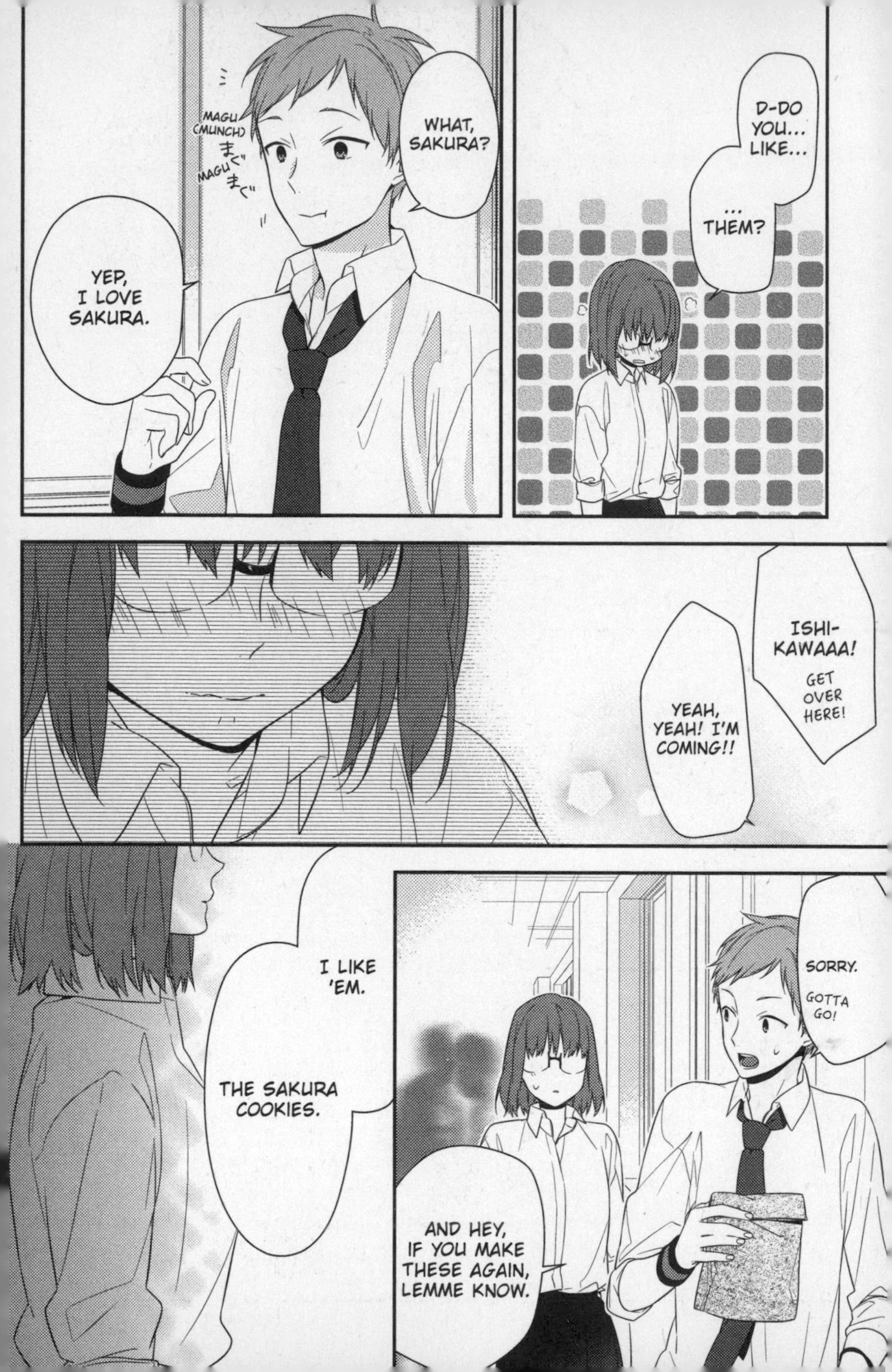
D-DO YOU... LIKE...
... THEM?
WHAT, SAKURA?
MAGU (MUNCH) まぐ MAGU まぐ
YEP, I LOVE SAKURA.
ISHI-KAWAAA!
GET OVER HERE!
YEAH, YEAH! I'M COMING!!
SORRY.
GOTTA GO!
AND HEY, IF YOU MAKE THESE AGAIN, LEMME KNOW.
I LIKE 'EM.
THE SAKURA COOKIES.

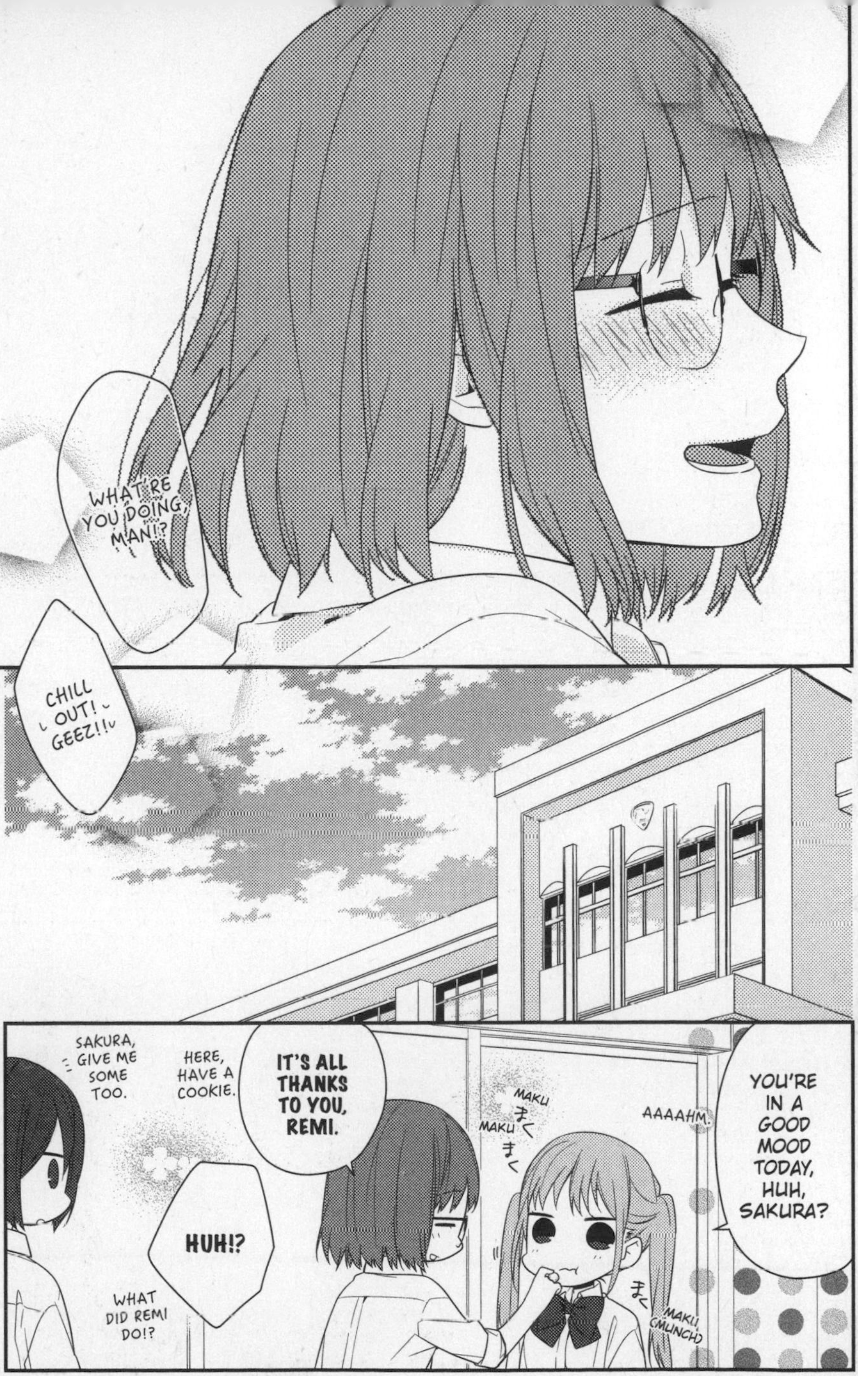
WHAT'RE YOU DOING, MANI?
CHILL OUT! GEEZ!!
YOU'RE IN A GOOD MOOD TODAY, HUH, SAKURA?
AAAAHM.
MAKU まく
MAKU まく
IT'S ALL THANKS TO YOU, REMI.
HERE, HAVE A COOKIE.
SAKURA, GIVE ME SOME TOO.
HUH!?
WHAT DID REMI DO!?
まく MAKU (MUNCH)

HORIMIYA

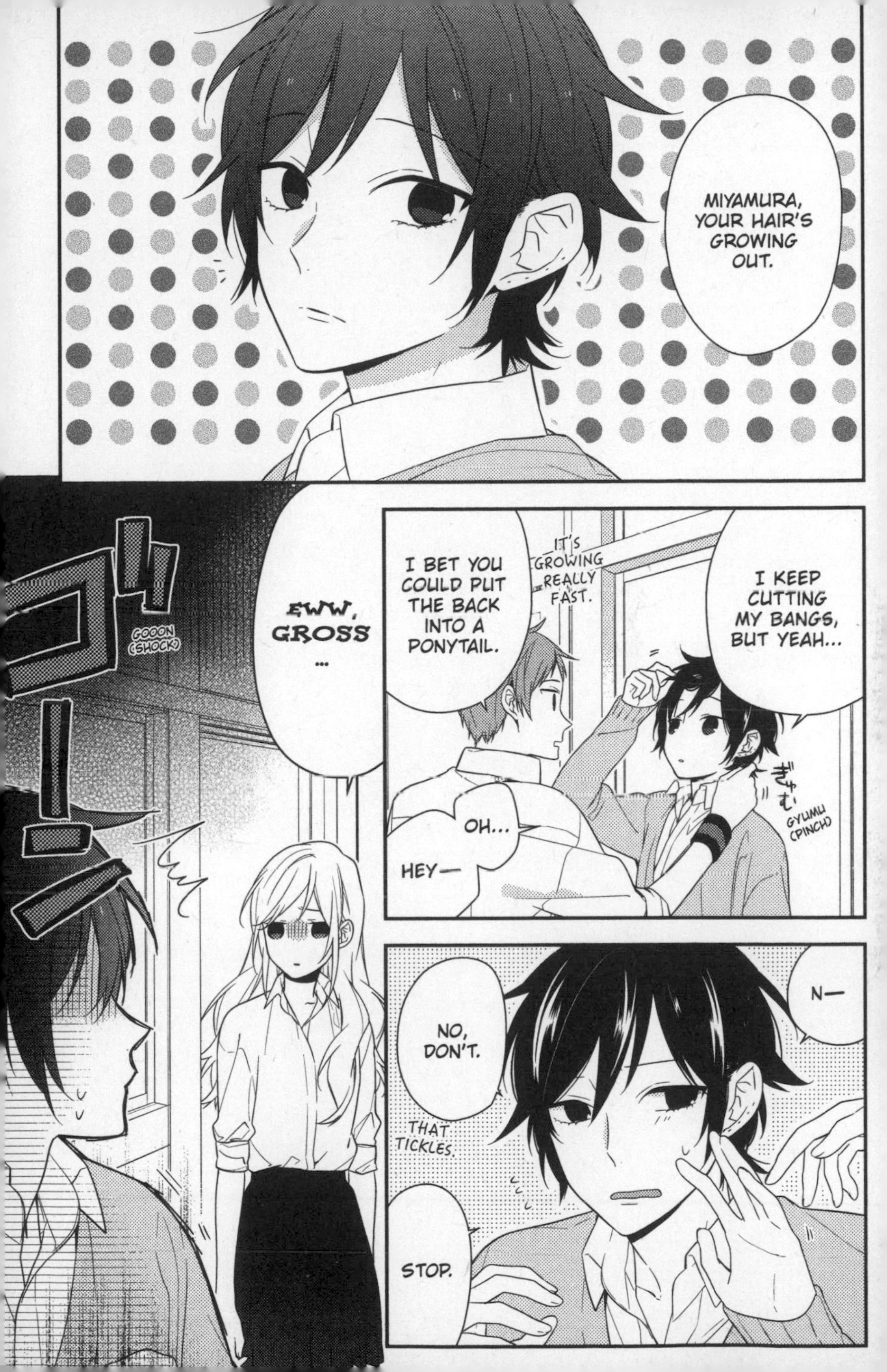
MIYAMURA, YOUR HAIR'S GROWING OUT.
I KEEP CUTTING MY BANGS, BUT YEAH...
IT'S GROWING REALLY FAST.
I BET YOU COULD PUT THE BACK INTO A PONYTAIL.
ぎゅむ
GYUMU (PINCH)
OH...
HEY—
N—
NO, DON'T.
THAT TICKLES.
STOP.
EWW, GROSS ...
GOOON (SHOCK)

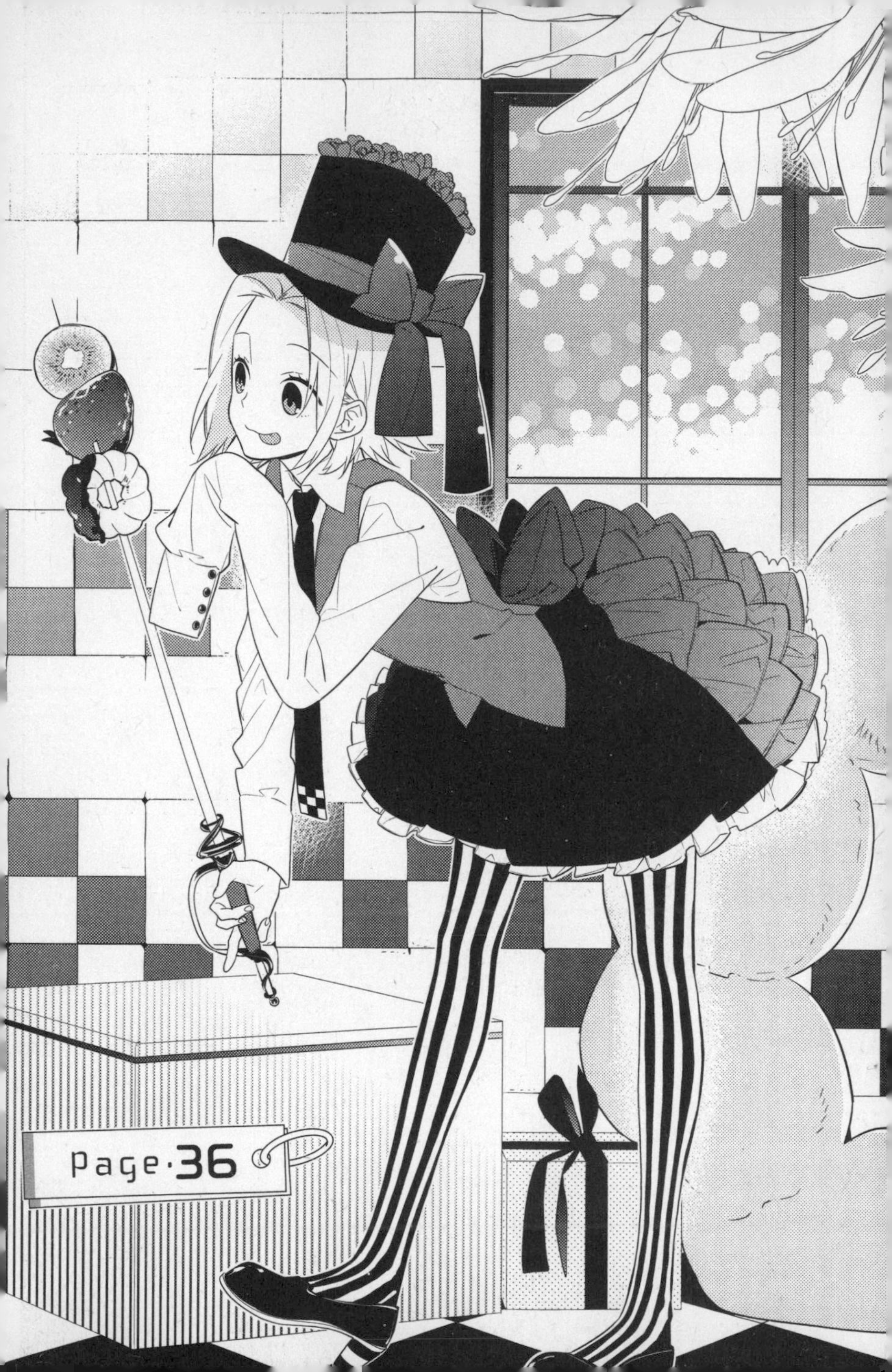
page·36

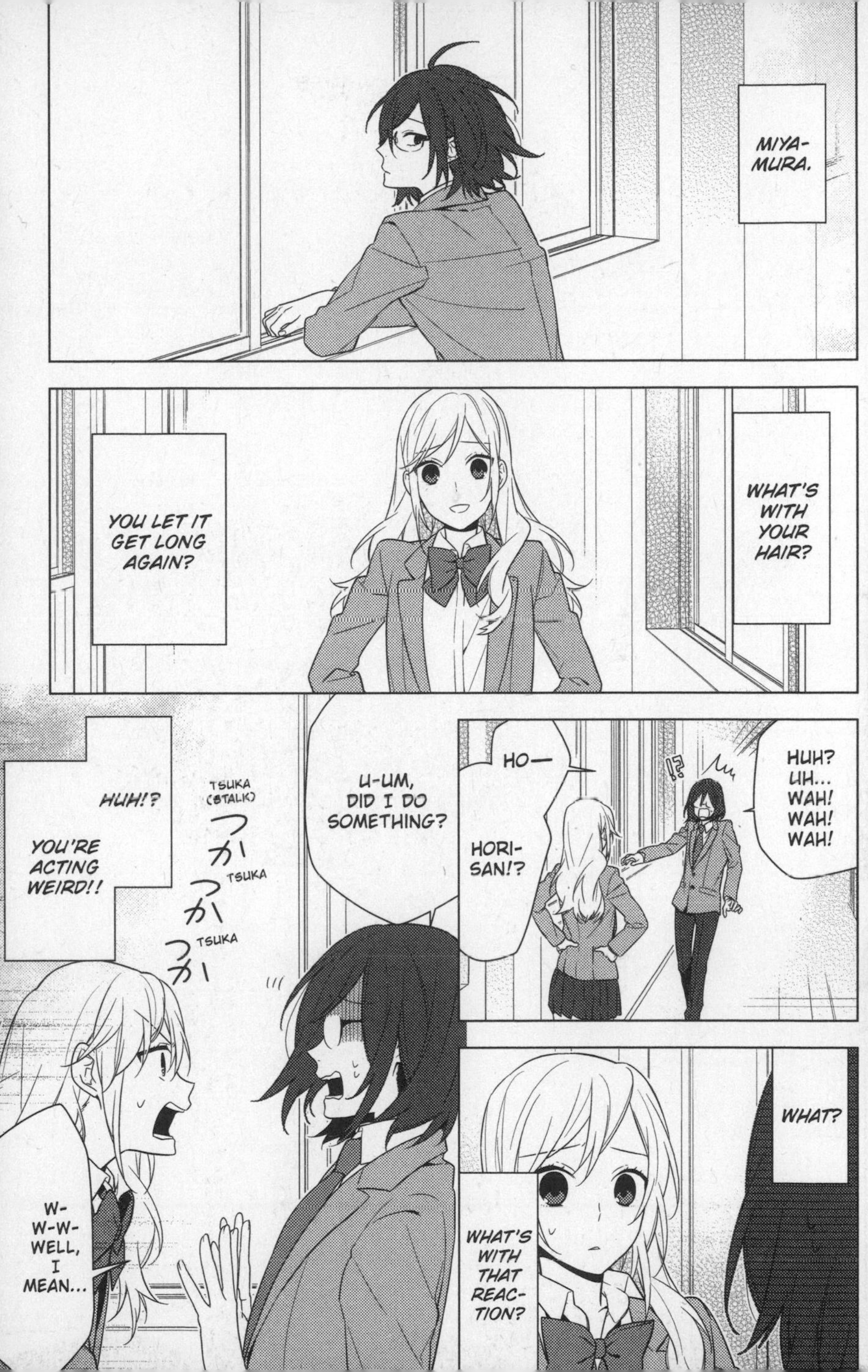

MIYA-MURA.
WHAT'S WITH YOUR HAIR?
YOU LET IT GET LONG AGAIN?
HUH? UH... WAH! WAH! WAH!
!?
HO—
HORI-SAN!?
WHAT?
WHAT'S WITH THAT REACTION?
U-UM, DID I DO SOMETHING?
TSUKA (STALK)
つか
TSUKA
つか
TSUKA
つか
HUH!?
YOU'RE ACTING WEIRD!!
W-W-W-WELL, I MEAN...

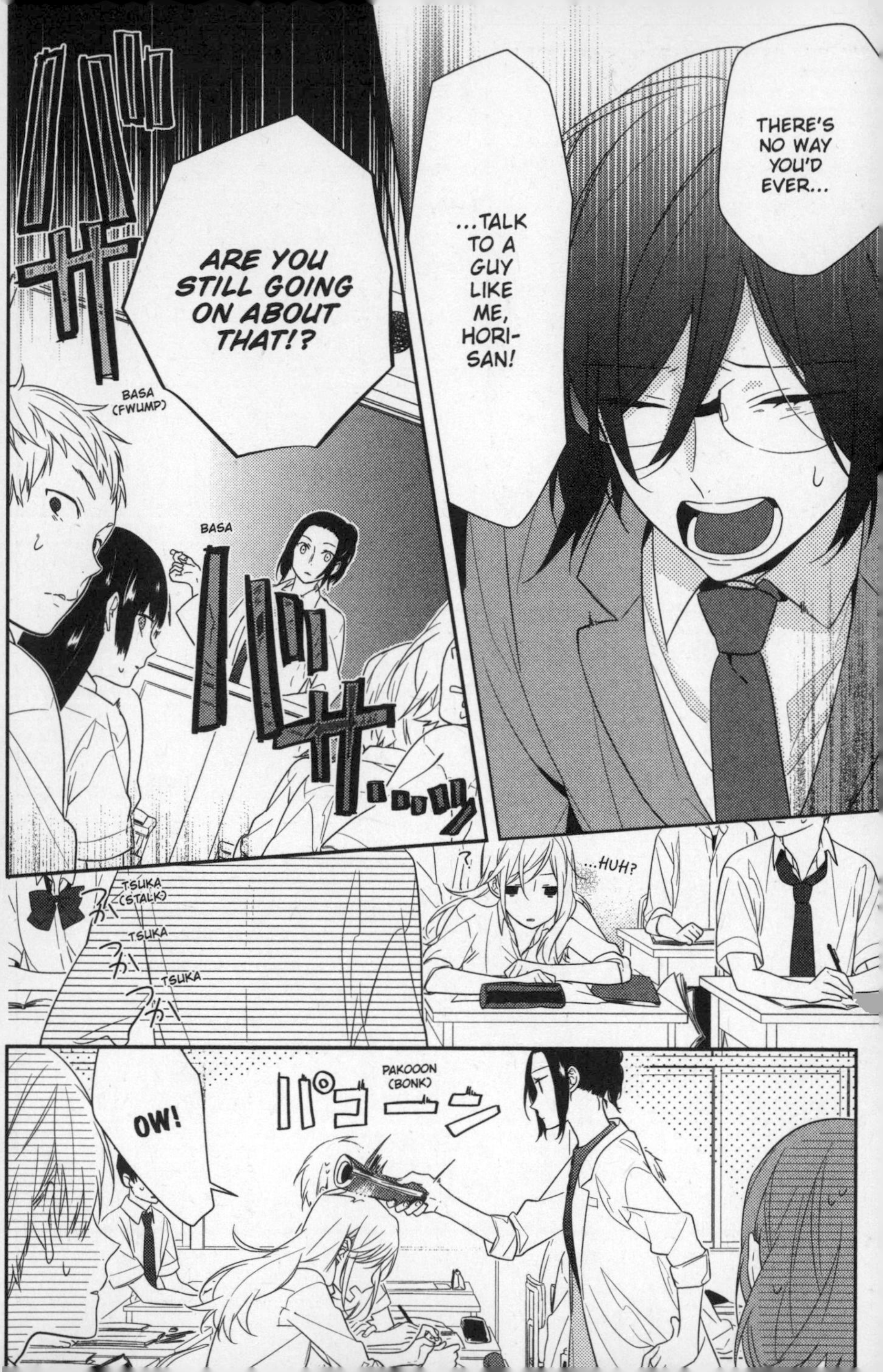
THERE'S NO WAY YOU'D EVER...
...TALK TO A GUY LIKE ME, HORI-SAN!
ARE YOU STILL GOING ON ABOUT THAT!?
BASA (FWUMP)
BASA
?
...HUH?
TSUKA (STALK)
TSUKA
TSUKA
PAKOOON (BONK)
OW!

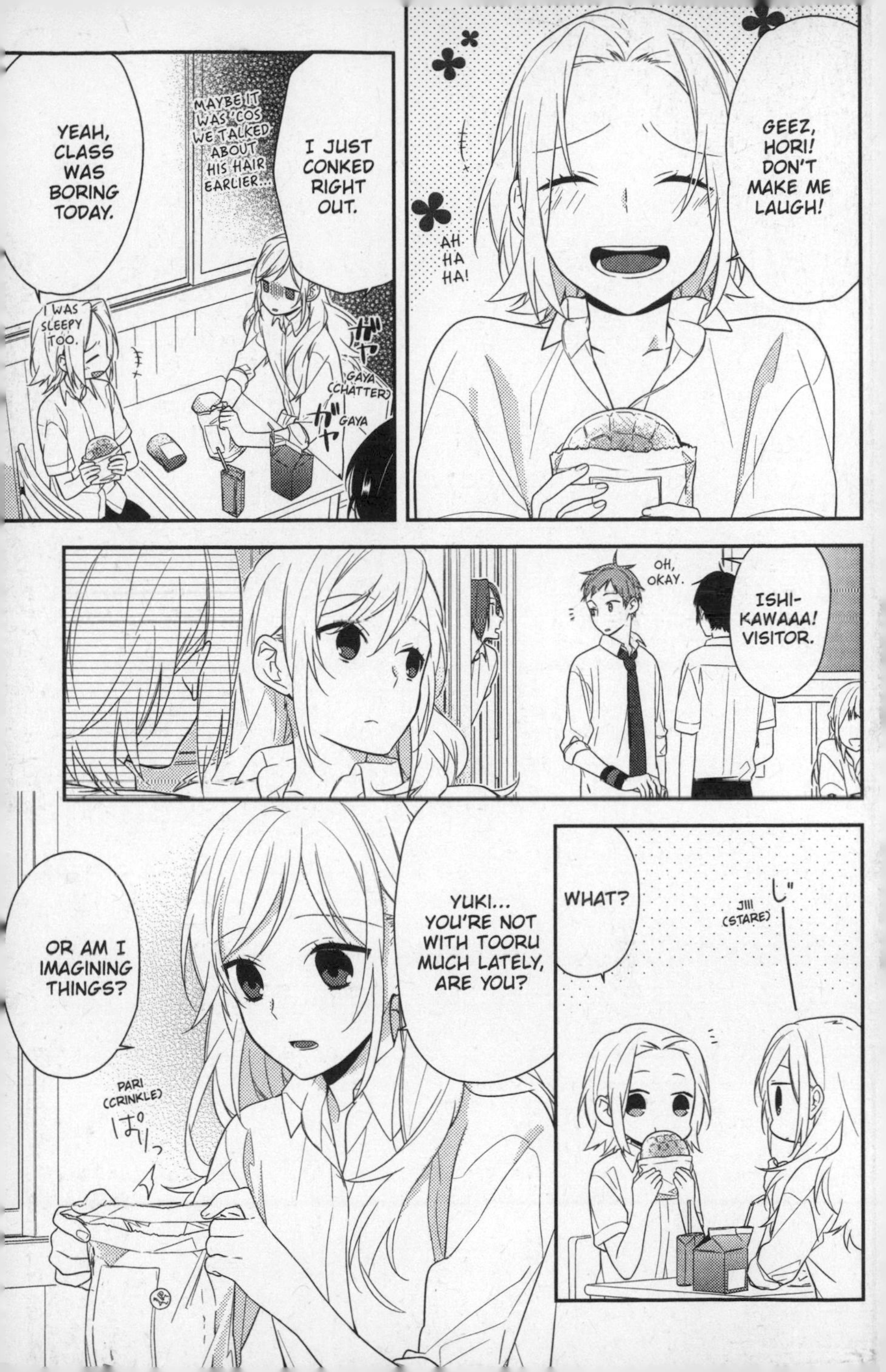
GEEZ, HORI! DON'T MAKE ME LAUGH!
AH HA HA!
I JUST CONKED RIGHT OUT.
MAYBE IT WAS 'COS WE TALKED ABOUT HIS HAIR EARLIER...
YEAH, CLASS WAS BORING TODAY.
I WAS SLEEPY TOO.
ガヤ
GAYA (CHATTER)
ガヤ
GAYA
ISHI-KAWAAA! VISITOR.
OH, OKAY.
JIII (STARE)
WHAT?
YUKI... YOU'RE NOT WITH TOORU MUCH LATELY, ARE YOU?
OR AM I IMAGINING THINGS?
PARI (CRINKLE)
ぱりっ

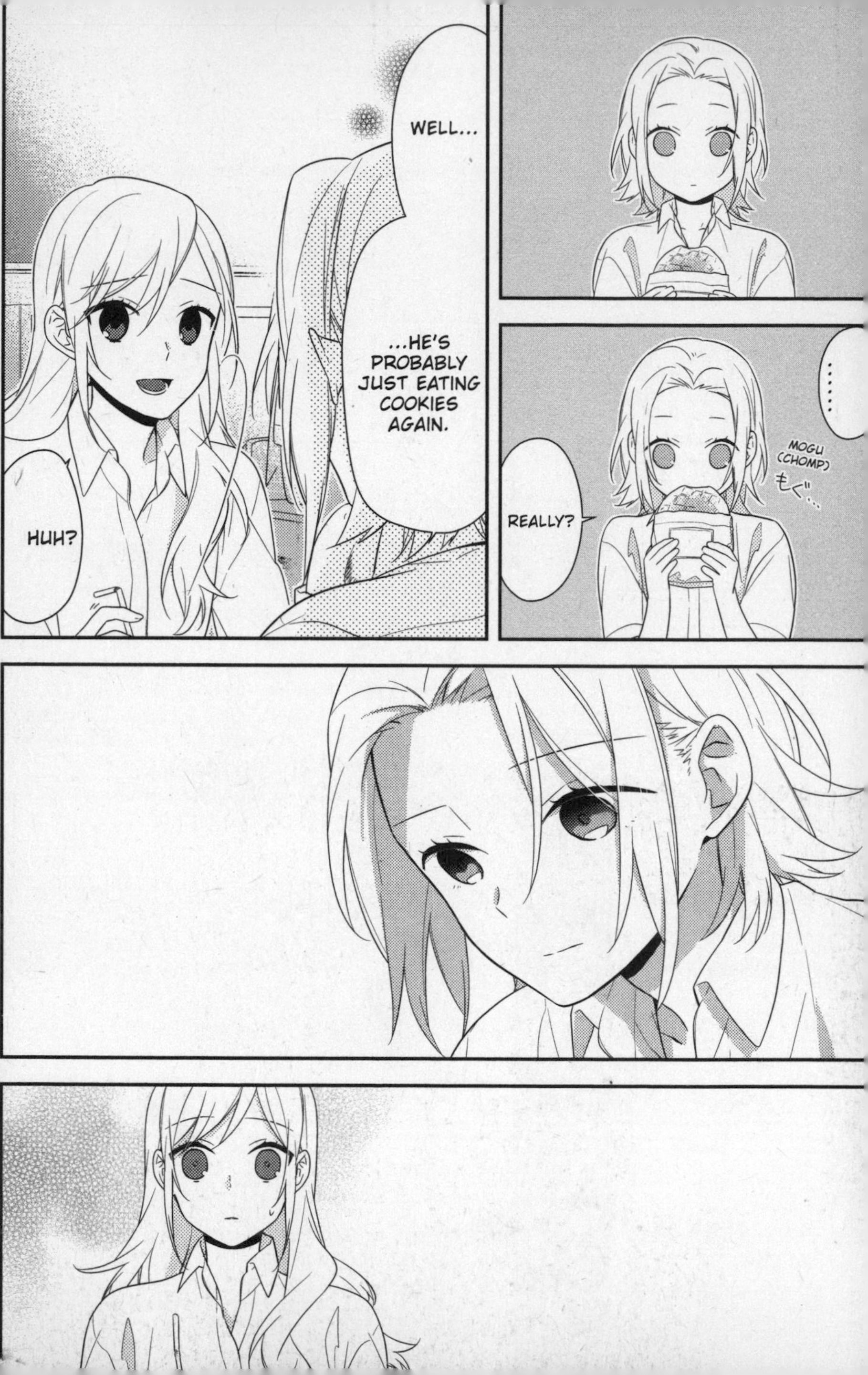
……
MOGU (CHOMP)
もぐ…
REALLY?
WELL…
…HE'S PROBABLY JUST EATING COOKIES AGAIN.
HUH?

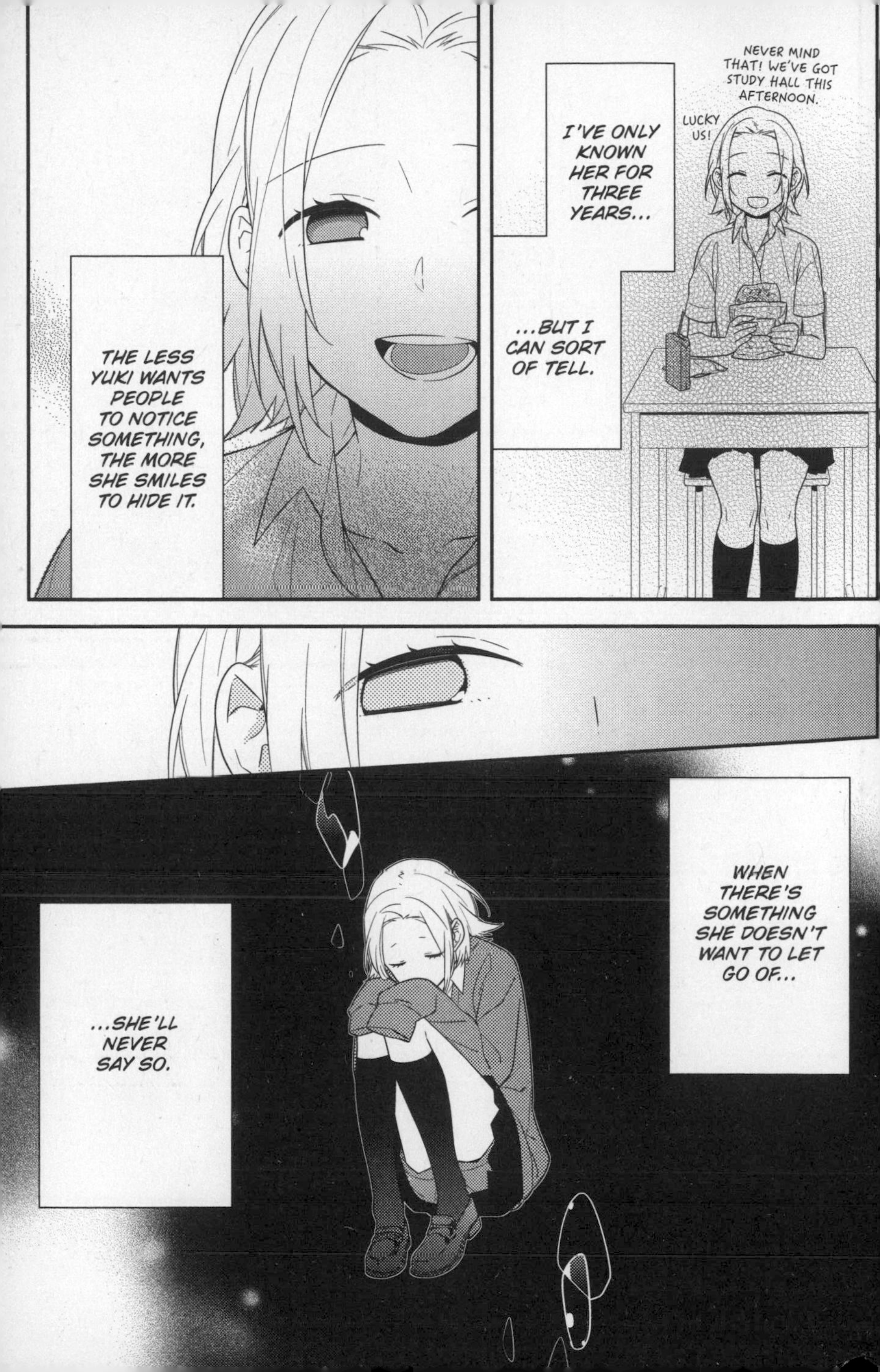
NEVER MIND THAT! WE'VE GOT STUDY HALL THIS AFTERNOON.
LUCKY US!
I'VE ONLY KNOWN HER FOR THREE YEARS...
...BUT I CAN SORT OF TELL.
THE LESS YUKI WANTS PEOPLE TO NOTICE SOMETHING, THE MORE SHE SMILES TO HIDE IT.
WHEN THERE'S SOMETHING SHE DOESN'T WANT TO LET GO OF...
...SHE'LL NEVER SAY SO.

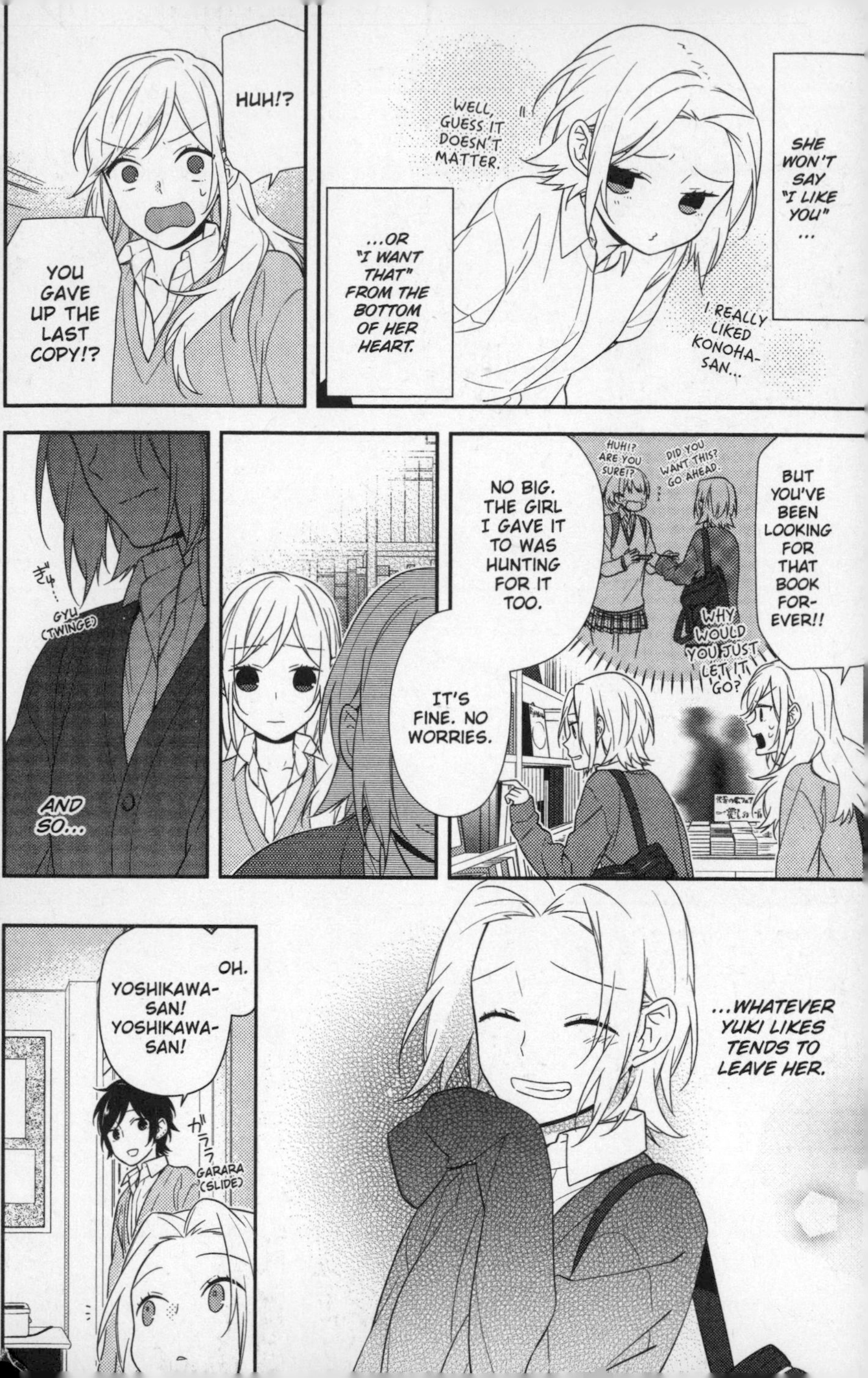
SHE WON'T SAY "I LIKE YOU"...
WELL, GUESS IT DOESN'T MATTER.
I REALLY LIKED KONOHA-SAN...
...OR "I WANT THAT" FROM THE BOTTOM OF HER HEART.
HUH!?
YOU GAVE UP THE LAST COPY!?
BUT YOU'VE BEEN LOOKING FOR THAT BOOK FOR-EVER!!
DID YOU WANT THIS? GO AHEAD.
HUH!? ARE YOU SURE!?
NO BIG. THE GIRL I GAVE IT TO WAS HUNTING FOR IT TOO.
WHY WOULD YOU JUST LET IT GO?
IT'S FINE. NO WORRIES.
ぎゅ…
GYU (TWINGE)
AND SO...
...WHATEVER YUKI LIKES TENDS TO LEAVE HER.
OH. YOSHIKAWA-SAN! YOSHIKAWA-SAN!
ガララ
GARARA (SLIDE)

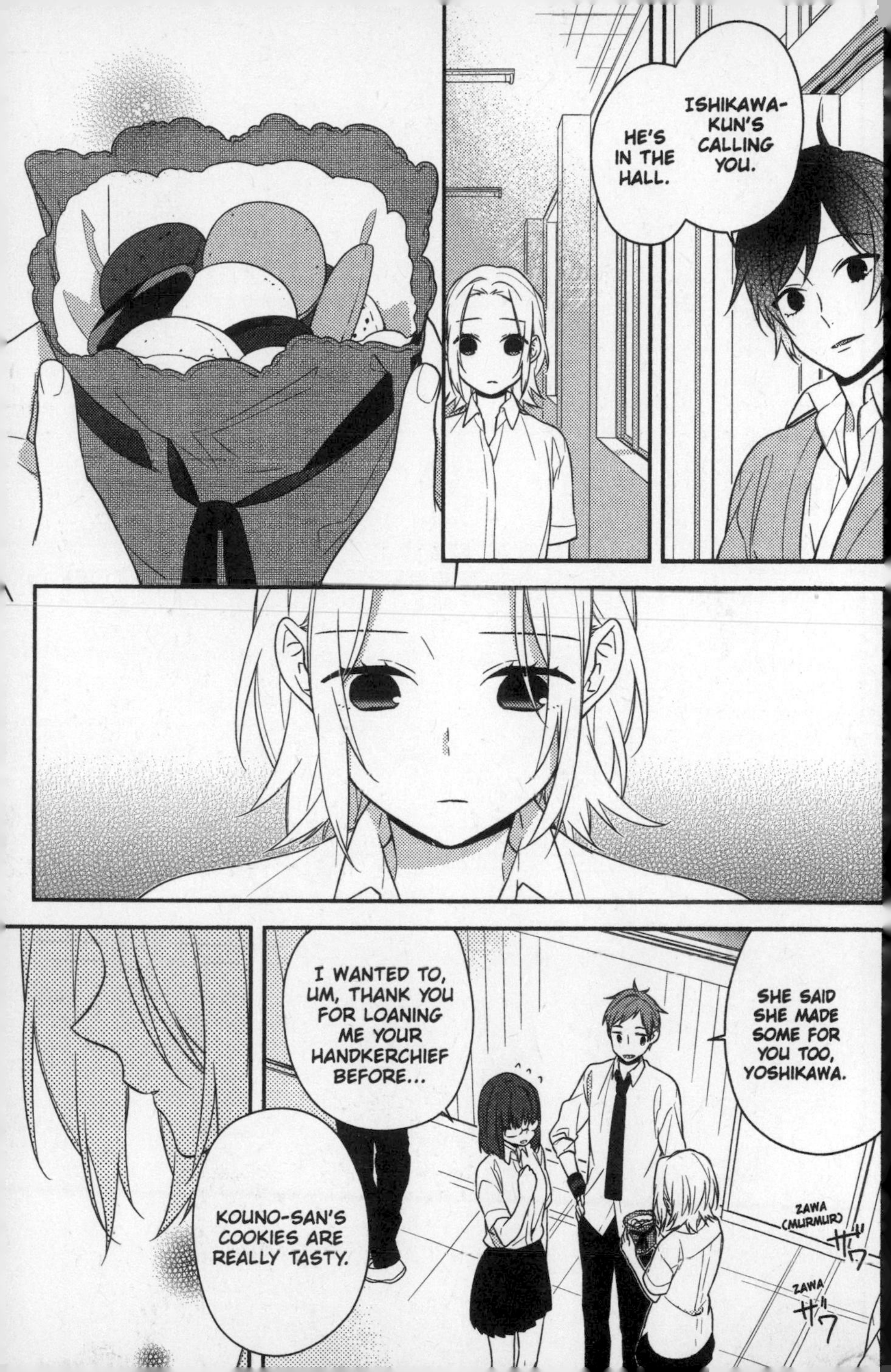
ISHIKAWA-KUN'S CALLING YOU.
HE'S IN THE HALL.
SHE SAID SHE MADE SOME FOR YOU TOO, YOSHIKAWA.
I WANTED TO, UM, THANK YOU FOR LOANING ME YOUR HANDKERCHIEF BEFORE...
KOUNO-SAN'S COOKIES ARE REALLY TASTY.
ZAWA (MURMUR) ザワ
ZAWA ザワ

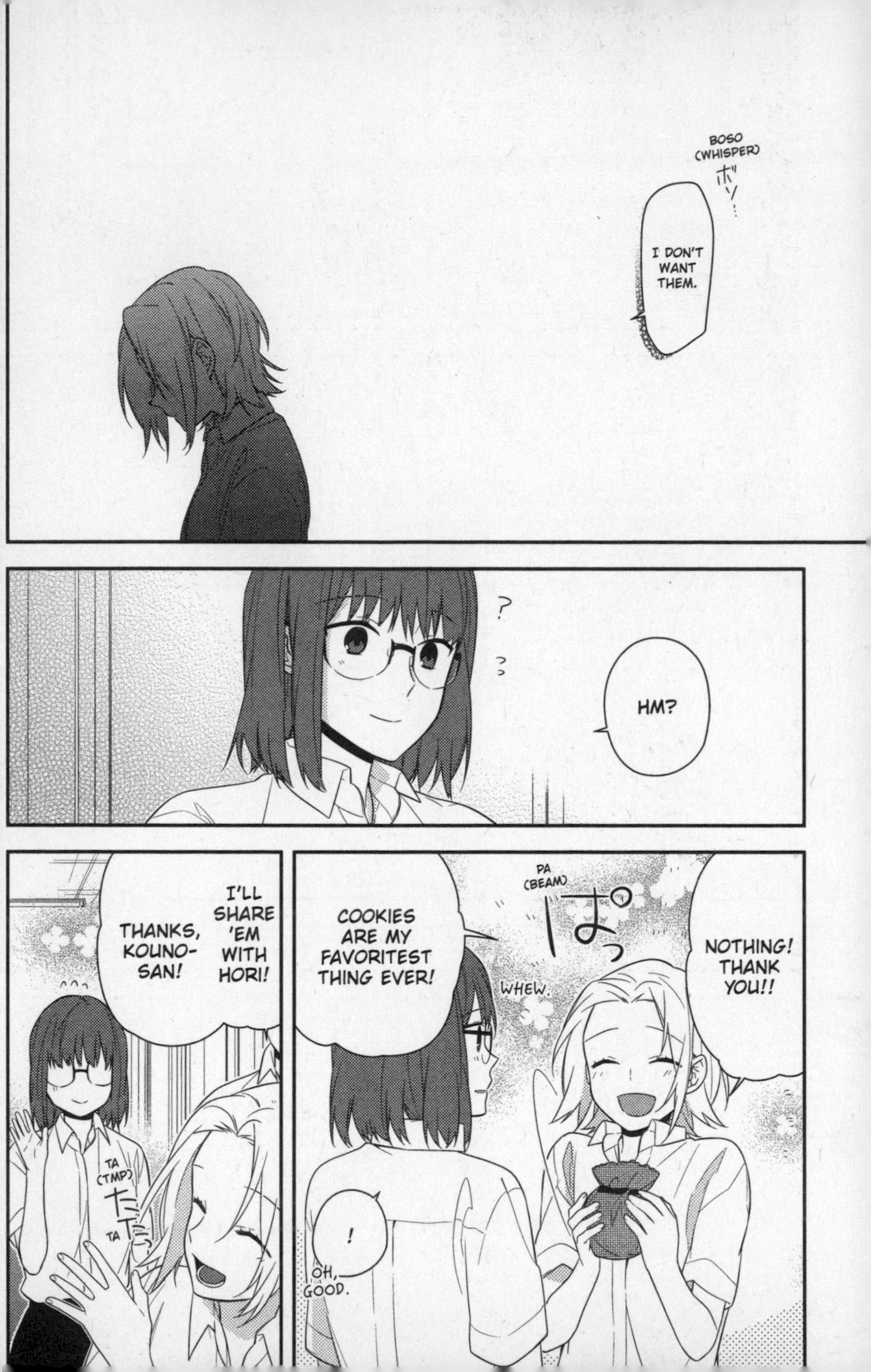
BOSO (WHISPER)
ボソ…
I DON'T WANT THEM.
?
HM?
PA (BEAM)
ぱっ
NOTHING! THANK YOU!!
COOKIES ARE MY FAVORITEST THING EVER!
WHEW.
!
OH, GOOD.
I'LL SHARE 'EM WITH HORI!
THANKS, KOUNO-SAN!
TA (TMP)
TA

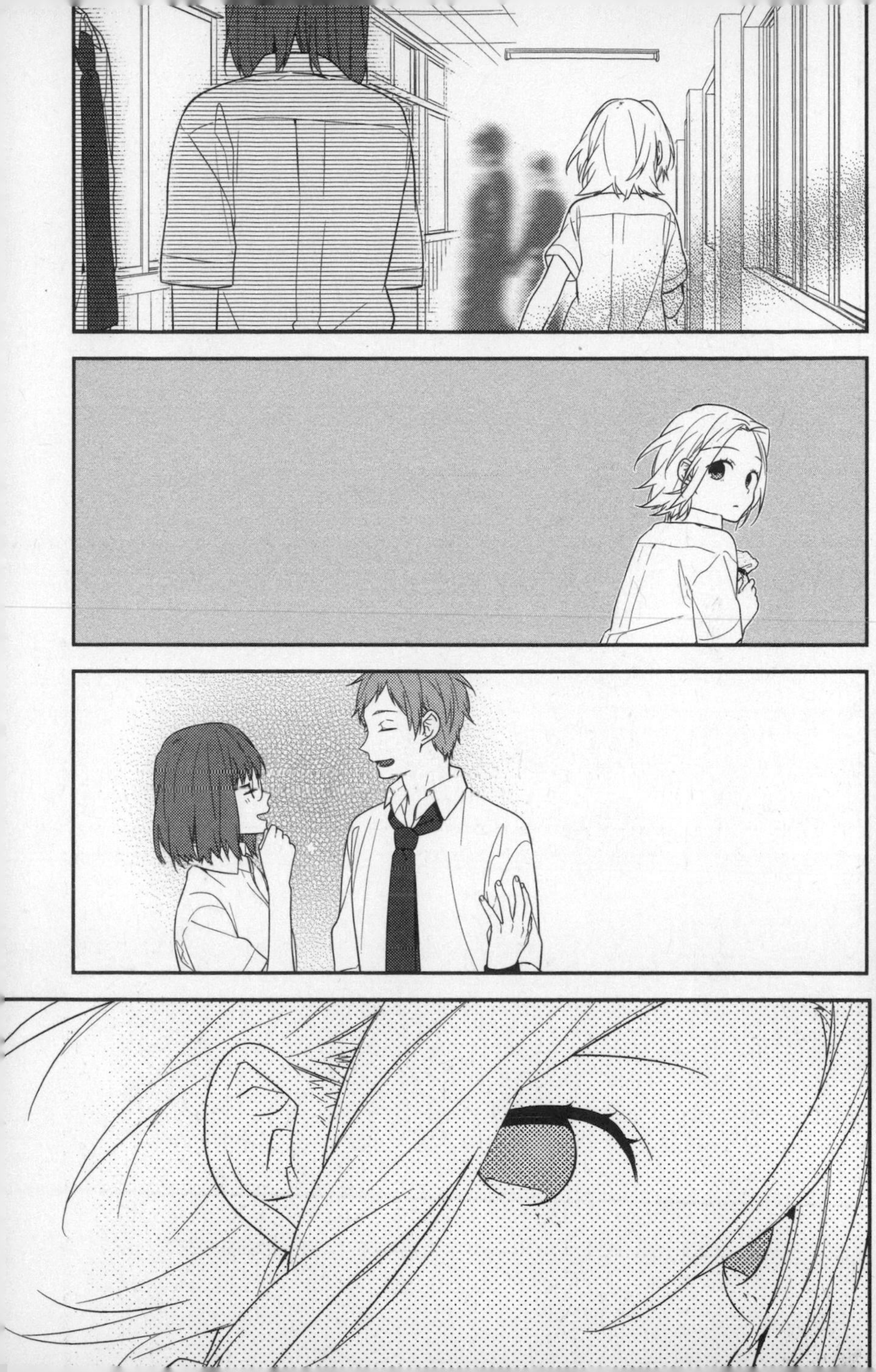

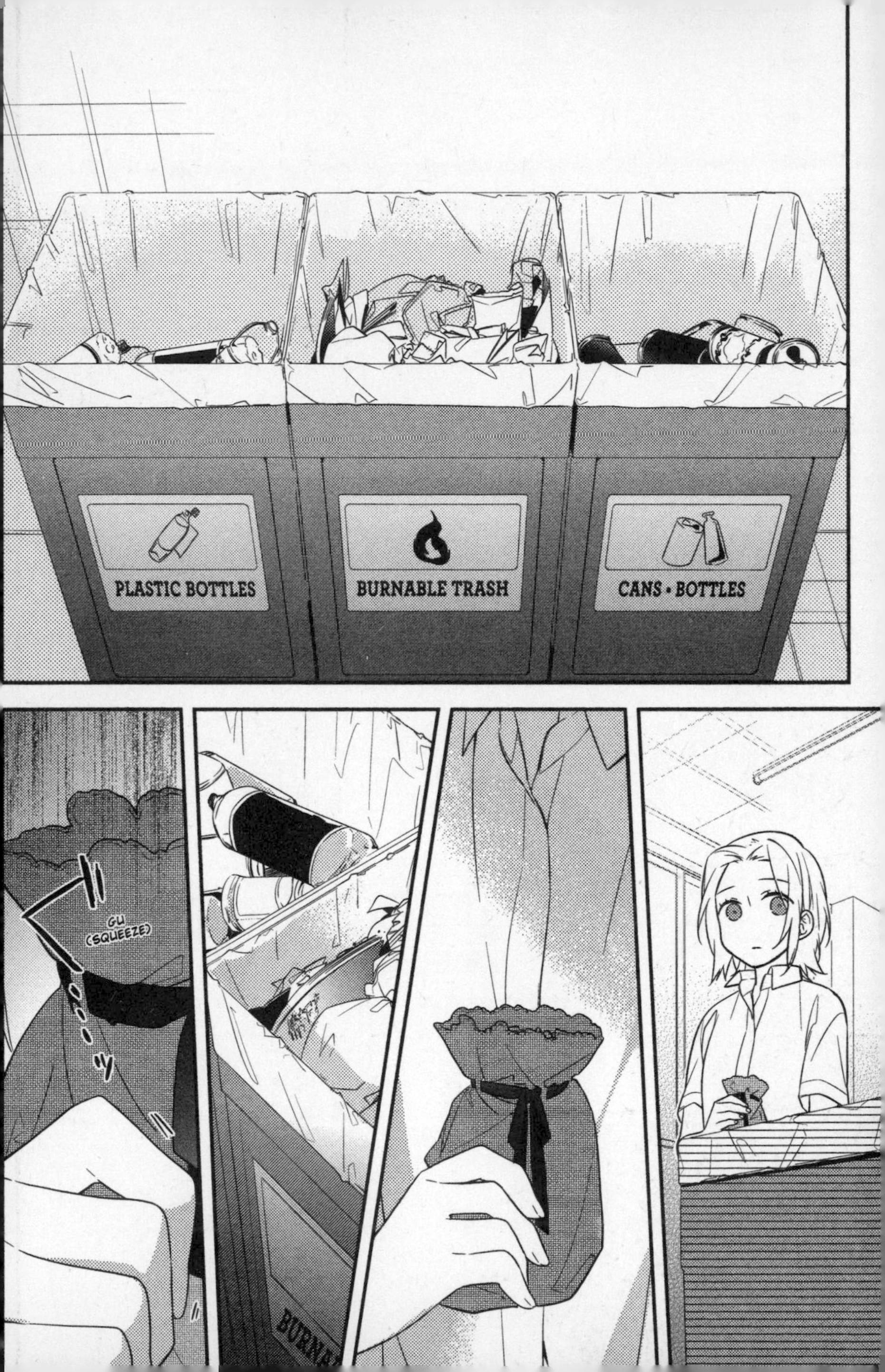
PLASTIC BOTTLES
BURNABLE TRASH
CANS • BOTTLES
GU (SQUEEZE)

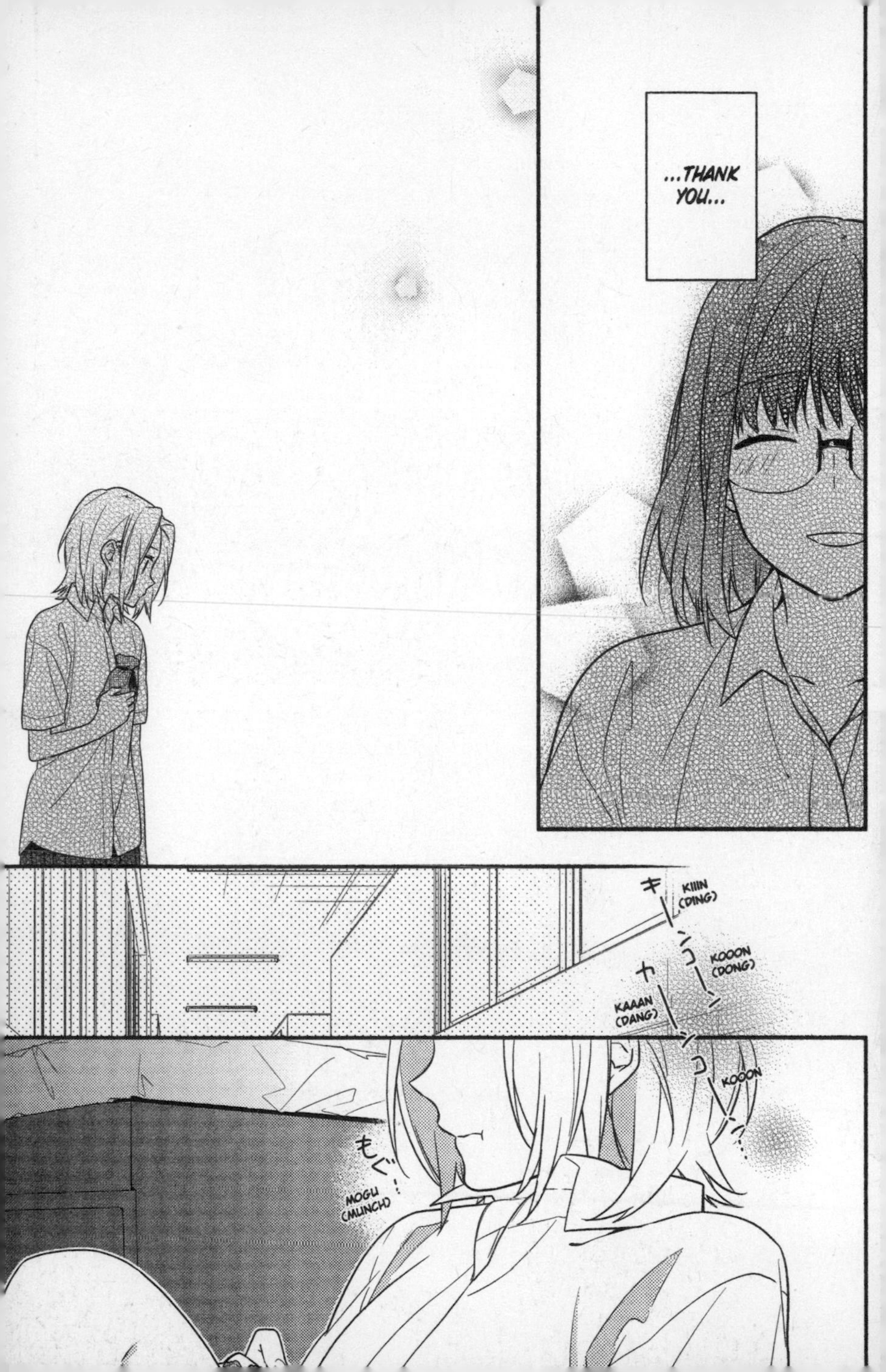
...THANK YOU...
キーンコーン
KIIIN (DING)
KOOON (DONG)
カーンコーン
KAAAN (DANG)
KOOON
もぐ
MOGU (MUNCH)

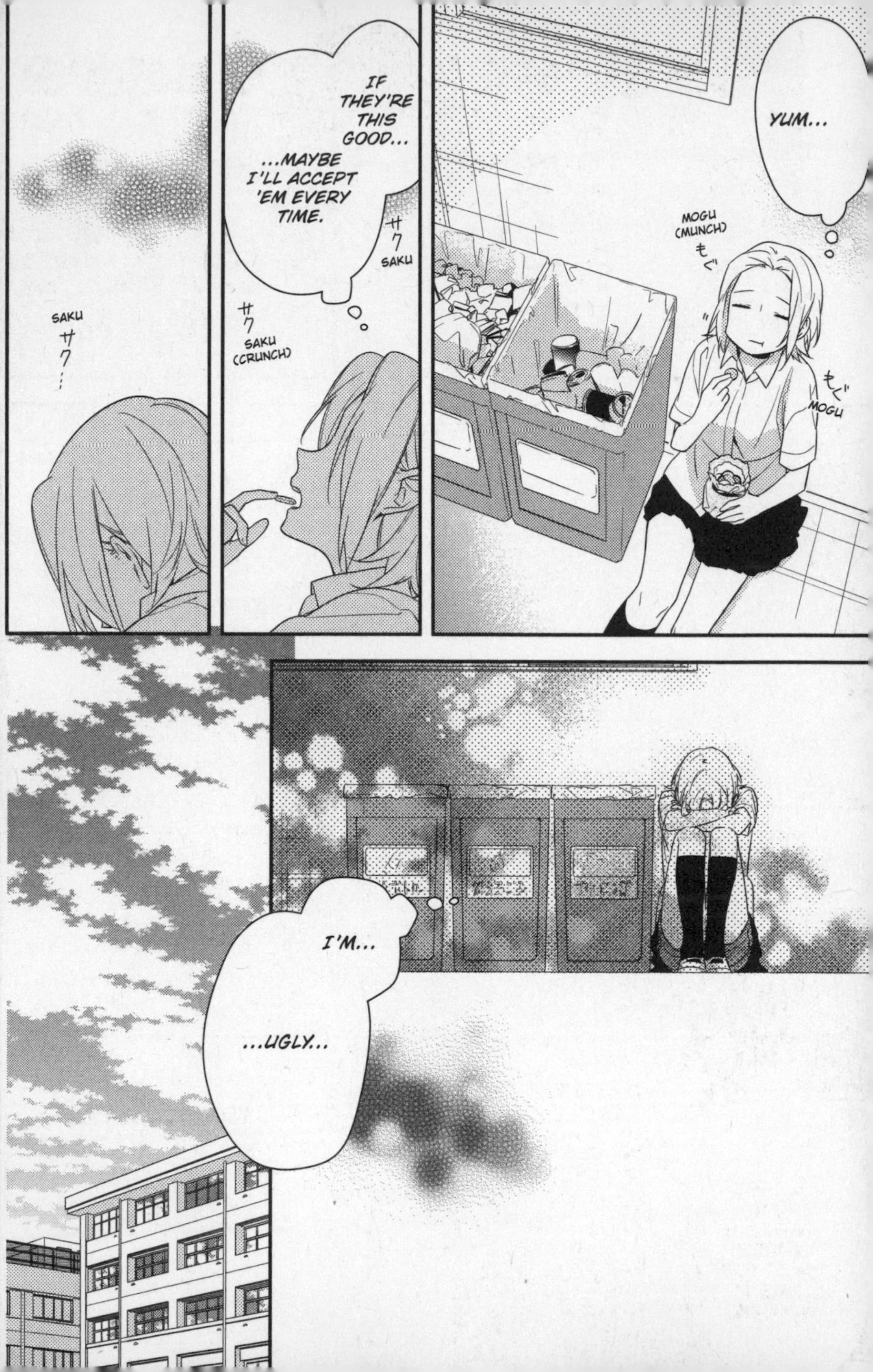
YUM...
MOGU (MUNCH)
もぐ
もぐ
MOGU
IF THEY'RE THIS GOOD...
...MAYBE I'LL ACCEPT 'EM EVERY TIME.
サク
SAKU
サク
SAKU (CRUNCH)
SAKU
サク...
I'M...
...UGLY...

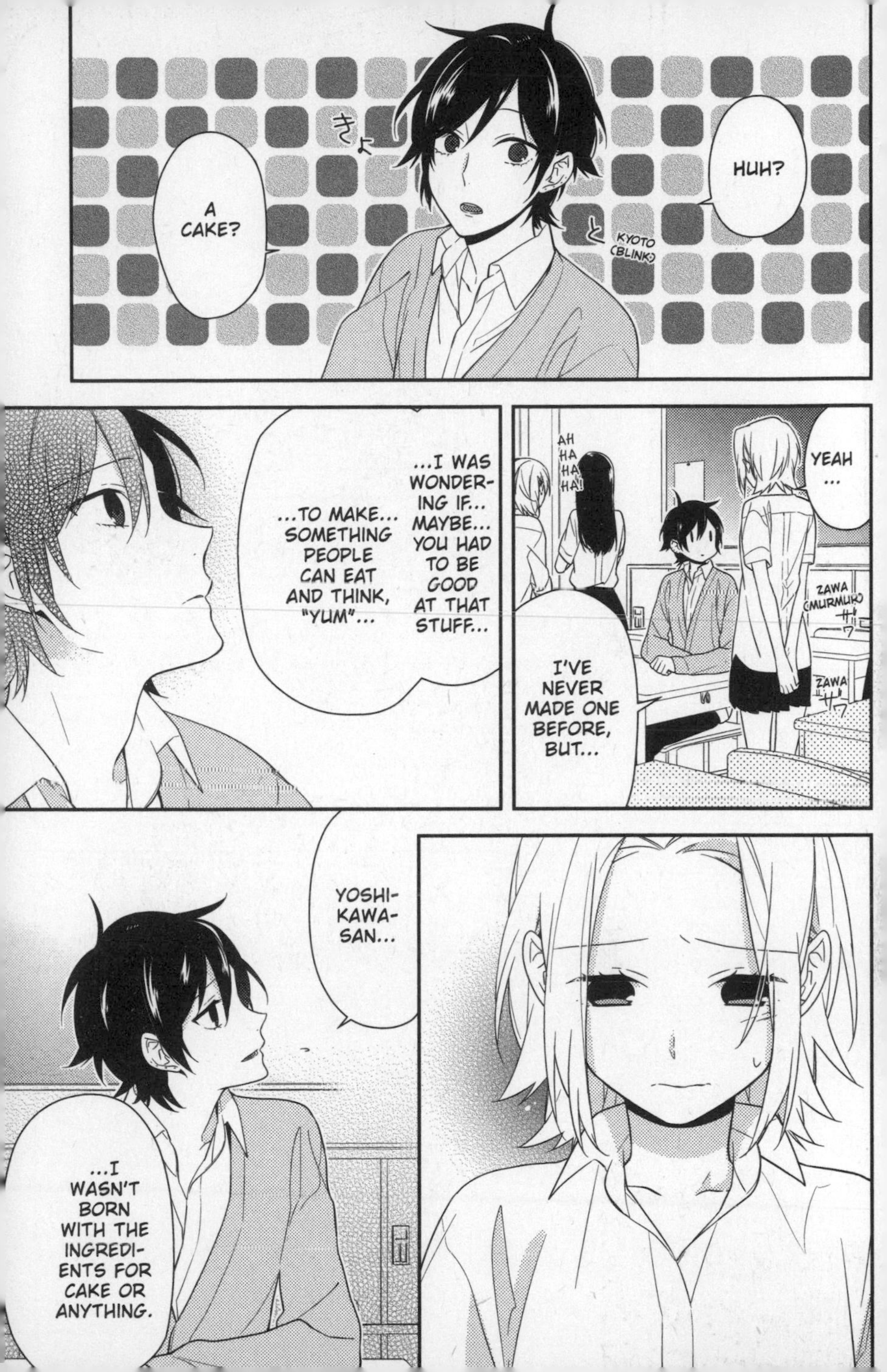
HUH?
と
KYOTO (BLINK)
きょ
A CAKE?
YEAH...
AH HA HA HA!
ZAWA (MURMUR)
ザワ
ZAWA
ザワ
I'VE NEVER MADE ONE BEFORE, BUT...
...I WAS WONDERING IF... MAYBE... YOU HAD TO BE GOOD AT THAT STUFF...
...TO MAKE... SOMETHING PEOPLE CAN EAT AND THINK, "YUM"...
YOSHIKAWA-SAN...
...I WASN'T BORN WITH THE INGREDIENTS FOR CAKE OR ANYTHING.

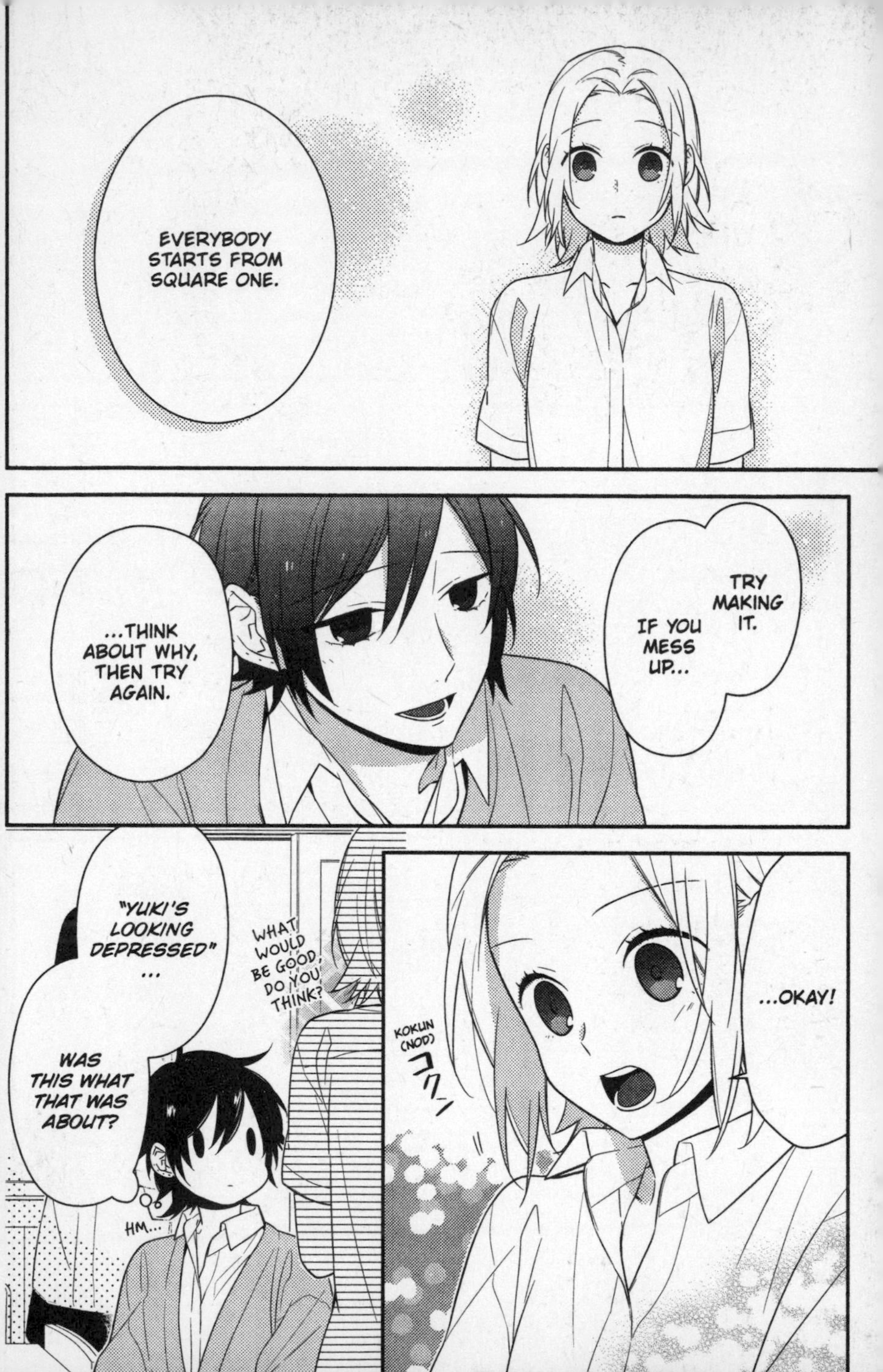
EVERYBODY STARTS FROM SQUARE ONE.
TRY MAKING IT.
IF YOU MESS UP...
...THINK ABOUT WHY, THEN TRY AGAIN.
...OKAY!
KOKUN (NOD)
WHAT WOULD BE GOOD, DO YOU THINK?
"YUKI'S LOOKING DEPRESSED"...
WAS THIS WHAT THAT WAS ABOUT?
HM...

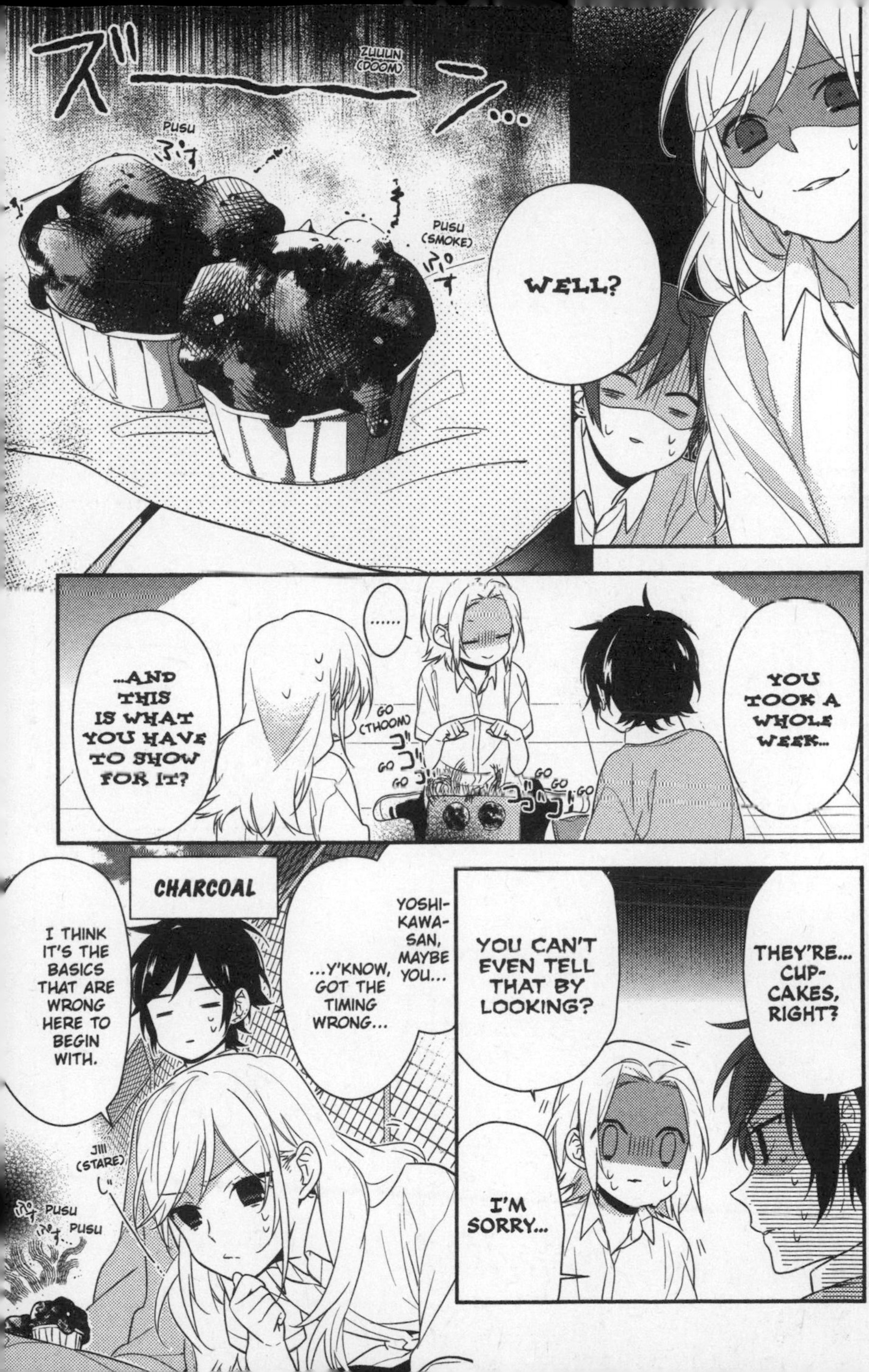
WELL?
ZUUUN (DOOM)
PUSU
PUSU (SMOKE)
YOU TOOK A WHOLE WEEK...
......
...AND THIS IS WHAT YOU HAVE TO SHOW FOR IT?
GO (THOOM) GO GO
GO GO GO
THEY'RE... CUP-CAKES, RIGHT?
YOU CAN'T EVEN TELL THAT BY LOOKING?
I'M SORRY...
YOSHI-KAWA-SAN, MAYBE YOU...
...Y'KNOW, GOT THE TIMING WRONG...
CHARCOAL
I THINK IT'S THE BASICS THAT ARE WRONG HERE TO BEGIN WITH.
JIII (STARE)
PUSU PUSU

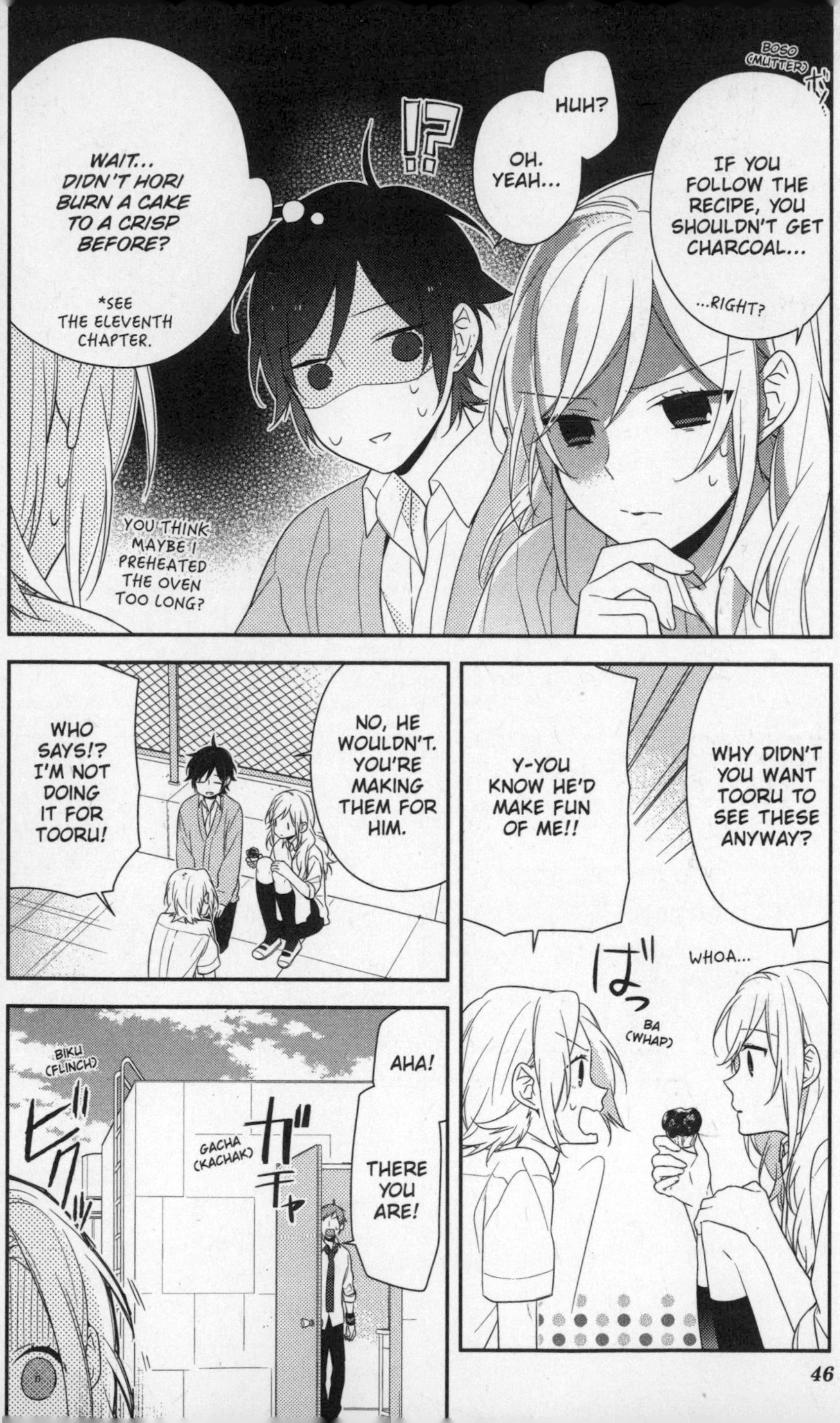
BOSO (MUTTER)
IF YOU FOLLOW THE RECIPE, YOU SHOULDN'T GET CHARCOAL...
...RIGHT?
HUH?
OH. YEAH...
!?
WAIT... DIDN'T HORI BURN A CAKE TO A CRISP BEFORE?
*SEE THE ELEVENTH CHAPTER.
YOU THINK MAYBE I PREHEATED THE OVEN TOO LONG?
WHY DIDN'T YOU WANT TOORU TO SEE THESE ANYWAY?
Y-YOU KNOW HE'D MAKE FUN OF ME!!
WHOA...
BA (WHAP)
NO, HE WOULDN'T. YOU'RE MAKING THEM FOR HIM.
WHO SAYS!? I'M NOT DOING IT FOR TOORU!
AHA!
THERE YOU ARE!
GACHA (KACHAK)
BIKU (FLINCH)

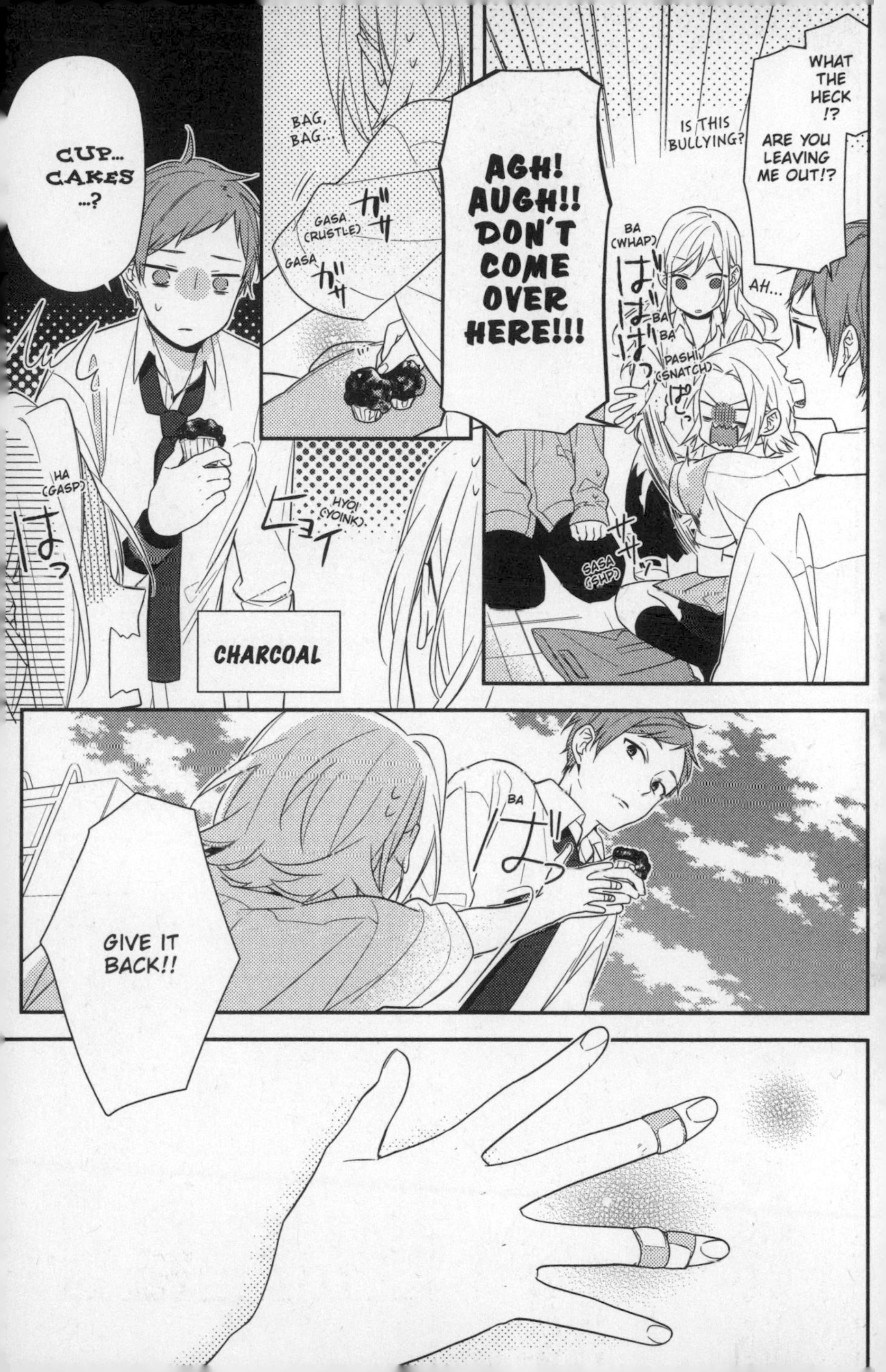
WHAT THE HECK!?
ARE YOU LEAVING ME OUT!?
IS THIS BULLYING?
AGH! AUGH!! DON'T COME OVER HERE!!!
BA (WHAP)
BA
BA
AH...
PASHI (SNATCH)
SASA (SHP)
BAG, BAG...
GASA (RUSTLE)
GASA
CUP... CAKES ...?
HYOI (YOINK)
HA (GASP)
CHARCOAL
BA
GIVE IT BACK!!

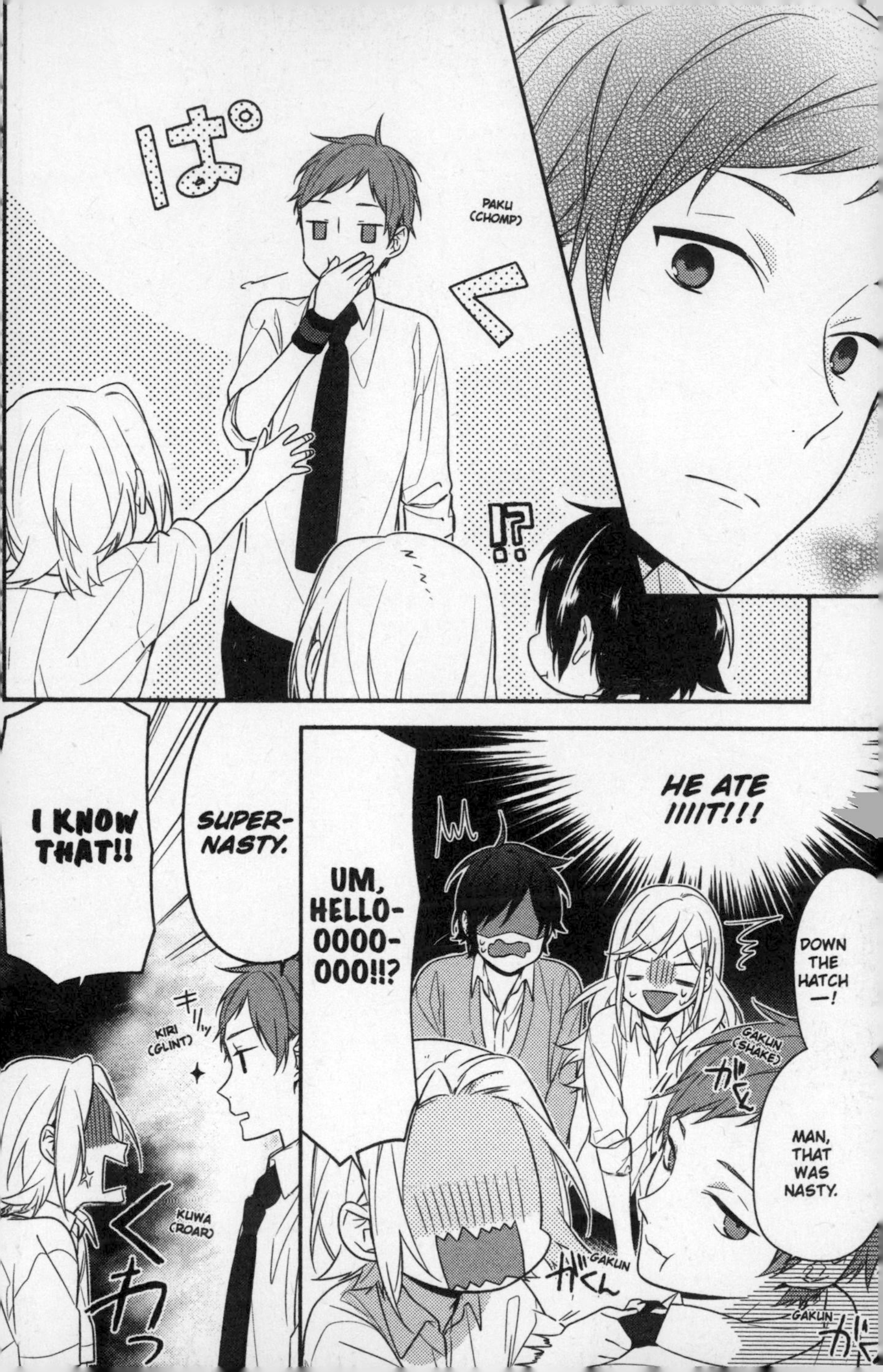
ぱく
PAKU (CHOMP)
!?
HE ATE IIIIT!!!
DOWN THE HATCH—!
GAKUN (SHAKE)
がくん
MAN, THAT WAS NASTY.
GAKUN
GAKUN
UM, HELLO-OOOO-OOO!!?
SUPER-NASTY.
I KNOW THAT!!
KIRI (GLINT)
KUWA (ROAR)

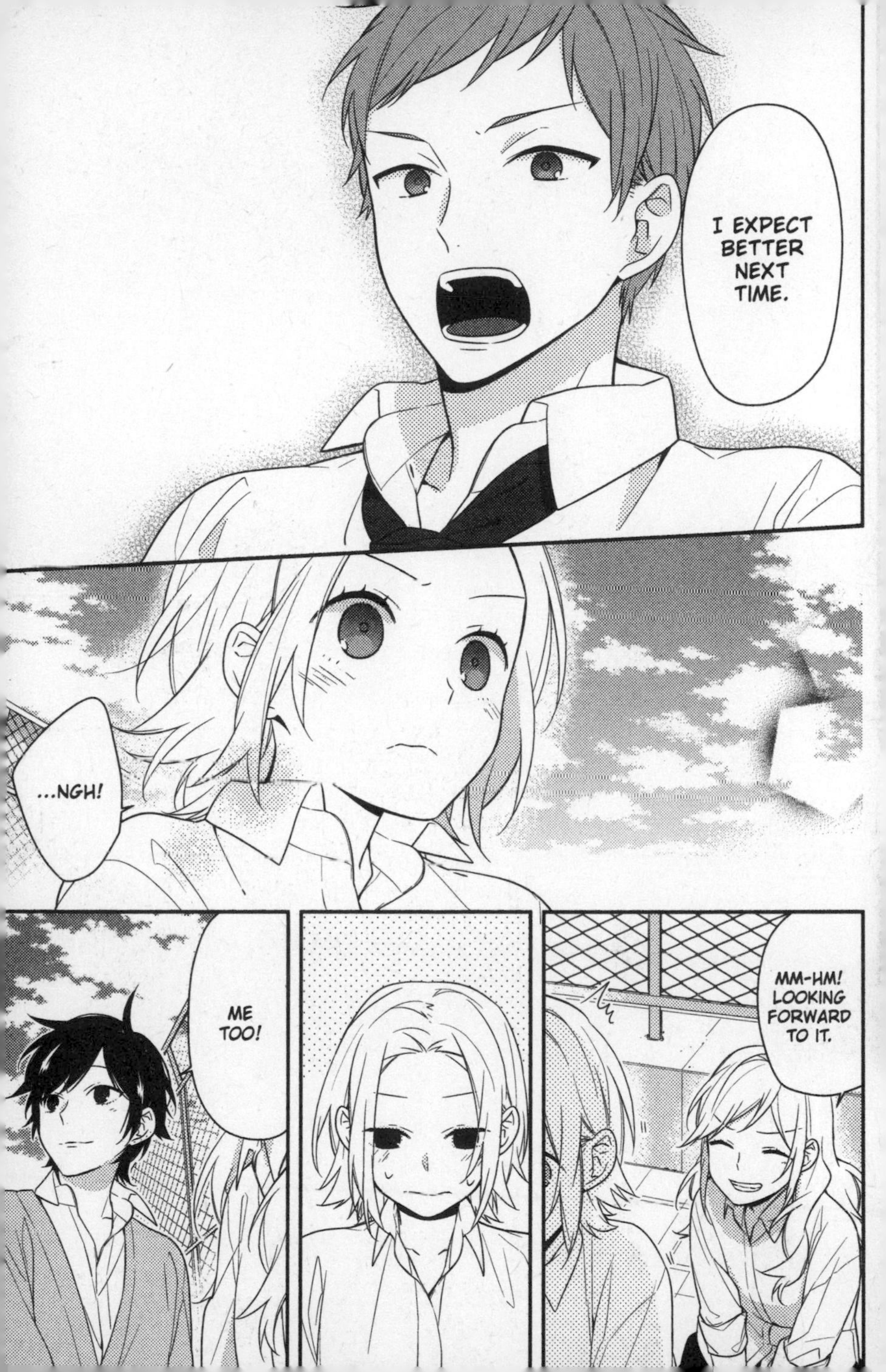
I EXPECT BETTER NEXT TIME.
...NGH!
MM-HM! LOOKING FORWARD TO IT.
ME TOO!

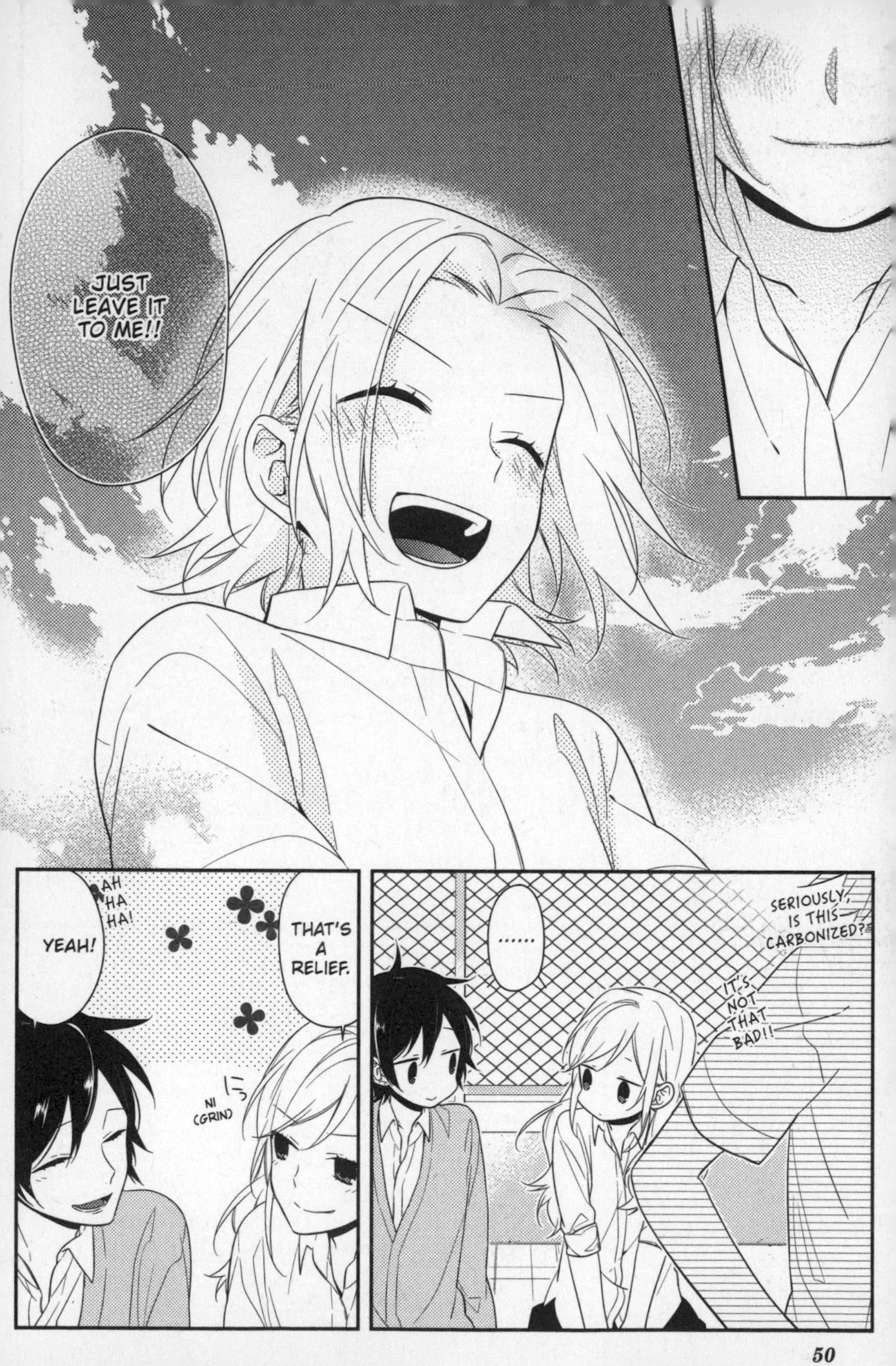
JUST LEAVE IT TO ME!!
SERIOUSLY, IS THIS CARBONIZED?
IT'S NOT THAT BAD!!
......
THAT'S A RELIEF.
AH HA HA!
YEAH!
NI (GRIN)

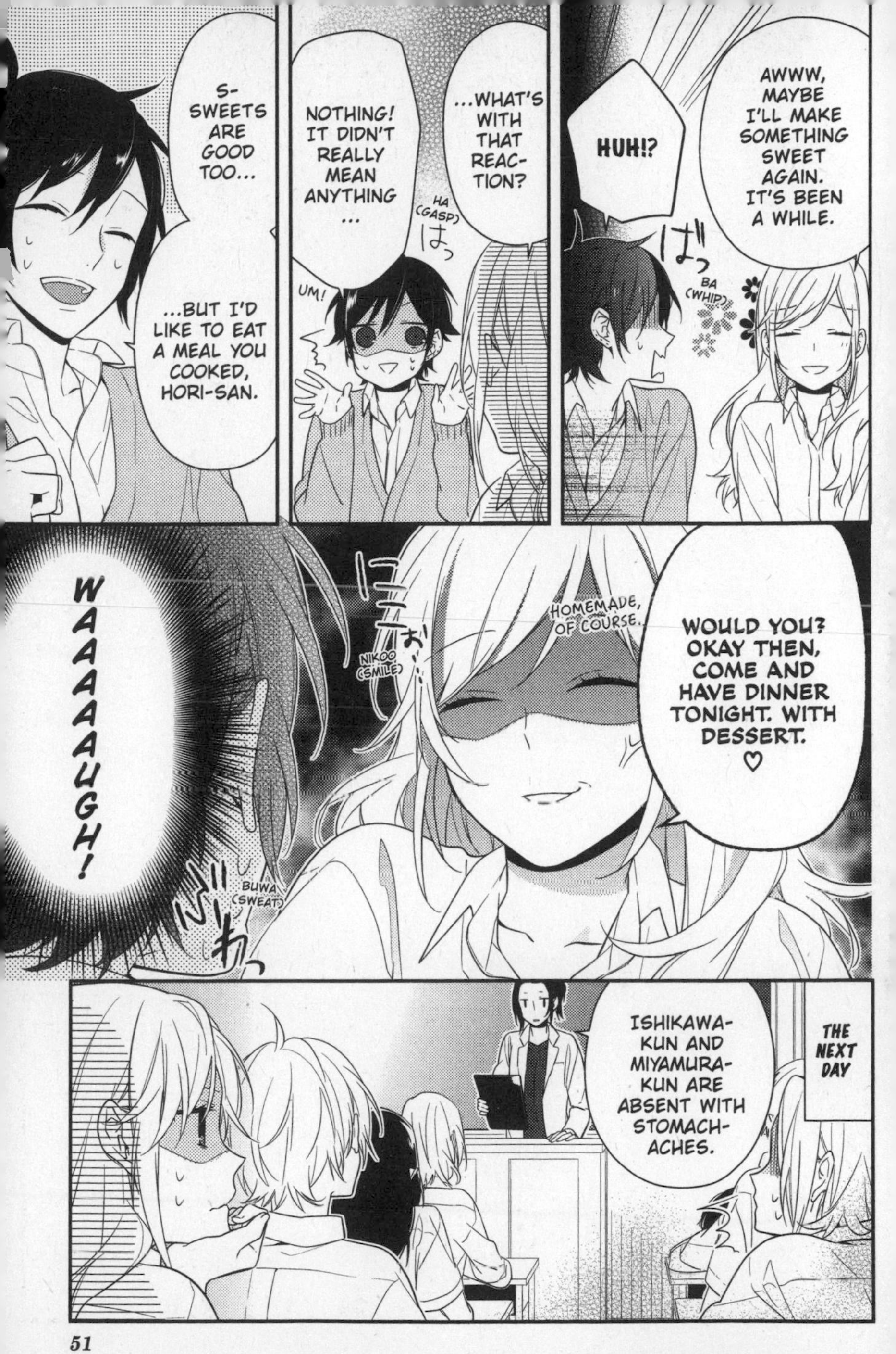
AWWW, MAYBE I'LL MAKE SOMETHING SWEET AGAIN. IT'S BEEN A WHILE.
HUH!?
BA (WHIP)
...WHAT'S WITH THAT REACTION?
HA (GASP)
NOTHING! IT DIDN'T REALLY MEAN ANYTHING...
UM!
S-SWEETS ARE GOOD TOO...
...BUT I'D LIKE TO EAT A MEAL YOU COOKED, HORI-SAN.
WOULD YOU? OKAY THEN, COME AND HAVE DINNER TONIGHT. WITH DESSERT. ♡
HOMEMADE, OF COURSE.
NIKOO (SMILE)
BUWA (SWEAT)
WAAAAAAUGH!
THE NEXT DAY
ISHIKAWA-KUN AND MIYAMURA-KUN ARE ABSENT WITH STOMACHACHES.

HORIMIYA

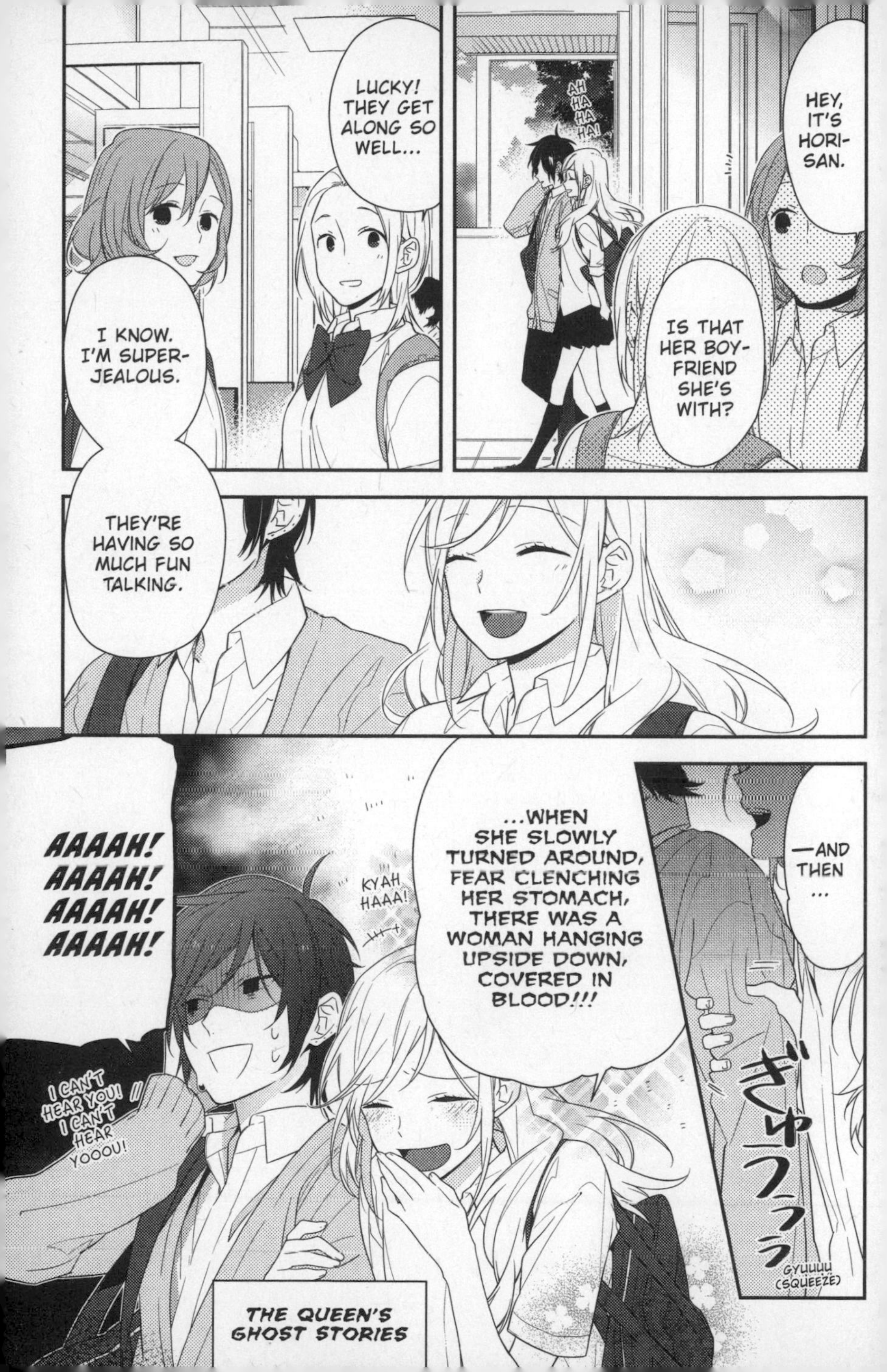
HEY, IT'S HORI-SAN.
AH HA HA HA!
IS THAT HER BOY-FRIEND SHE'S WITH?
LUCKY! THEY GET ALONG SO WELL...
I KNOW. I'M SUPER-JEALOUS.
THEY'RE HAVING SO MUCH FUN TALKING.
—AND THEN ...
ぎゅううう
GYUUUU (SQUEEZE)
...WHEN SHE SLOWLY TURNED AROUND, FEAR CLENCHING HER STOMACH, THERE WAS A WOMAN HANGING UPSIDE DOWN, COVERED IN BLOOD!!!
KYAH HAAA!
AAAAH! AAAAH! AAAAH! AAAAH!
I CAN'T HEAR YOU! I CAN'T HEAR YOOOU!
THE QUEEN'S GHOST STORIES

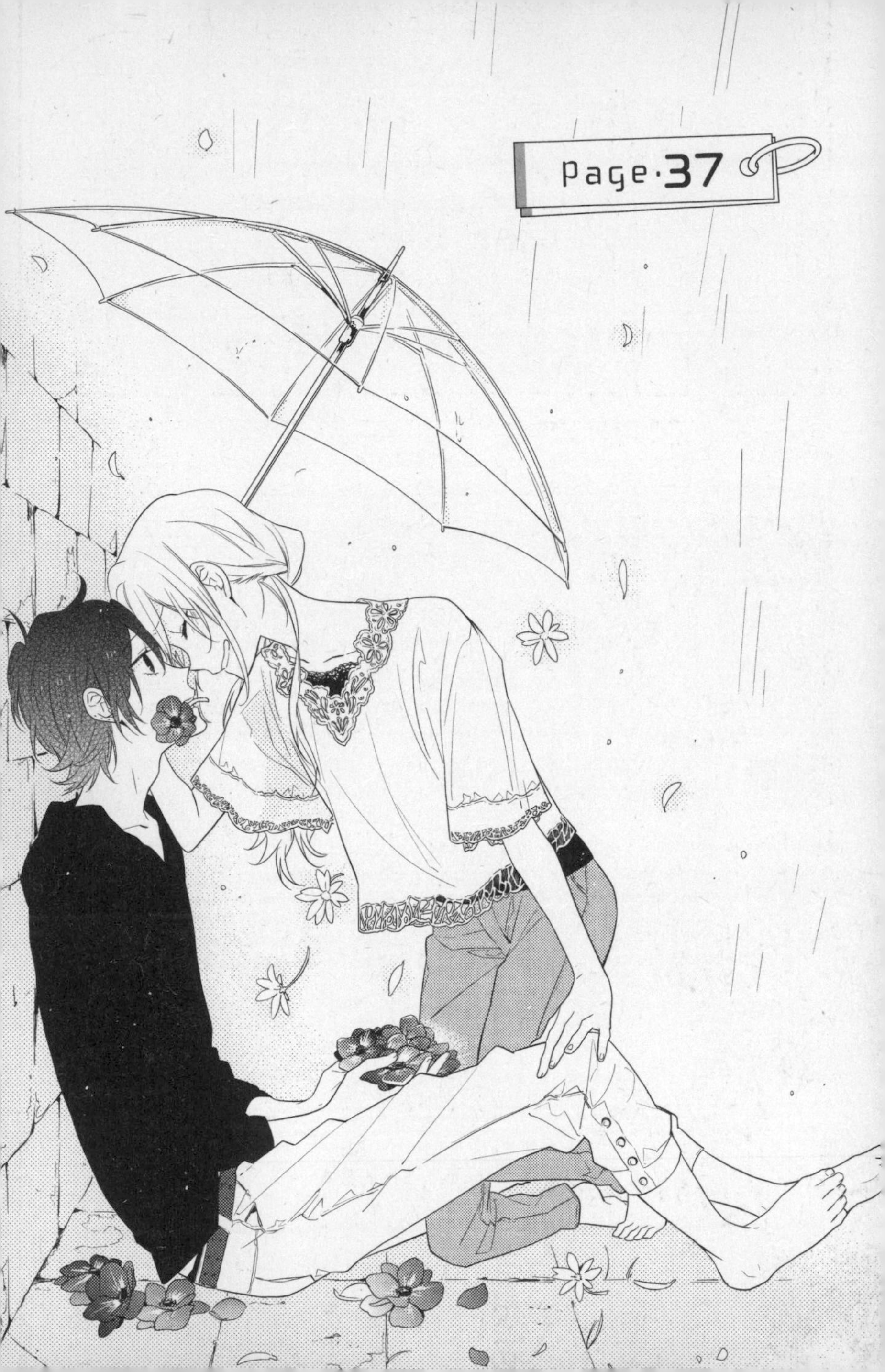
page.37

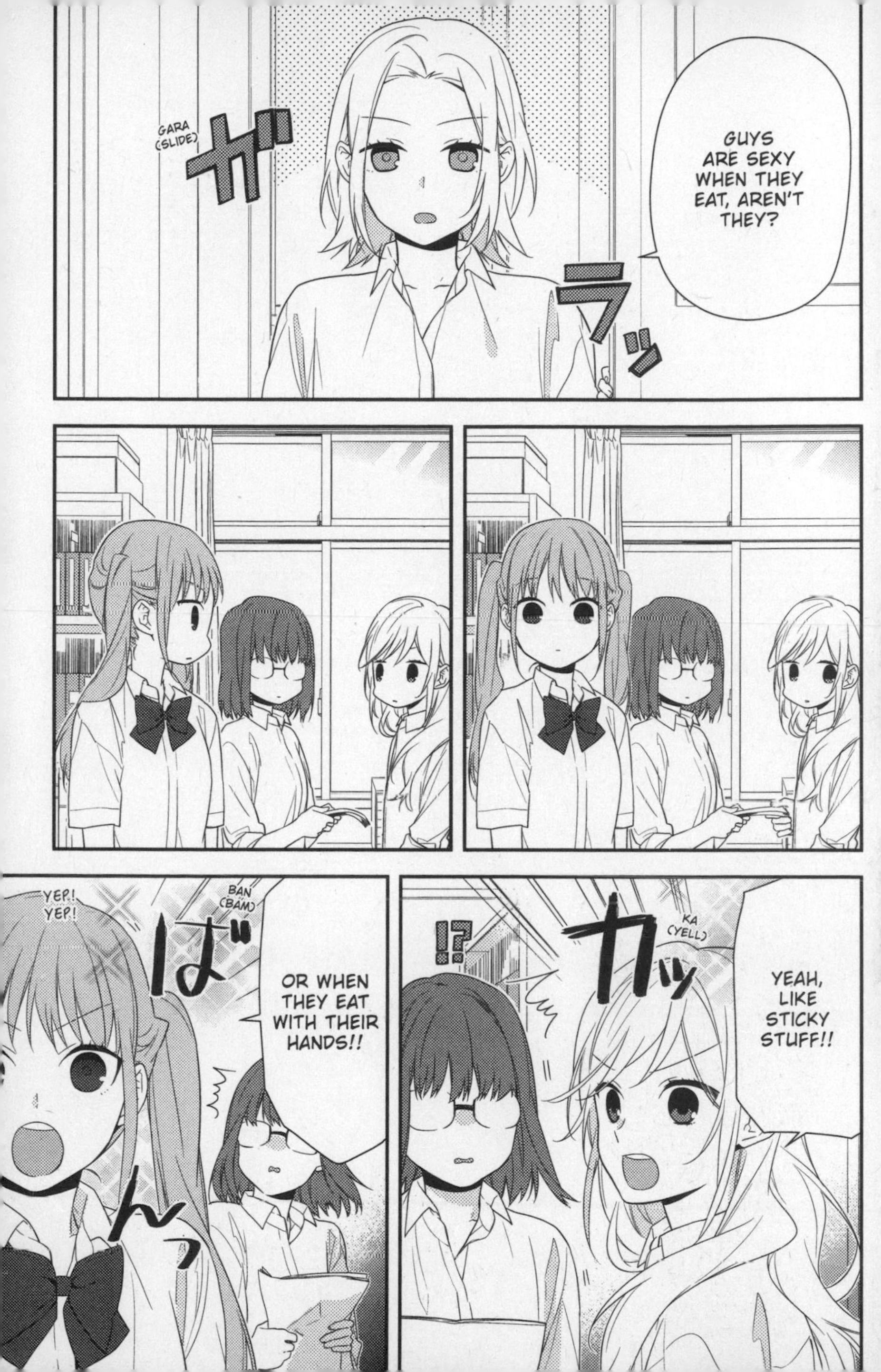
GUYS ARE SEXY WHEN THEY EAT, AREN'T THEY?
GARA (SLIDE)
YEAH, LIKE STICKY STUFF!!
KA (YELL)
!?
OR WHEN THEY EAT WITH THEIR HANDS!!
BAN (BAM)
YEP! YEP!

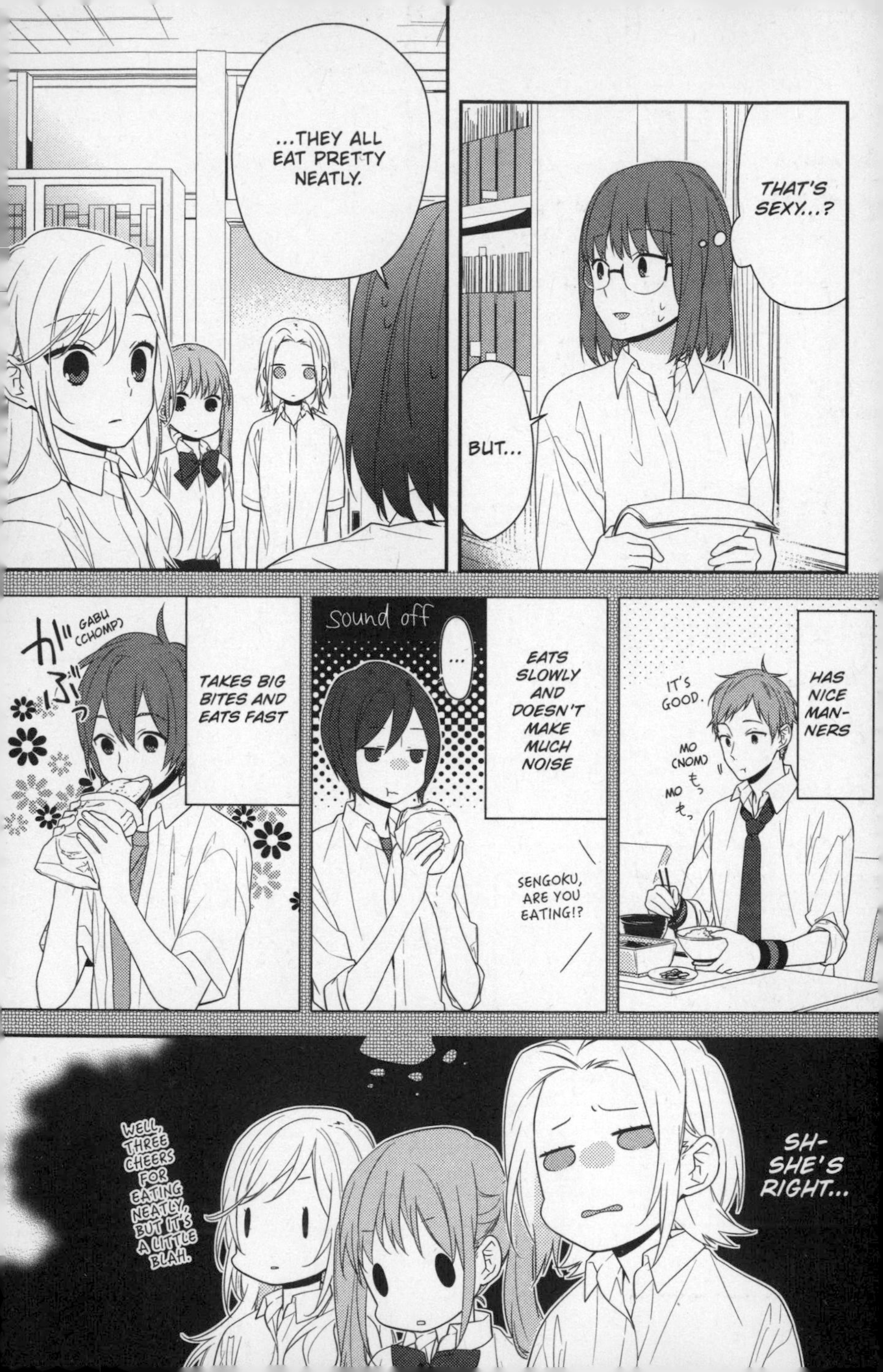
THAT'S SEXY...?
BUT...
...THEY ALL EAT PRETTY NEATLY.
HAS NICE MAN-NERS
IT'S GOOD.
MO (NOM)
MO
EATS SLOWLY AND DOESN'T MAKE MUCH NOISE
...
SENGOKU, ARE YOU EATING!?
sound off
TAKES BIG BITES AND EATS FAST
GABU (CHOMP)
SH-SHE'S RIGHT...
WELL, THREE CHEERS FOR EATING NEATLY, BUT IT'S A LITTLE BLAH.

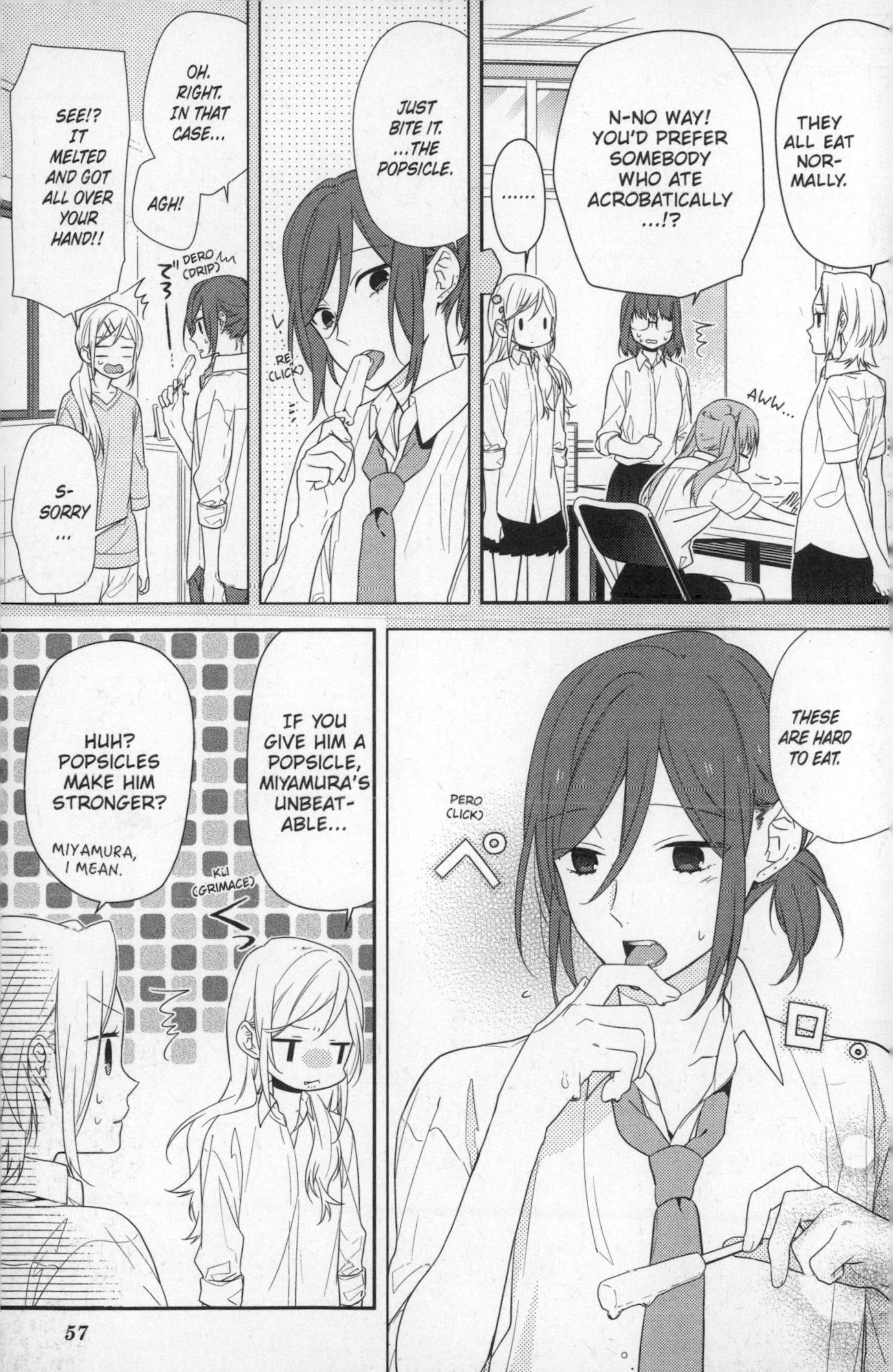
THEY ALL EAT NOR-MALLY.
N-NO WAY! YOU'D PREFER SOMEBODY WHO ATE ACROBATICALLY ...!?
......
AWW...
JUST BITE IT. ...THE POPSICLE.
RE (CLICK)
OH. RIGHT. IN THAT CASE...
AGH!
SEE!? IT MELTED AND GOT ALL OVER YOUR HAND!!
DERO (DRIP)
S-SORRY...
THESE ARE HARD TO EAT.
PERO (CLICK)
IF YOU GIVE HIM A POPSICLE, MIYAMURA'S UNBEAT-ABLE...
HUH? POPSICLES MAKE HIM STRONGER?
MIYAMURA, I MEAN.
KII (GRIMACE)

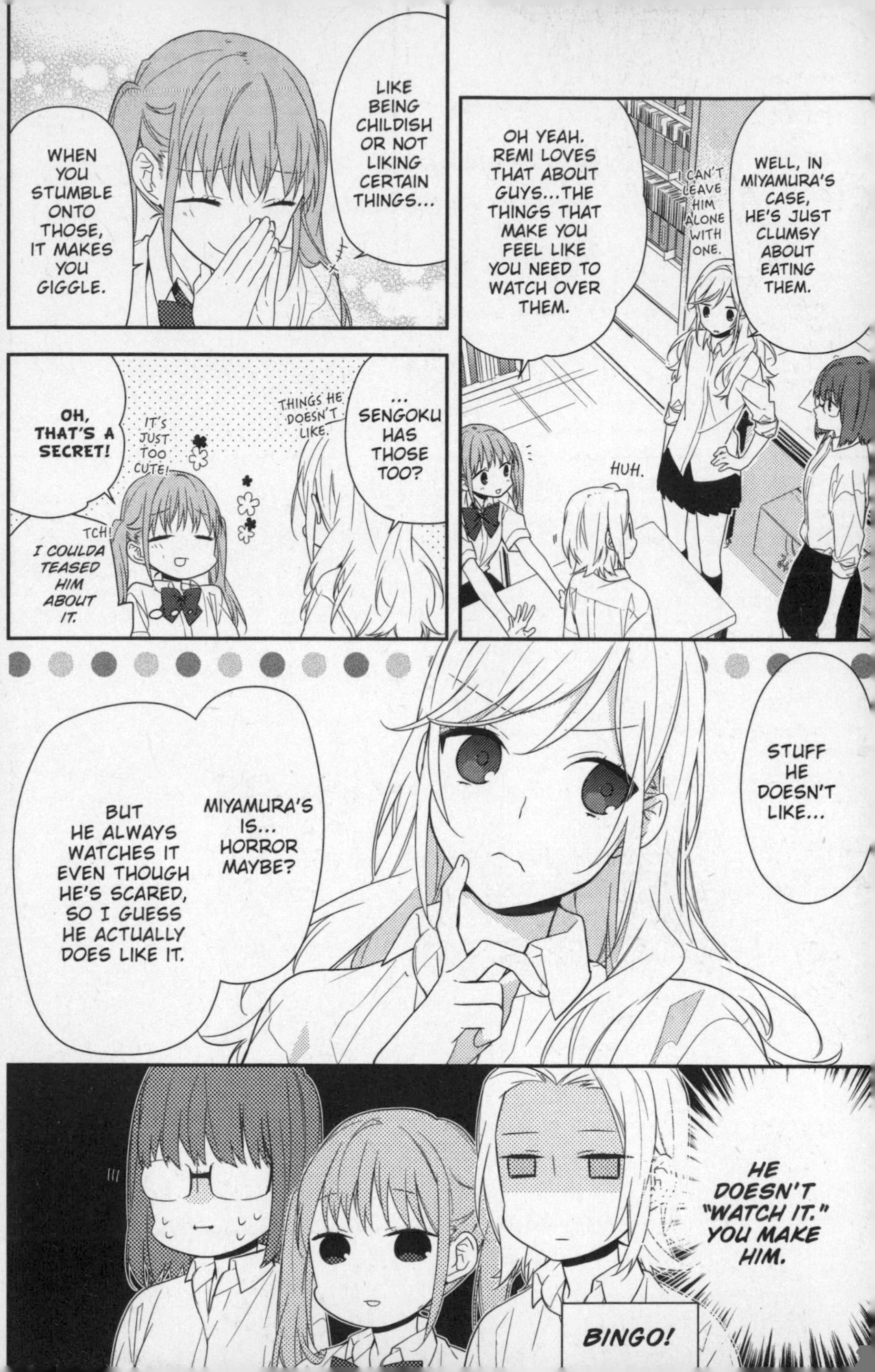
WELL, IN MIYAMURA'S CASE, HE'S JUST CLUMSY ABOUT EATING THEM.
I CAN'T LEAVE HIM ALONE WITH ONE.
OH YEAH. REMI LOVES THAT ABOUT GUYS...THE THINGS THAT MAKE YOU FEEL LIKE YOU NEED TO WATCH OVER THEM.
HUH.
LIKE BEING CHILDISH OR NOT LIKING CERTAIN THINGS...
WHEN YOU STUMBLE ONTO THOSE, IT MAKES YOU GIGGLE.
...SENGOKU HAS THOSE TOO?
THINGS HE DOESN'T LIKE.
OH, THAT'S A SECRET!
IT'S JUST TOO CUTE!
TCH! I COULDA TEASED HIM ABOUT IT.
STUFF HE DOESN'T LIKE...
MIYAMURA'S IS... HORROR MAYBE?
BUT HE ALWAYS WATCHES IT EVEN THOUGH HE'S SCARED, SO I GUESS HE ACTUALLY DOES LIKE IT.
HE DOESN'T "WATCH IT." YOU MAKE HIM.
BINGO!

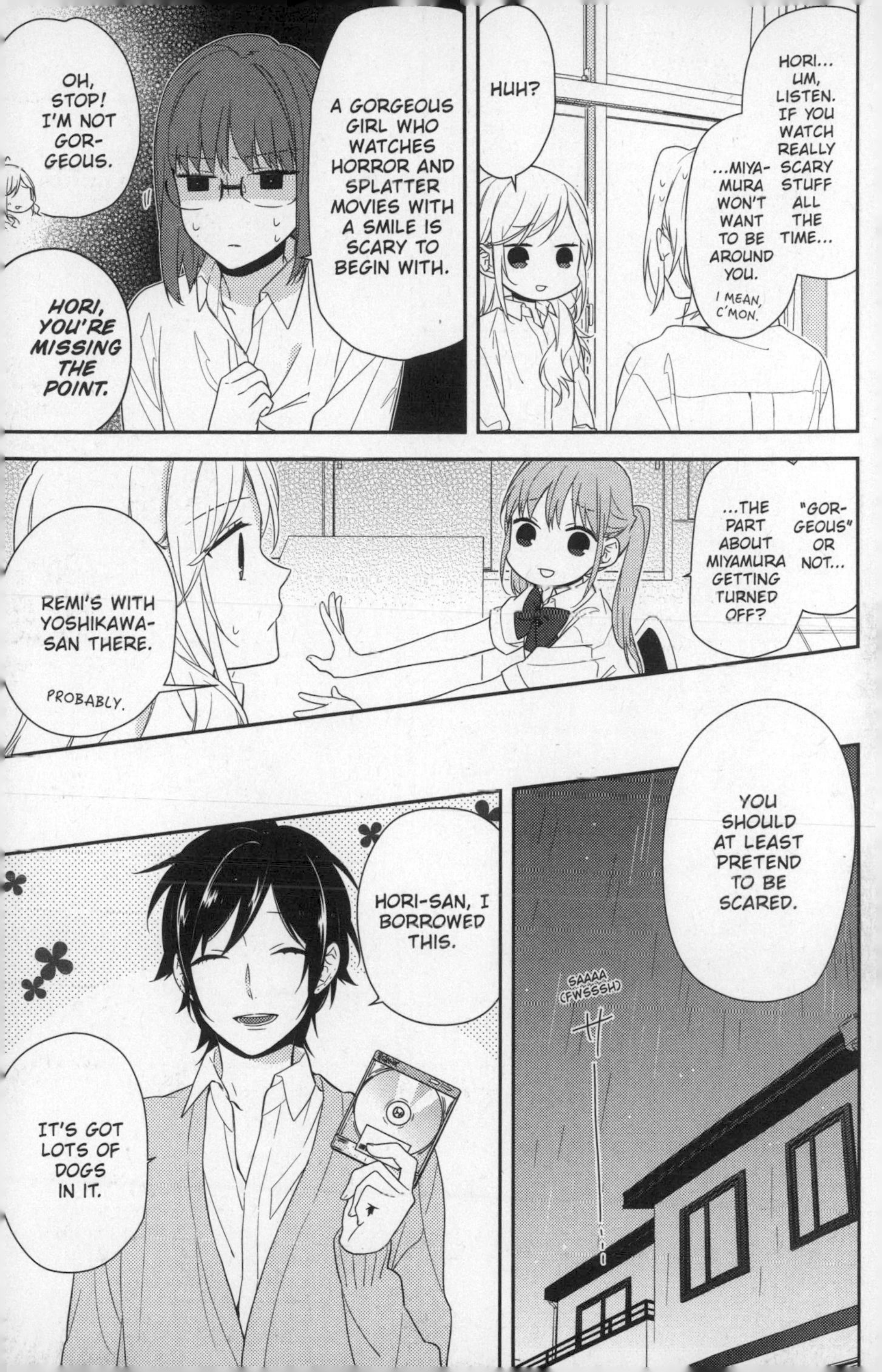
HORI... UM, LISTEN. IF YOU WATCH REALLY SCARY STUFF ALL THE TIME...
...MIYAMURA WON'T WANT TO BE AROUND YOU.
I MEAN, C'MON.
HUH?
A GORGEOUS GIRL WHO WATCHES HORROR AND SPLATTER MOVIES WITH A SMILE IS SCARY TO BEGIN WITH.
OH, STOP! I'M NOT GORGEOUS.
HORI, YOU'RE MISSING THE POINT.
"GORGEOUS" OR NOT...
...THE PART ABOUT MIYAMURA GETTING TURNED OFF?
REMI'S WITH YOSHIKAWA-SAN THERE.
PROBABLY.
YOU SHOULD AT LEAST PRETEND TO BE SCARED.
SAAAA (FWSSSH)
HORI-SAN, I BORROWED THIS.
IT'S GOT LOTS OF DOGS IN IT.

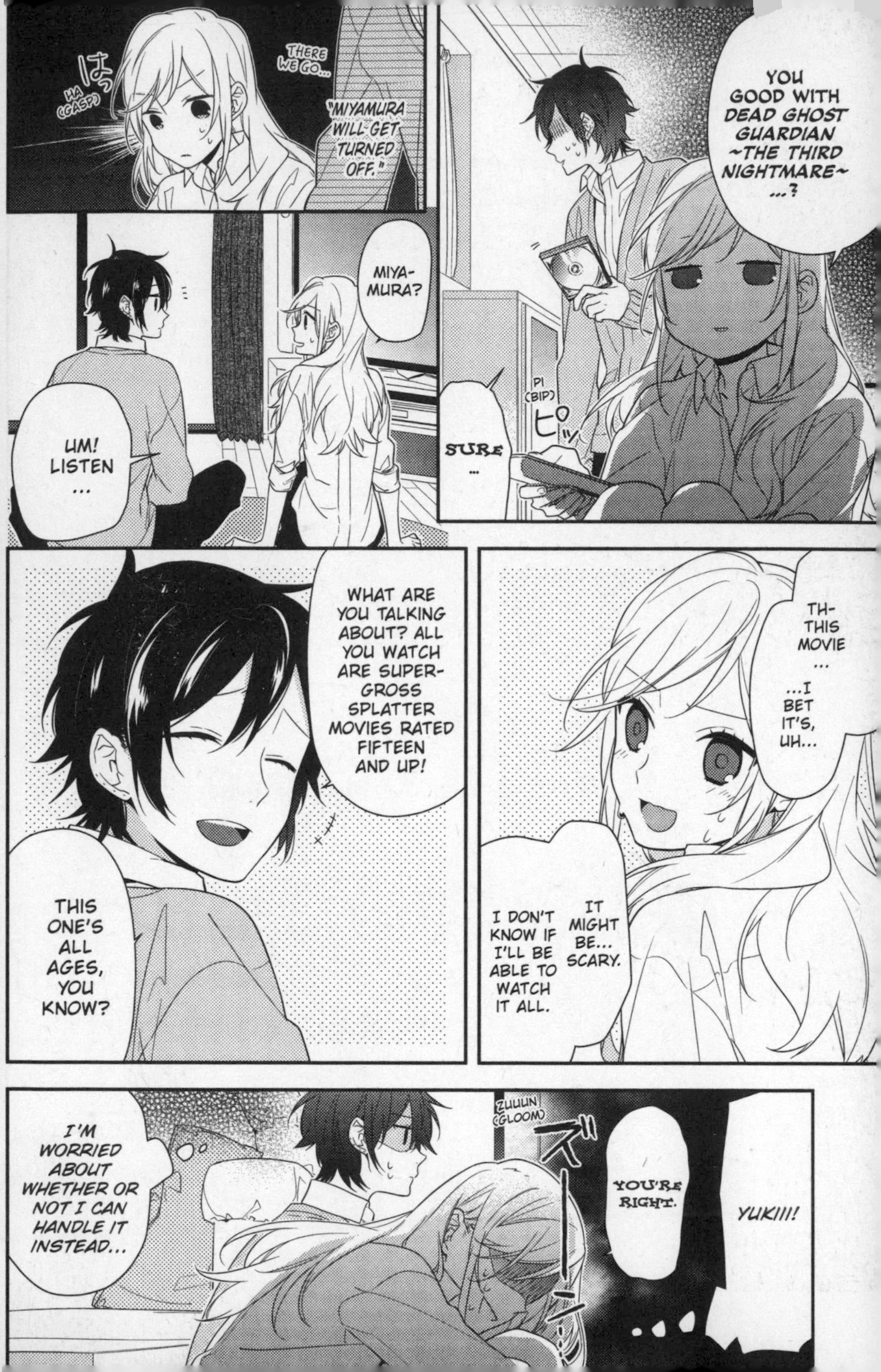
YOU GOOD WITH DEAD GHOST GUARDIAN ~THE THIRD NIGHTMARE~ ...?
PI (BIP)
SURE...
HA (GASP)
THERE WE GO...
"MIYAMURA WILL GET TURNED OFF."
MIYA-MURA?
UM! LISTEN...
TH-THIS MOVIE...
...I BET IT'S, UH...
IT MIGHT BE... SCARY.
I DON'T KNOW IF I'LL BE ABLE TO WATCH IT ALL.
WHAT ARE YOU TALKING ABOUT? ALL YOU WATCH ARE SUPER-GROSS SPLATTER MOVIES RATED FIFTEEN AND UP!
THIS ONE'S ALL AGES, YOU KNOW?
YUKIII!
YOU'RE RIGHT.
ZUUUN (GLOOM)
I'M WORRIED ABOUT WHETHER OR NOT I CAN HANDLE IT INSTEAD...

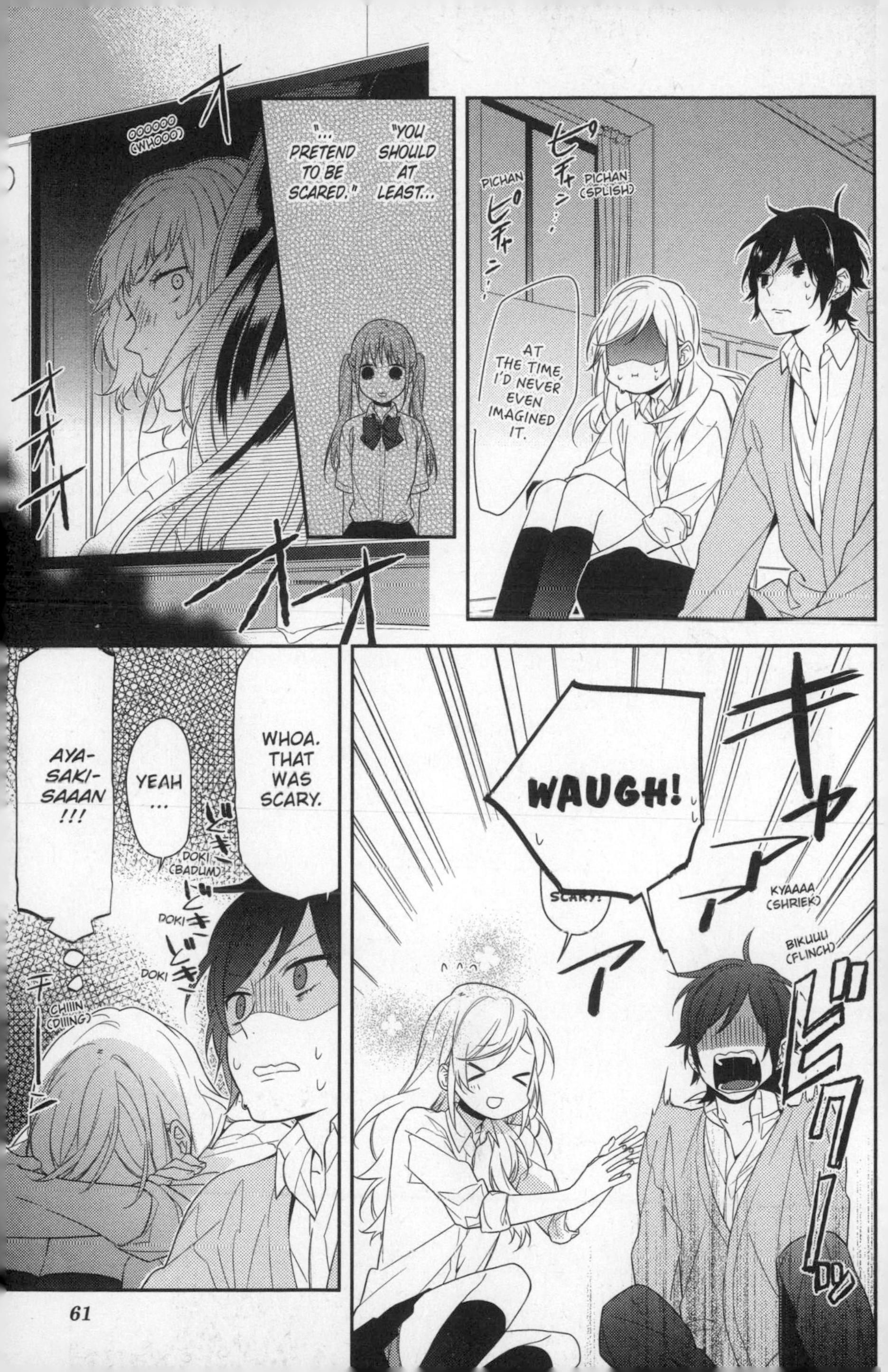
PICHAN (SPLISH)
PICHAN
AT THE TIME, I'D NEVER EVEN IMAGINED IT.
"YOU SHOULD AT LEAST...
"... PRETEND TO BE SCARED."
OOOOOO (WHOOO)
KYAAAA (SHRIEK)
WAUGH!
SCARY!
BIKUUU (FLINCH)
WHOA. THAT WAS SCARY.
YEAH ...
DOKI (BADUM)
DOKI
DOKI
AYA-SAKI-SAAAN !!!
CHIIIN (DIIING)

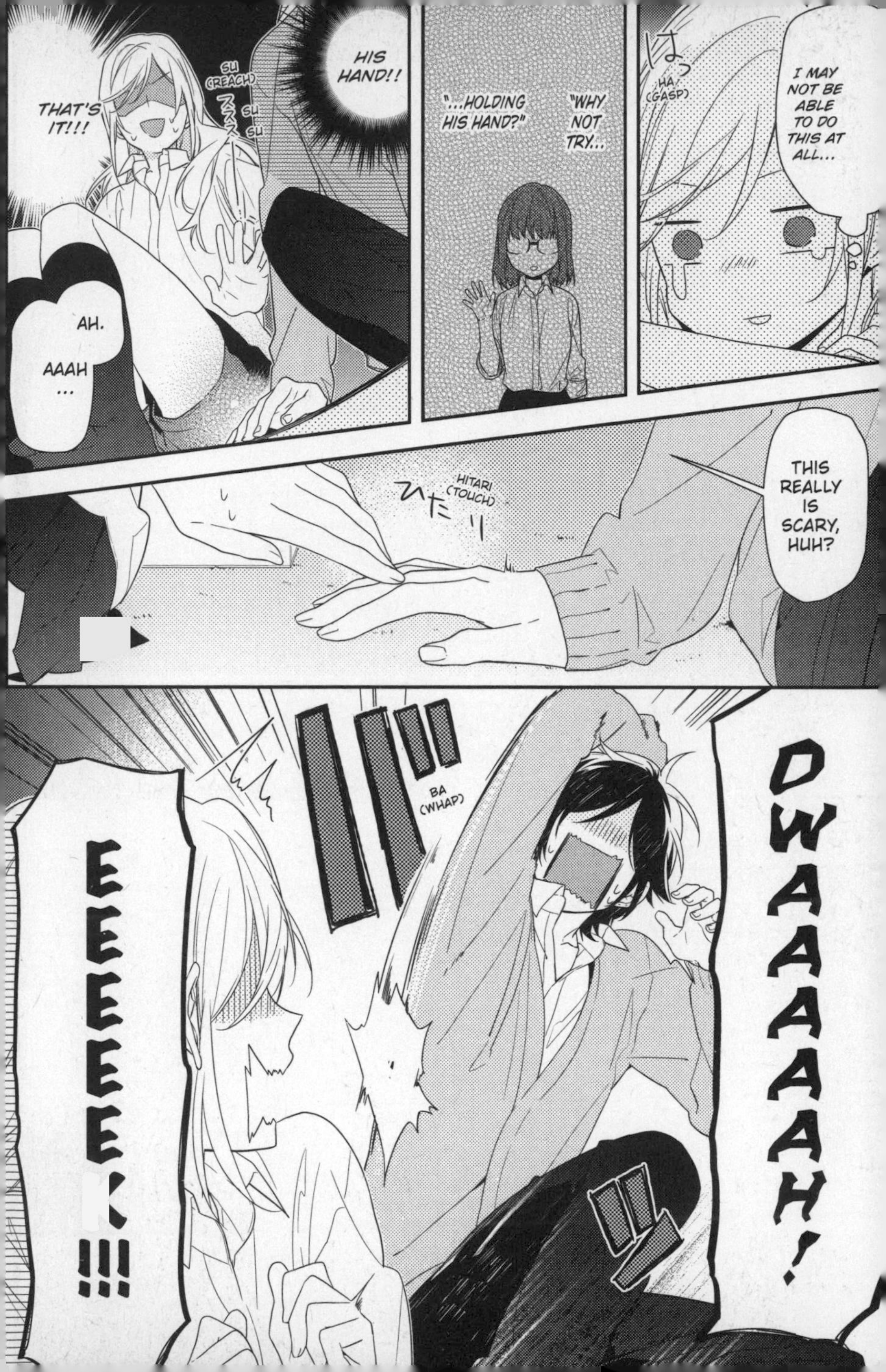
I MAY NOT BE ABLE TO DO THIS AT ALL...
はっ
HA (GASP)
"WHY NOT TRY...
"...HOLDING HIS HAND?"
HIS HAND!!
SU (REACH)
スススス
SU SU
THAT'S IT!!!
AH.
AAAH ...
THIS REALLY IS SCARY, HUH?
ひたり
HITARI (TOUCH)
DWAAAAH!
BA (WHAP)
EEEEEK!!!

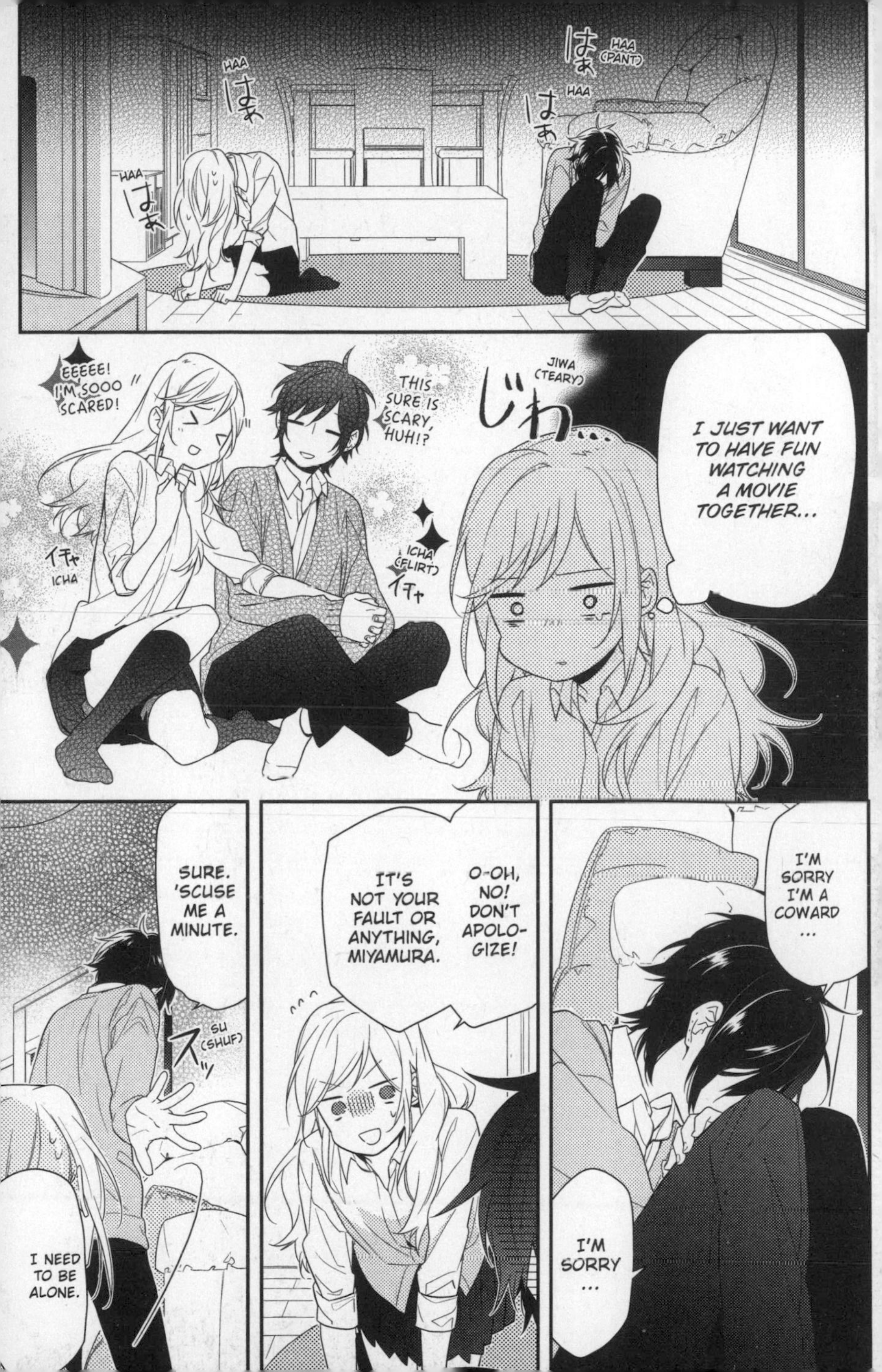
はぁ
HAA (PANT)
はぁ
HAA
HAA
はぁ
HAA
はぁ
I JUST WANT TO HAVE FUN WATCHING A MOVIE TOGETHER...
じわ
JIWA (TEARY)
THIS SURE IS SCARY, HUH!?
EEEEE! I'M SOOO SCARED!
イチャ
ICHA (FLIRT)
イチャ
ICHA
I'M SORRY I'M A COWARD ...
I'M SORRY ...
O-OH, NO! DON'T APOLOGIZE!
IT'S NOT YOUR FAULT OR ANYTHING, MIYAMURA.
SURE. 'SCUSE ME A MINUTE.
ス
SU (SHUF)
I NEED TO BE ALONE.

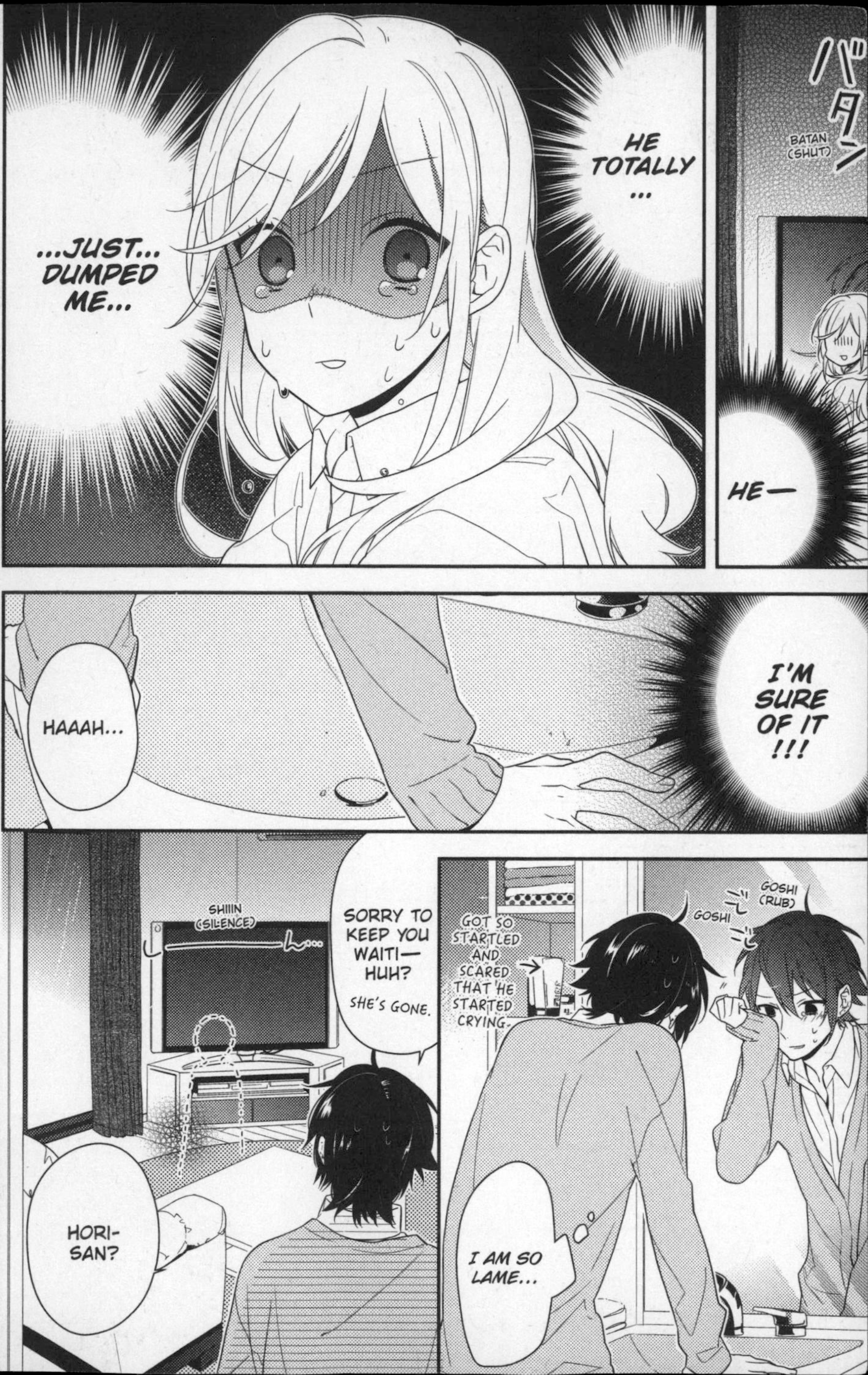
バタン
BATAN (SHUT)
HE—
HE TOTALLY ...
...JUST... DUMPED ME...
I'M SURE OF IT !!!
HAAAH...
GOSHI (RUB)
GOSHI
GOT SO STARTLED AND SCARED THAT HE STARTED CRYING.
I AM SO LAME...
SORRY TO KEEP YOU WAITI— HUH?
SHE'S GONE.
SHIIIN (SILENCE)
HORI-SAN?

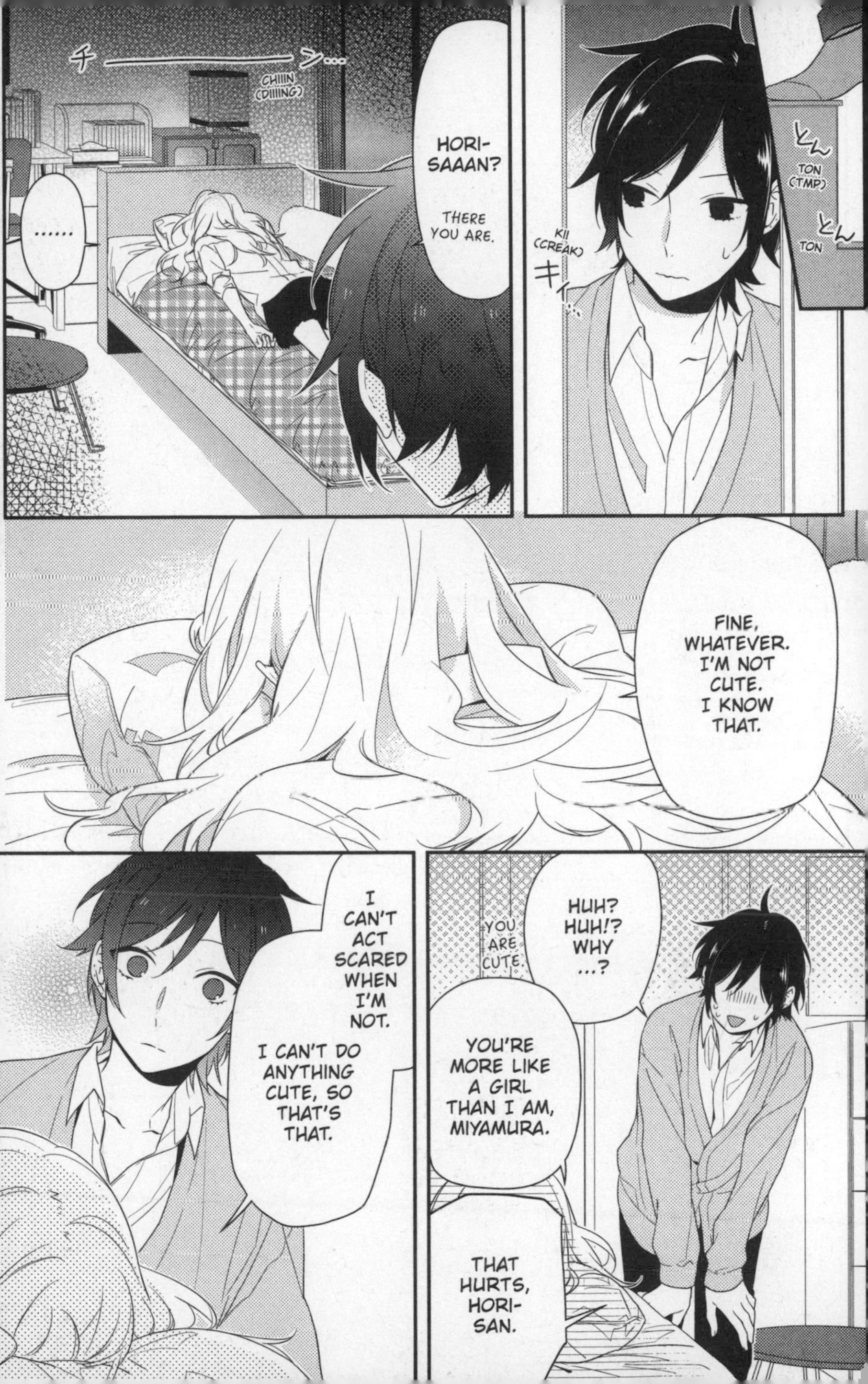
とん
TON (TMP)
とん
TON
キィ…
KII (CREAK)
HORI-SAAAN?
THERE YOU ARE.
チーーーーン…
CHIIIN (DIIIING)
……
FINE, WHATEVER. I'M NOT CUTE. I KNOW THAT.
HUH? HUH!? WHY …?
YOU ARE CUTE.
YOU'RE MORE LIKE A GIRL THAN I AM, MIYAMURA.
THAT HURTS, HORI-SAN.
I CAN'T ACT SCARED WHEN I'M NOT.
I CAN'T DO ANYTHING CUTE, SO THAT'S THAT.

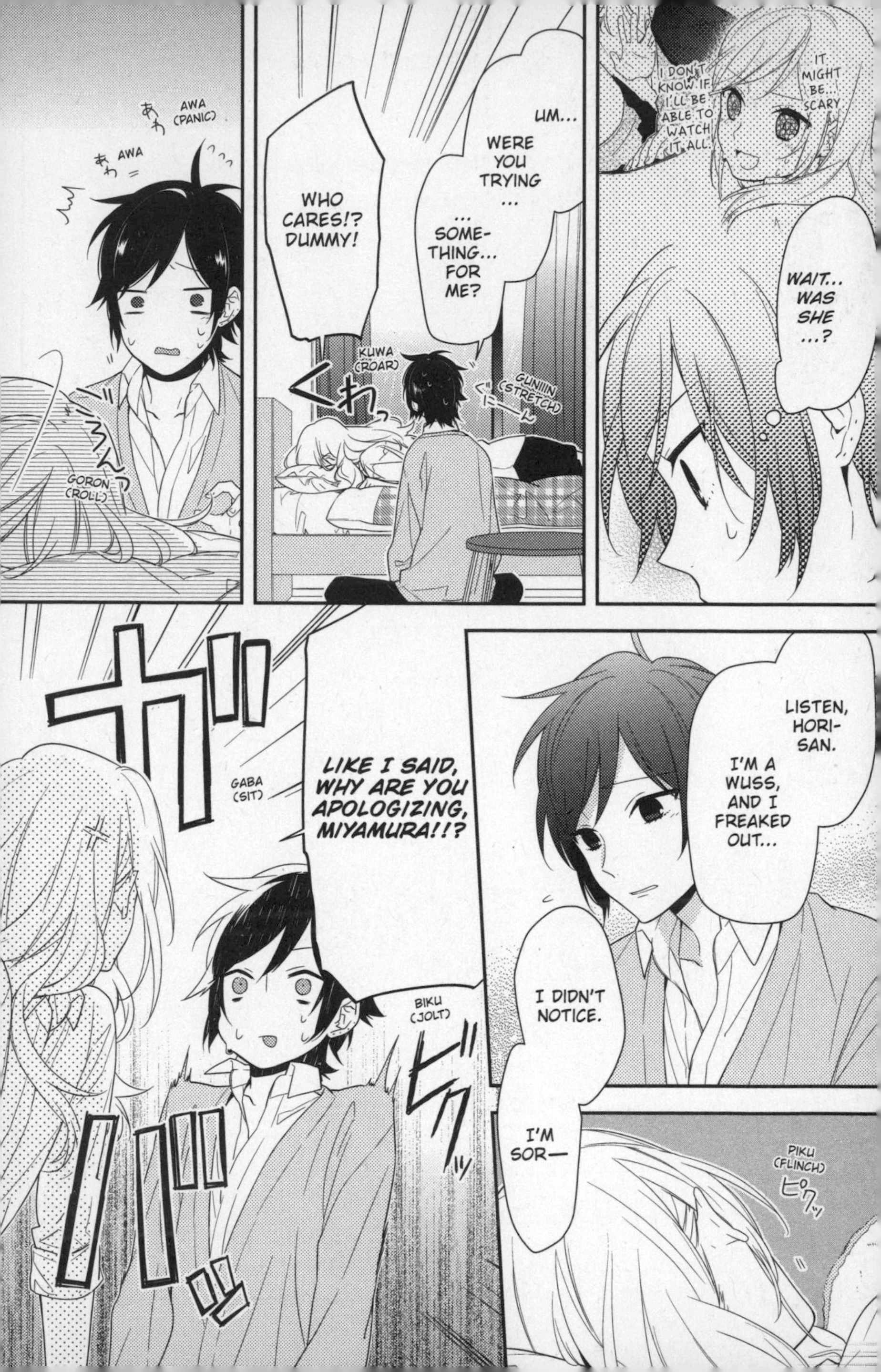

IT MIGHT BE... SCARY
I DON'T KNOW IF I'LL BE ABLE TO WATCH IT ALL
WAIT... WAS SHE ...?
UM...
WERE YOU TRYING ...
... SOMETHING... FOR ME?
WHO CARES!? DUMMY!
GUNIIIN (STRETCH)
KUWA (ROAR)
AWA (PANIC)
AWA
GORON (ROLL)
LISTEN, HORI-SAN.
I'M A WUSS, AND I FREAKED OUT...
I DIDN'T NOTICE.
I'M SOR—
PIKU (FLINCH)
LIKE I SAID, WHY ARE YOU APOLOGIZING, MIYAMURA!!?
GABA (SIT)
BIKU (JOLT)

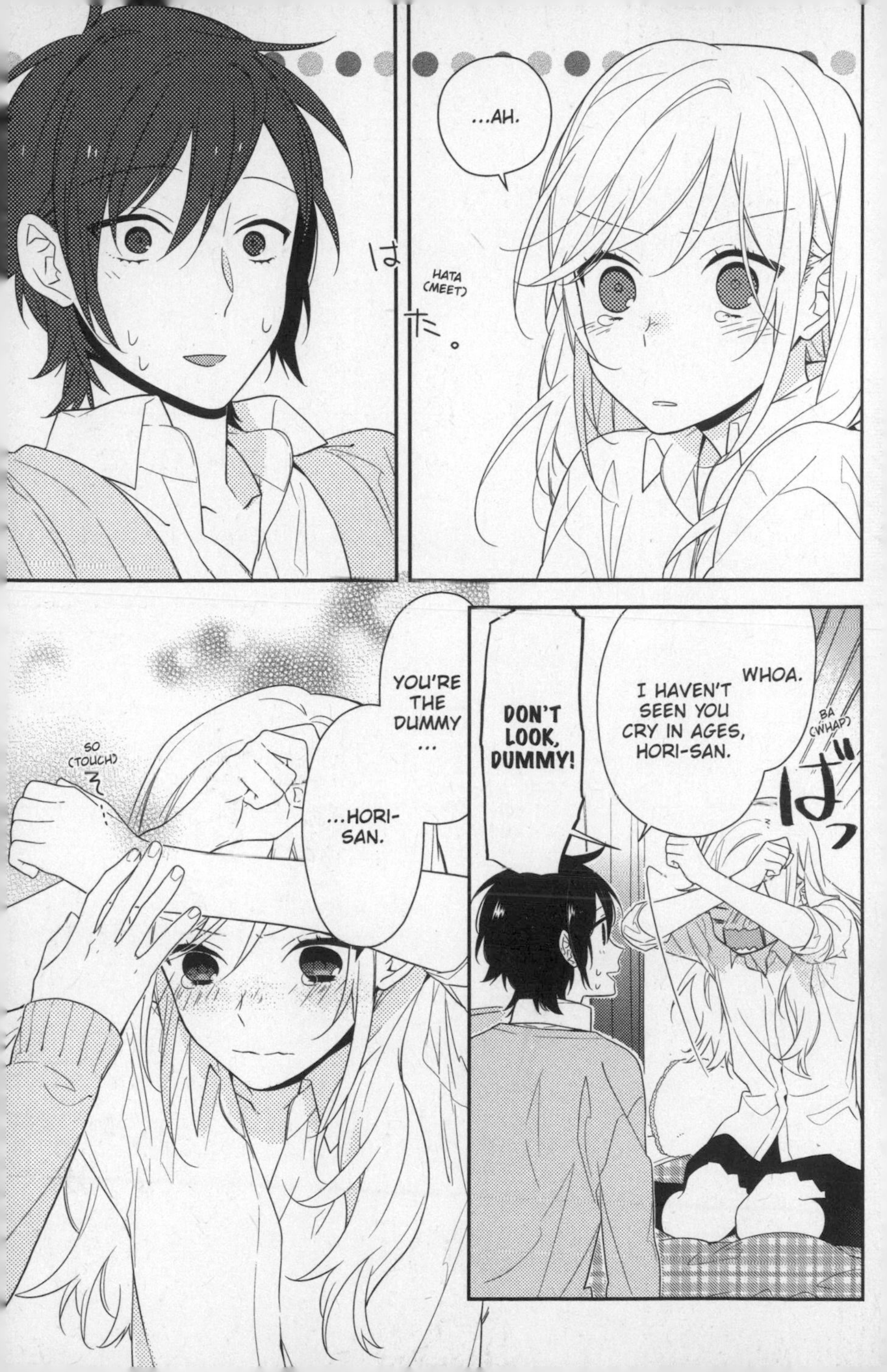
...AH.
はた。
HATA (MEET)
WHOA. I HAVEN'T SEEN YOU CRY IN AGES, HORI-SAN.
ばっ
BA (WHAP)
DON'T LOOK, DUMMY!
YOU'RE THE DUMMY...
...HORI-SAN.
SO (TOUCH)

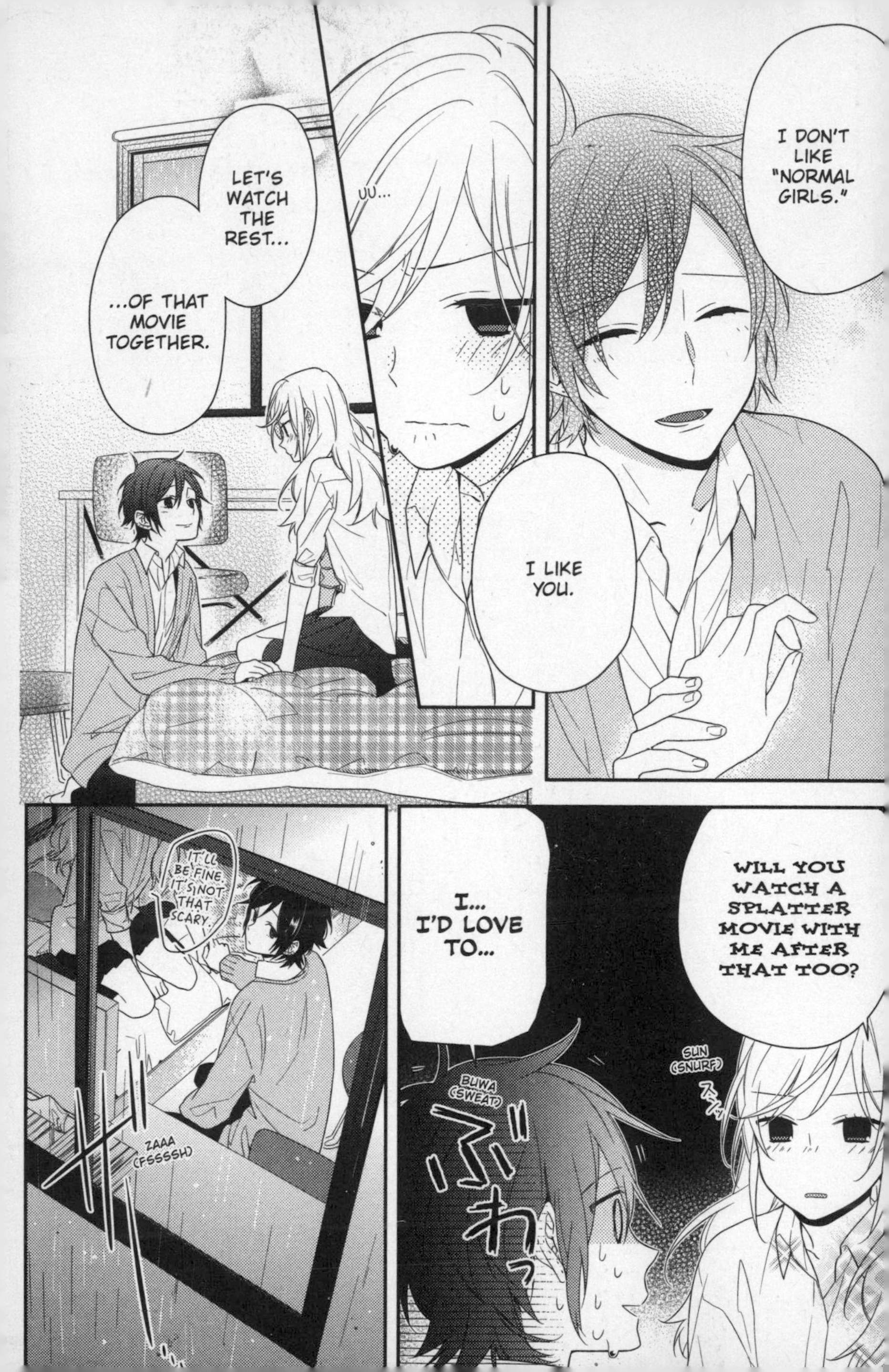

I DON'T LIKE "NORMAL GIRLS."
I LIKE YOU.
UU...
LET'S WATCH THE REST...
...OF THAT MOVIE TOGETHER.
WILL YOU WATCH A SPLATTER MOVIE WITH ME AFTER THAT TOO?
I... I'D LOVE TO...
SUN (SNURF)
BUWA (SWEAT)
ぶわっ
IT'LL BE FINE. IT'S NOT THAT SCARY.
ZAAA (FSSSSH)

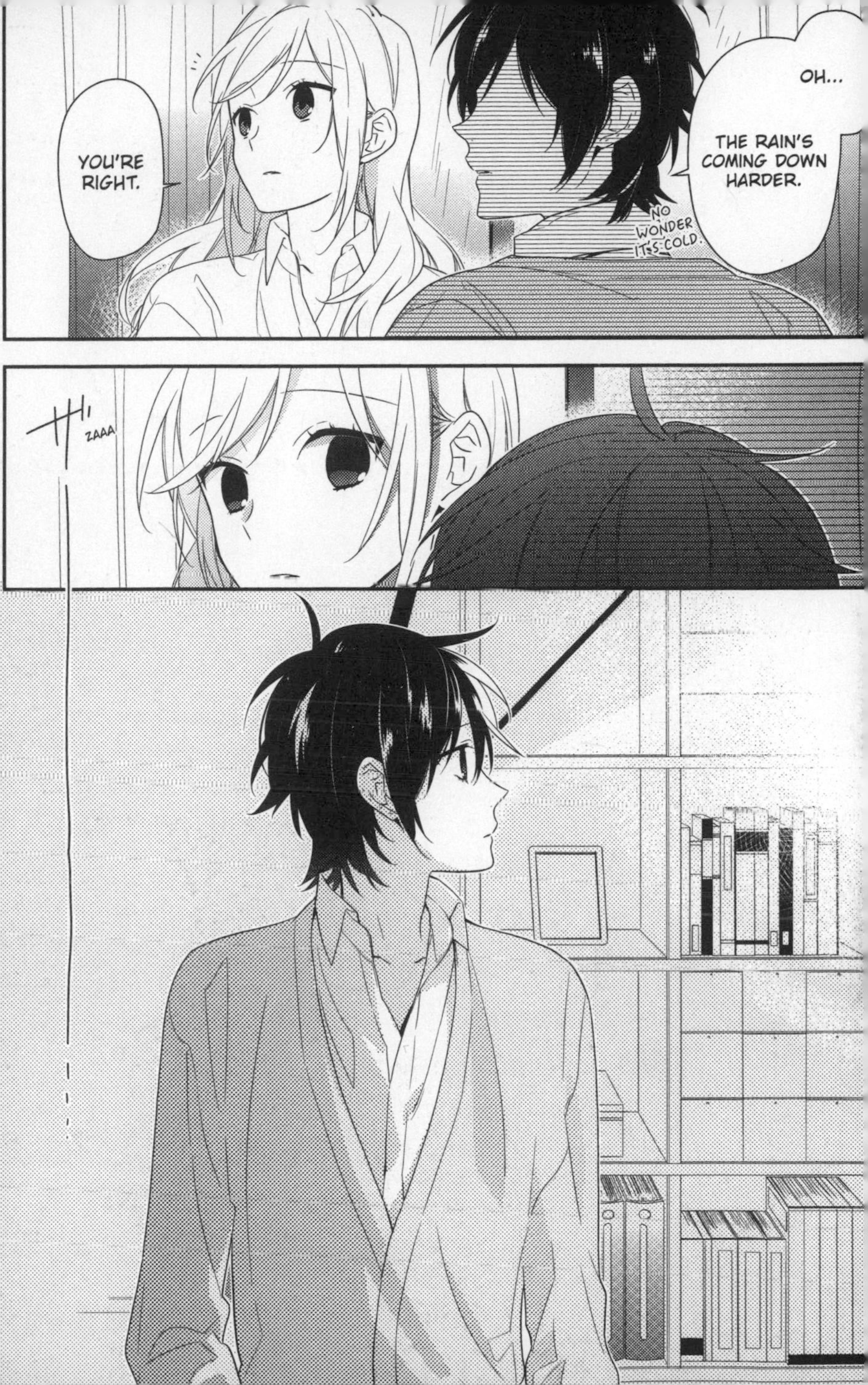
OH...
THE RAIN'S COMING DOWN HARDER.
NO WONDER IT'S COLD.
YOU'RE RIGHT.
ZAAA

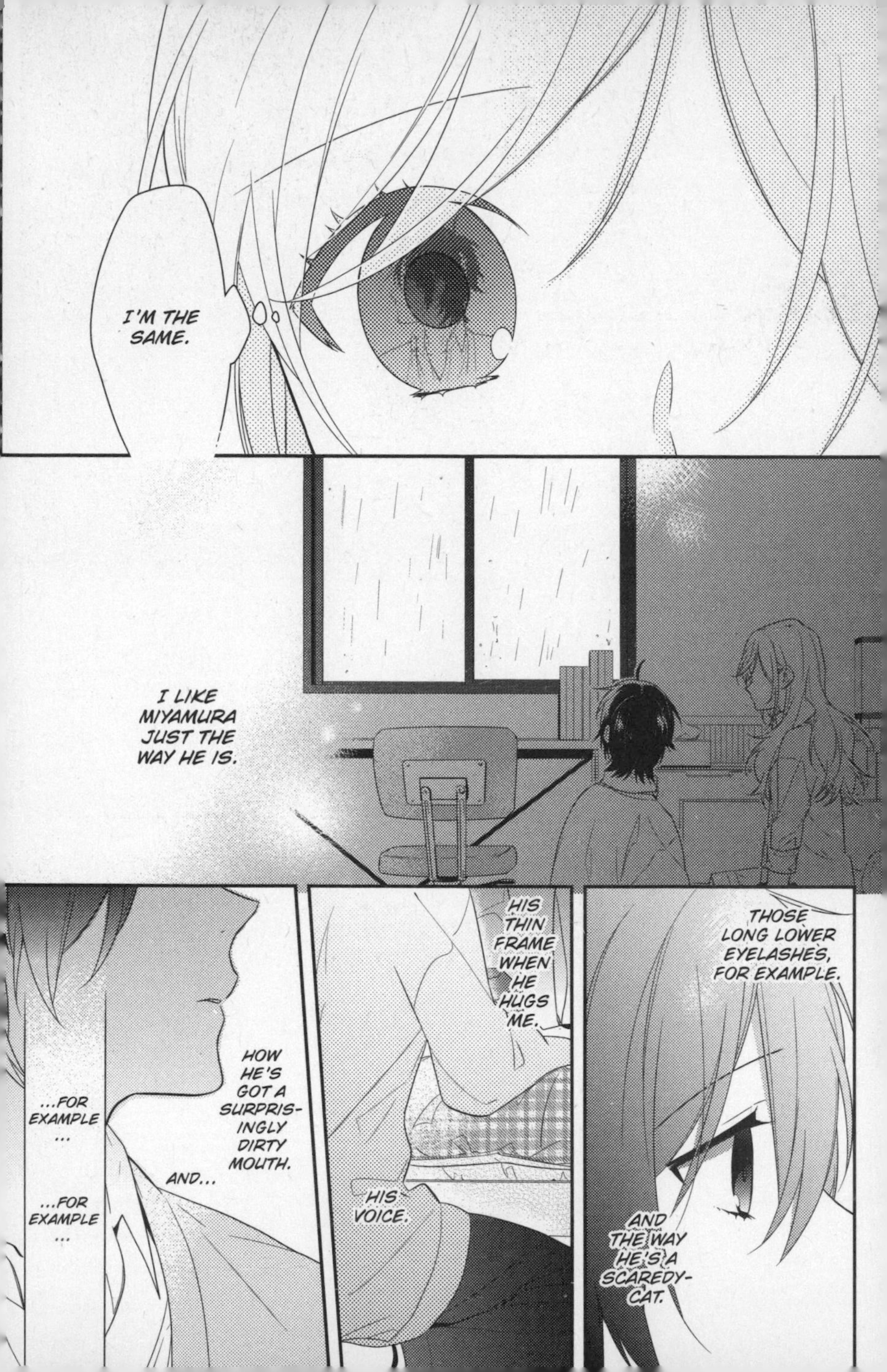
I'M THE SAME.
I LIKE MIYAMURA JUST THE WAY HE IS.
THOSE LONG LOWER EYELASHES, FOR EXAMPLE.
AND THE WAY HE'S A SCAREDY-CAT.
HIS THIN FRAME WHEN HE HUGS ME.
HIS VOICE.
HOW HE'S GOT A SURPRISINGLY DIRTY MOUTH.
...FOR EXAMPLE...
AND...
...FOR EXAMPLE...

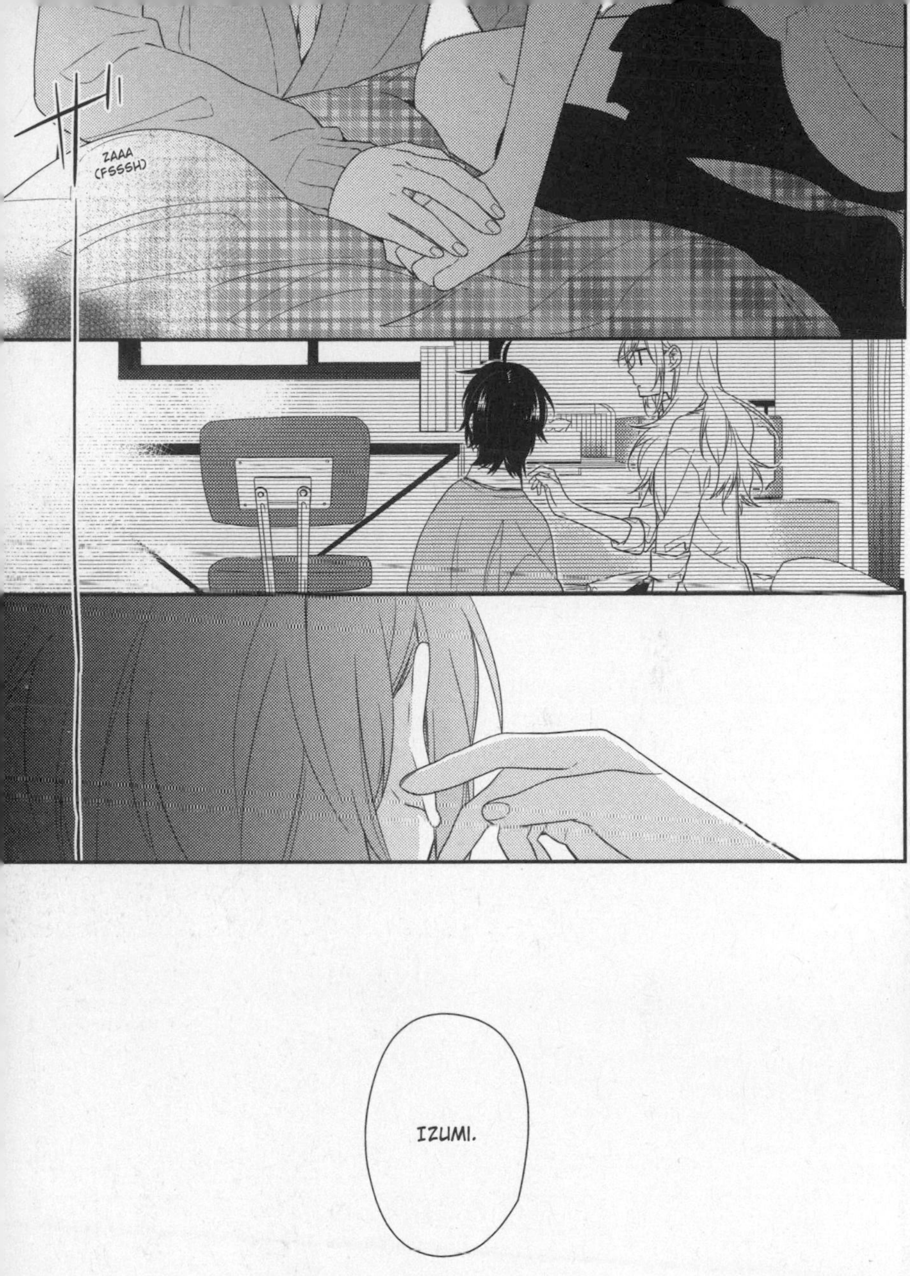
ZAAA
(FSSSH)
IZUMI.

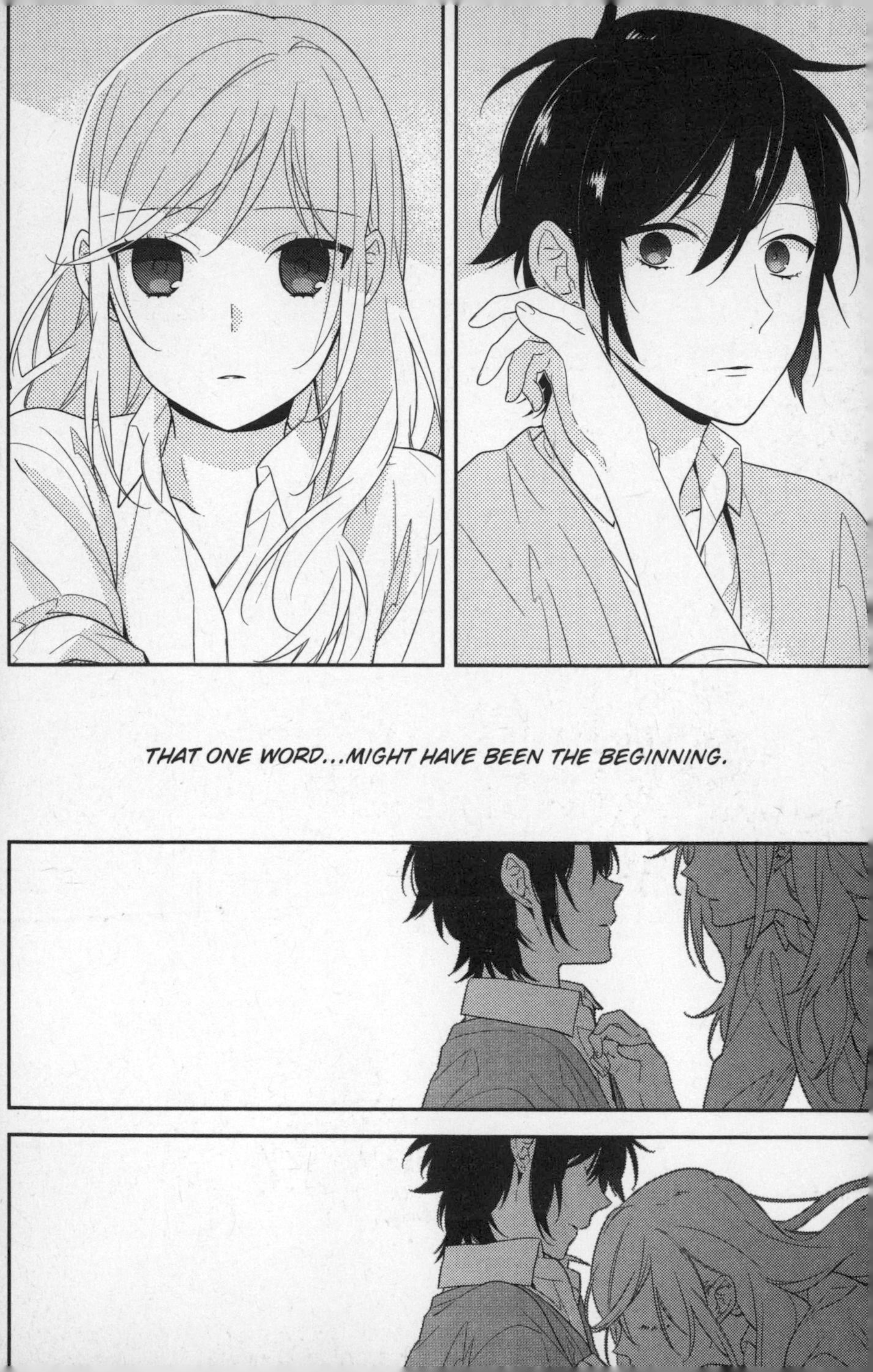
THAT ONE WORD...MIGHT HAVE BEEN THE BEGINNING.

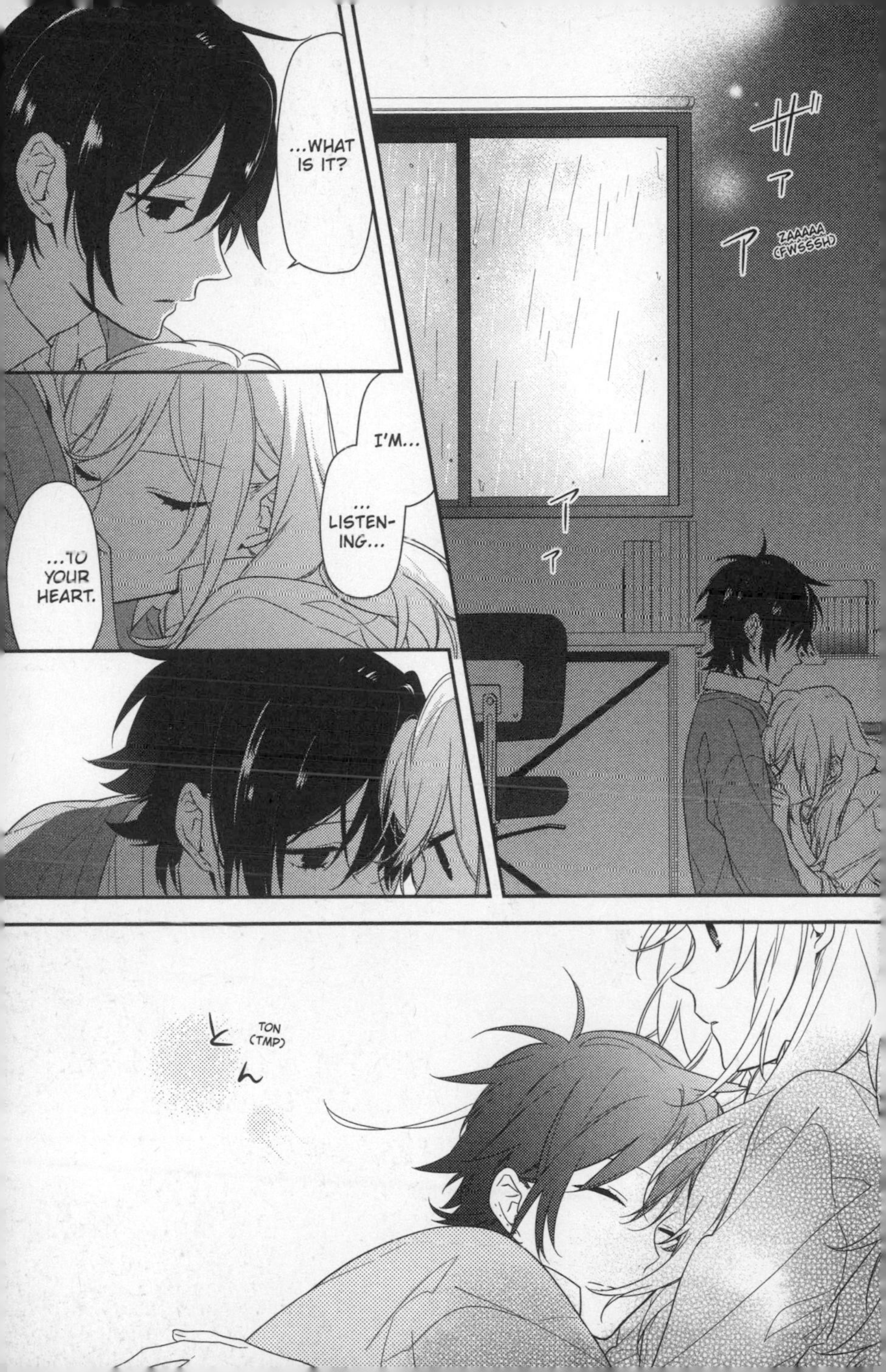
ZAAAAA (FWSSSH)
...WHAT IS IT?
I'M...
...LISTENING...
...TO YOUR HEART.
TON (TMP)

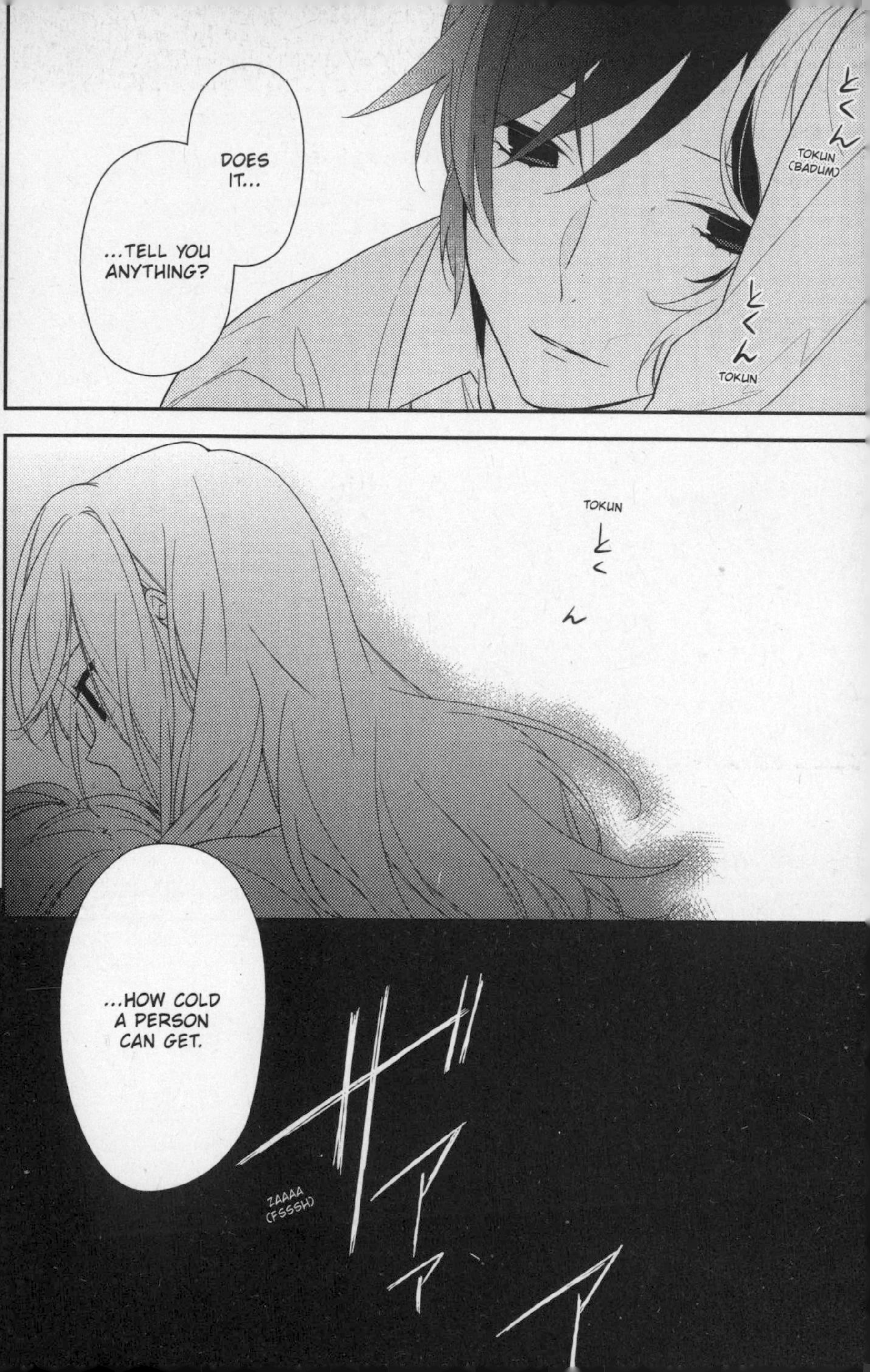
とくん
TOKUN (BADUM)
DOES IT...
...TELL YOU ANYTHING?
とくん
TOKUN
TOKUN
とくん
...HOW COLD A PERSON CAN GET.
ZAAAA (FSSSH)

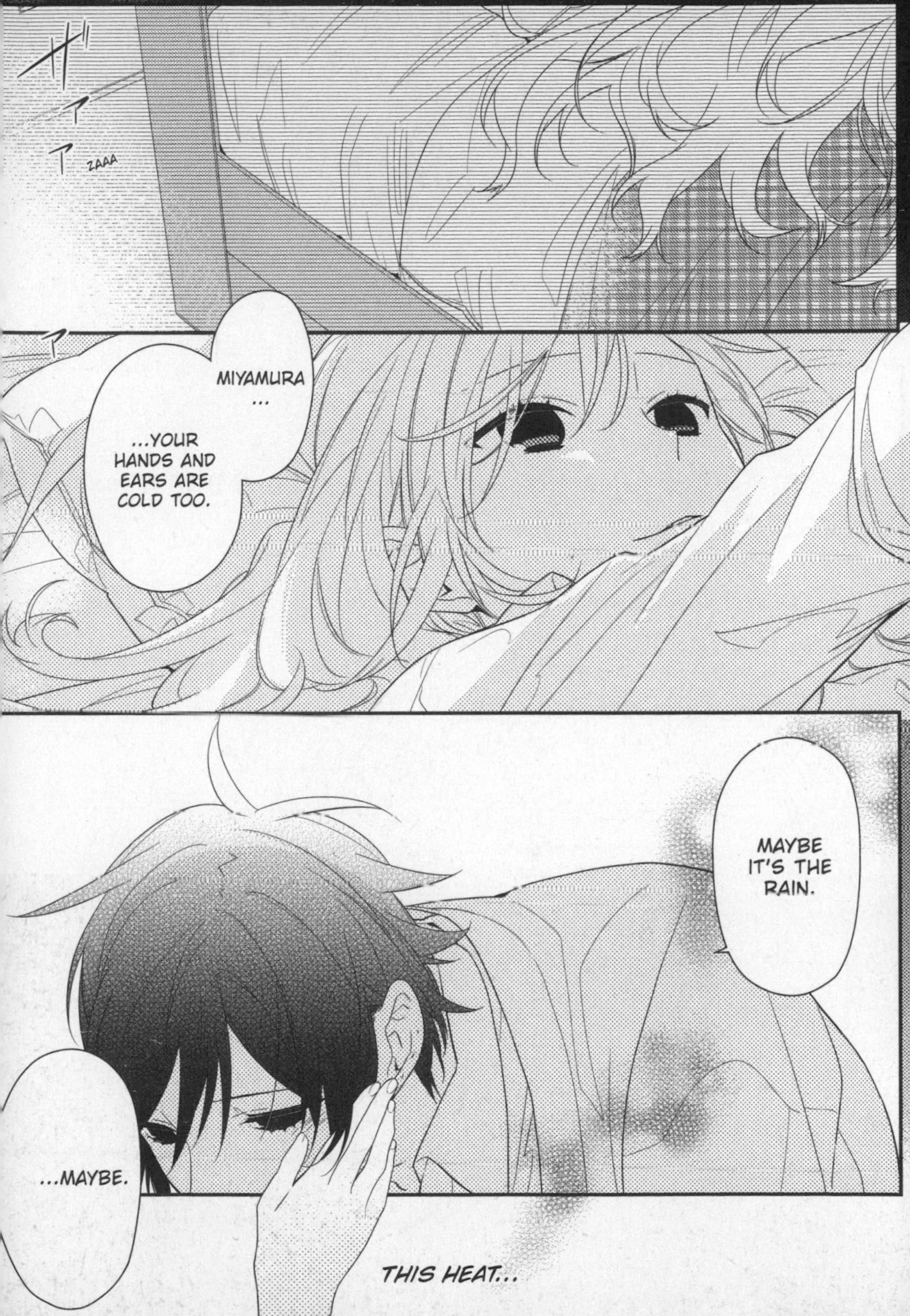
ザァァ
ZAAA
MIYAMURA ...
...YOUR HANDS AND EARS ARE COLD TOO.
MAYBE IT'S THE RAIN.
...MAYBE.
THIS HEAT...

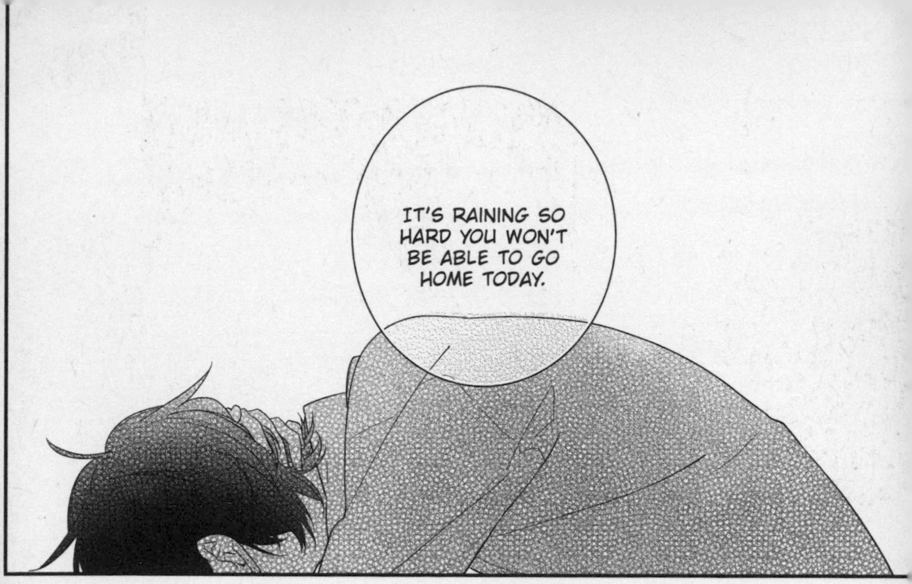
IT'S RAINING SO HARD YOU WON'T BE ABLE TO GO HOME TODAY.

...I WANTED MIYAMURA TO FEEL IT TOO.

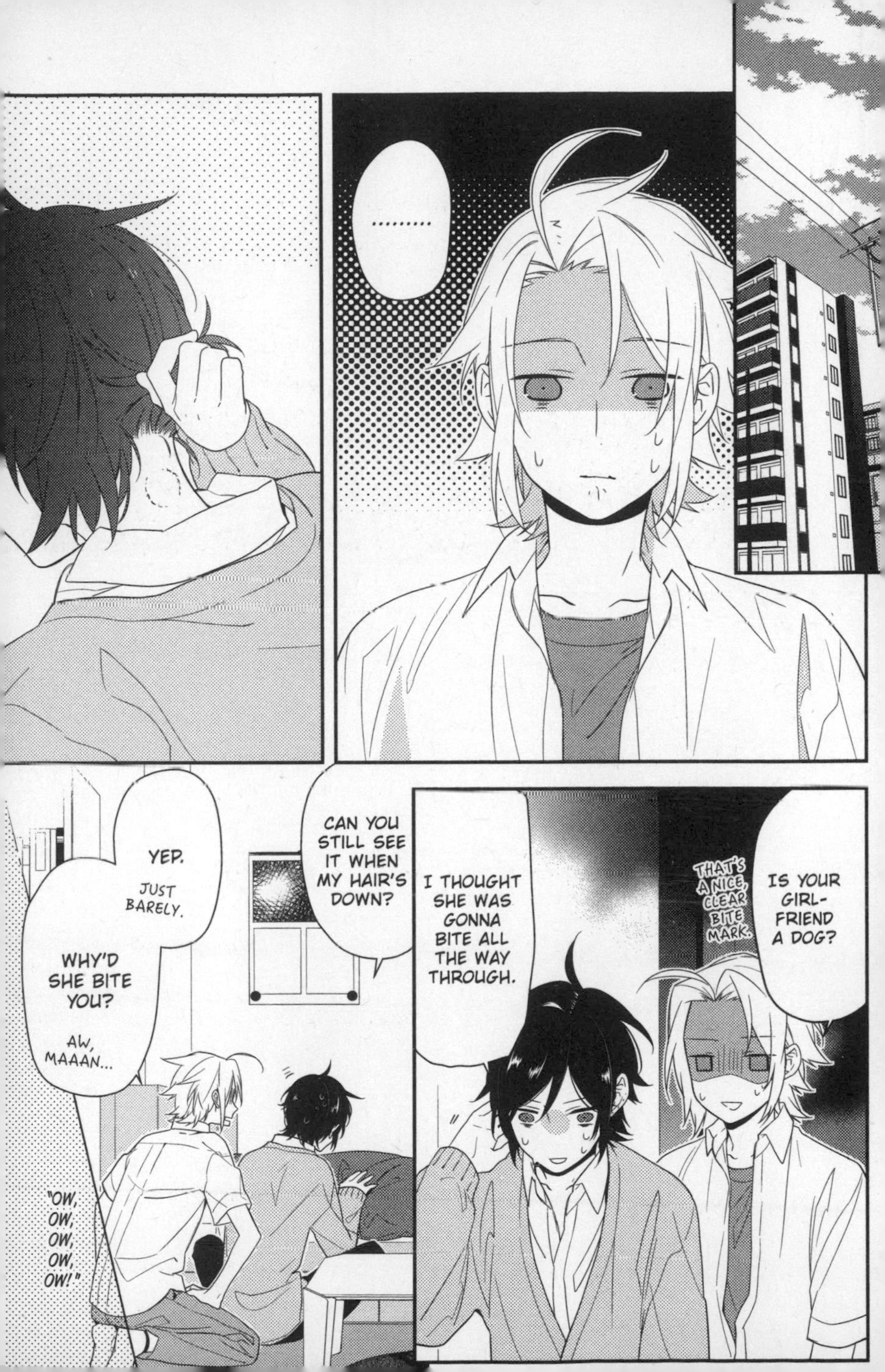
....
IS YOUR GIRL-FRIEND A DOG?
THAT'S A NICE, CLEAR BITE MARK.
I THOUGHT SHE WAS GONNA BITE ALL THE WAY THROUGH.
CAN YOU STILL SEE IT WHEN MY HAIR'S DOWN?
YEP.
JUST BARELY.
WHY'D SHE BITE YOU?
AW, MAAAN...
"OW, OW, OW, OW, OW!"

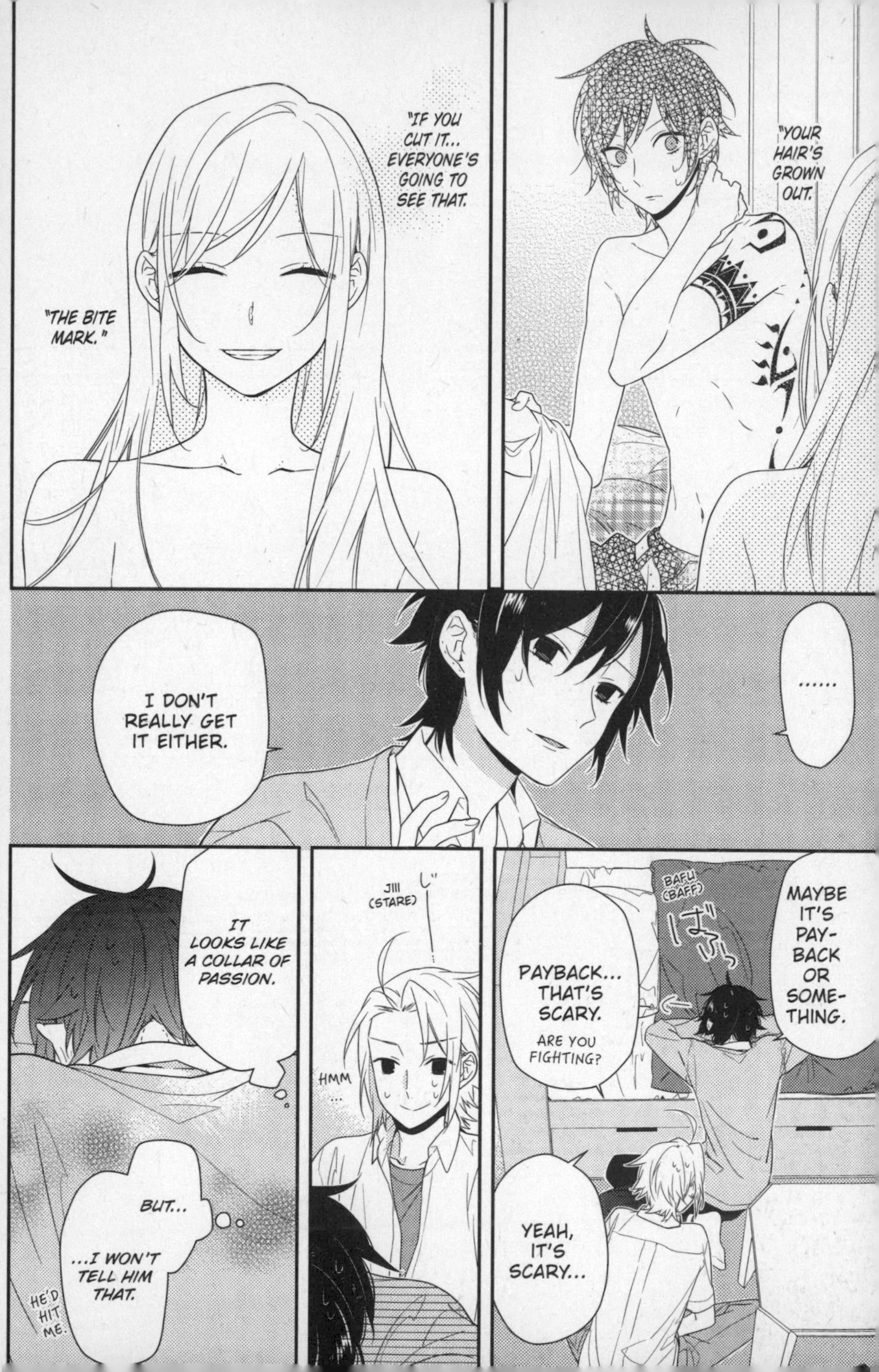
"YOUR HAIR'S GROWN OUT.
"IF YOU CUT IT... EVERYONE'S GOING TO SEE THAT.
"THE BITE MARK."
......
I DON'T REALLY GET IT EITHER.
MAYBE IT'S PAY-BACK OR SOME-THING.
BAFU (BAFF)
ばふっ
PAYBACK... THAT'S SCARY.
ARE YOU FIGHTING?
YEAH, IT'S SCARY...
JIII (STARE)
じー
HMM...
IT LOOKS LIKE A COLLAR OF PASSION.
BUT...
...I WON'T TELL HIM THAT.
HE'D HIT ME.

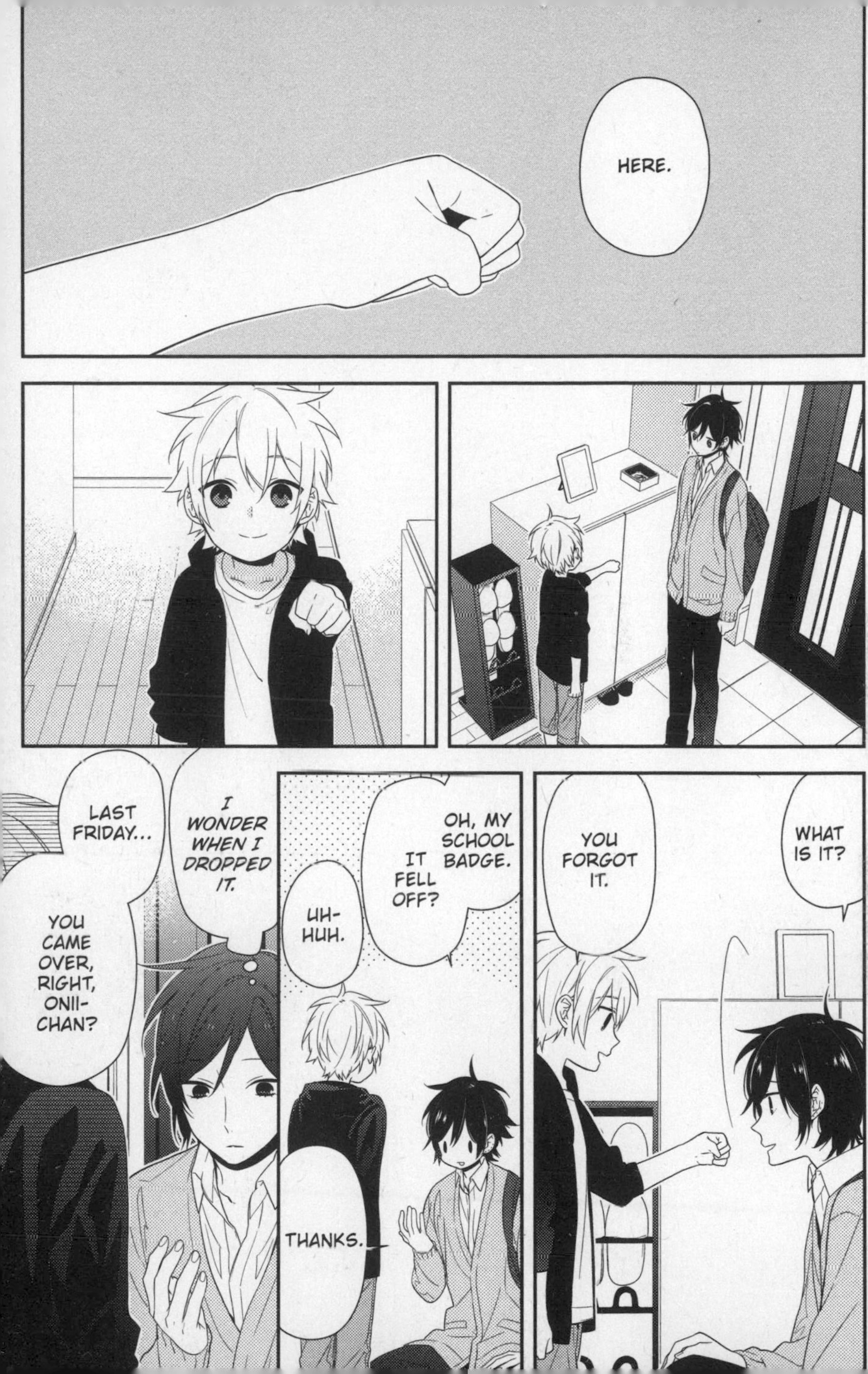
HERE.
WHAT IS IT?
YOU FORGOT IT.
OH, MY SCHOOL BADGE.
IT FELL OFF?
UH-HUH.
THANKS.
I WONDER WHEN I DROPPED IT.
LAST FRIDAY...
YOU CAME OVER, RIGHT, ONII-CHAN?

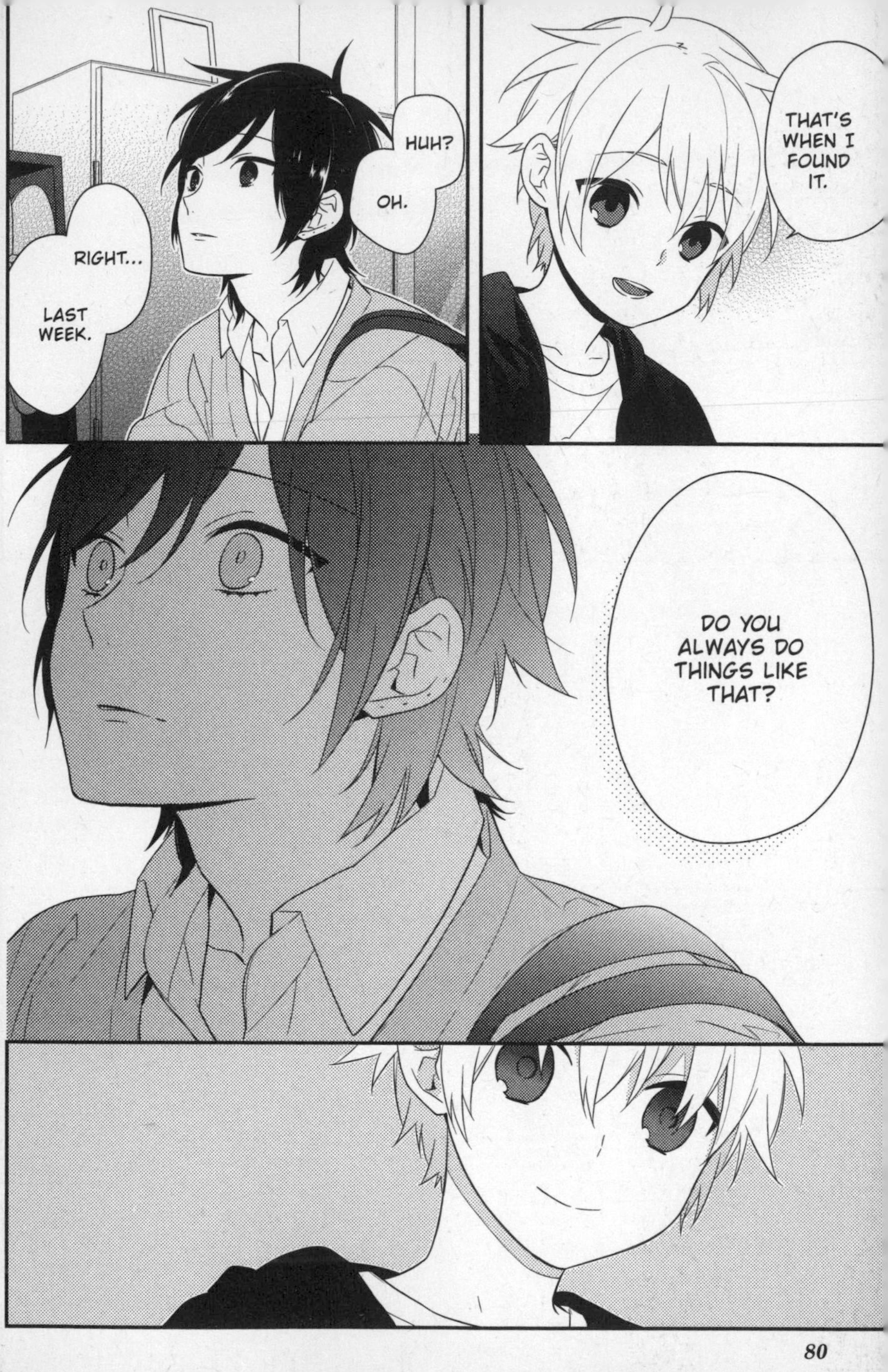
THAT'S WHEN I FOUND IT.
HUH?
OH.
RIGHT...
LAST WEEK.
DO YOU ALWAYS DO THINGS LIKE THAT?

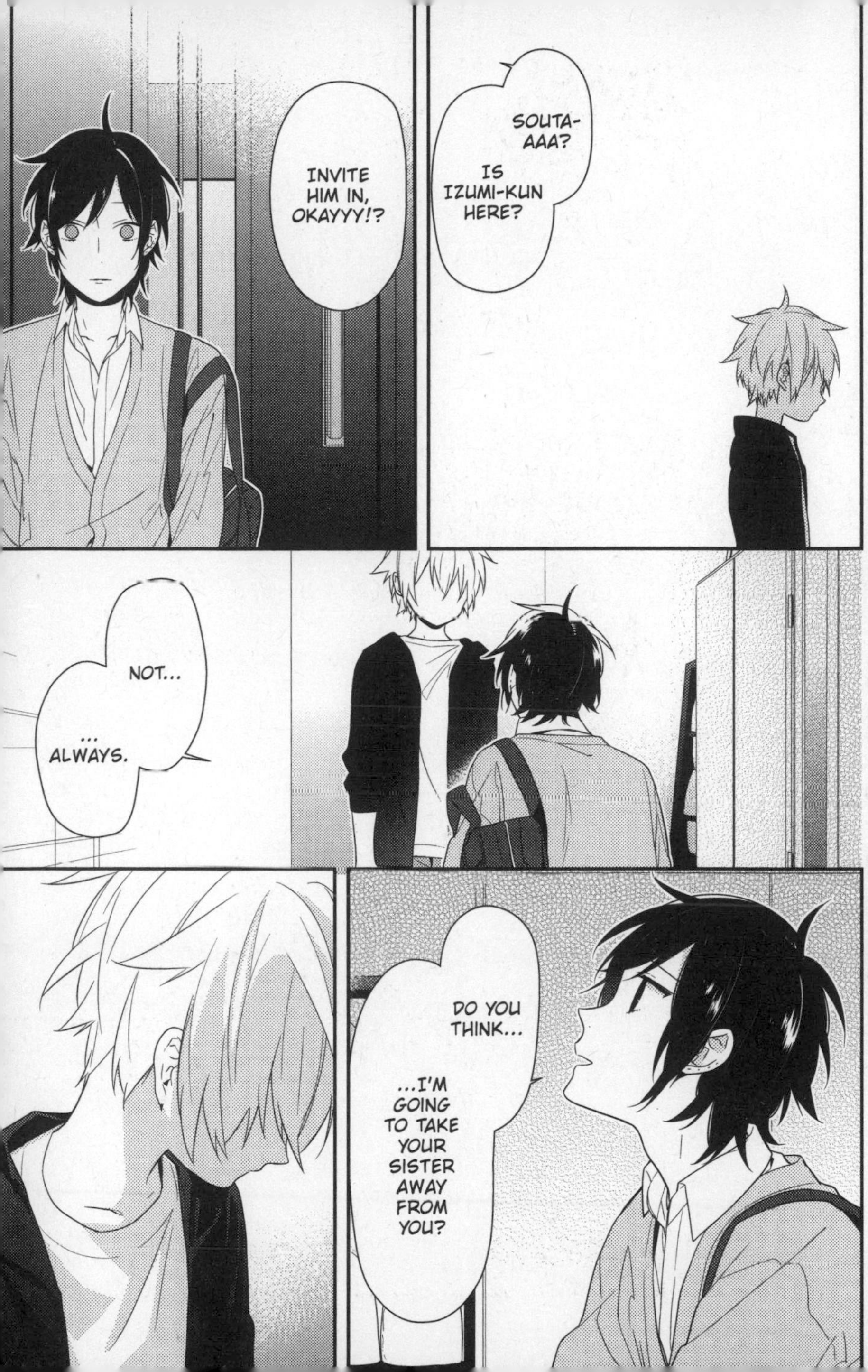
SOUTA-AAA?
IS IZUMI-KUN HERE?
INVITE HIM IN, OKAYYY!?
NOT... ...ALWAYS.
DO YOU THINK...
...I'M GOING TO TAKE YOUR SISTER AWAY FROM YOU?

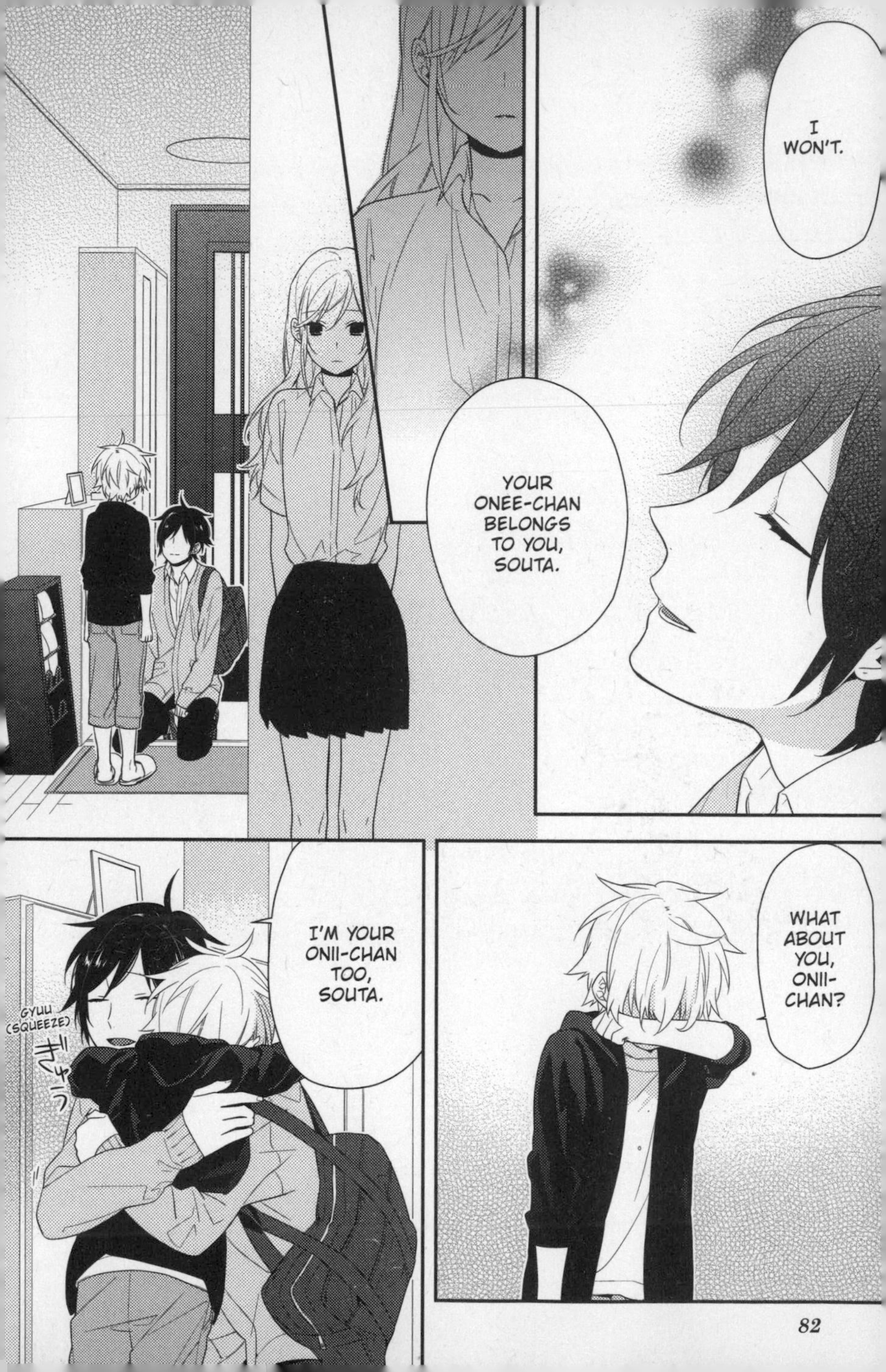
I WON'T.
YOUR ONEE-CHAN BELONGS TO YOU, SOUTA.
WHAT ABOUT YOU, ONII-CHAN?
I'M YOUR ONII-CHAN TOO, SOUTA.
GYUU (SQUEEZE)
ぎゅう

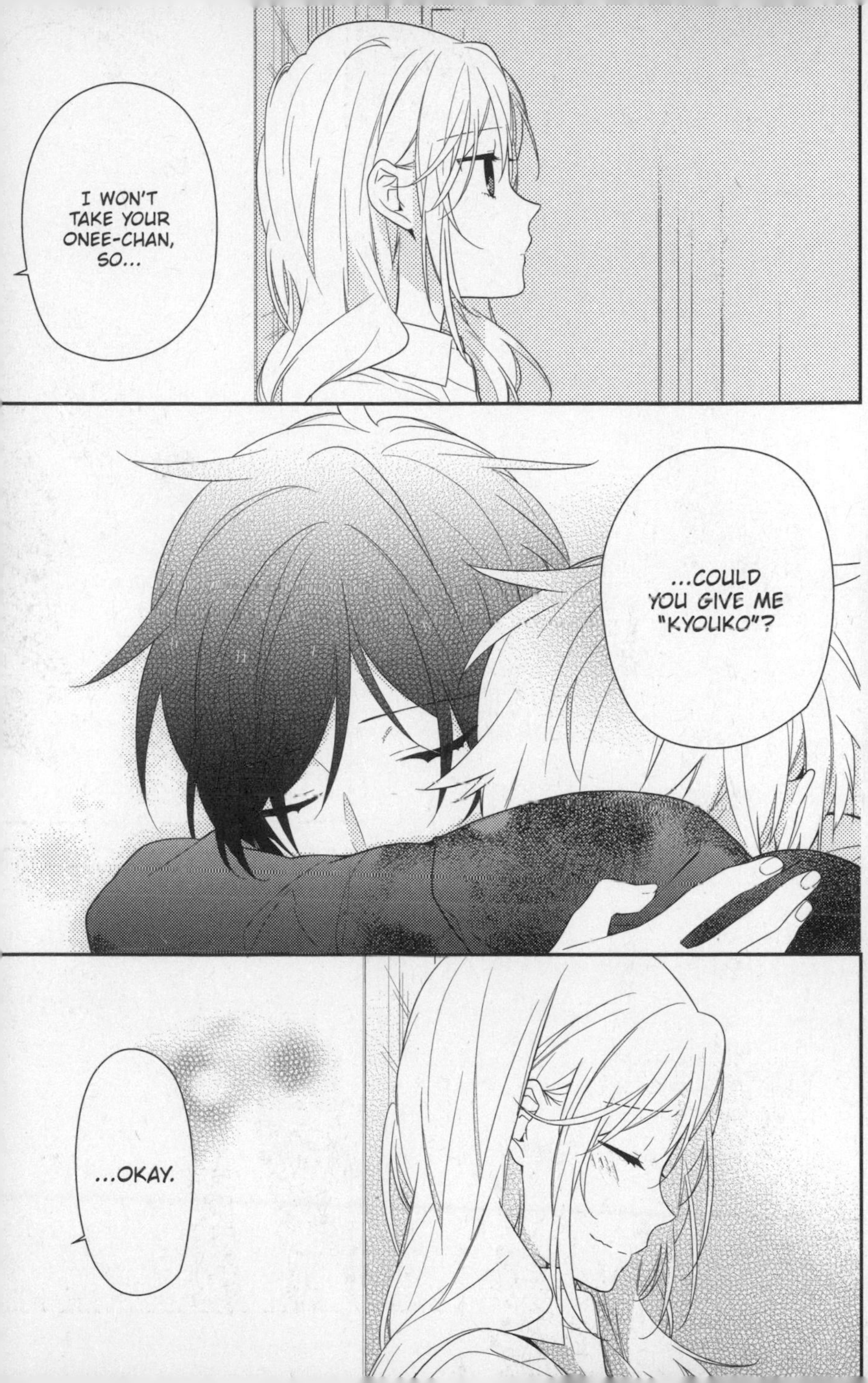
I WON'T TAKE YOUR ONEE-CHAN, SO...
...COULD YOU GIVE ME "KYOUKO"?
...OKAY.

HORIMIYA

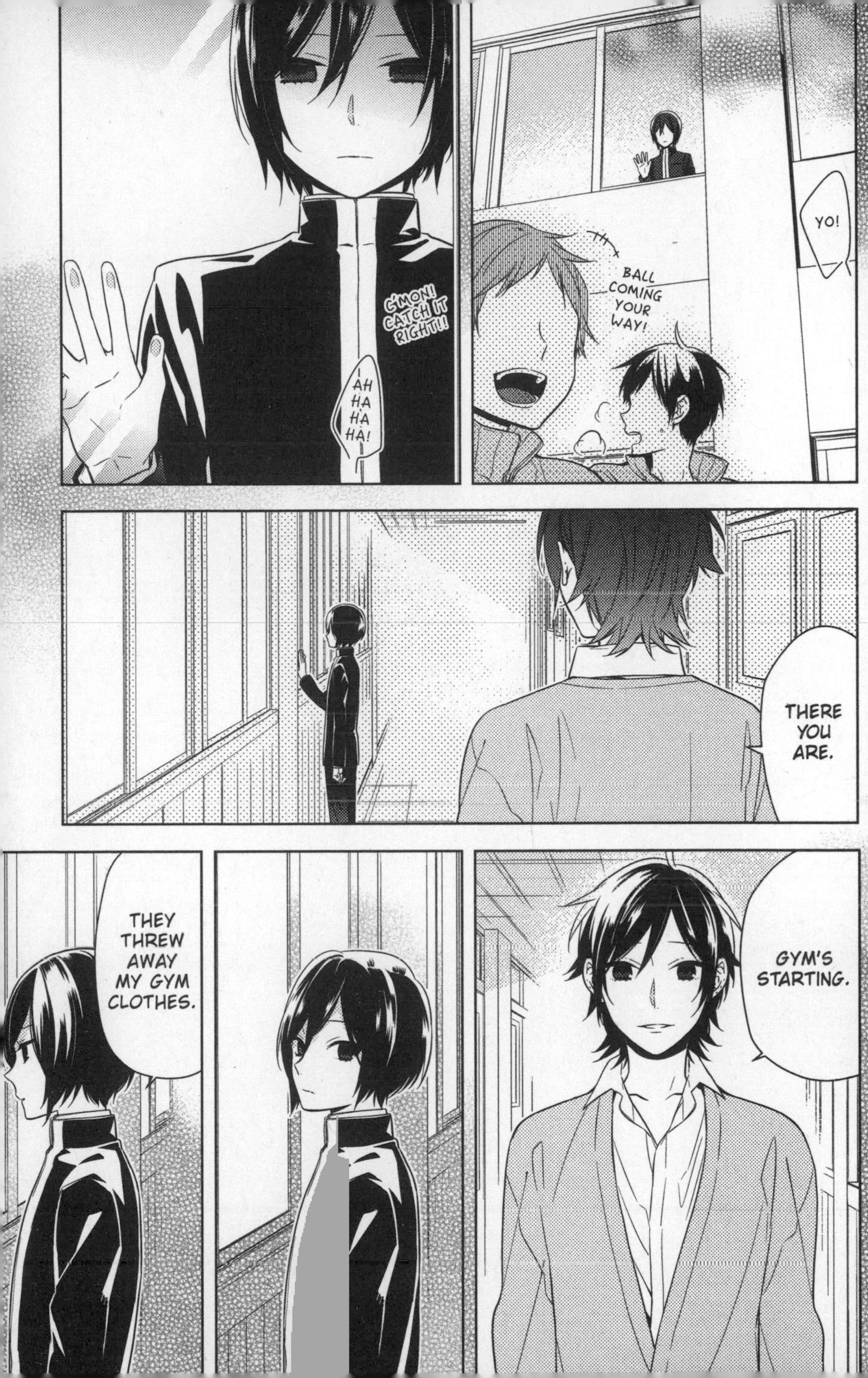
YO!
BALL COMING YOUR WAY!
C'MON! CATCH IT RIGHT!!
AH HA HA HA!
THERE YOU ARE.
GYM'S STARTING.
THEY THREW AWAY MY GYM CLOTHES.

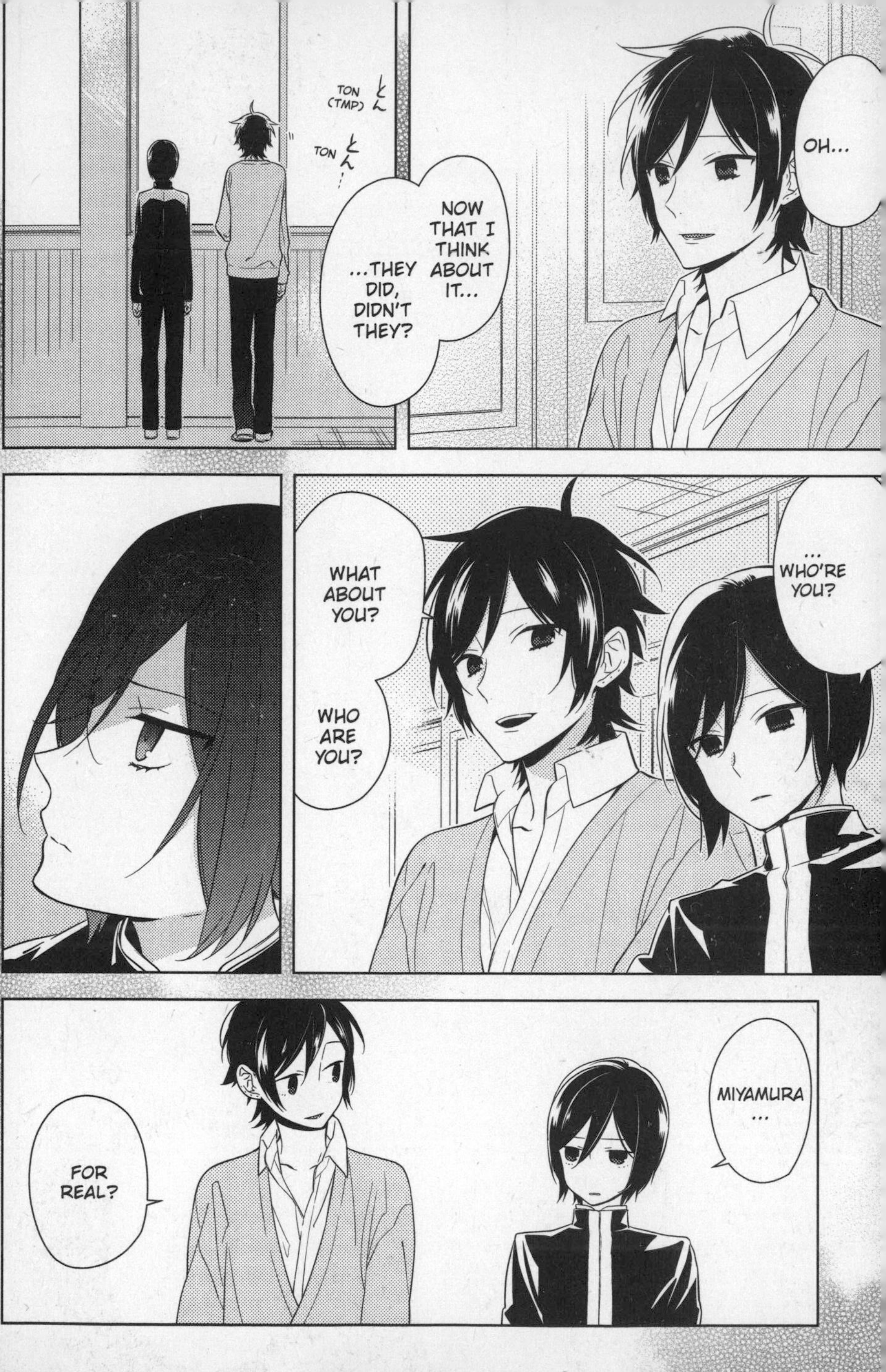
OH...
NOW THAT I THINK ABOUT IT...
...THEY DID, DIDN'T THEY?
TON (TMP) とん
TON とん
...WHO'RE YOU?
WHAT ABOUT YOU?
WHO ARE YOU?
MIYAMURA...
FOR REAL?

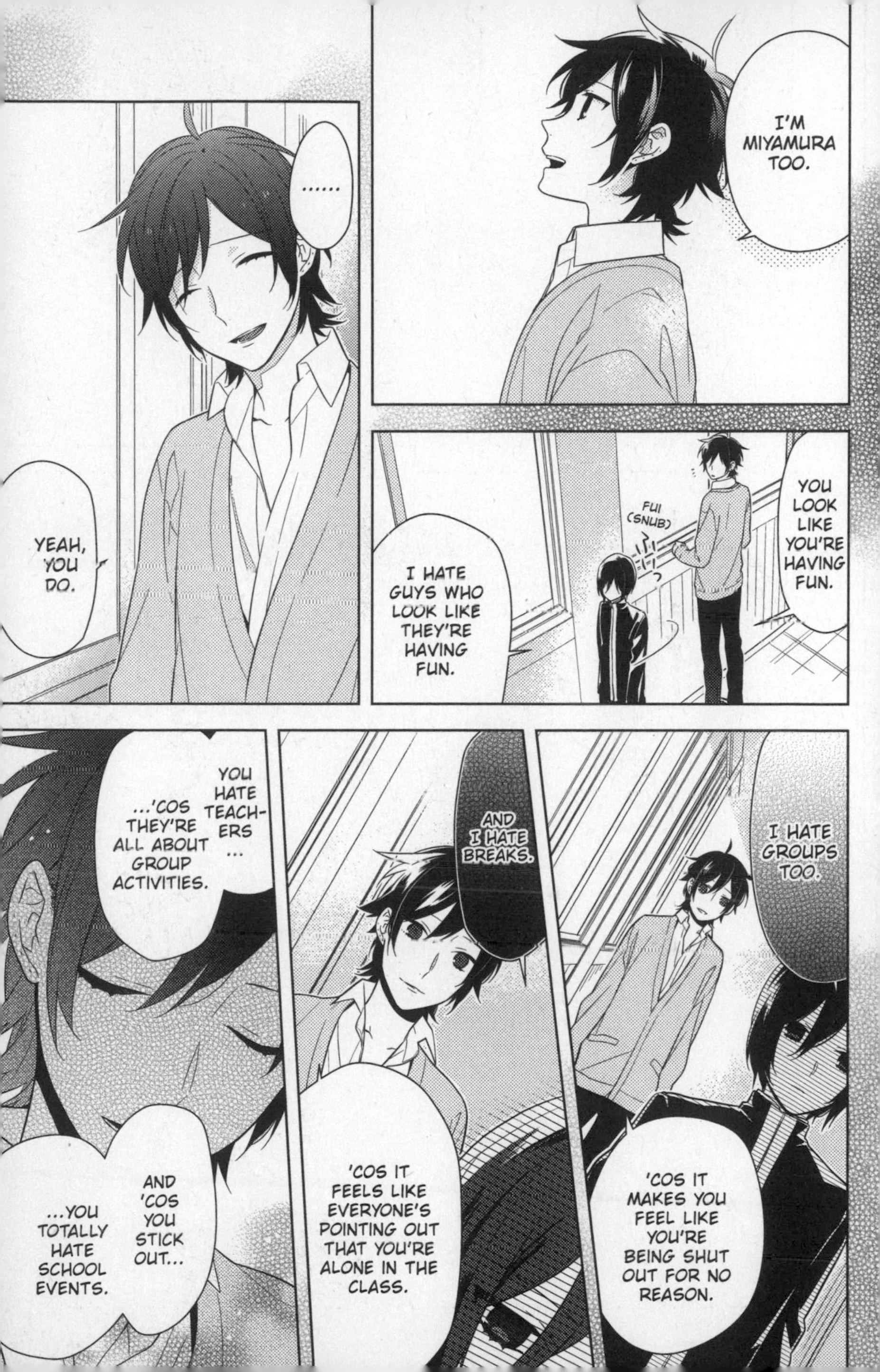
I'M MIYAMURA TOO.
YOU LOOK LIKE YOU'RE HAVING FUN.
FUI (SNUB)
I HATE GUYS WHO LOOK LIKE THEY'RE HAVING FUN.
......
YEAH, YOU DO.
I HATE GROUPS TOO.
'COS IT MAKES YOU FEEL LIKE YOU'RE BEING SHUT OUT FOR NO REASON.
AND I HATE BREAKS.
'COS IT FEELS LIKE EVERYONE'S POINTING OUT THAT YOU'RE ALONE IN THE CLASS.
YOU HATE TEACHERS...
...'COS THEY'RE ALL ABOUT GROUP ACTIVITIES.
AND 'COS YOU STICK OUT...
...YOU TOTALLY HATE SCHOOL EVENTS.

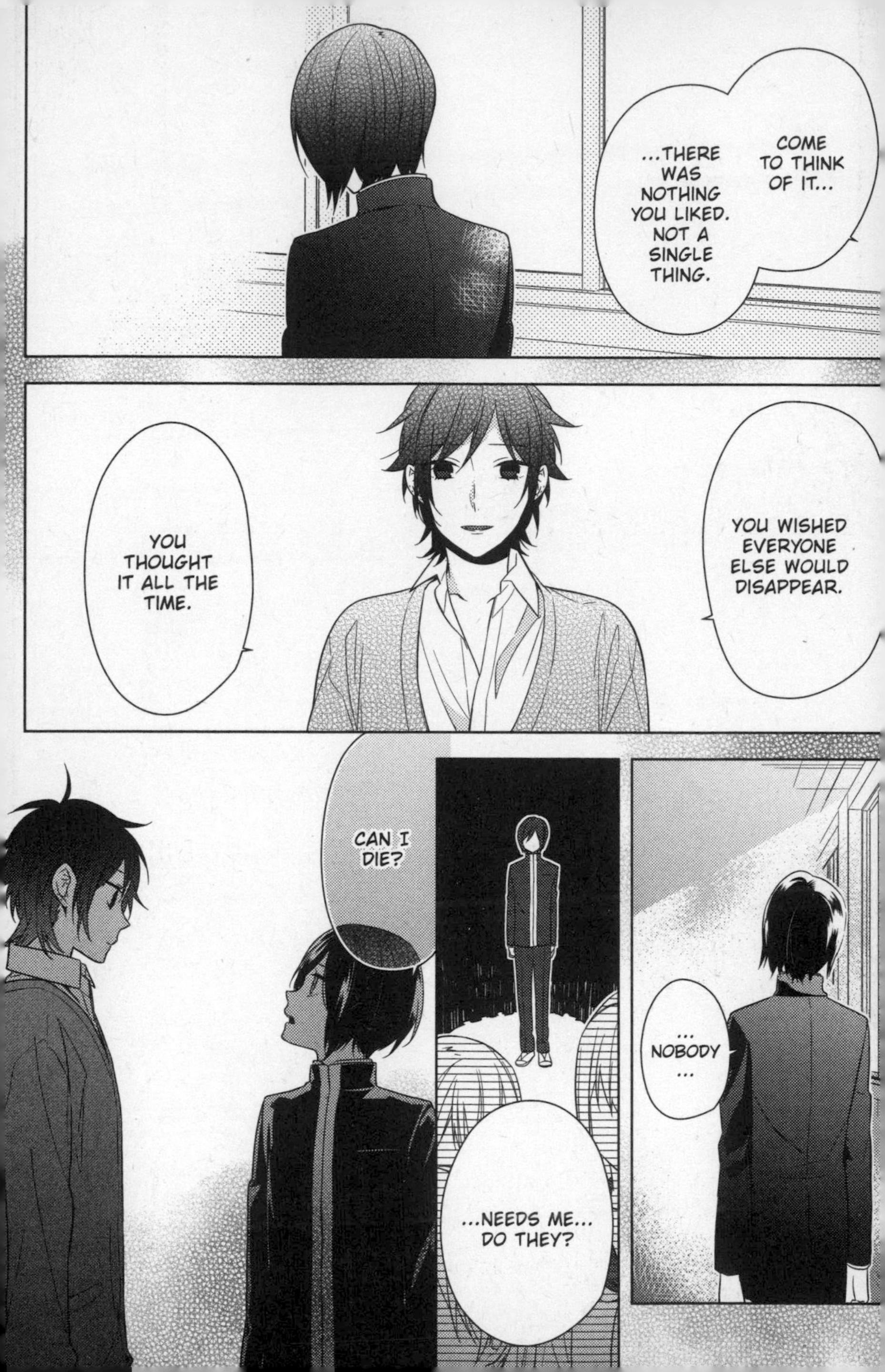
COME TO THINK OF IT...
...THERE WAS NOTHING YOU LIKED. NOT A SINGLE THING.
YOU WISHED EVERYONE ELSE WOULD DISAPPEAR.
YOU THOUGHT IT ALL THE TIME.
... NOBODY ...
...NEEDS ME... DO THEY?
CAN I DIE?

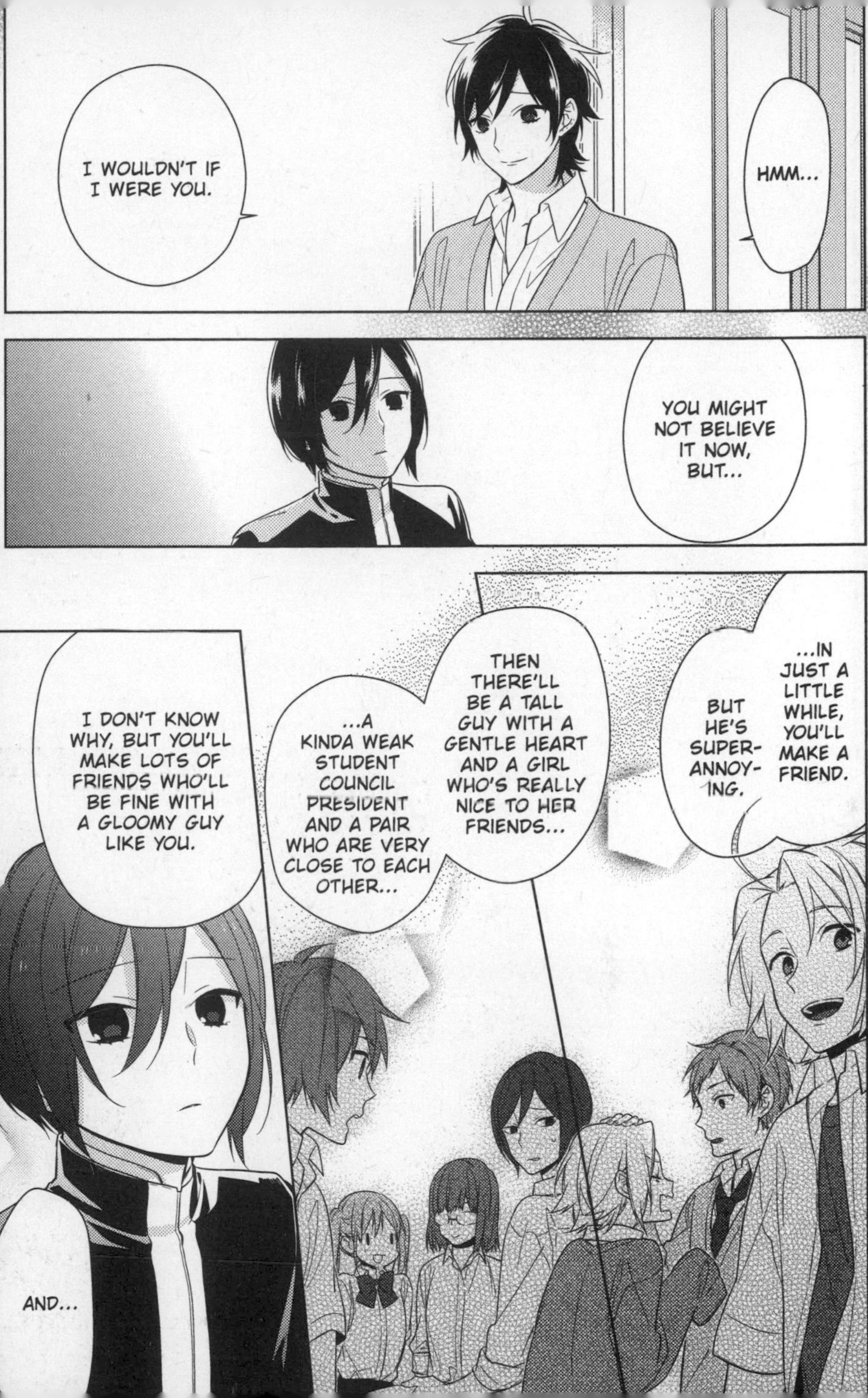
HMM...
I WOULDN'T IF I WERE YOU.
YOU MIGHT NOT BELIEVE IT NOW, BUT...
...IN JUST A LITTLE WHILE, YOU'LL MAKE A FRIEND.
BUT HE'S SUPER-ANNOYING.
THEN THERE'LL BE A TALL GUY WITH A GENTLE HEART AND A GIRL WHO'S REALLY NICE TO HER FRIENDS...
...A KINDA WEAK STUDENT COUNCIL PRESIDENT AND A PAIR WHO ARE VERY CLOSE TO EACH OTHER...
I DON'T KNOW WHY, BUT YOU'LL MAKE LOTS OF FRIENDS WHO'LL BE FINE WITH A GLOOMY GUY LIKE YOU.
AND...

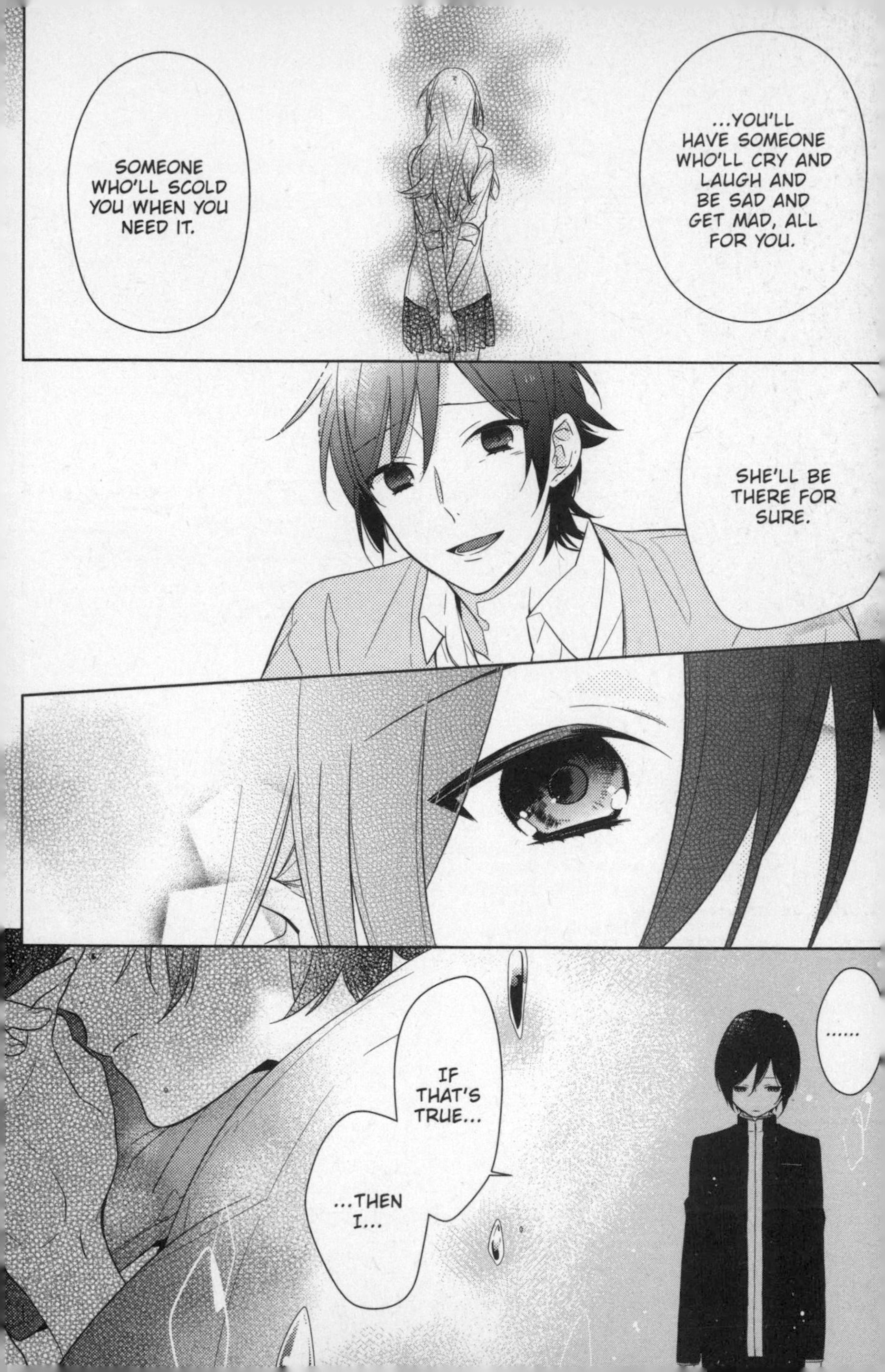
...YOU'LL HAVE SOMEONE WHO'LL CRY AND LAUGH AND BE SAD AND GET MAD, ALL FOR YOU.
SOMEONE WHO'LL SCOLD YOU WHEN YOU NEED IT.
SHE'LL BE THERE FOR SURE.
......
IF THAT'S TRUE...
...THEN I...

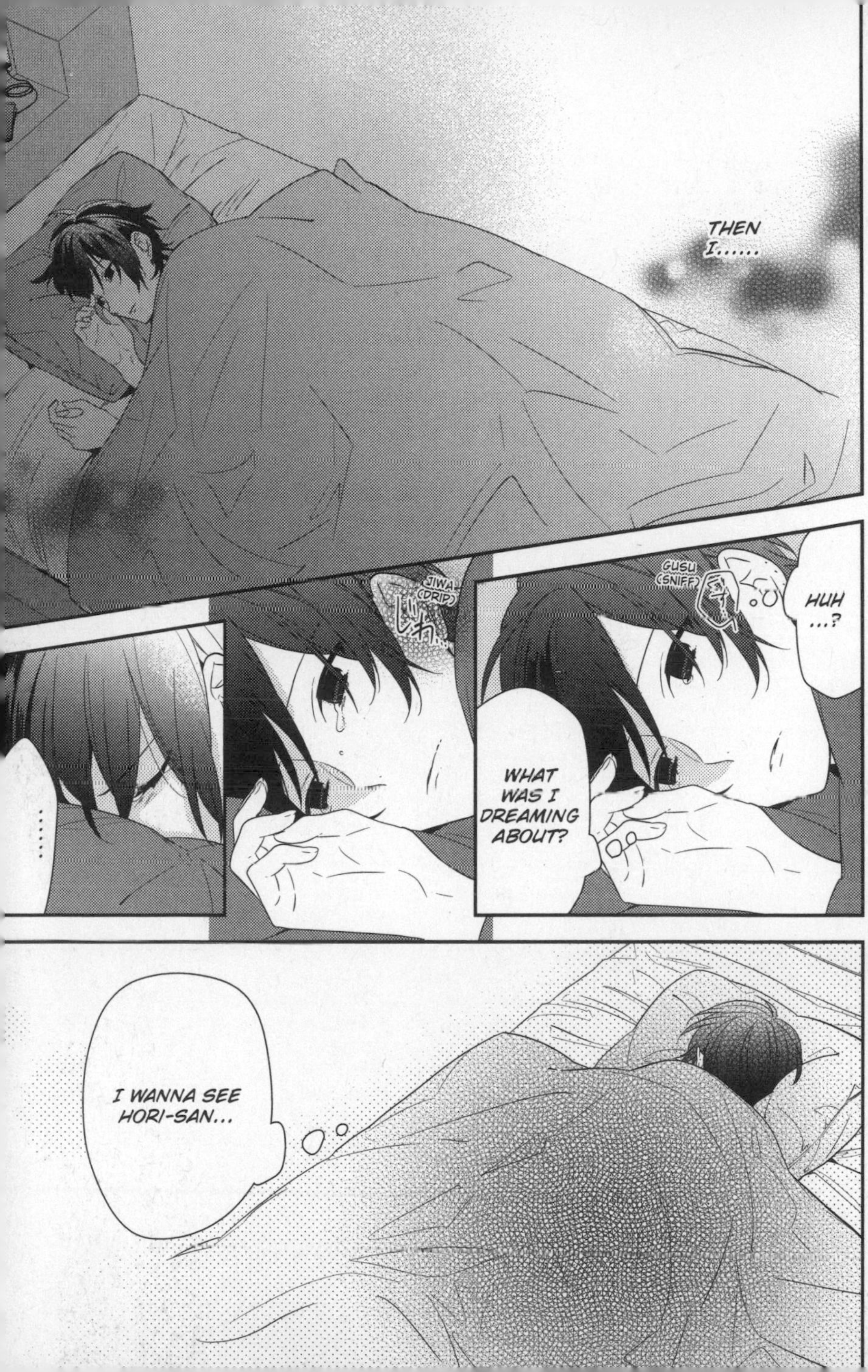
THEN I......
GUSU (SNIFF)
HUH ...?
WHAT WAS I DREAMING ABOUT?
JIWA (DRIP)
じわ...
......
I WANNA SEE HORI-SAN...

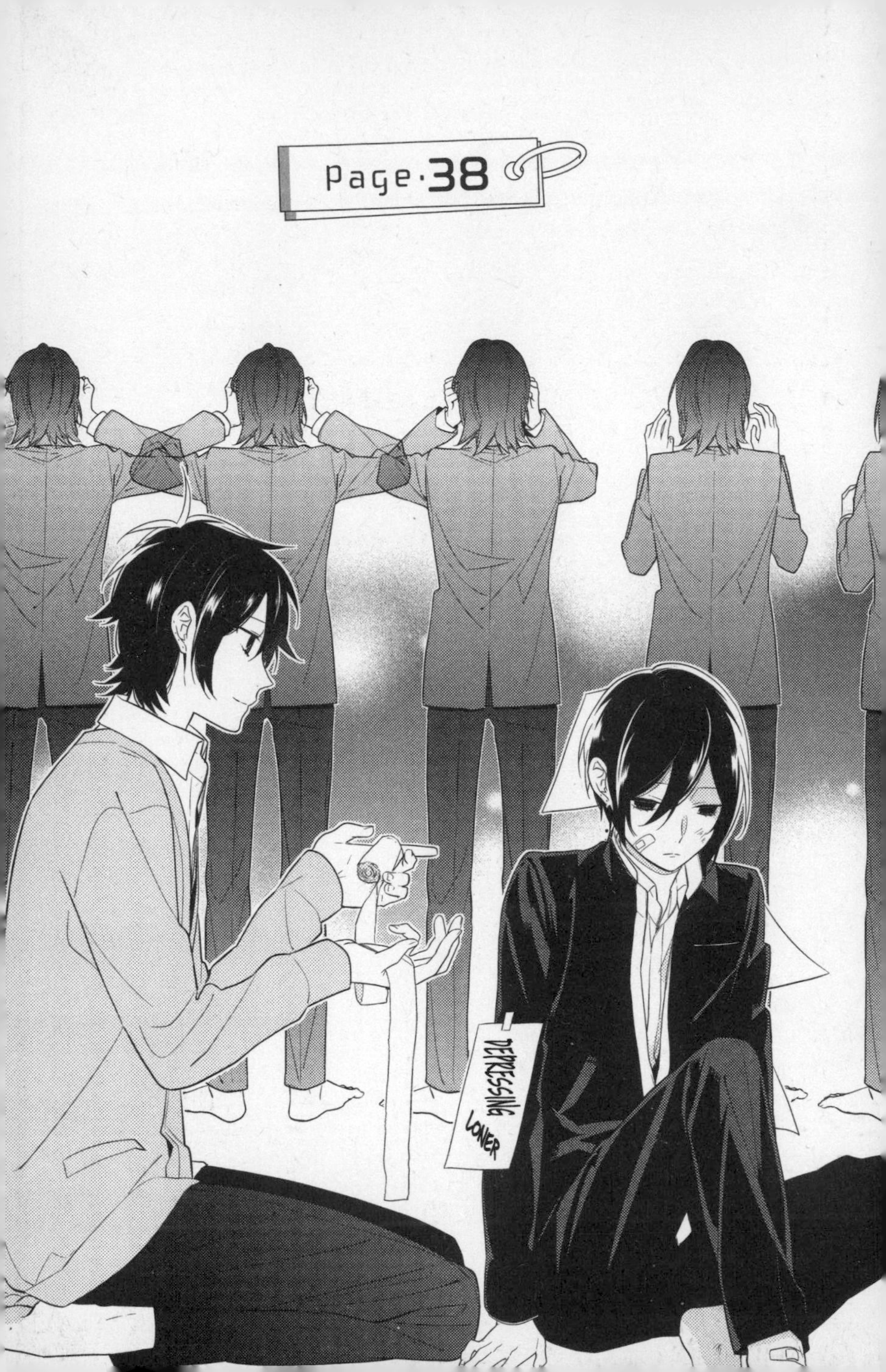
page.38
DEPRESSING LONER

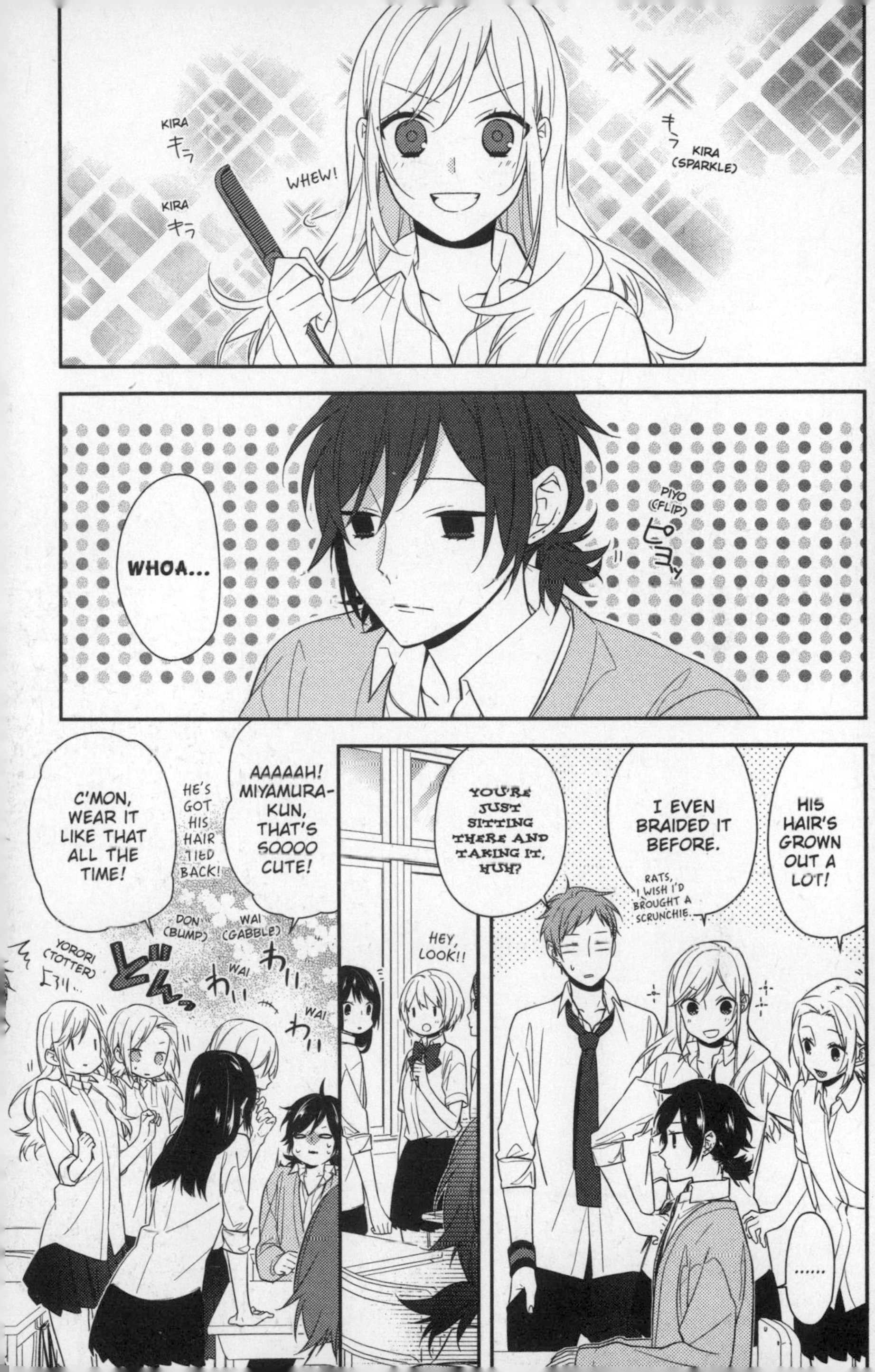
キラ KIRA (SPARKLE)
WHEW!
KIRA キラ
KIRA キラ
PIYO (FLIP) ピョッ
WHOA...
HIS HAIR'S GROWN OUT A LOT!
I EVEN BRAIDED IT BEFORE.
RATS, I WISH I'D BROUGHT A SCRUNCHIE.
YOU'RE JUST SITTING THERE AND TAKING IT, HUH?
......
HEY, LOOK!!
AAAAAH! MIYAMURA-KUN, THAT'S SOOOO CUTE!
WAI (GABBLE) わい
WAI わい
WAI わい
HE'S GOT HIS HAIR TIED BACK!
C'MON, WEAR IT LIKE THAT ALL THE TIME!
DON (BUMP) どんっ
YORORI (TOTTER) よろり...

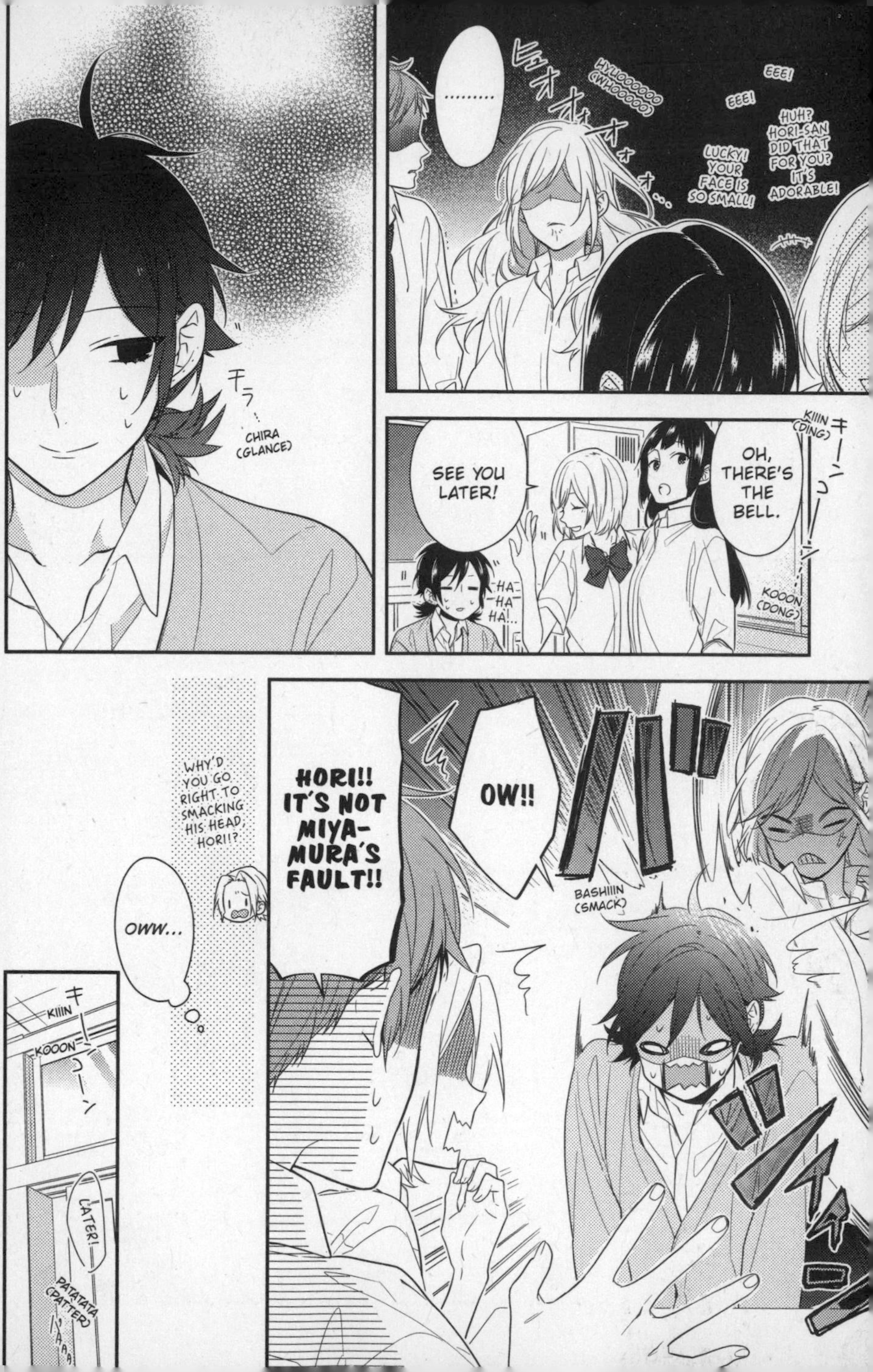
....
HYUOOOOOO (WHOOOOO)
EEE!
EEE!
HUH? HORI-SAN DID THAT FOR YOU? IT'S ADORABLE!
LUCKY! YOUR FACE IS SO SMALL!
KIIIN (DING)
OH, THERE'S THE BELL.
SEE YOU LATER!
HA HA HA...
KOOON (DONG)
CHIRA (GLANCE)
BASHIIIN (SMACK)
OW!!
HORI!! IT'S NOT MIYAMURA'S FAULT!!
WHY'D YOU GO RIGHT TO SMACKING HIS HEAD, HORI!?
OWW...
KIIIN
KOOON
LATER!
PATATATA (PATTER)

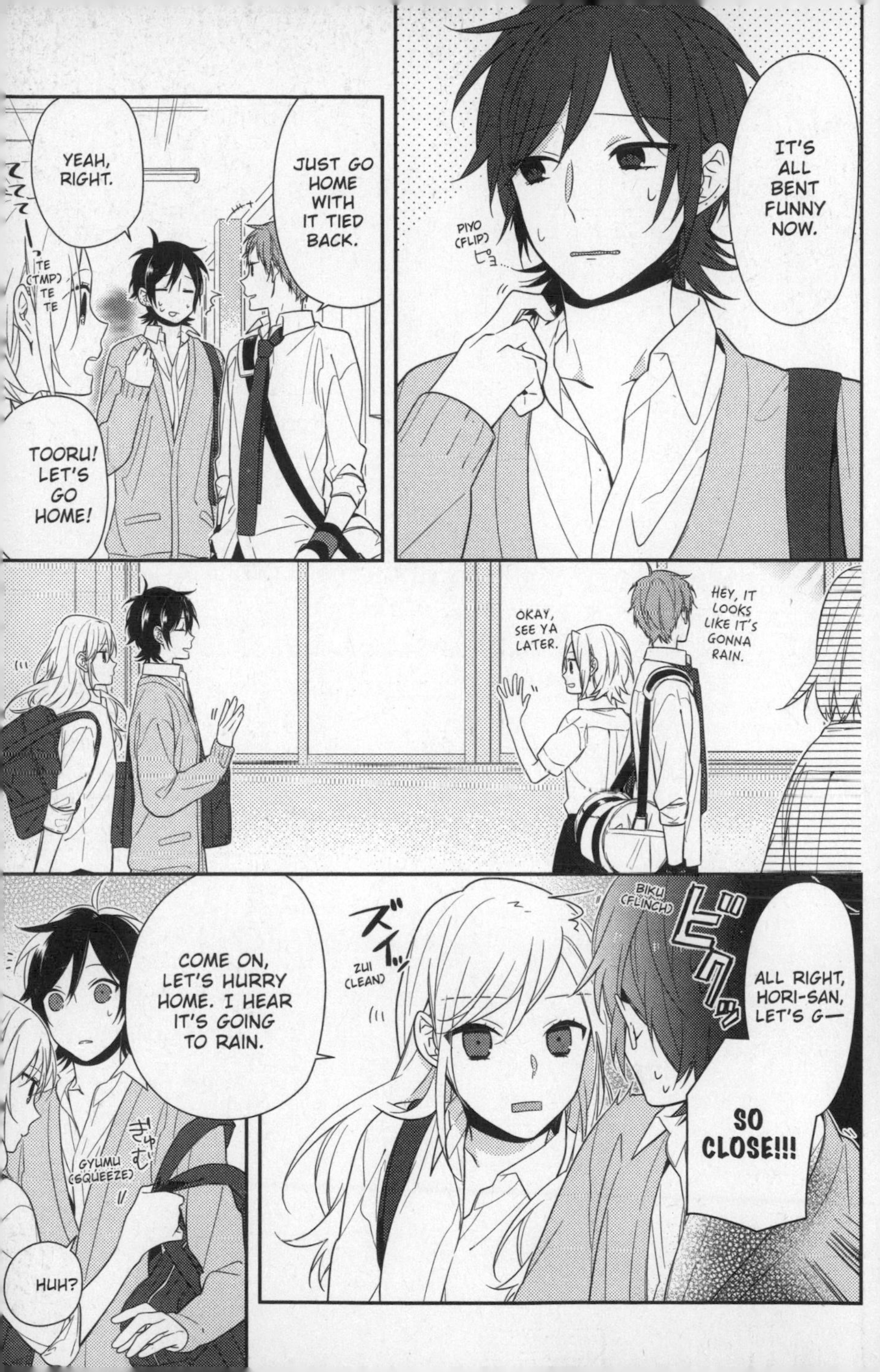
IT'S ALL BENT FUNNY NOW.
PIYO (FLIP)
ピョ
JUST GO HOME WITH IT TIED BACK.
YEAH, RIGHT.
TE (TMP) TE TE
TOORU! LET'S GO HOME!
HEY, IT LOOKS LIKE IT'S GONNA RAIN.
OKAY, SEE YA LATER.
BIKU (FLINCH)
ビクッ
ALL RIGHT, HORI-SAN, LET'S G—
SO CLOSE!!!
ズイッ
ZUI (LEAN)
COME ON, LET'S HURRY HOME. I HEAR IT'S GOING TO RAIN.
ぎゅむ
GYUMU (SQUEEZE)
HUH?

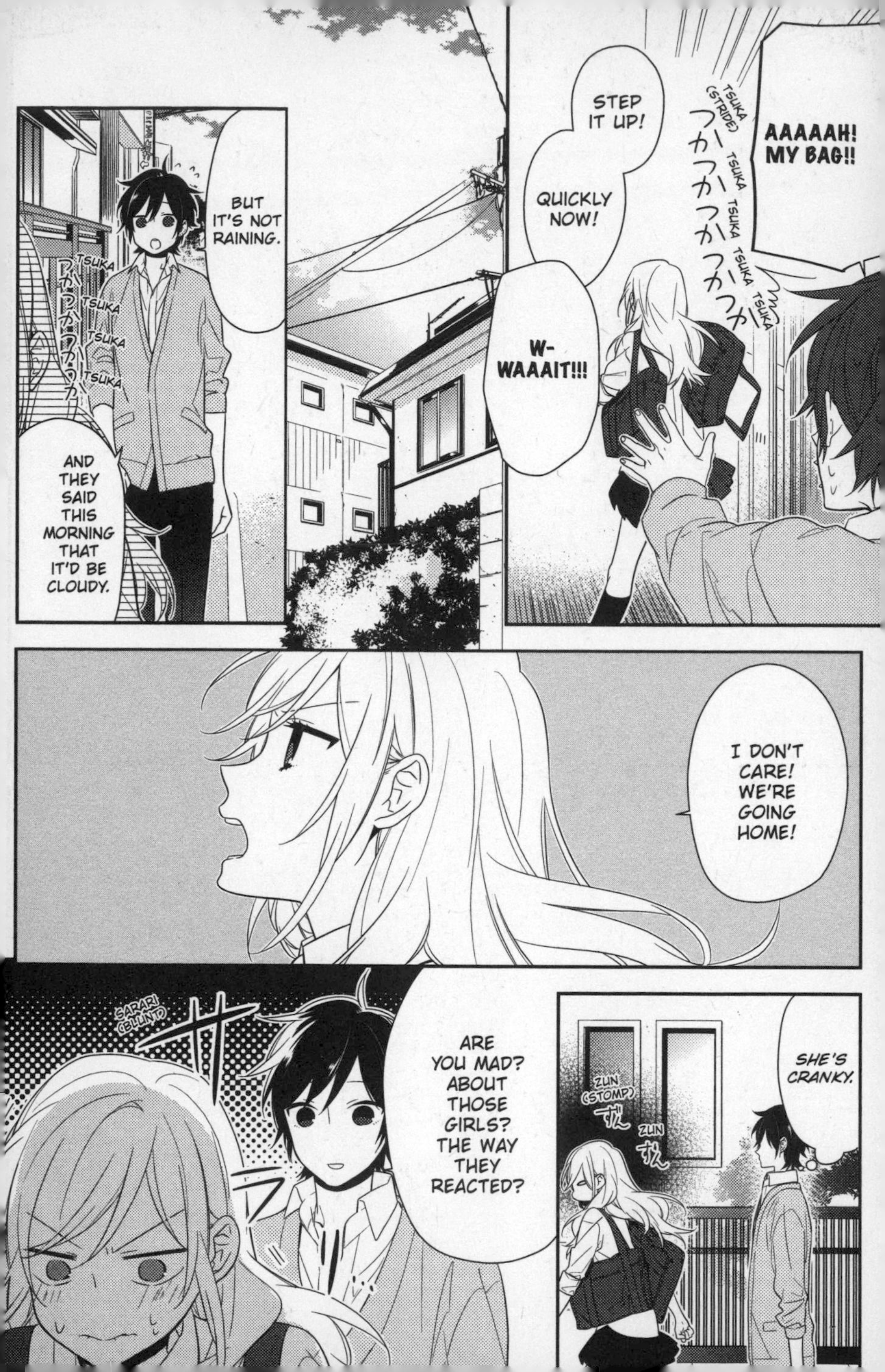
AAAAAH! MY BAG!!
TSUKA (STRIDE) TSUKA TSUKA TSUKA TSUKA
STEP IT UP!
QUICKLY NOW!
W-WAAAIT!!!
BUT IT'S NOT RAINING.
TSUKA TSUKA TSUKA TSUKA
AND THEY SAID THIS MORNING THAT IT'D BE CLOUDY.
I DON'T CARE! WE'RE GOING HOME!
SHE'S CRANKY.
ZUN (STOMP) ずん
ZUN ずん
SARARI (BLUNT)
ARE YOU MAD? ABOUT THOSE GIRLS? THE WAY THEY REACTED?

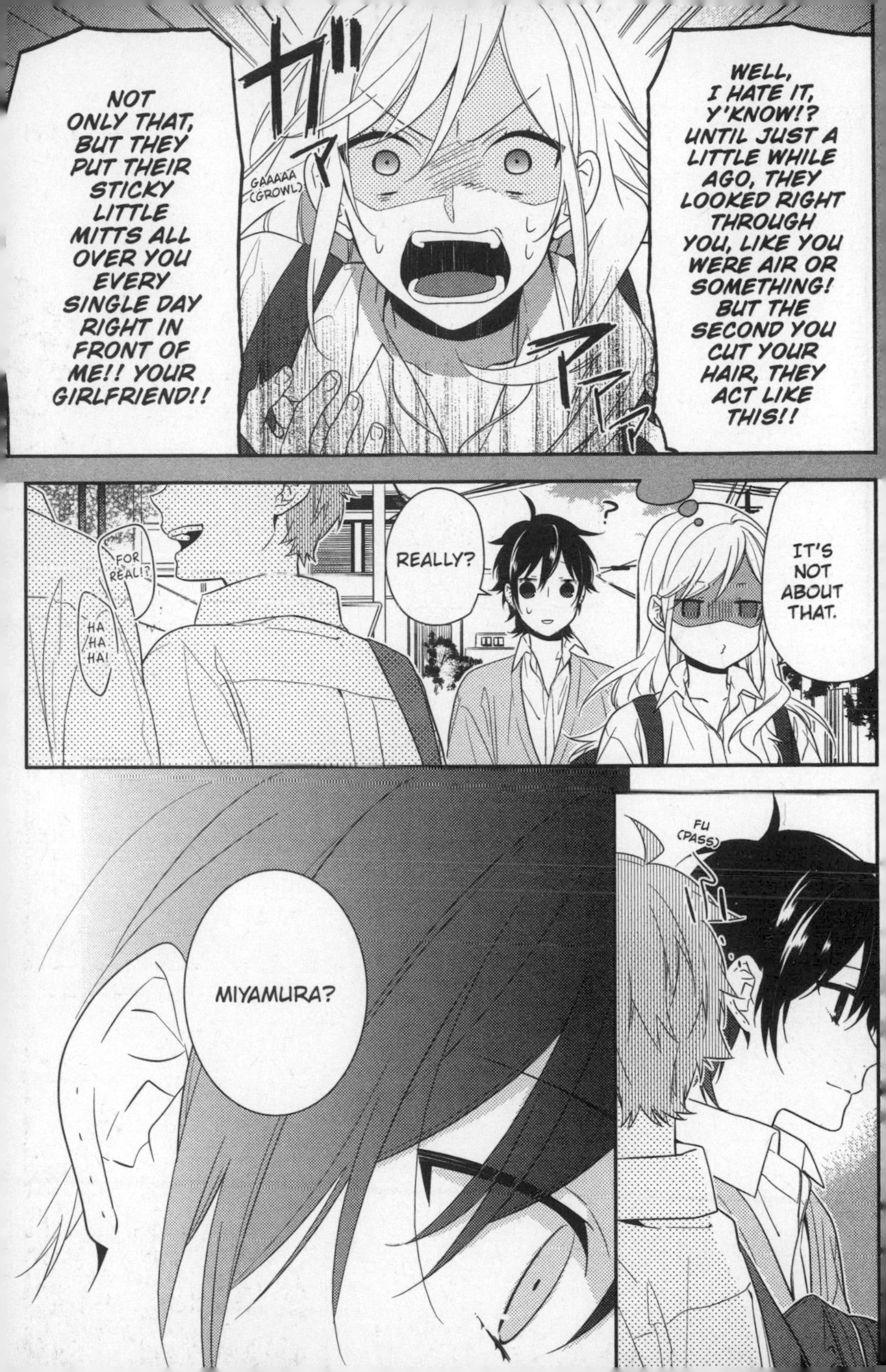
WELL, I HATE IT, Y'KNOW!? UNTIL JUST A LITTLE WHILE AGO, THEY LOOKED RIGHT THROUGH YOU, LIKE YOU WERE AIR OR SOMETHING! BUT THE SECOND YOU CUT YOUR HAIR, THEY ACT LIKE THIS!!
GAAAAA (GROWL)
NOT ONLY THAT, BUT THEY PUT THEIR STICKY LITTLE MITTS ALL OVER YOU EVERY SINGLE DAY RIGHT IN FRONT OF ME!! YOUR GIRLFRIEND!!
IT'S NOT ABOUT THAT.
?
REALLY?
FOR REAL!?
HA HA HA!
FU (PASS)
MIYAMURA?

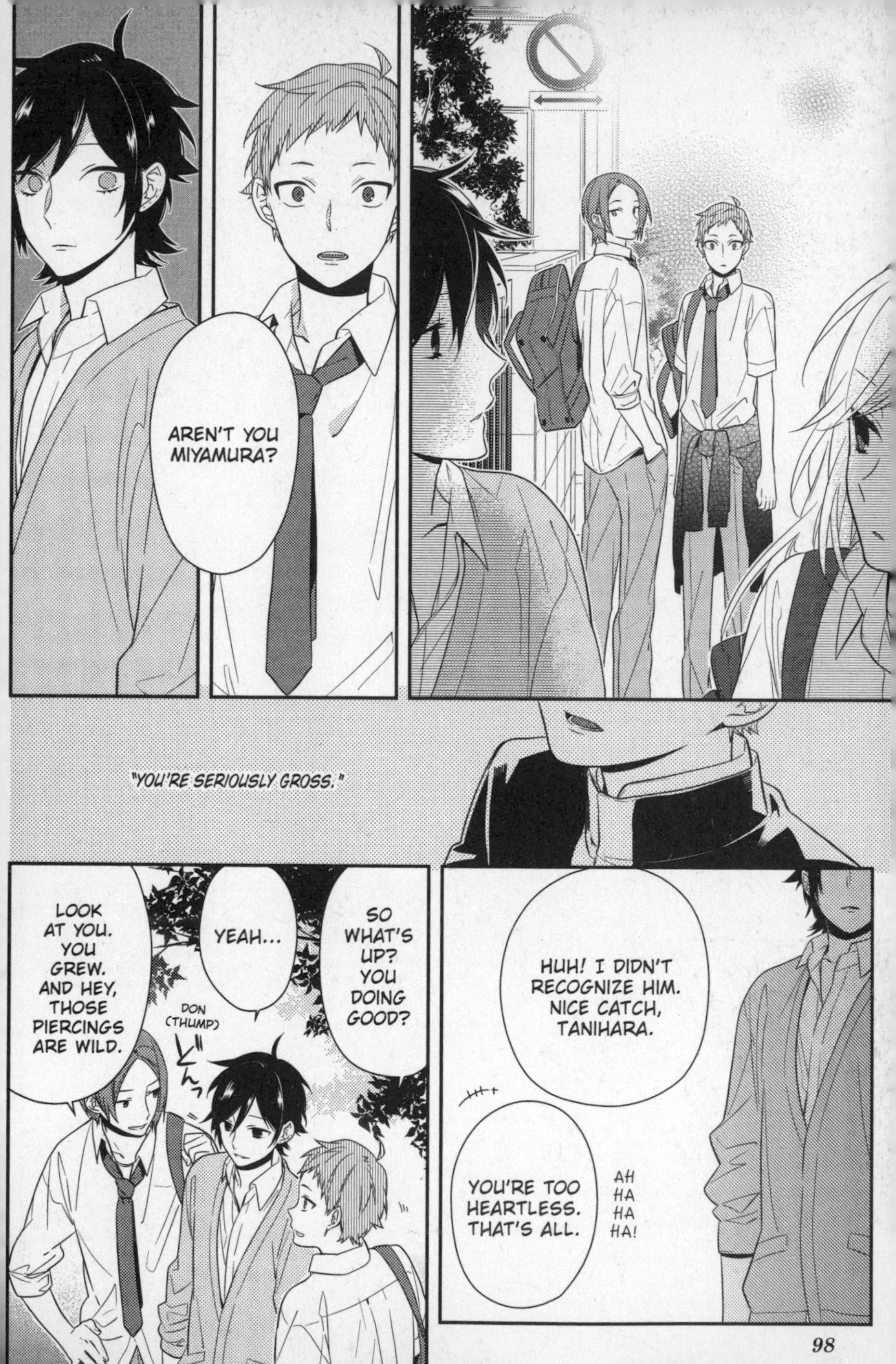
AREN'T YOU MIYAMURA?
"YOU'RE SERIOUSLY GROSS."
HUH! I DIDN'T RECOGNIZE HIM. NICE CATCH, TANIHARA.
YOU'RE TOO HEARTLESS. THAT'S ALL.
AH HA HA HA!
SO WHAT'S UP? YOU DOING GOOD?
YEAH...
LOOK AT YOU. YOU GREW. AND HEY, THOSE PIERCINGS ARE WILD.
DON (THUMP)

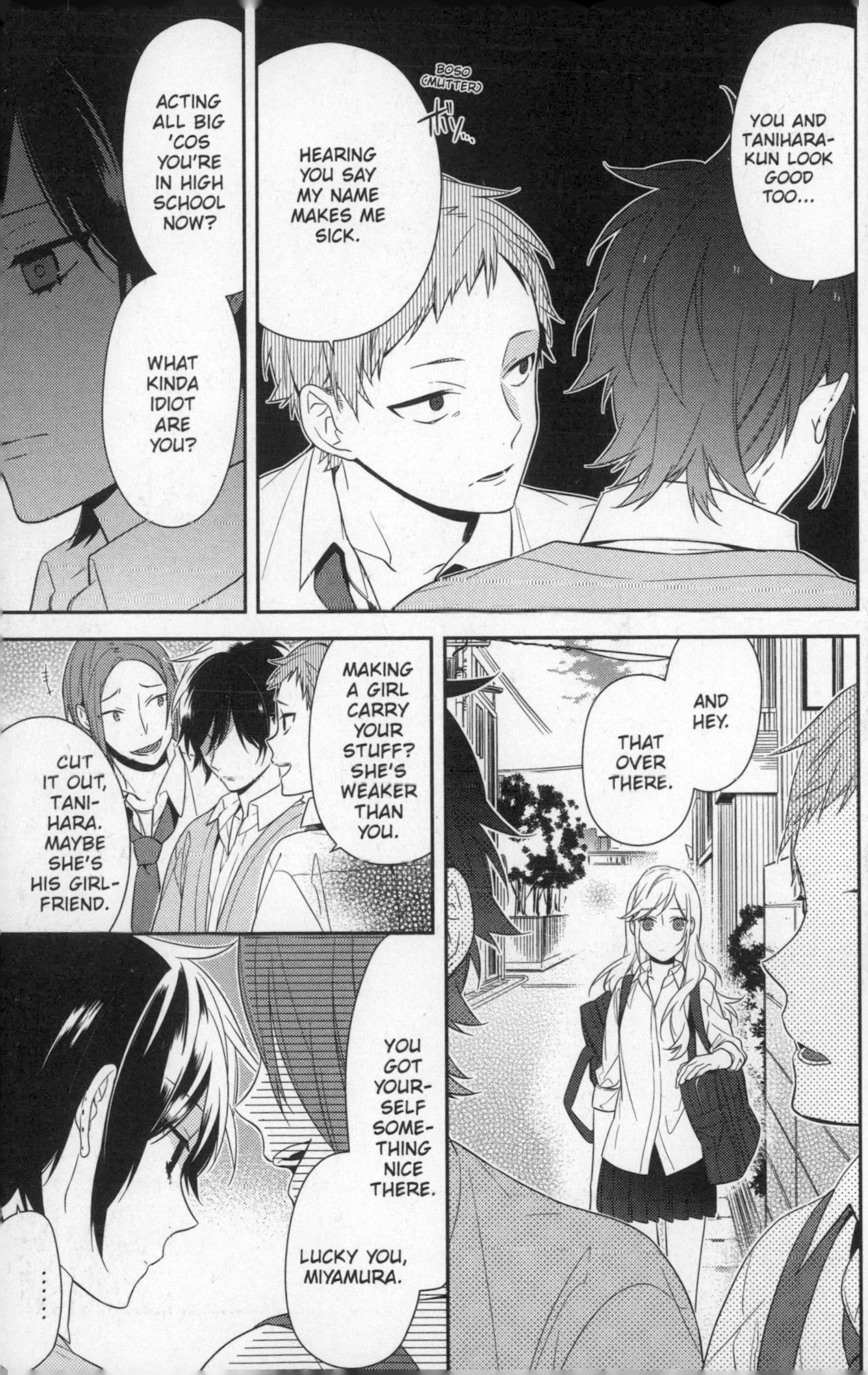
YOU AND TANIHARA-KUN LOOK GOOD TOO...
BOSO (MUTTER)
HEARING YOU SAY MY NAME MAKES ME SICK.
ACTING ALL BIG 'COS YOU'RE IN HIGH SCHOOL NOW?
WHAT KINDA IDIOT ARE YOU?
AND HEY. THAT OVER THERE.
MAKING A GIRL CARRY YOUR STUFF? SHE'S WEAKER THAN YOU.
CUT IT OUT, TANIHARA. MAYBE SHE'S HIS GIRLFRIEND.
YOU GOT YOURSELF SOMETHING NICE THERE.
LUCKY YOU, MIYAMURA.
......

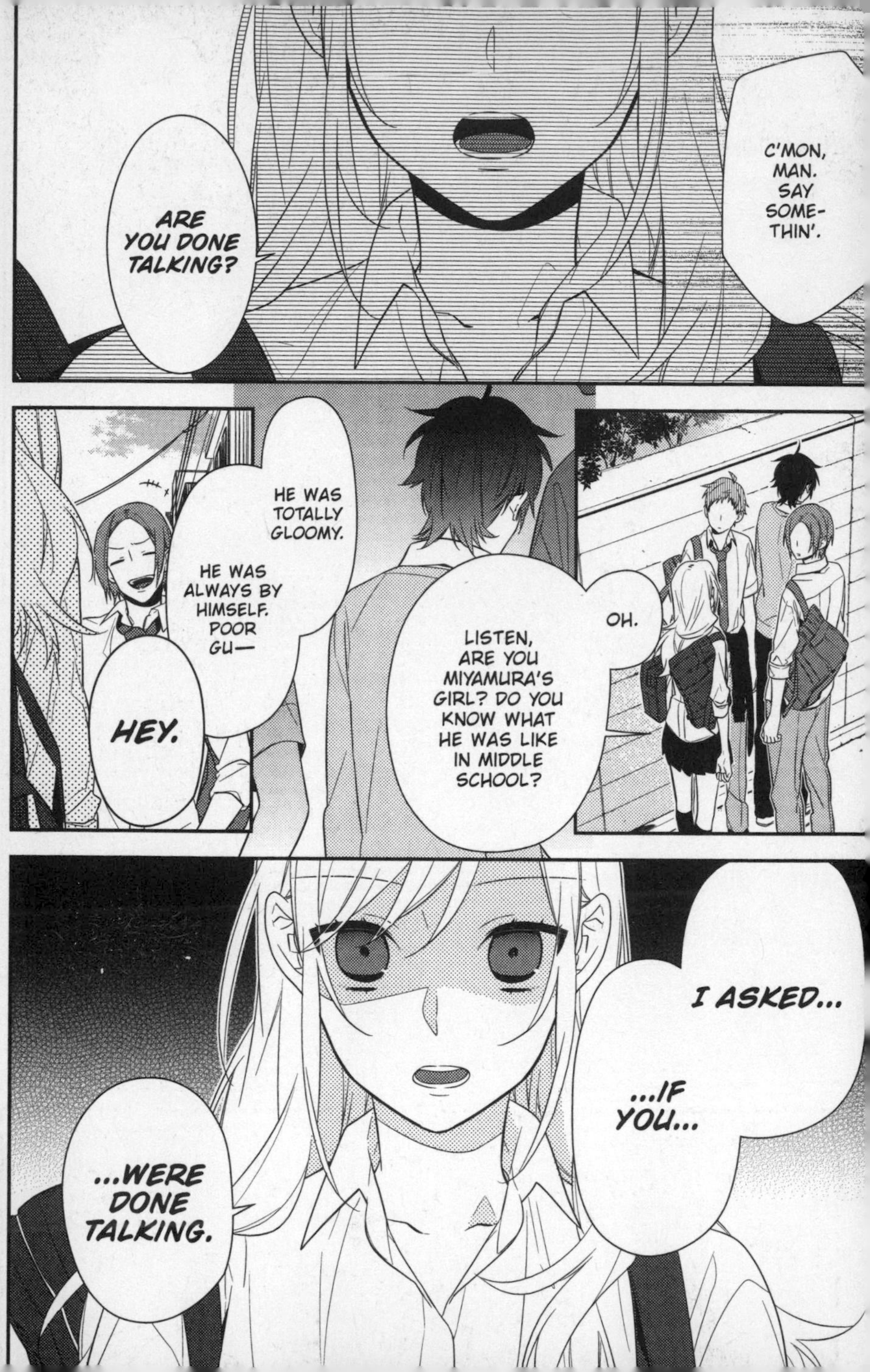
C'MON, MAN. SAY SOMETHIN'.
ARE YOU DONE TALKING?
OH.
LISTEN, ARE YOU MIYAMURA'S GIRL? DO YOU KNOW WHAT HE WAS LIKE IN MIDDLE SCHOOL?
HE WAS TOTALLY GLOOMY.
HE WAS ALWAYS BY HIMSELF. POOR GU—
HEY.
I ASKED...
...IF YOU...
...WERE DONE TALKING.

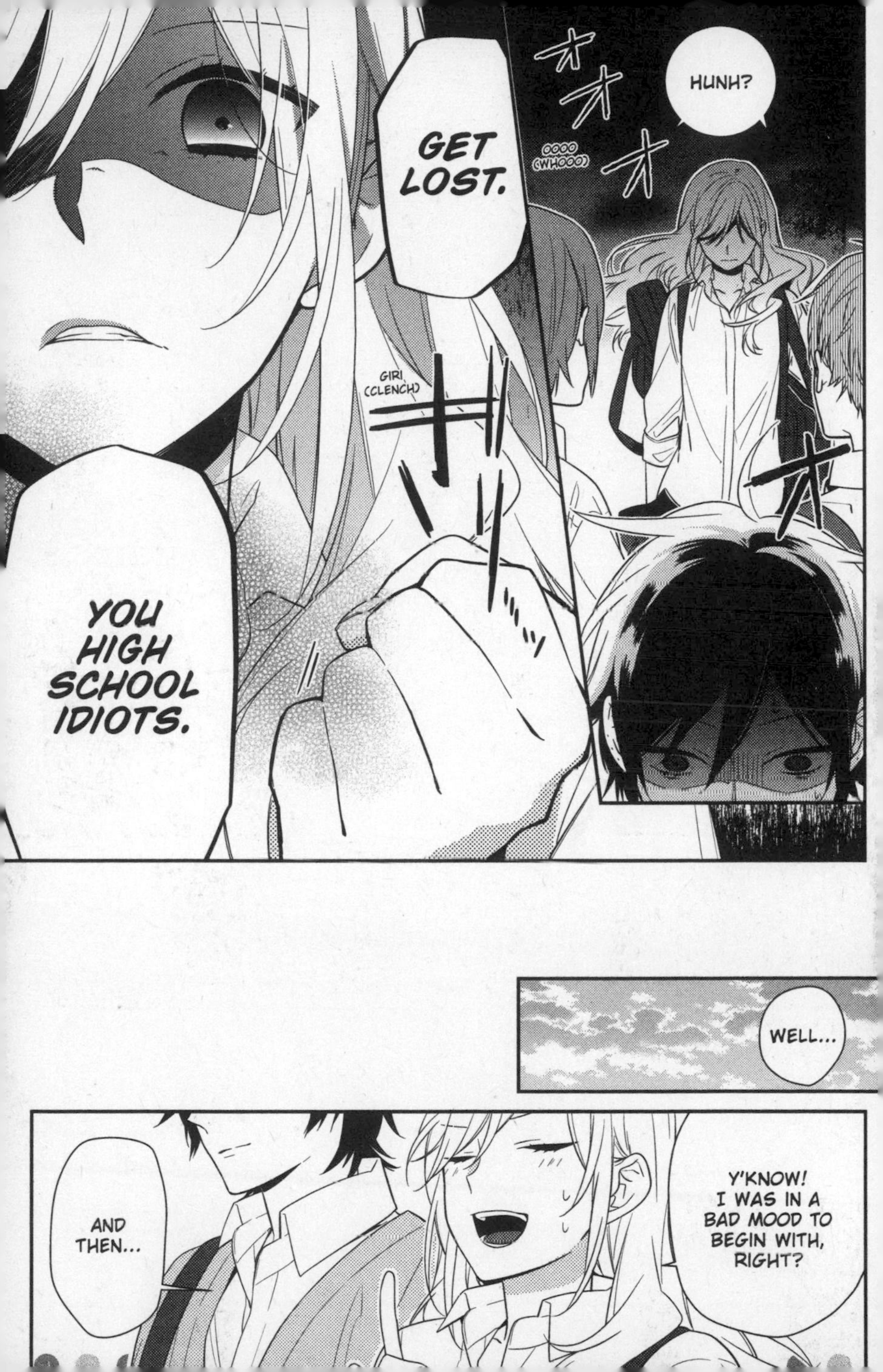
HUNH?
OOOO (WHOOO)
GET LOST.
GIRI (CLENCH)
YOU HIGH SCHOOL IDIOTS.
WELL...
Y'KNOW! I WAS IN A BAD MOOD TO BEGIN WITH, RIGHT?
AND THEN...

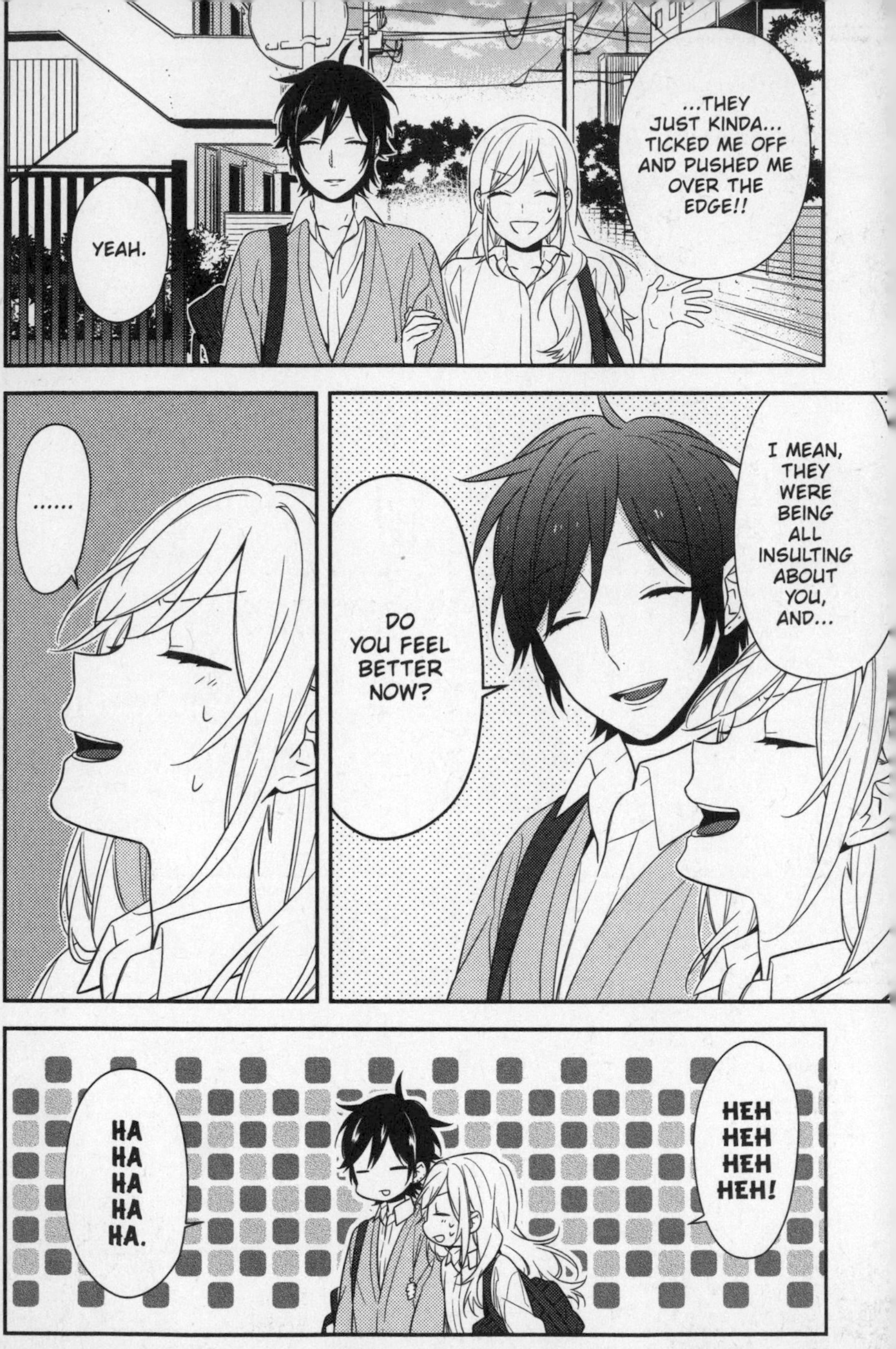
...THEY JUST KINDA... TICKED ME OFF AND PUSHED ME OVER THE EDGE!!
YEAH.
I MEAN, THEY WERE BEING ALL INSULTING ABOUT YOU, AND...
DO YOU FEEL BETTER NOW?
......
HEH HEH HEH HEH!
HA HA HA HA HA.

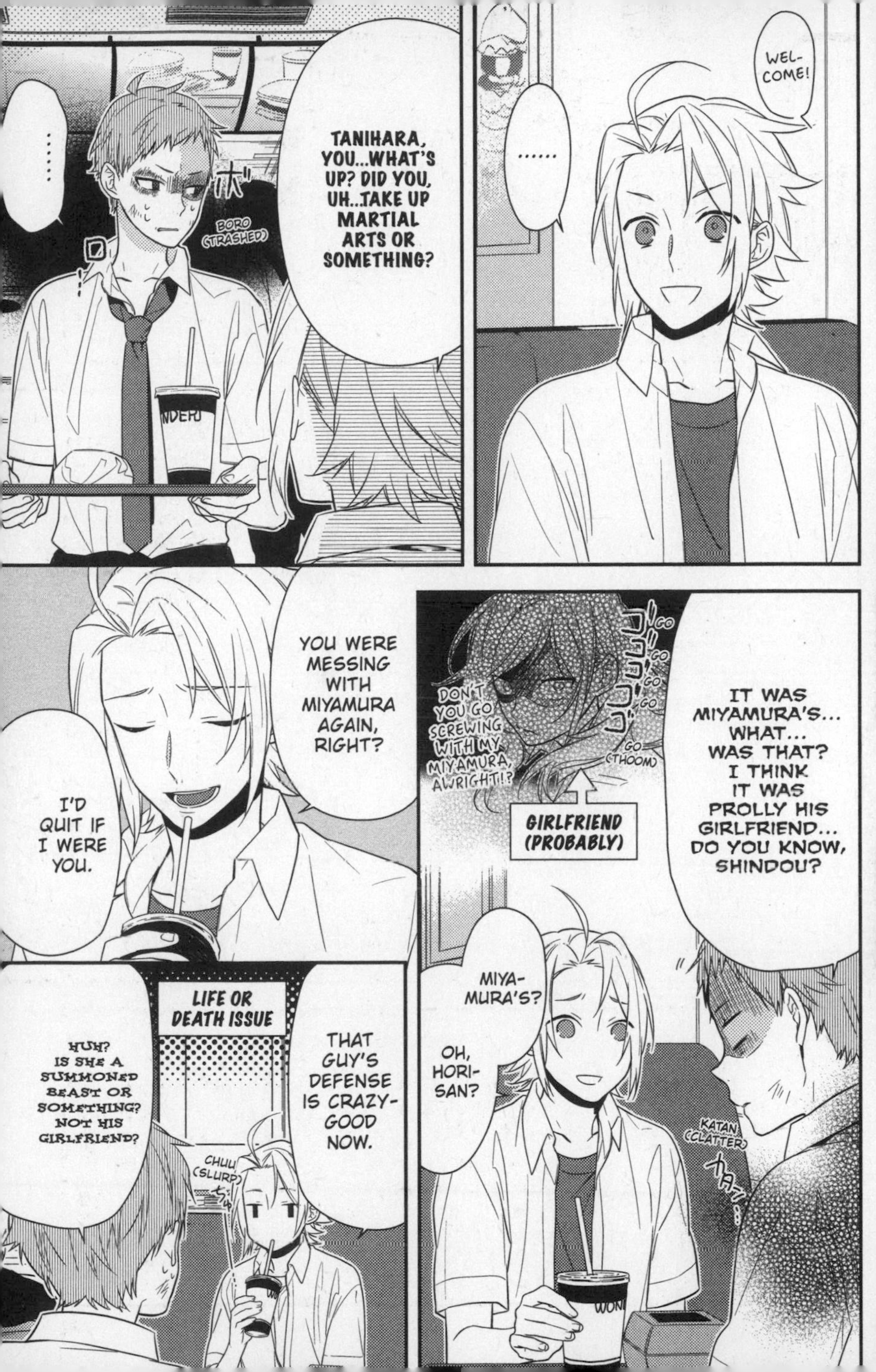
WEL-COME!
......
TANIHARA, YOU...WHAT'S UP? DID YOU, UH...TAKE UP MARTIAL ARTS OR SOMETHING?
BORO (TRASHED)
......
IT WAS MIYAMURA'S... WHAT... WAS THAT? I THINK IT WAS PROLLY HIS GIRLFRIEND... DO YOU KNOW, SHINDOU?
GO GO GO GO GO (THOOM)
DON'T YOU GO SCREWING WITH MY MIYAMURA, AWRIGHT!?
GIRLFRIEND (PROBABLY)
YOU WERE MESSING WITH MIYAMURA AGAIN, RIGHT?
I'D QUIT IF I WERE YOU.
KATAN (CLATTER)
MIYA-MURA'S?
OH, HORI-SAN?
THAT GUY'S DEFENSE IS CRAZY-GOOD NOW.
LIFE OR DEATH ISSUE
HUH? IS SHE A SUMMONED BEAST OR SOMETHING? NOT HIS GIRLFRIEND?
CHUU (SLURP)

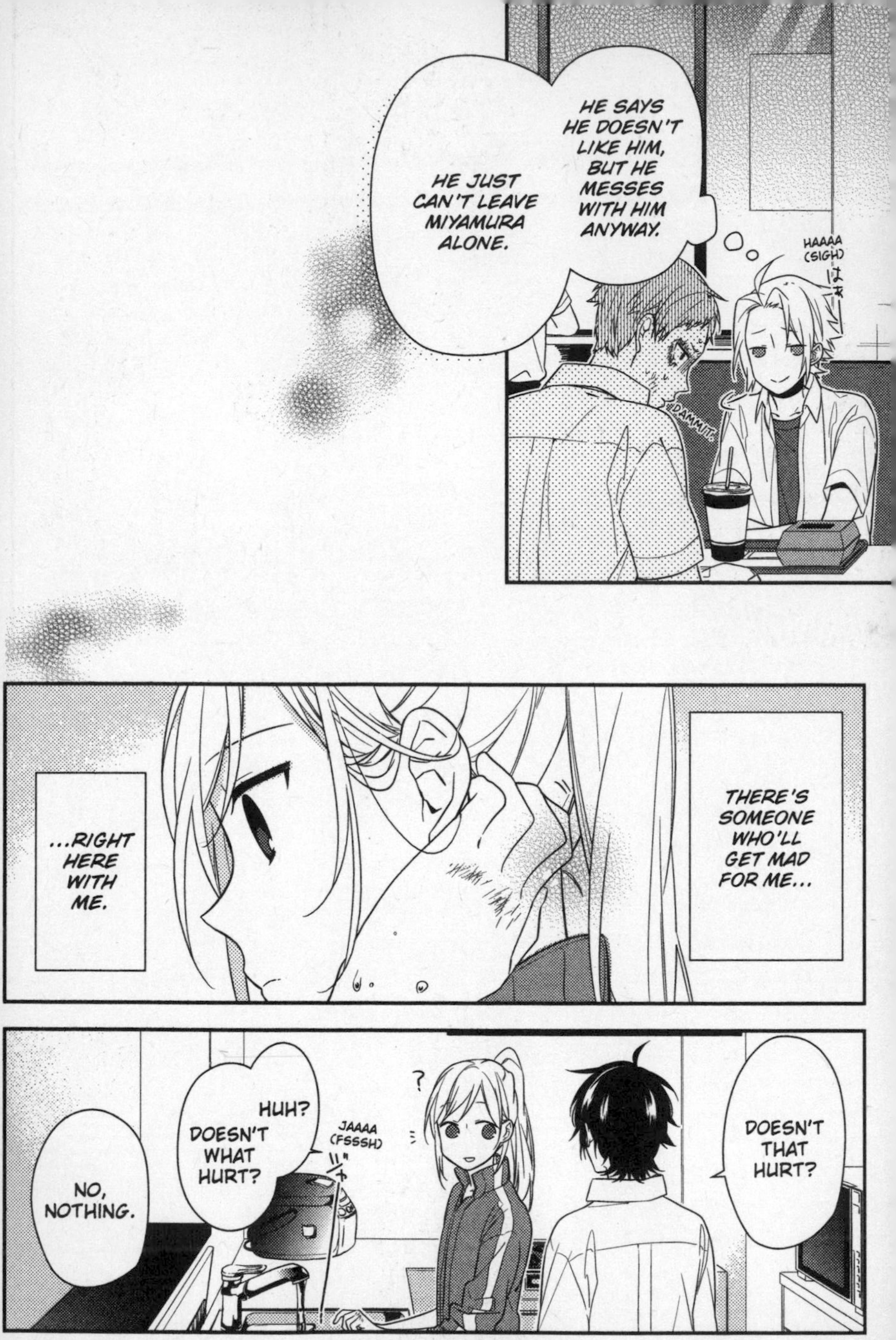
HE SAYS HE DOESN'T LIKE HIM, BUT HE MESSES WITH HIM ANYWAY.
HE JUST CAN'T LEAVE MIYAMURA ALONE.
HAAAA (SIGH)
はぁ
DAMMIT.
THERE'S SOMEONE WHO'LL GET MAD FOR ME...
...RIGHT HERE WITH ME.
DOESN'T THAT HURT?
?
JAAAA (FSSSH)
HUH? DOESN'T WHAT HURT?
NO, NOTHING.

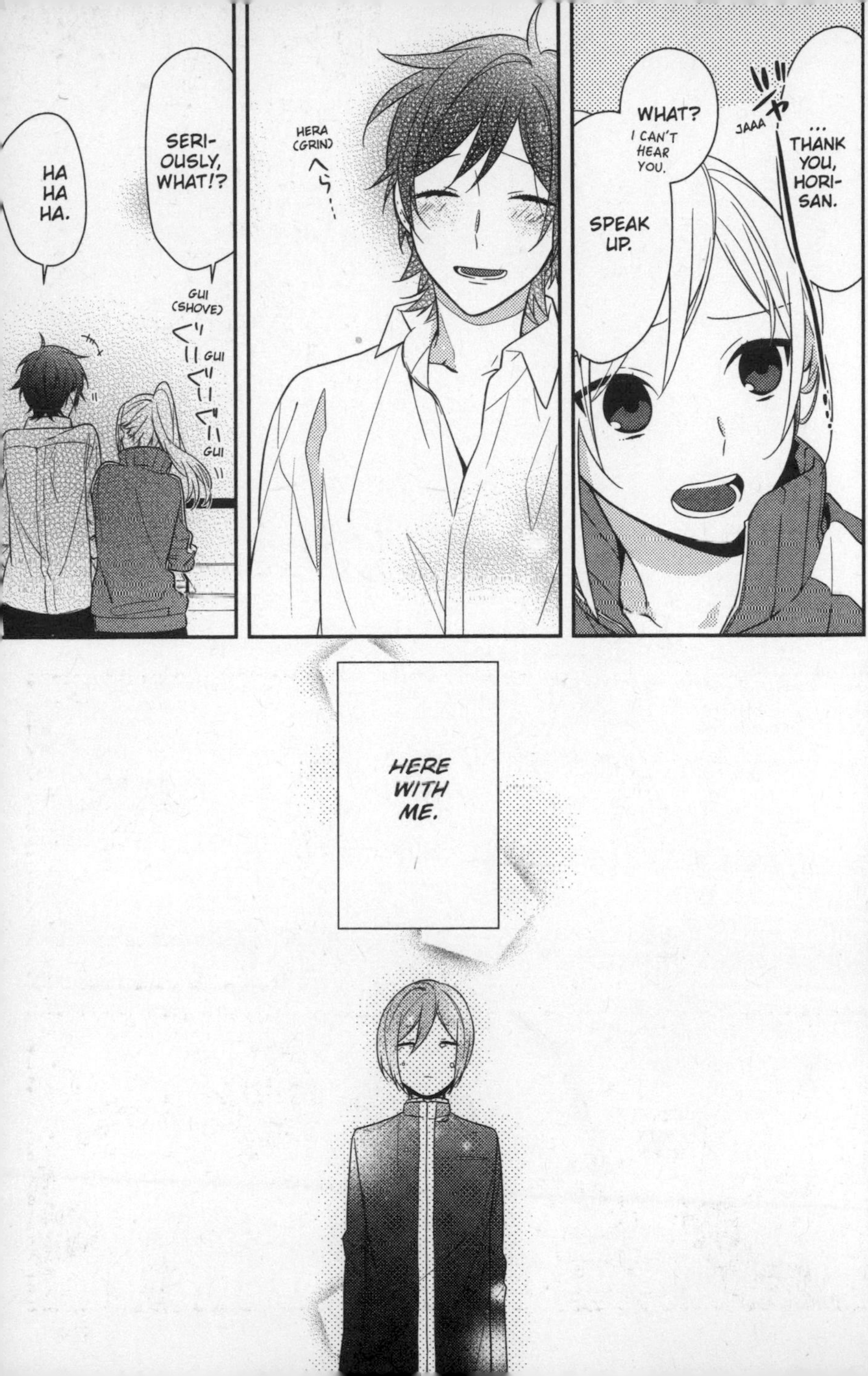
JAAA
... THANK YOU, HORI-SAN.
WHAT? I CAN'T HEAR YOU.
SPEAK UP.
HERA (GRIN)
SERI-OUSLY, WHAT!?
GUI (SHOVE)
GUI
GUI
HA HA HA.
HERE WITH ME.

HORIMIYA

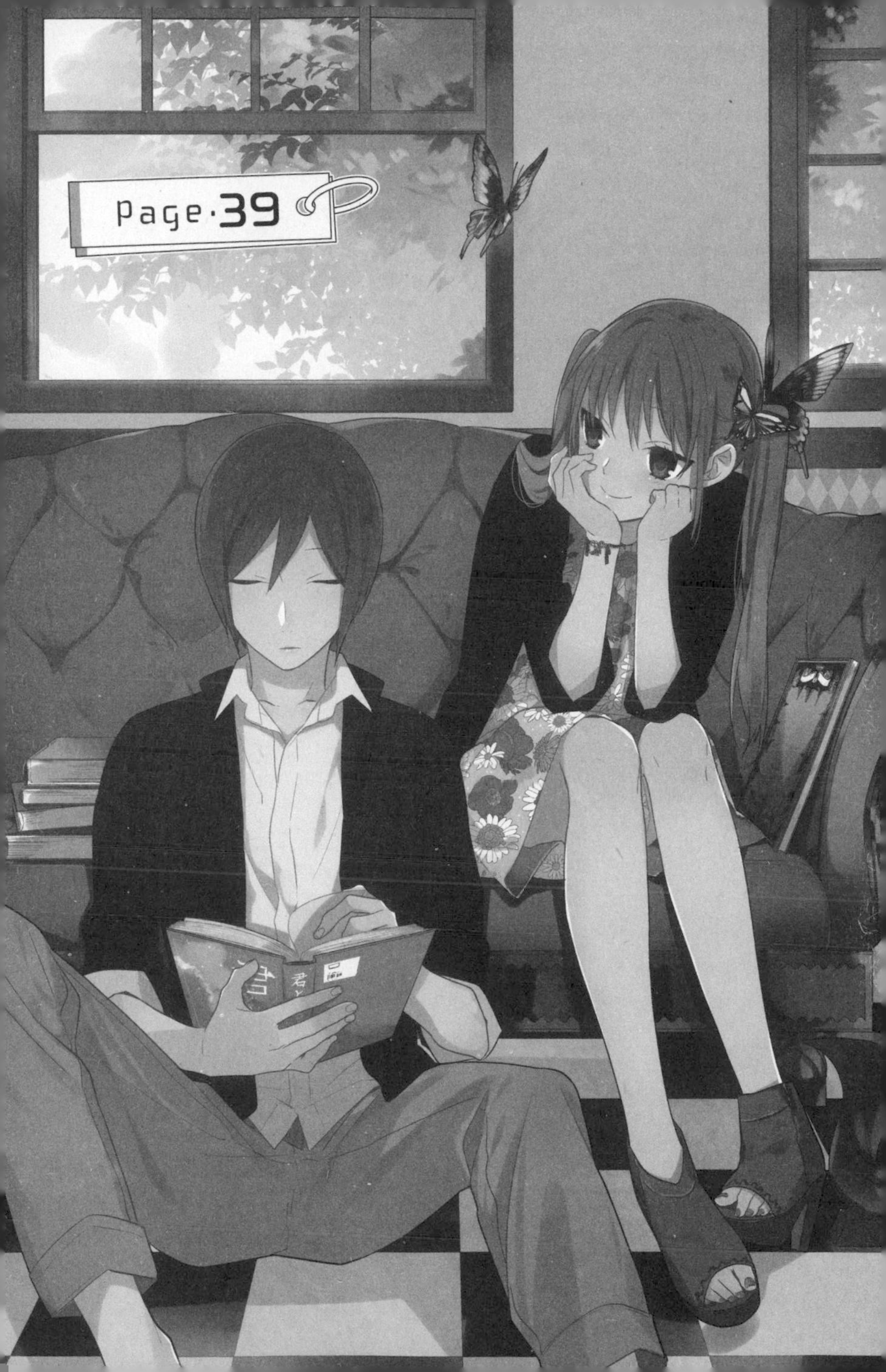
page·39

HORIMIYA

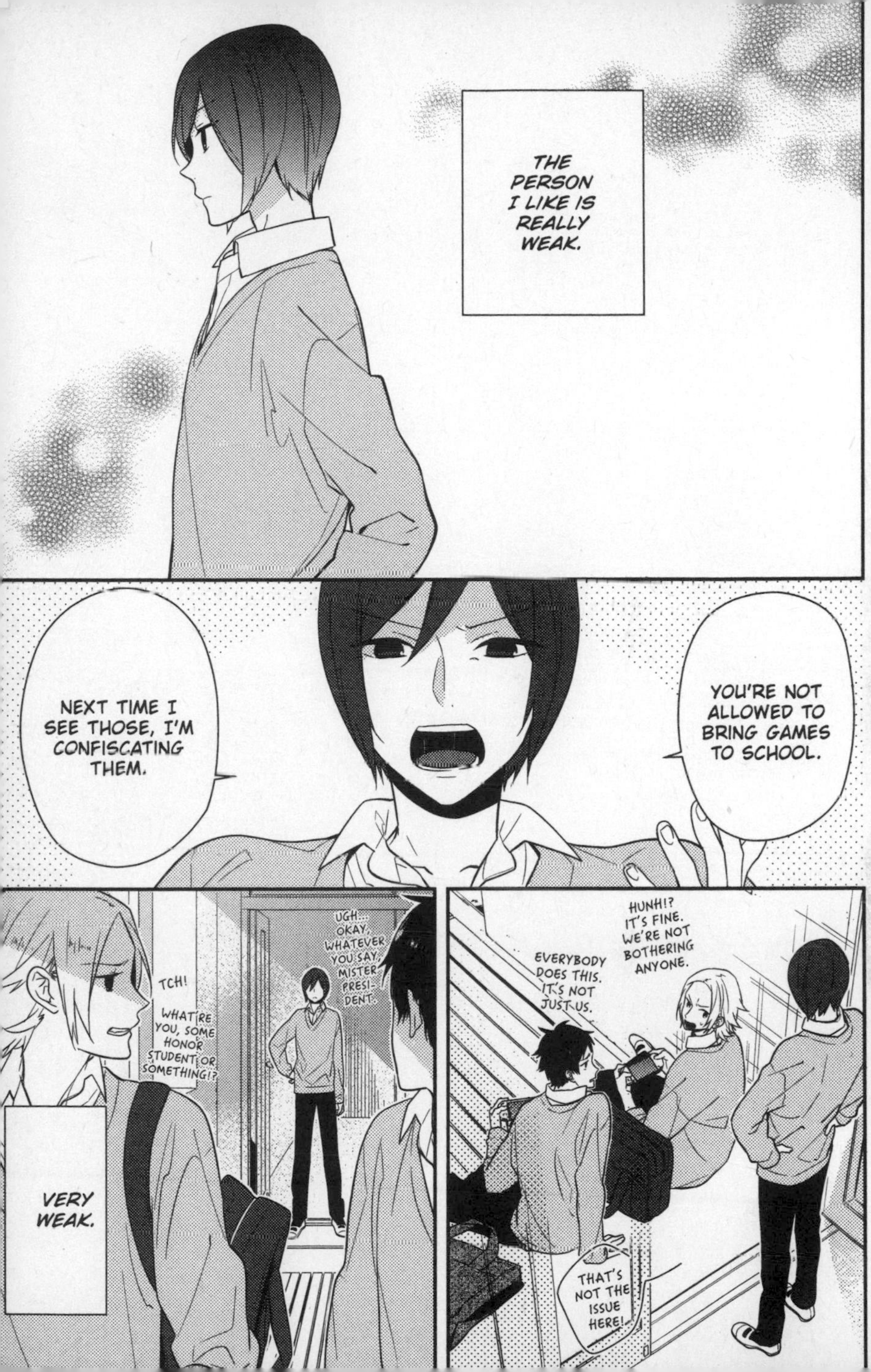
THE PERSON I LIKE IS REALLY WEAK.
YOU'RE NOT ALLOWED TO BRING GAMES TO SCHOOL.
NEXT TIME I SEE THOSE, I'M CONFISCATING THEM.
HUNH!? IT'S FINE. WE'RE NOT BOTHERING ANYONE.
EVERYBODY DOES THIS. IT'S NOT JUST US.
THAT'S NOT THE ISSUE HERE!
UGH... OKAY, WHATEVER YOU SAY, MISTER PRESIDENT.
TCH!
WHAT'RE YOU, SOME HONOR STUDENT OR SOMETHING!?
VERY WEAK.

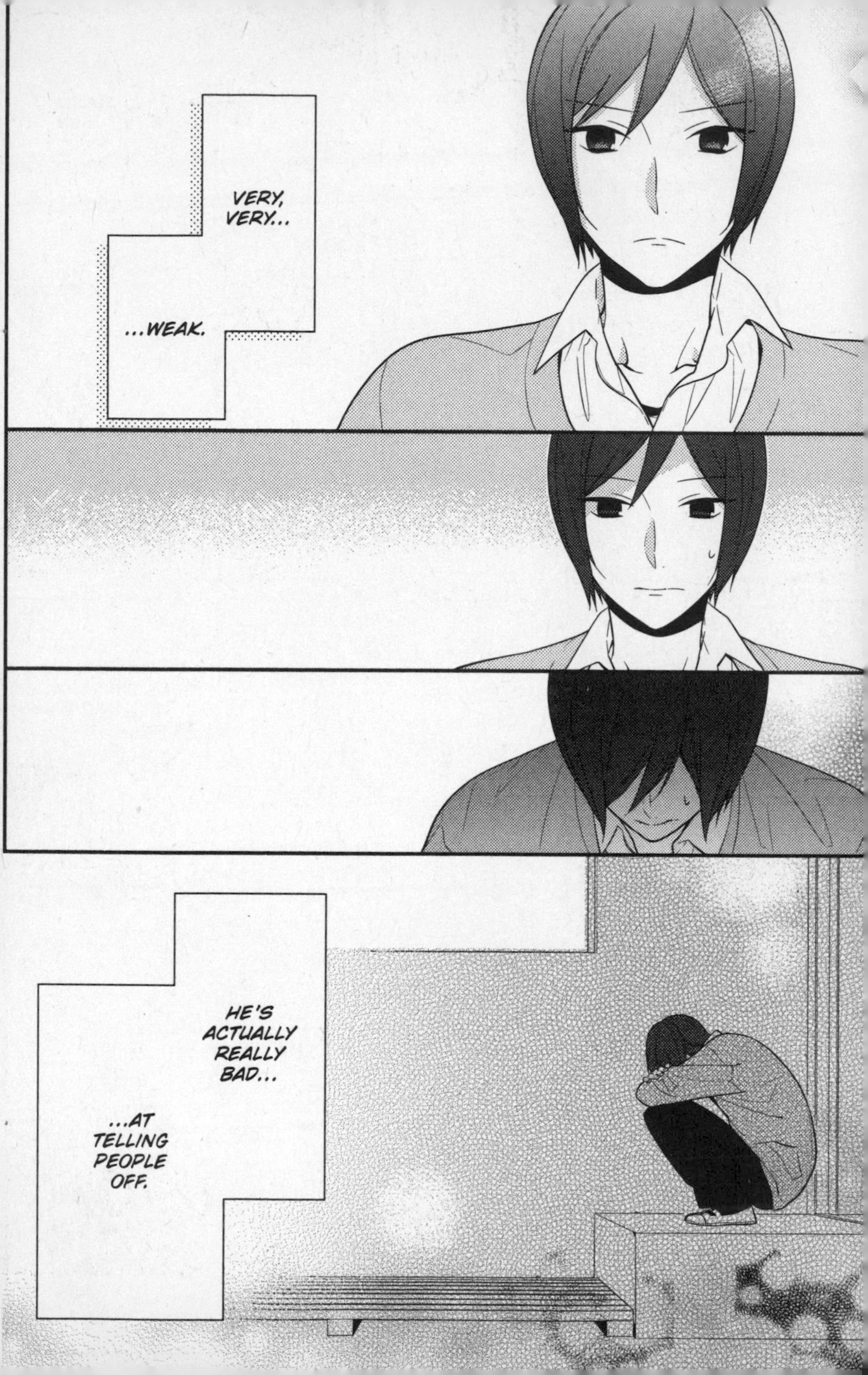
VERY, VERY...
...WEAK.
HE'S ACTUALLY REALLY BAD...
...AT TELLING PEOPLE OFF.

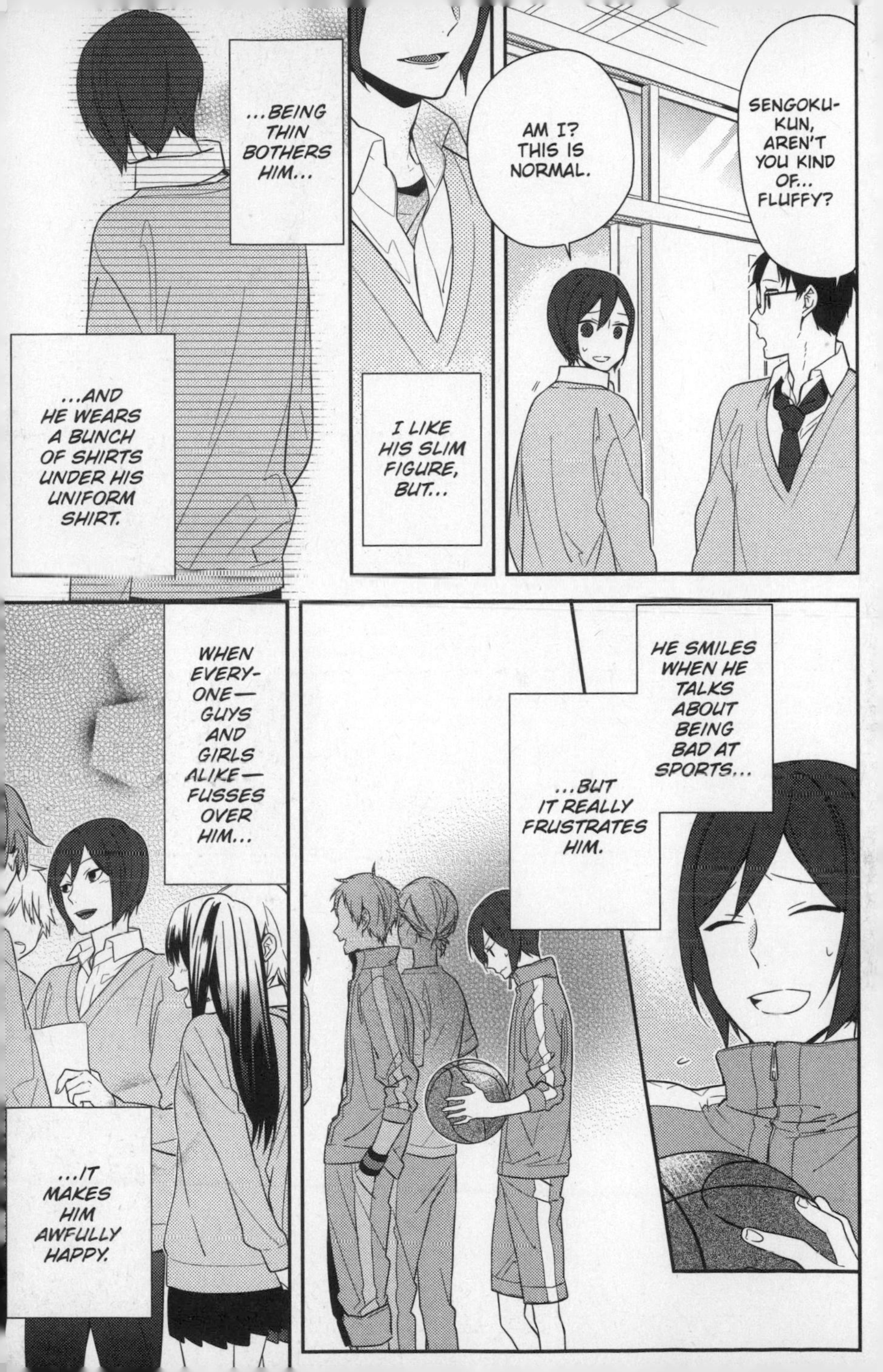
SENGOKU-KUN, AREN'T YOU KIND OF... FLUFFY?
AM I? THIS IS NORMAL.
I LIKE HIS SLIM FIGURE, BUT...
...BEING THIN BOTHERS HIM...
...AND HE WEARS A BUNCH OF SHIRTS UNDER HIS UNIFORM SHIRT.
HE SMILES WHEN HE TALKS ABOUT BEING BAD AT SPORTS...
...BUT IT REALLY FRUSTRATES HIM.
WHEN EVERY-ONE—GUYS AND GIRLS ALIKE—FUSSES OVER HIM...
...IT MAKES HIM AWFULLY HAPPY.

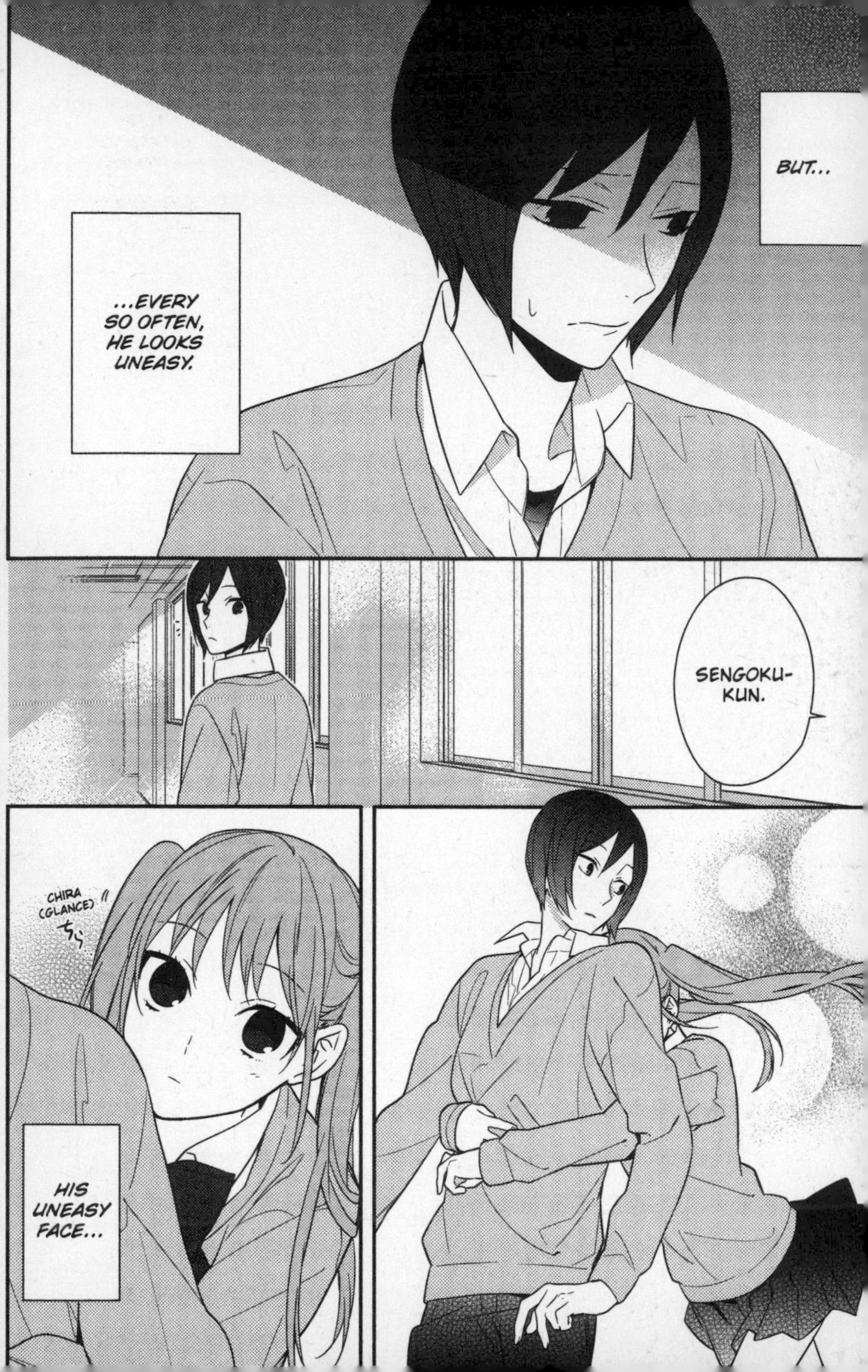
BUT...
...EVERY SO OFTEN, HE LOOKS UNEASY.
SENGOKU-KUN.
CHIRA (GLANCE)
HIS UNEASY FACE...

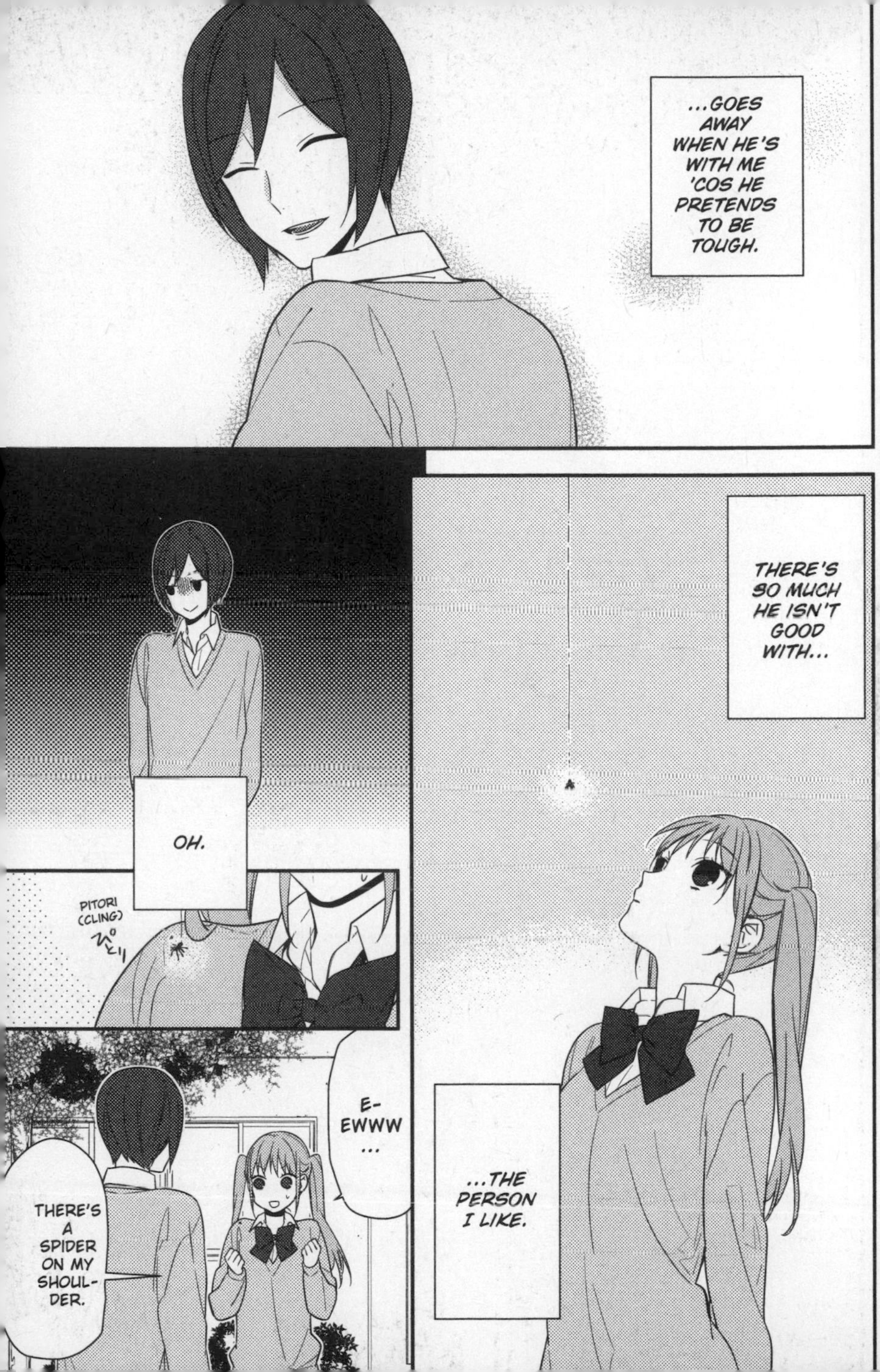
...GOES AWAY WHEN HE'S WITH ME 'COS HE PRETENDS TO BE TOUGH.
THERE'S SO MUCH HE ISN'T GOOD WITH...
...THE PERSON I LIKE.
OH.
PITORI (CLING)
E-EWWW...
THERE'S A SPIDER ON MY SHOUL-DER.

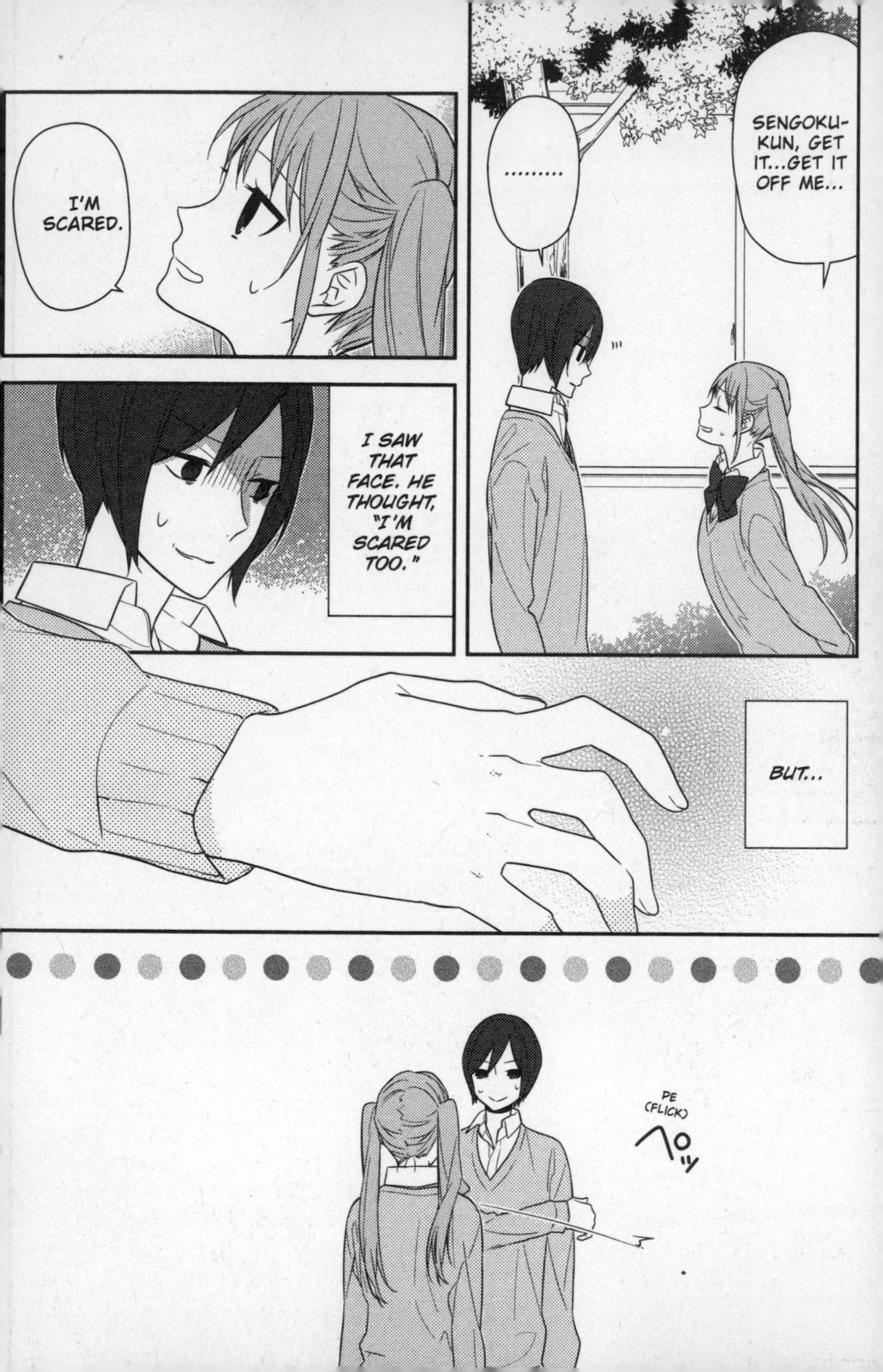
SENGOKU-KUN, GET IT...GET IT OFF ME...
....
I'M SCARED.
I SAW THAT FACE. HE THOUGHT, "I'M SCARED TOO."
BUT...
PE (FLICK)
ペッ

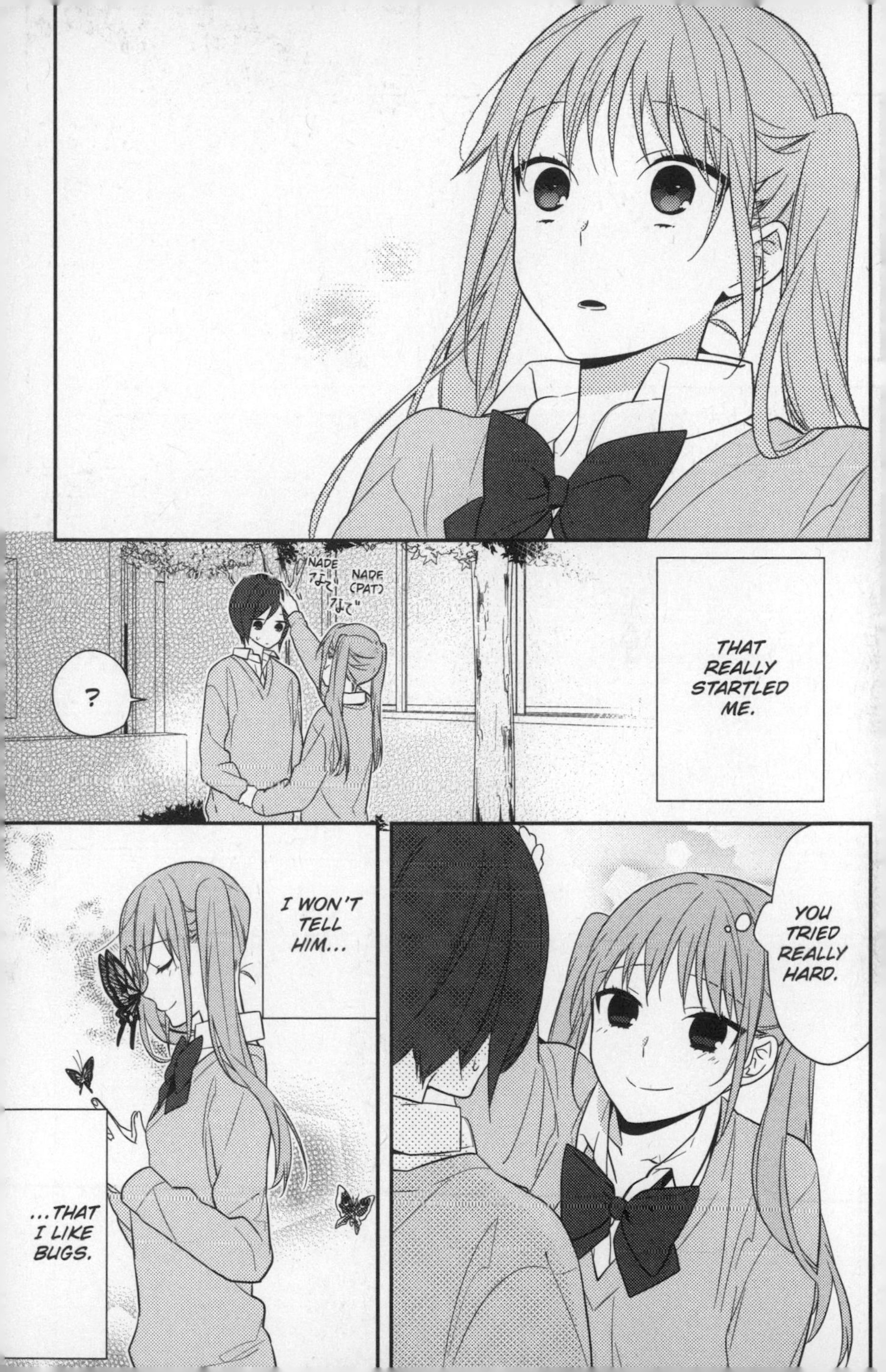
THAT REALLY STARTLED ME.
NADE
NADE (PAT)
?
YOU TRIED REALLY HARD.
I WON'T TELL HIM...
...THAT I LIKE BUGS.

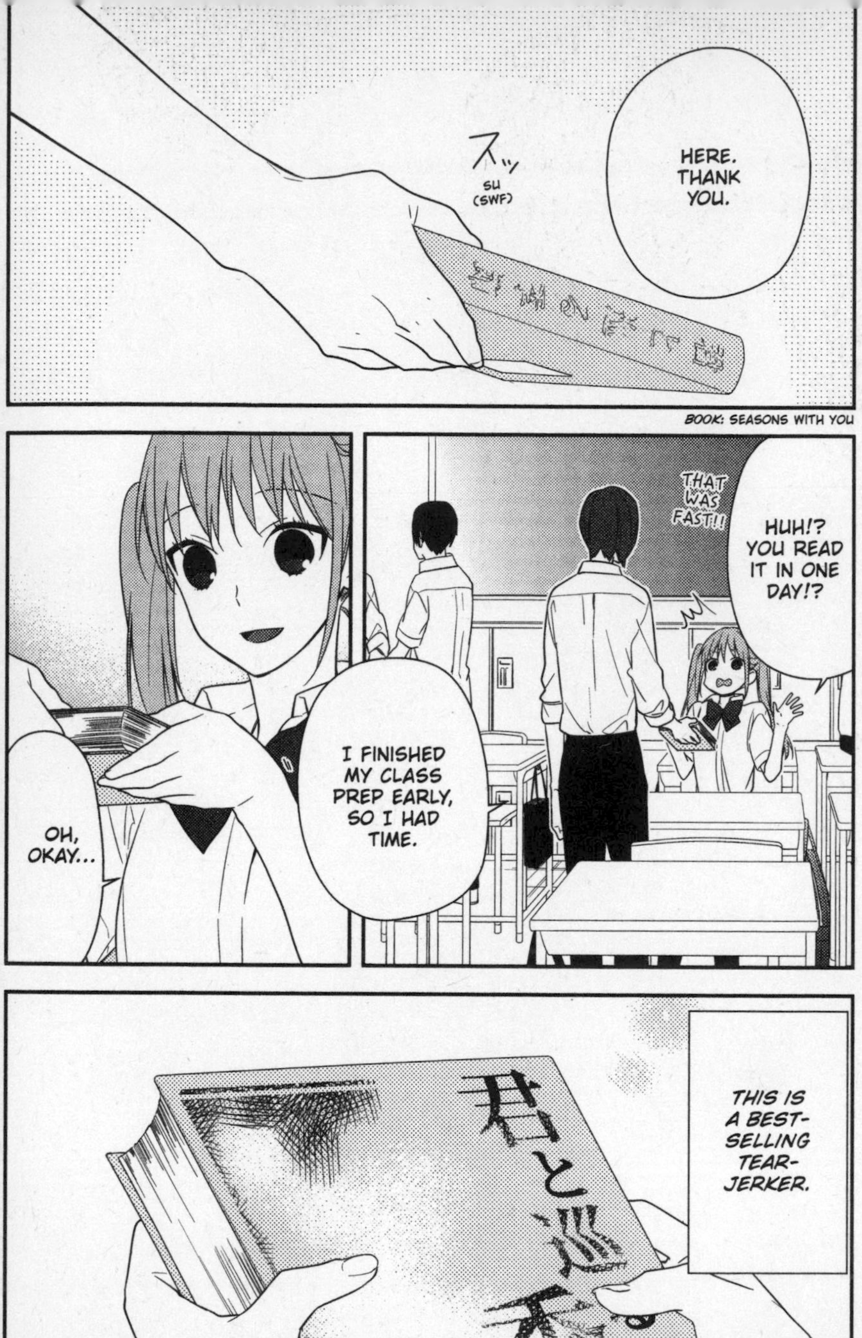

HERE. THANK YOU.
スッ
SU (SWF)
BOOK: SEASONS WITH YOU
HUH!? YOU READ IT IN ONE DAY!?
THAT WAS FAST!!
I FINISHED MY CLASS PREP EARLY, SO I HAD TIME.
OH, OKAY...
THIS IS A BEST-SELLING TEAR-JERKER.

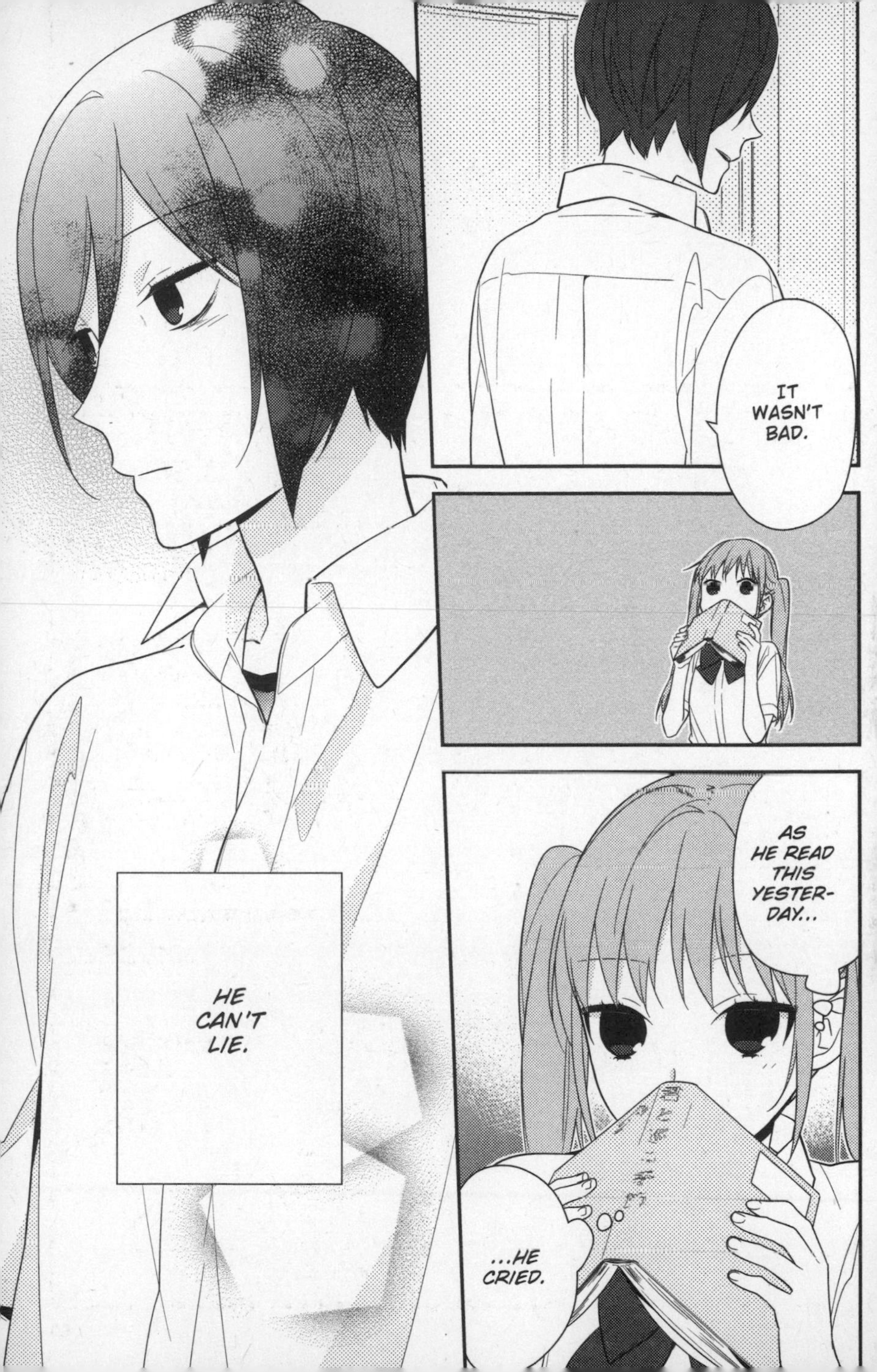
IT WASN'T BAD.
AS HE READ THIS YESTER-DAY...
...HE CRIED.
HE CAN'T LIE.

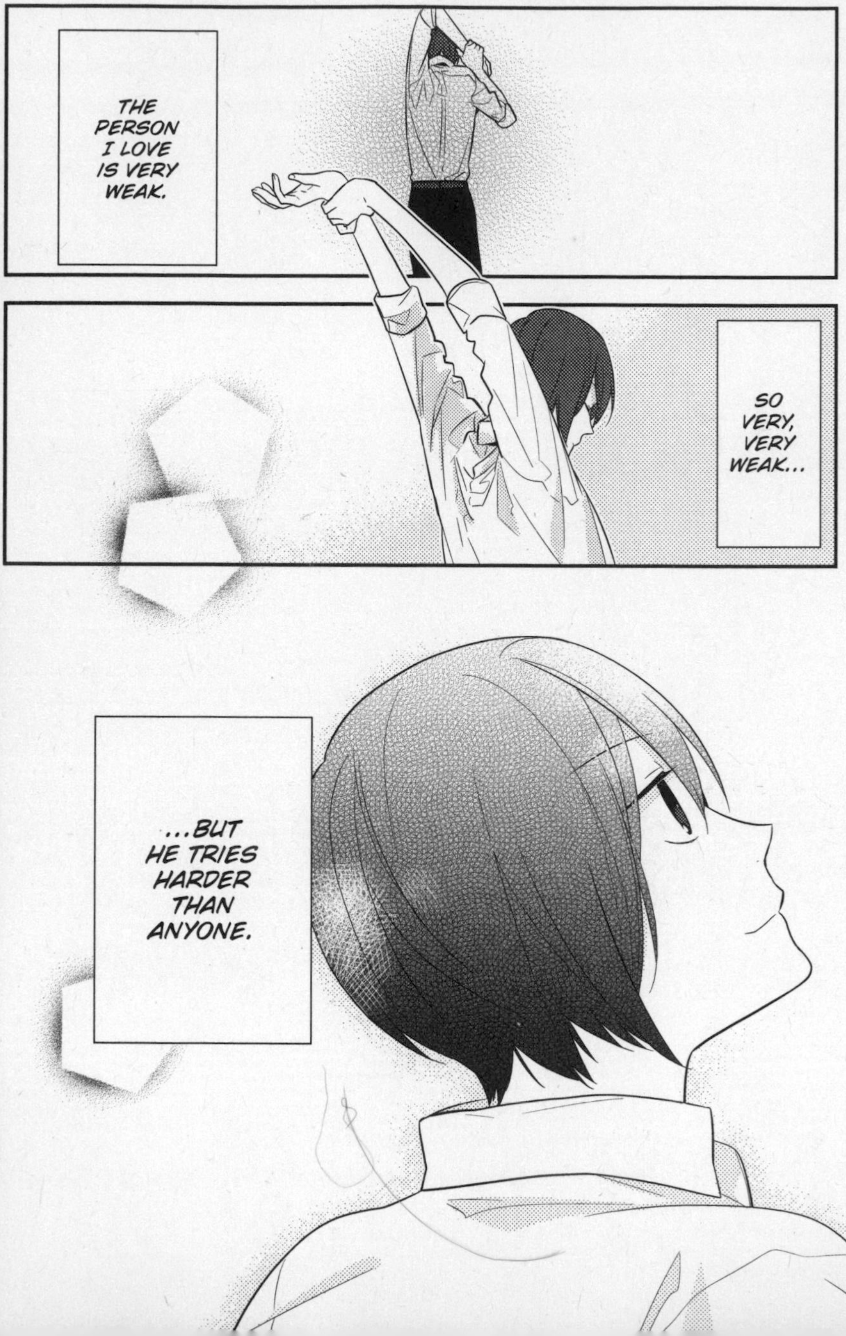
THE PERSON I LOVE IS VERY WEAK.
SO VERY, VERY WEAK...
...BUT HE TRIES HARDER THAN ANYONE.

HORIMIYA

HORIMIYA

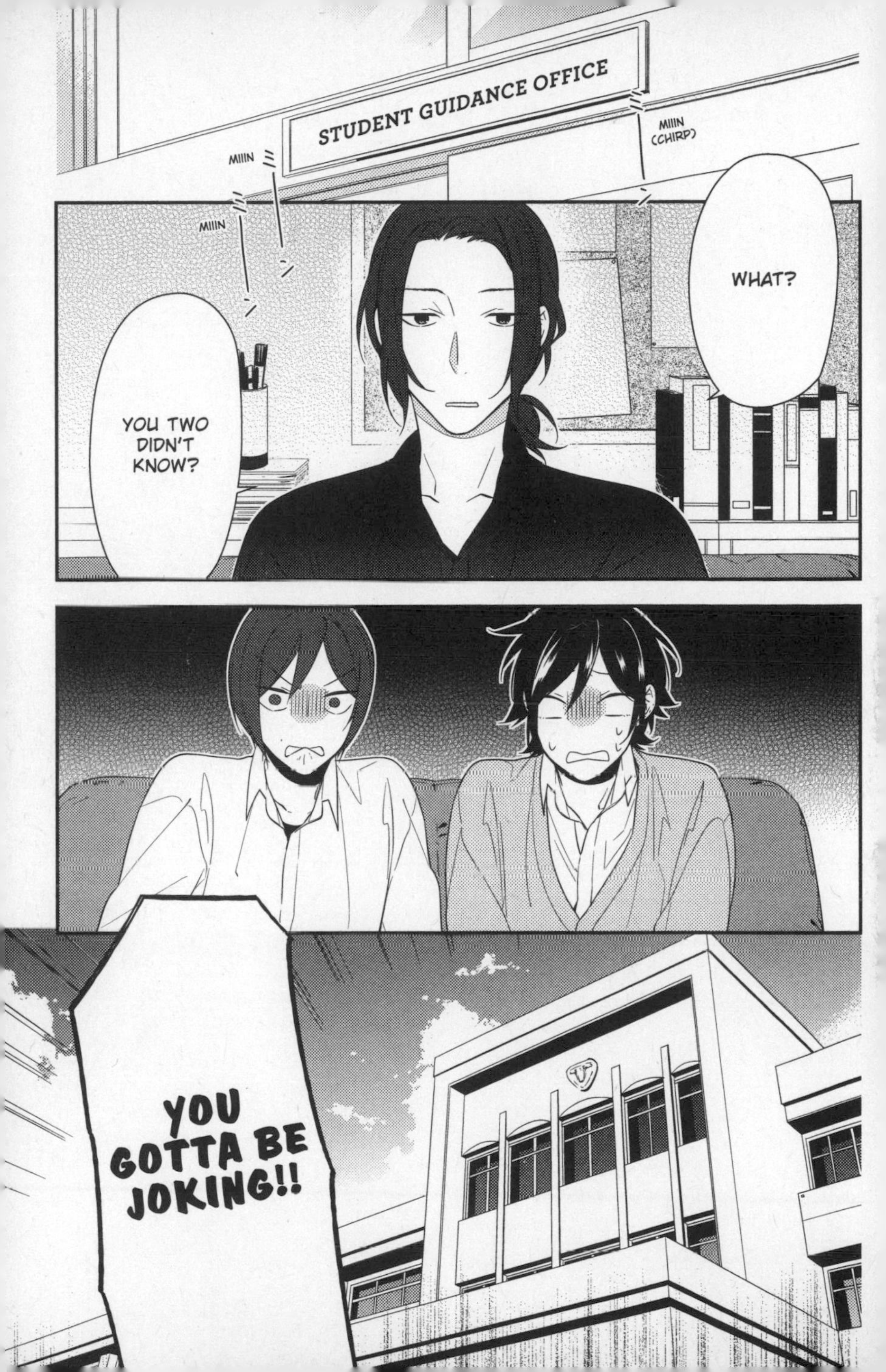
STUDENT GUIDANCE OFFICE
MIIIN (CHIRP)
MIIIN
MIIIN
WHAT?
YOU TWO DIDN'T KNOW?
YOU GOTTA BE JOKING!!

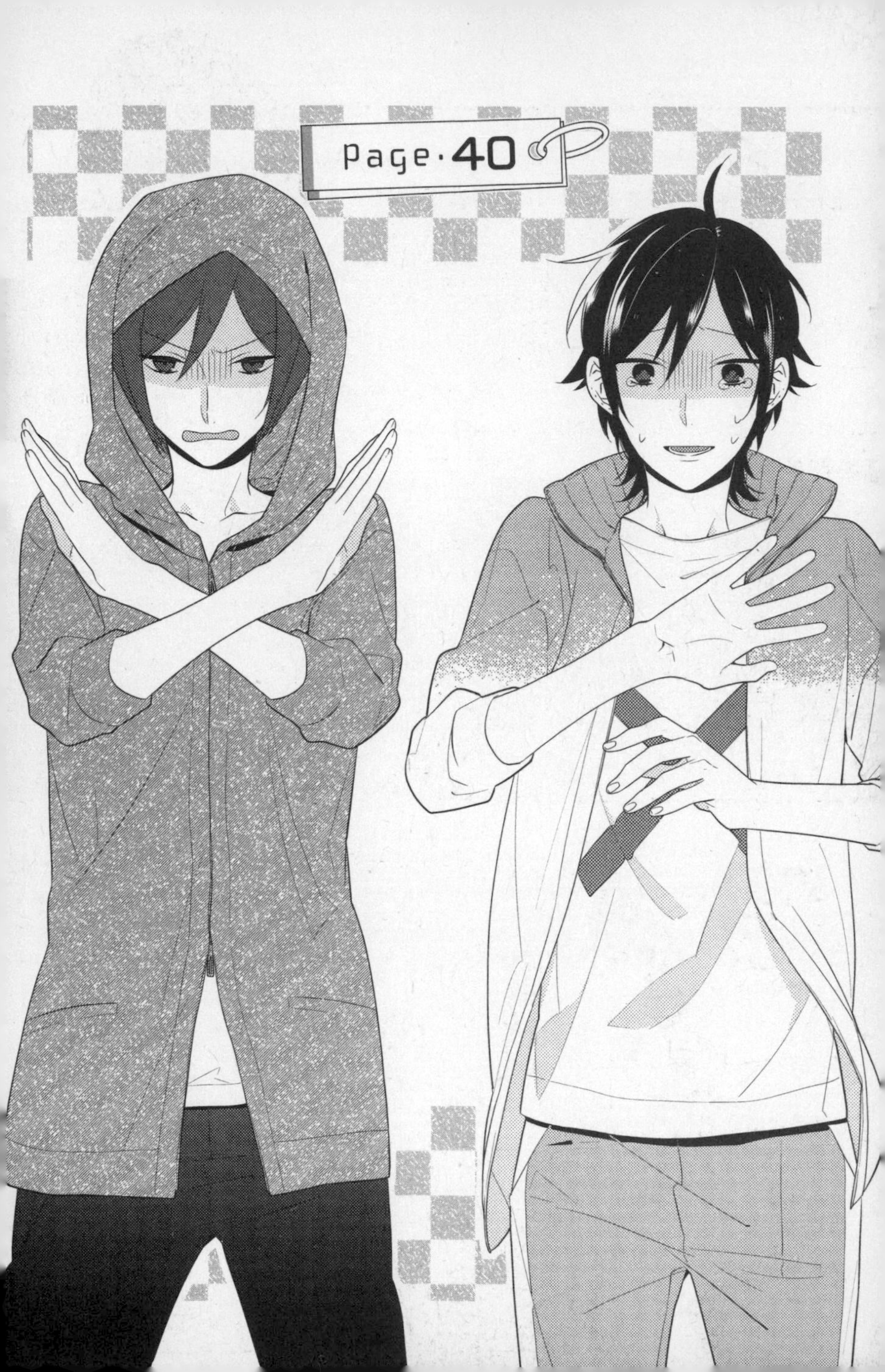
Page·40

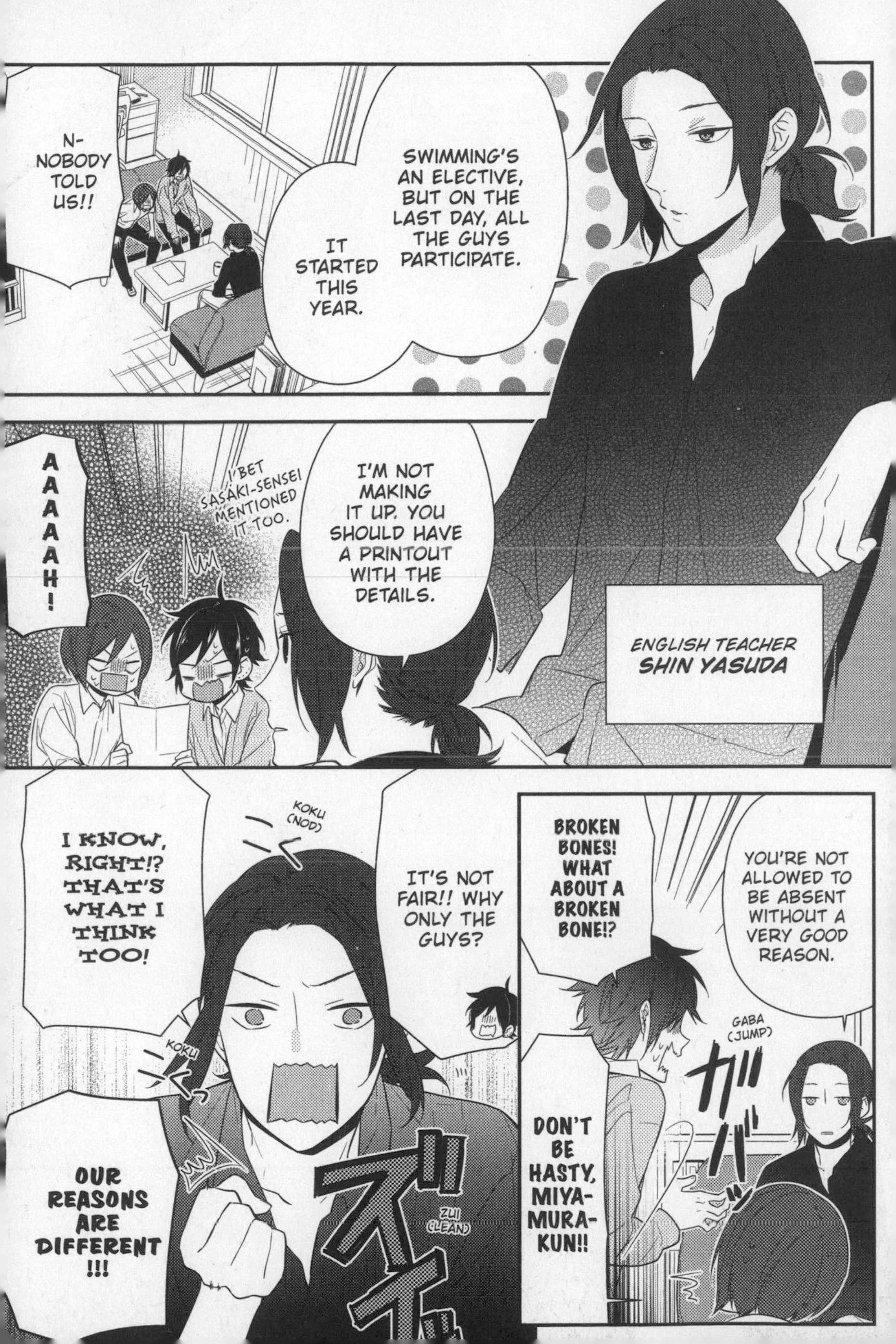
ENGLISH TEACHER SHIN YASUDA
SWIMMING'S AN ELECTIVE, BUT ON THE LAST DAY, ALL THE GUYS PARTICIPATE.
IT STARTED THIS YEAR.
N-NOBODY TOLD US!!
I'M NOT MAKING IT UP. YOU SHOULD HAVE A PRINTOUT WITH THE DETAILS.
I BET SASAKI-SENSEI MENTIONED IT TOO.
AAAAAAH!
YOU'RE NOT ALLOWED TO BE ABSENT WITHOUT A VERY GOOD REASON.
BROKEN BONES! WHAT ABOUT A BROKEN BONE!?
GABA (JUMP)
DON'T BE HASTY, MIYAMURA-KUN!!
IT'S NOT FAIR!! WHY ONLY THE GUYS?
KOKU (NOD)
I KNOW, RIGHT!? THAT'S WHAT I THINK TOO!
KOKU
ZUI (LEAN)
OUR REASONS ARE DIFFERENT!!!

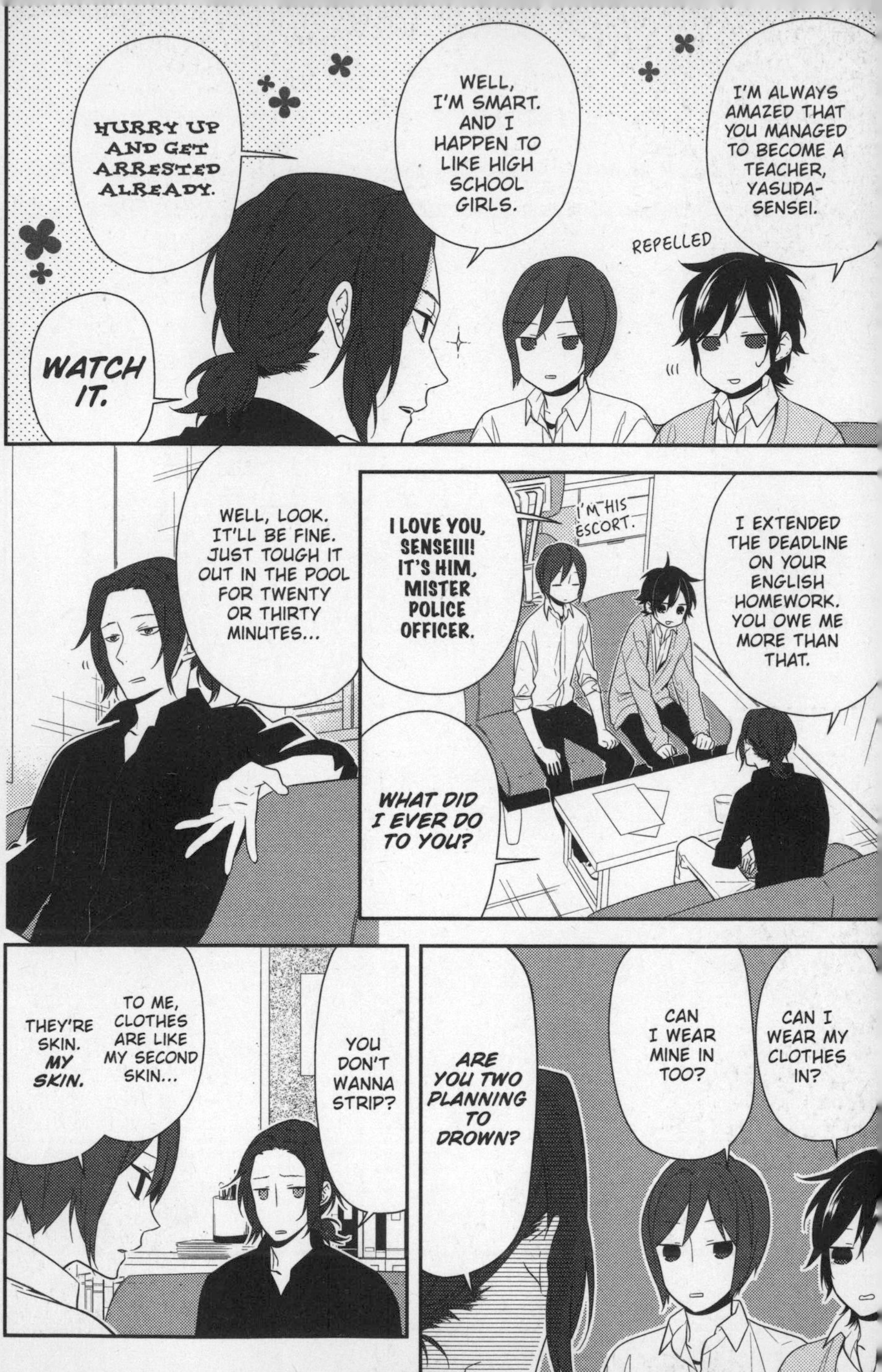
I'M ALWAYS AMAZED THAT YOU MANAGED TO BECOME A TEACHER, YASUDA-SENSEI.
WELL, I'M SMART. AND I HAPPEN TO LIKE HIGH SCHOOL GIRLS.
REPELLED
HURRY UP AND GET ARRESTED ALREADY.
WATCH IT.
I EXTENDED THE DEADLINE ON YOUR ENGLISH HOMEWORK. YOU OWE ME MORE THAN THAT.
I'M HIS ESCORT.
I LOVE YOU, SENSEIII! IT'S HIM, MISTER POLICE OFFICER.
WHAT DID I EVER DO TO YOU?
WELL, LOOK. IT'LL BE FINE. JUST TOUGH IT OUT IN THE POOL FOR TWENTY OR THIRTY MINUTES...
CAN I WEAR MY CLOTHES IN?
CAN I WEAR MINE IN TOO?
ARE YOU TWO PLANNING TO DROWN?
YOU DON'T WANNA STRIP?
TO ME, CLOTHES ARE LIKE MY SECOND SKIN...
THEY'RE SKIN. MY SKIN.

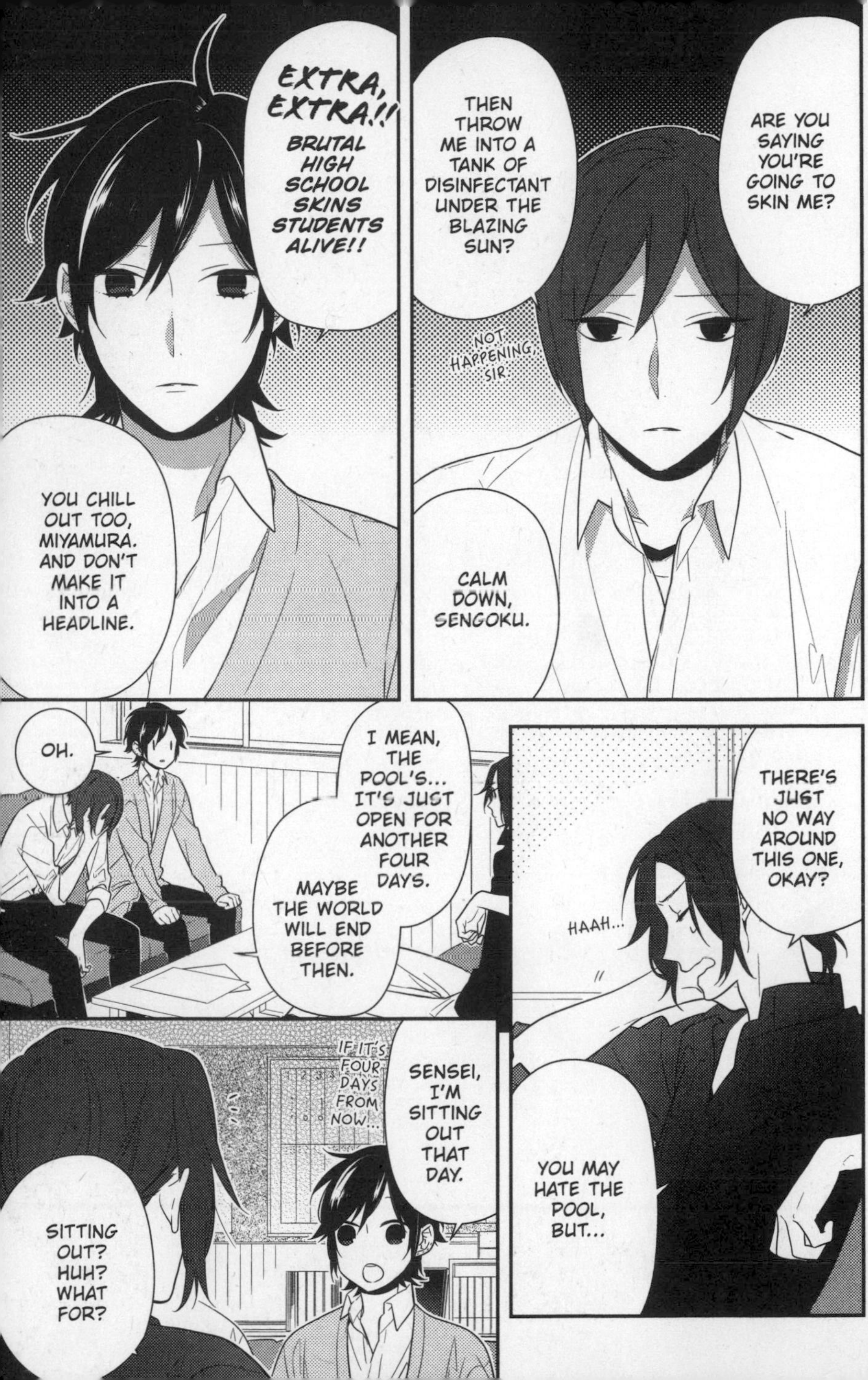
ARE YOU SAYING YOU'RE GOING TO SKIN ME?
THEN THROW ME INTO A TANK OF DISINFECTANT UNDER THE BLAZING SUN?
NOT HAPPENING, SIR.
CALM DOWN, SENGOKU.
EXTRA, EXTRA!! BRUTAL HIGH SCHOOL SKINS STUDENTS ALIVE!!
YOU CHILL OUT TOO, MIYAMURA. AND DON'T MAKE IT INTO A HEADLINE.
THERE'S JUST NO WAY AROUND THIS ONE, OKAY?
HAAH...
YOU MAY HATE THE POOL, BUT...
I MEAN, THE POOL'S... IT'S JUST OPEN FOR ANOTHER FOUR DAYS.
MAYBE THE WORLD WILL END BEFORE THEN.
OH.
IF IT'S FOUR DAYS FROM NOW...
SENSEI, I'M SITTING OUT THAT DAY.
SITTING OUT? HUH? WHAT FOR?

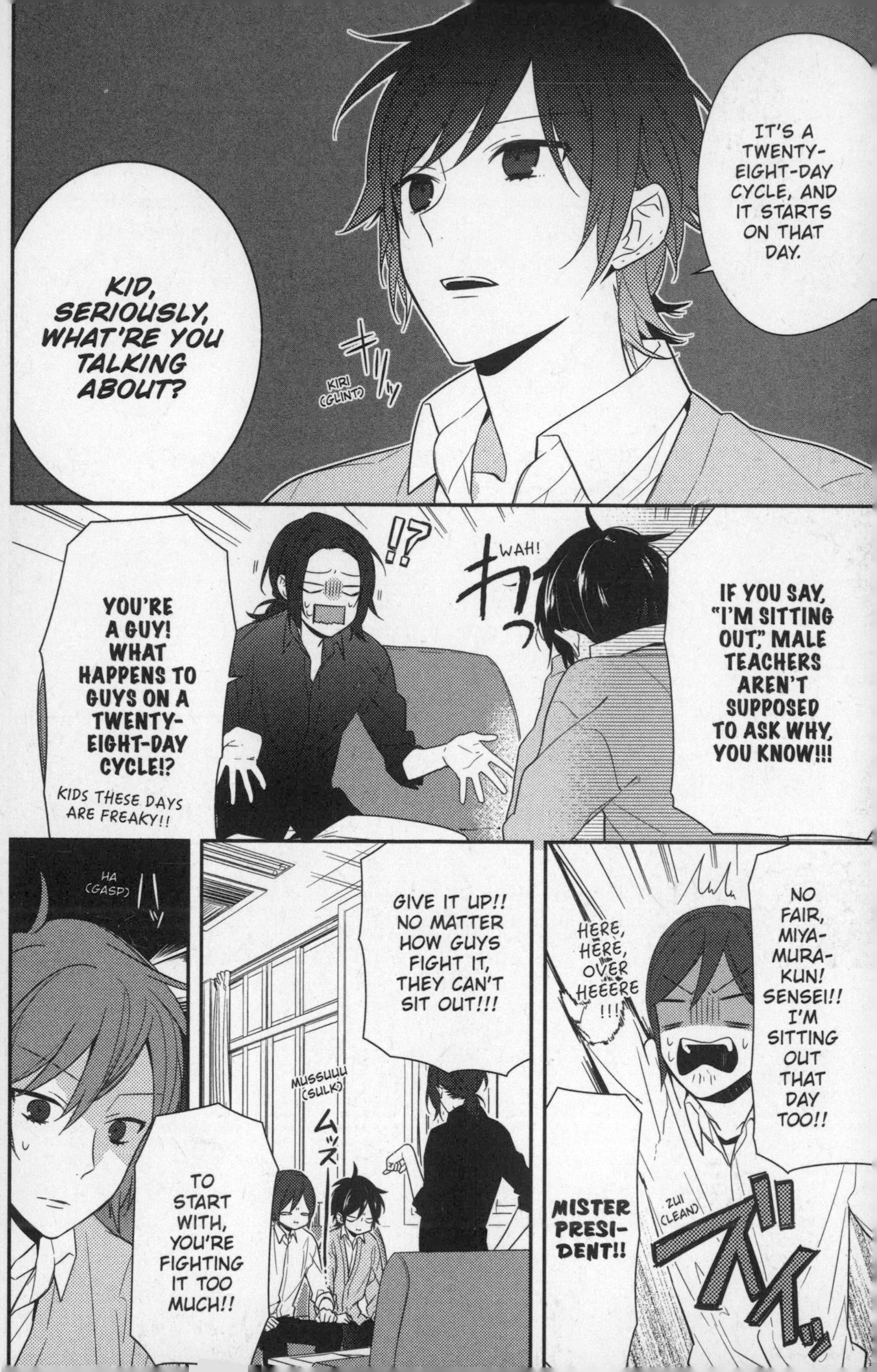
IT'S A TWENTY-EIGHT-DAY CYCLE, AND IT STARTS ON THAT DAY.
KIRI (GLINT)
KID, SERIOUSLY, WHAT'RE YOU TALKING ABOUT?
IF YOU SAY, "I'M SITTING OUT," MALE TEACHERS AREN'T SUPPOSED TO ASK WHY, YOU KNOW!!!
WAH!
!?
YOU'RE A GUY! WHAT HAPPENS TO GUYS ON A TWENTY-EIGHT-DAY CYCLE!?
KIDS THESE DAYS ARE FREAKY!!
NO FAIR, MIYAMURA-KUN! SENSEI!! I'M SITTING OUT THAT DAY TOO!!
HERE, HERE, OVER HEEERE!!!
ZUI (CLEAN)
MISTER PRESIDENT!!
GIVE IT UP!! NO MATTER HOW GUYS FIGHT IT, THEY CAN'T SIT OUT!!!
MUSSUUU (SULK)
TO START WITH, YOU'RE FIGHTING IT TOO MUCH!!
HA (GASP)

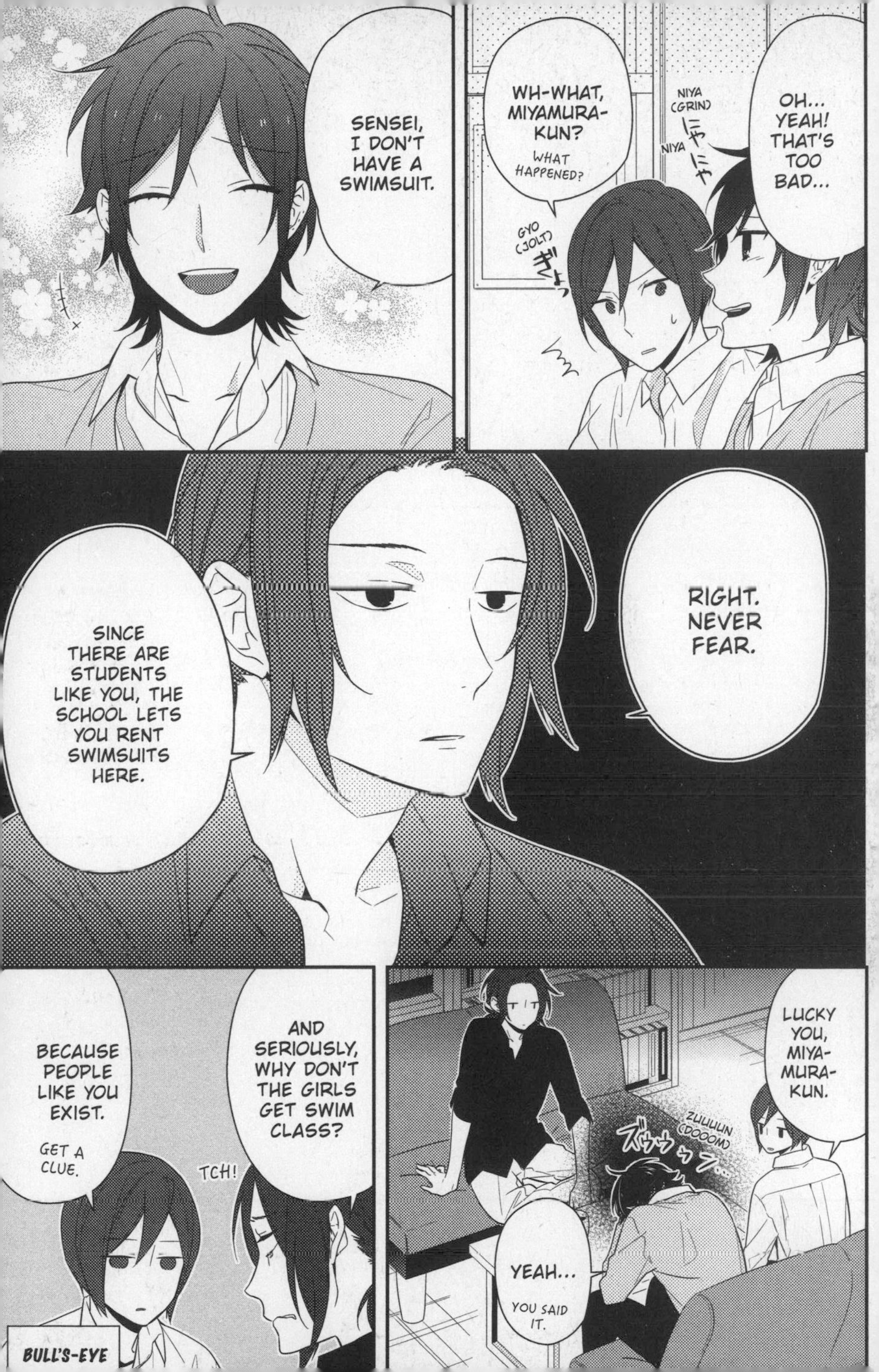
OH... YEAH! THAT'S TOO BAD...
NIYA (GRIN) NIYA
WH-WHAT, MIYAMURA-KUN?
WHAT HAPPENED?
GYO (JOLT)
SENSEI, I DON'T HAVE A SWIMSUIT.
RIGHT. NEVER FEAR.
SINCE THERE ARE STUDENTS LIKE YOU, THE SCHOOL LETS YOU RENT SWIMSUITS HERE.
LUCKY YOU, MIYA-MURA-KUN.
ZUUUUN (DOOOM)
YEAH...
YOU SAID IT.
AND SERIOUSLY, WHY DON'T THE GIRLS GET SWIM CLASS?
TCH!
BECAUSE PEOPLE LIKE YOU EXIST.
GET A CLUE.
BULL'S-EYE

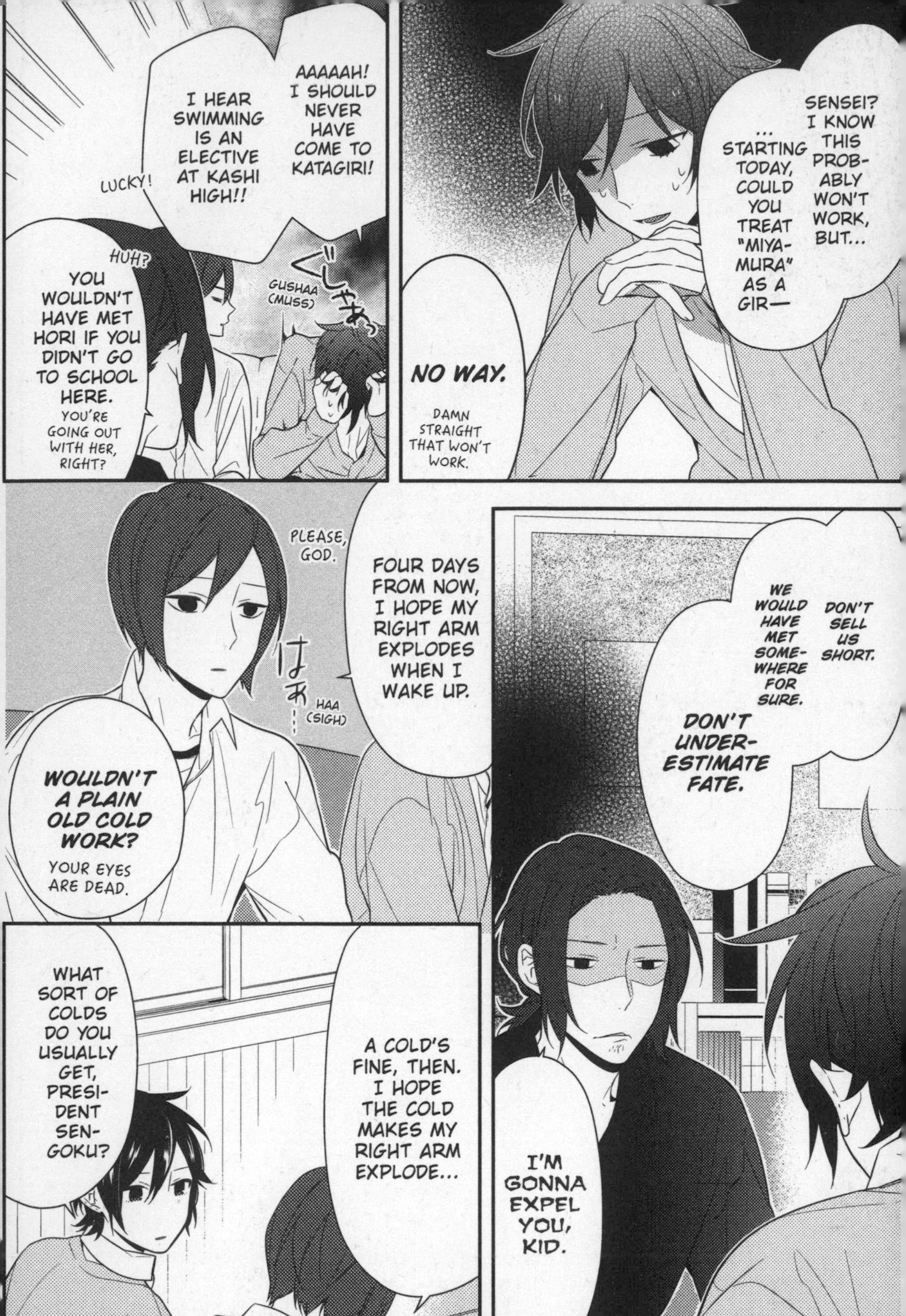
SENSEI? I KNOW THIS PROBABLY WON'T WORK, BUT...
...STARTING TODAY, COULD YOU TREAT "MIYAMURA" AS A GIR—
NO WAY.
DAMN STRAIGHT THAT WON'T WORK.
AAAAAH! I SHOULD NEVER HAVE COME TO KATAGIRI!
I HEAR SWIMMING IS AN ELECTIVE AT KASHI HIGH!!
LUCKY!
ぐしゃあっ
GUSHAA (MUSS)
HUH?
YOU WOULDN'T HAVE MET HORI IF YOU DIDN'T GO TO SCHOOL HERE.
YOU'RE GOING OUT WITH HER, RIGHT?
DON'T SELL US SHORT.
WE WOULD HAVE MET SOMEWHERE FOR SURE.
DON'T UNDERESTIMATE FATE.
I'M GONNA EXPEL YOU, KID.
FOUR DAYS FROM NOW, I HOPE MY RIGHT ARM EXPLODES WHEN I WAKE UP.
PLEASE, GOD.
はあ…
HAA (SIGH)
WOULDN'T A PLAIN OLD COLD WORK?
YOUR EYES ARE DEAD.
A COLD'S FINE, THEN. I HOPE THE COLD MAKES MY RIGHT ARM EXPLODE...
WHAT SORT OF COLDS DO YOU USUALLY GET, PRESIDENT SENGOKU?

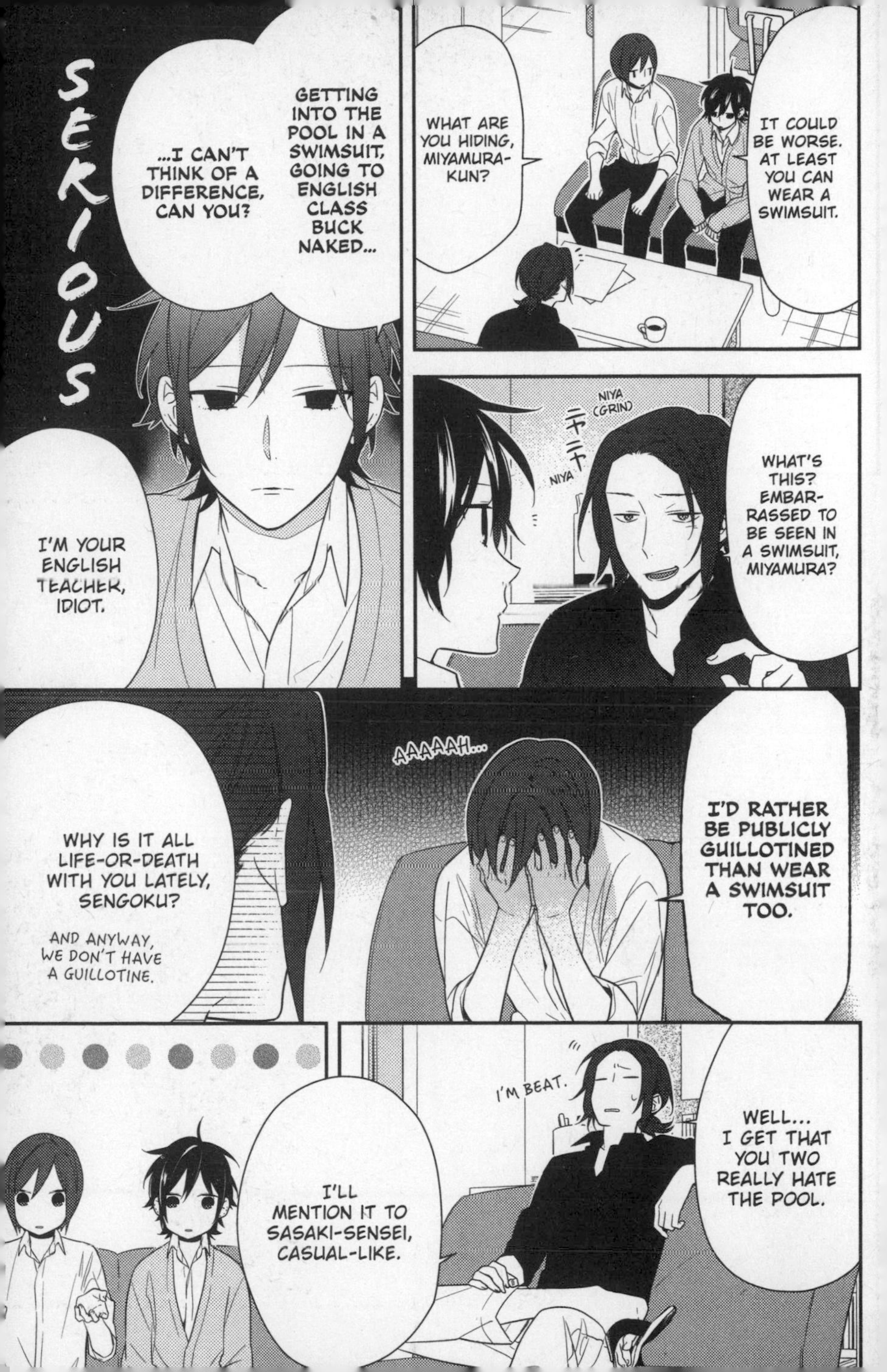
IT COULD BE WORSE. AT LEAST YOU CAN WEAR A SWIMSUIT.
WHAT ARE YOU HIDING, MIYAMURA-KUN?
WHAT'S THIS? EMBARRASSED TO BE SEEN IN A SWIMSUIT, MIYAMURA?
NIYA (GRIN)
NIYA
GETTING INTO THE POOL IN A SWIMSUIT, GOING TO ENGLISH CLASS BUCK NAKED...
...I CAN'T THINK OF A DIFFERENCE, CAN YOU?
SERIOUS
I'M YOUR ENGLISH TEACHER, IDIOT.
I'D RATHER BE PUBLICLY GUILLOTINED THAN WEAR A SWIMSUIT TOO.
AAAAAH...
WHY IS IT ALL LIFE-OR-DEATH WITH YOU LATELY, SENGOKU?
AND ANYWAY, WE DON'T HAVE A GUILLOTINE.
WELL... I GET THAT YOU TWO REALLY HATE THE POOL.
I'M BEAT.
I'LL MENTION IT TO SASAKI-SENSEI, CASUAL-LIKE.

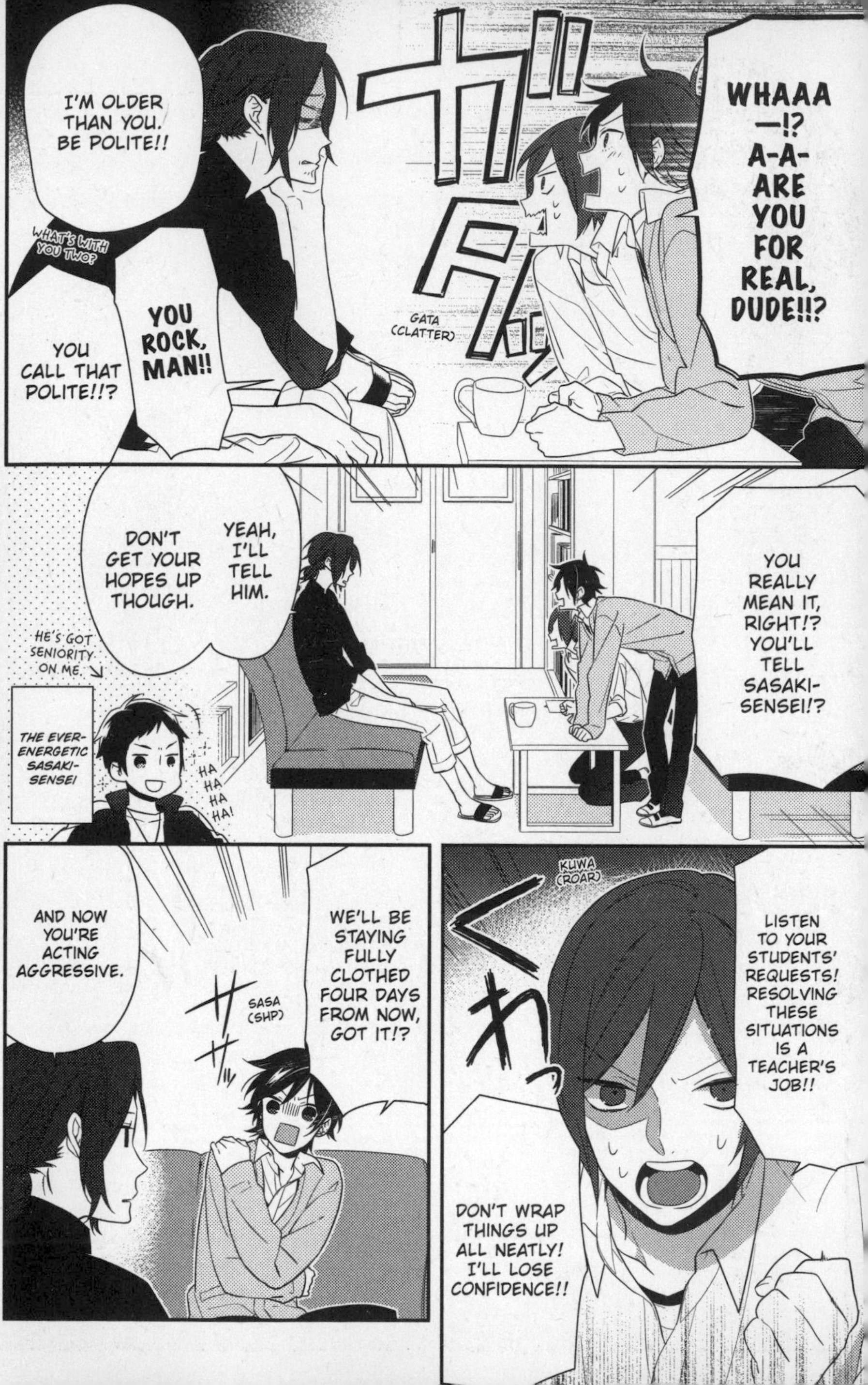
WHAAAA—!? A-A-ARE YOU FOR REAL, DUDE!!?
GATA (CLATTER)
I'M OLDER THAN YOU. BE POLITE!!
YOU ROCK, MAN!!
WHAT'S WITH YOU TWO?
YOU CALL THAT POLITE!!?
YOU REALLY MEAN IT, RIGHT!? YOU'LL TELL SASAKI-SENSEI!?
YEAH, I'LL TELL HIM.
DON'T GET YOUR HOPES UP THOUGH.
HE'S GOT SENIORITY ON ME.
THE EVER-ENERGETIC SASAKI-SENSEI
HA HA HA HA!
KUWA (ROAR)
LISTEN TO YOUR STUDENTS' REQUESTS! RESOLVING THESE SITUATIONS IS A TEACHER'S JOB!!
DON'T WRAP THINGS UP ALL NEATLY! I'LL LOSE CONFIDENCE!!
WE'LL BE STAYING FULLY CLOTHED FOUR DAYS FROM NOW, GOT IT!?
SASA (SHP)
AND NOW YOU'RE ACTING AGGRESSIVE.

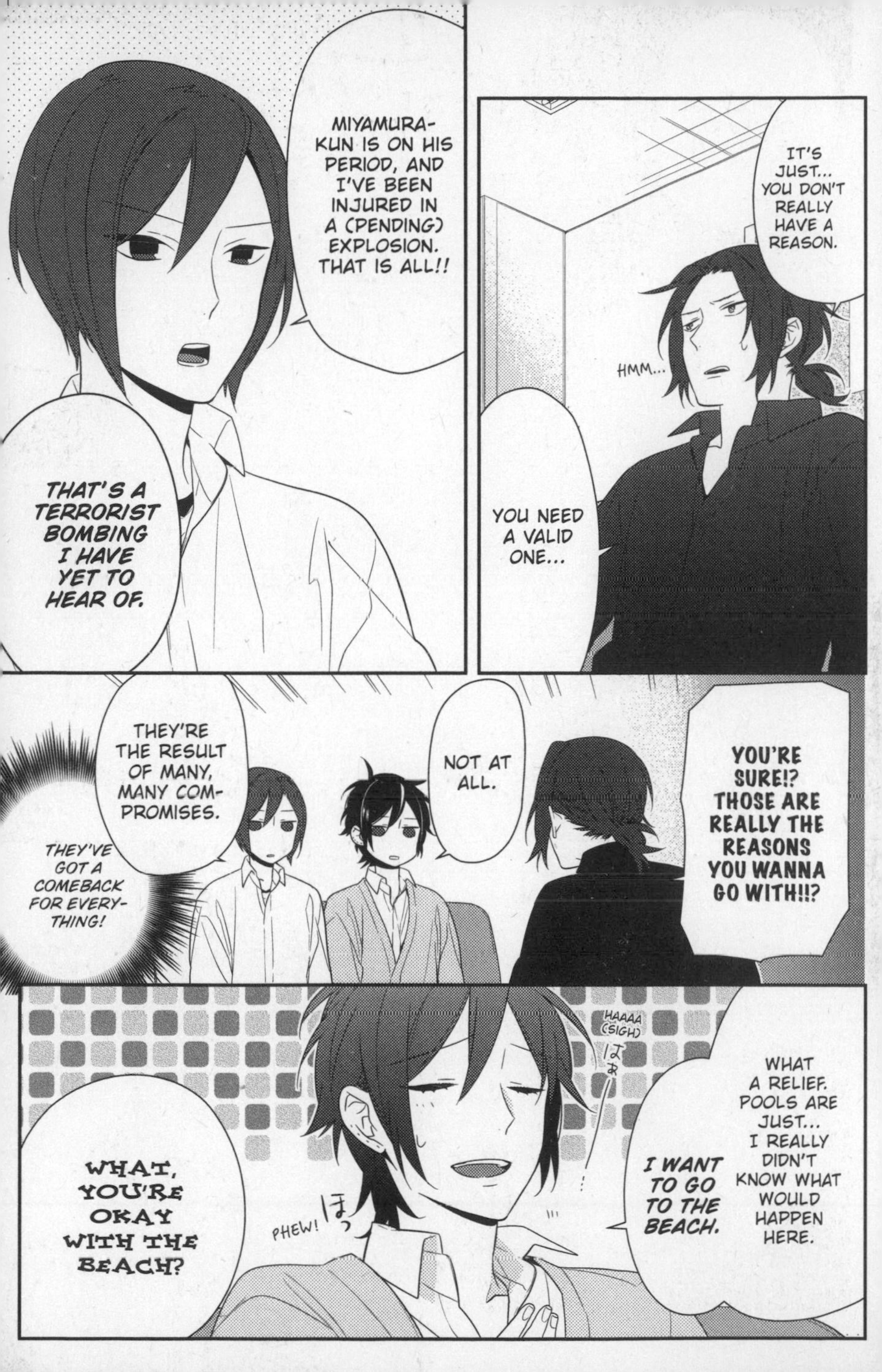
IT'S JUST... YOU DON'T REALLY HAVE A REASON.
HMM...
YOU NEED A VALID ONE...
MIYAMURA-KUN IS ON HIS PERIOD, AND I'VE BEEN INJURED IN A (PENDING) EXPLOSION. THAT IS ALL!!
THAT'S A TERRORIST BOMBING I HAVE YET TO HEAR OF.
YOU'RE SURE!? THOSE ARE REALLY THE REASONS YOU WANNA GO WITH!!?
NOT AT ALL.
THEY'RE THE RESULT OF MANY, MANY COMPROMISES.
THEY'VE GOT A COMEBACK FOR EVERYTHING!
WHAT A RELIEF. POOLS ARE JUST... I REALLY DIDN'T KNOW WHAT WOULD HAPPEN HERE.
I WANT TO GO TO THE BEACH.
HAAAA (SIGH)
はぁ
PHEW!
ほっ
WHAT, YOU'RE OKAY WITH THE BEACH?

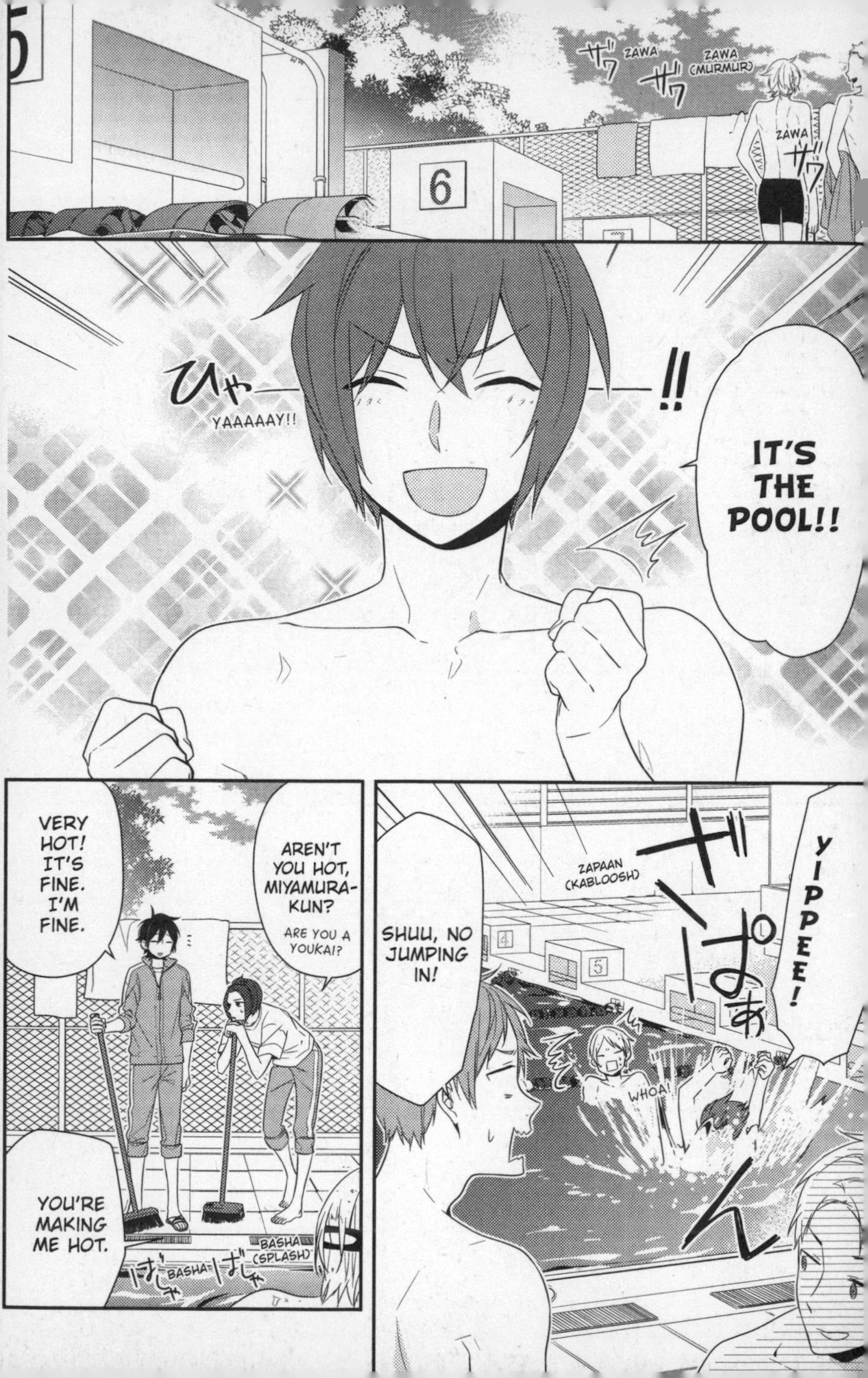
ZAWA
ザワ
ZAWA (MURMUR)
ザワ
ザワ
ZAWA
IT'S THE POOL!!
ひゃ——!!
YAAAAAY!!
YIPPEE!
ざぱあん
ZAPAAN (KABLOOSH)
SHUU, NO JUMPING IN!
WHOA!
AREN'T YOU HOT, MIYAMURA-KUN?
ARE YOU A YOUKAI?
VERY HOT! IT'S FINE. I'M FINE.
YOU'RE MAKING ME HOT.
BASHA (SPLASH)
ばしゃ
BASHA
ばしゃ

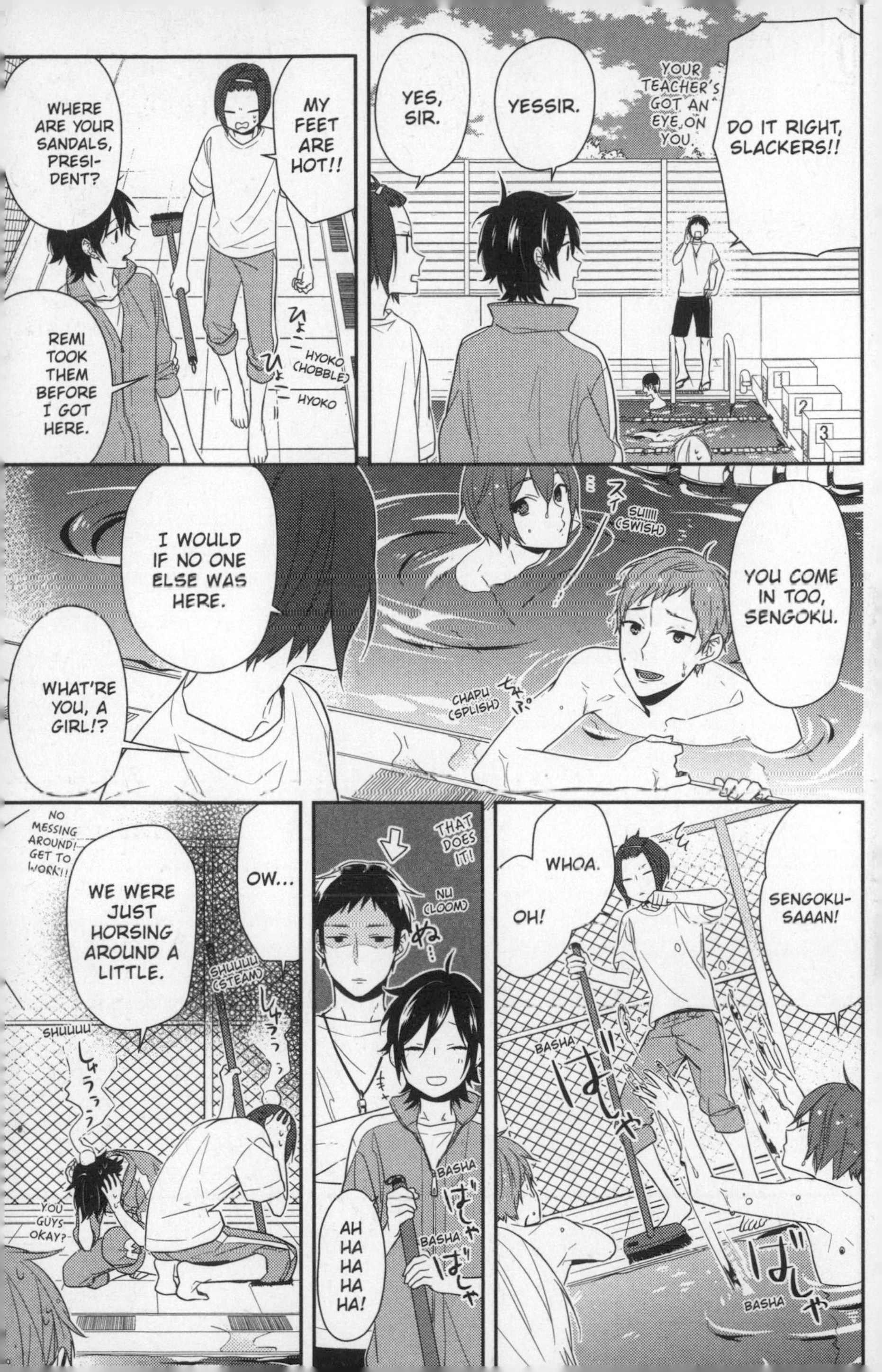
DO IT RIGHT, SLACKERS!!
YOUR TEACHER'S GOT AN EYE ON YOU.
YESSIR.
YES, SIR.
MY FEET ARE HOT!!
WHERE ARE YOUR SANDALS, PRESIDENT?
HYOKO (HOBBLE)
HYOKO
REMI TOOK THEM BEFORE I GOT HERE.
SUIII (SWISH)
YOU COME IN TOO, SENGOKU.
CHAPU (SPLISH)
I WOULD IF NO ONE ELSE WAS HERE.
WHAT'RE YOU, A GIRL!?
SENGOKU-SAAAN!
WHOA.
OH!
BASHA
BASHA
THAT DOES IT!
NU (LOOM)
BASHA
BASHA
AH HA HA HA HA HA!
OW...
NO MESSING AROUND! GET TO WORK!!
WE WERE JUST HORSING AROUND A LITTLE.
SHUUUU (STEAM)
SHUUUU
YOU GUYS OKAY?

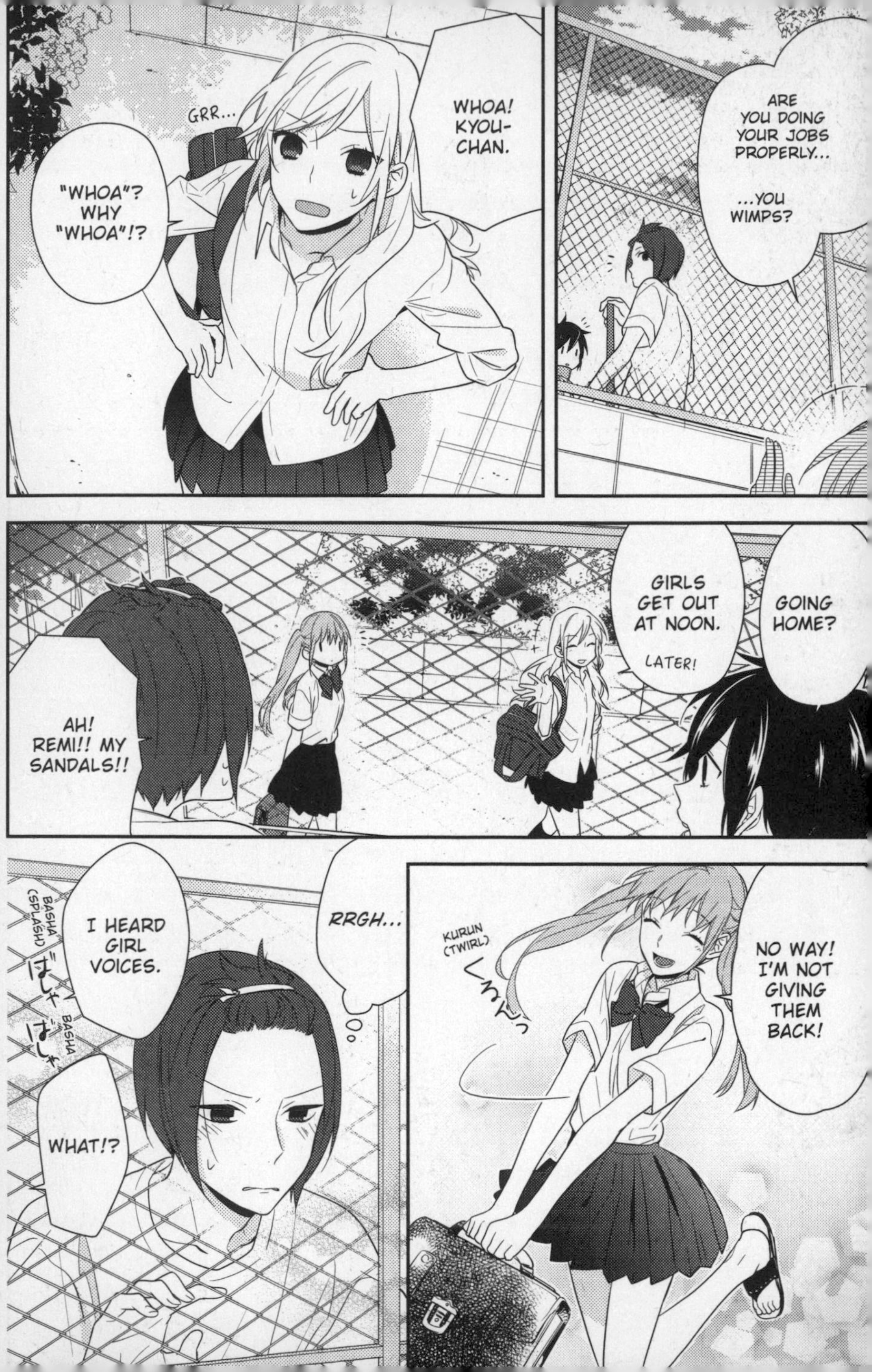
ARE YOU DOING YOUR JOBS PROPERLY...
...YOU WIMPS?
WHOA! KYOU-CHAN.
GRR...
"WHOA"? WHY "WHOA"!?
GOING HOME?
GIRLS GET OUT AT NOON.
LATER!
AH! REMI!! MY SANDALS!!
NO WAY! I'M NOT GIVING THEM BACK!
KURUN (TWIRL)
くるん
RRGH...
I HEARD GIRL VOICES.
BASHA (SPLASH)
ばしゃ
BASHA
ばしゃ
WHAT!?

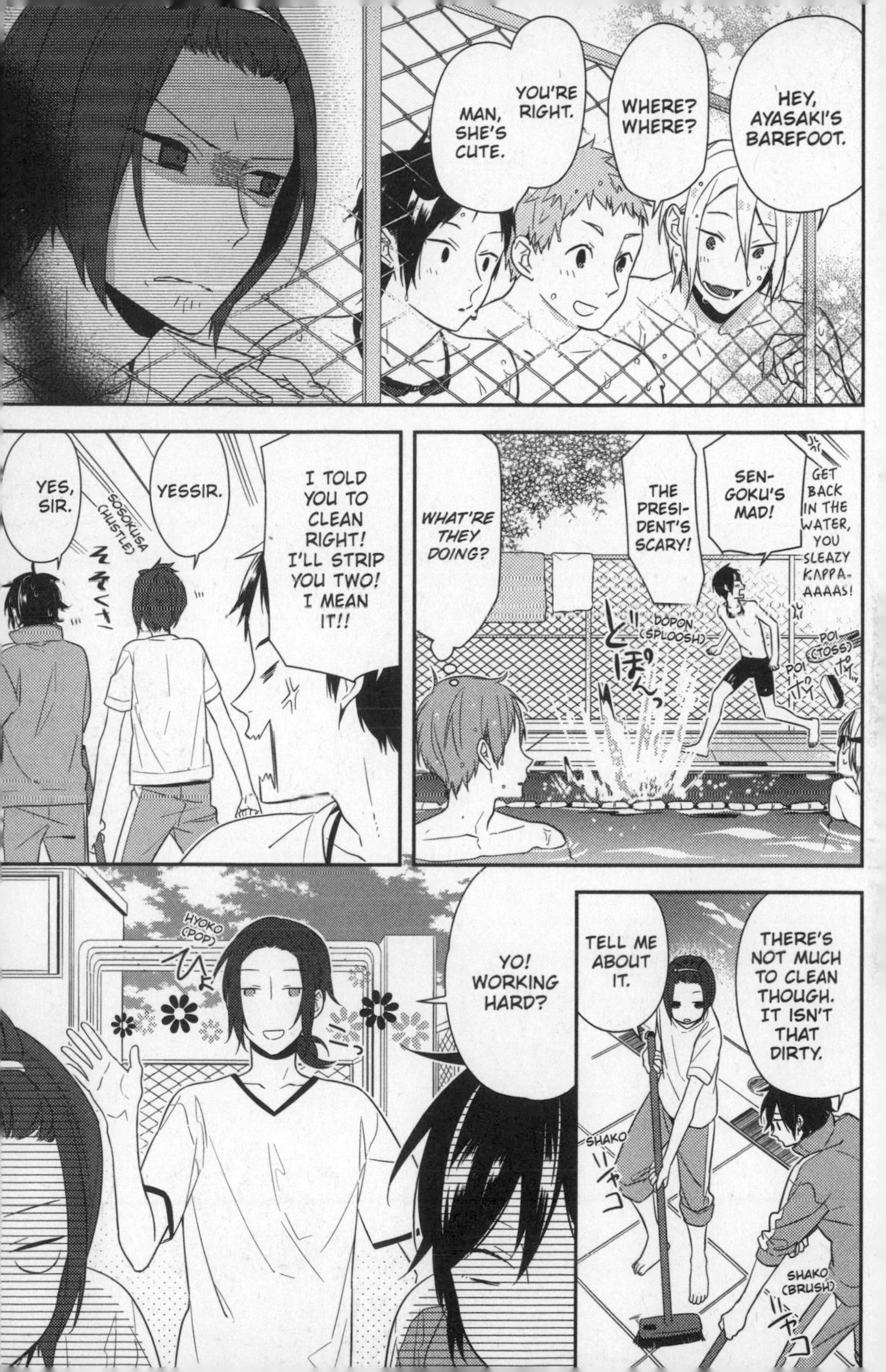
HEY, AYASAKI'S BAREFOOT.
WHERE? WHERE?
YOU'RE RIGHT.
MAN, SHE'S CUTE.
GET BACK IN THE WATER, YOU SLEAZY KAPPA-AAAAS!
POI (TOSS)
POI
SEN-GOKU'S MAD!
THE PRESI-DENT'S SCARY!
DOPON (SPLOOSH)
WHAT'RE THEY DOING?
I TOLD YOU TO CLEAN RIGHT! I'LL STRIP YOU TWO! I MEAN IT!!
YESSIR.
SOSOKUSA (HUSTLE)
YES, SIR.
THERE'S NOT MUCH TO CLEAN THOUGH. IT ISN'T THAT DIRTY.
TELL ME ABOUT IT.
SHAKO
SHAKO (BRUSH)
YO! WORKING HARD?
HYOKO (POP)

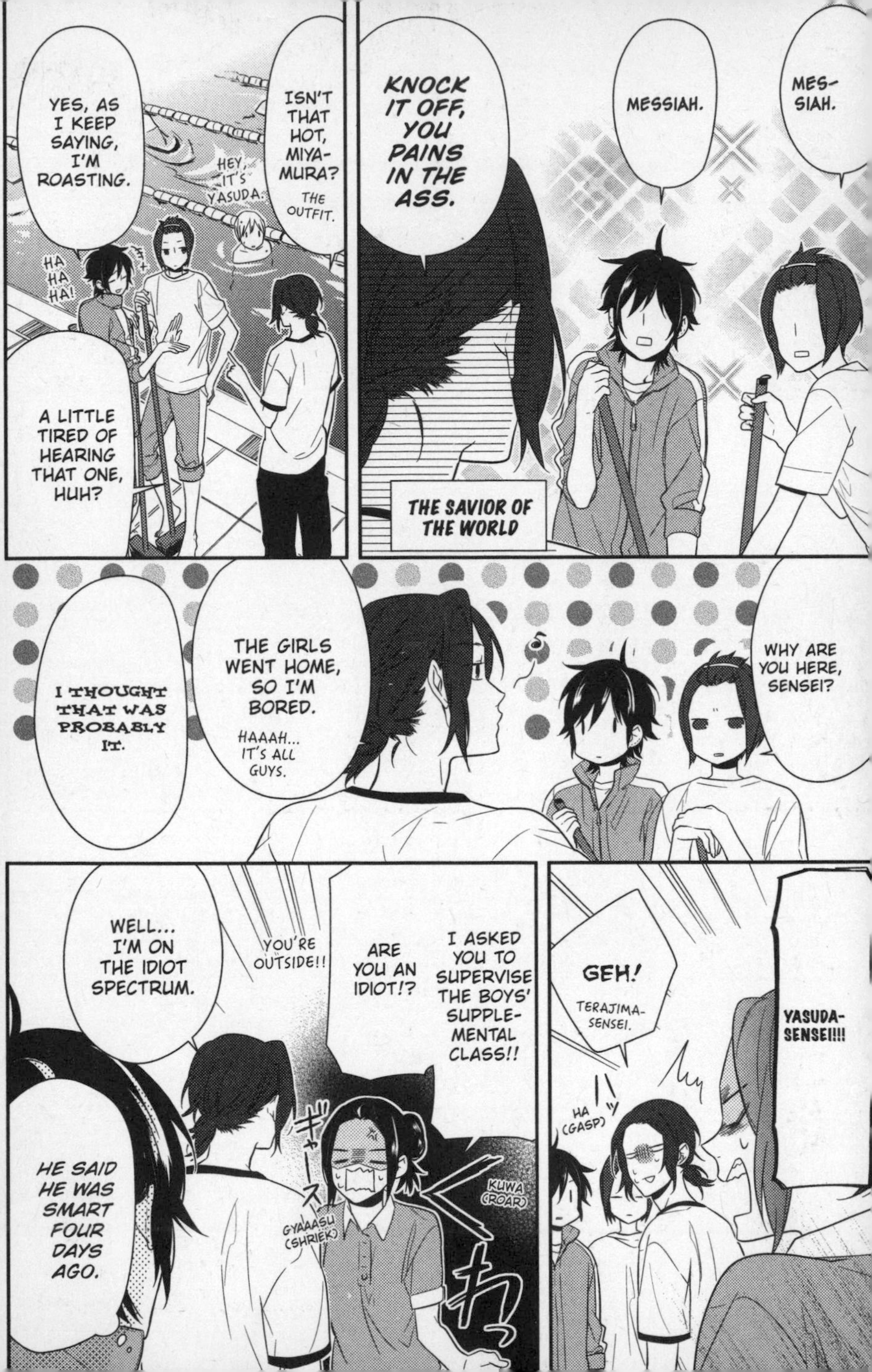
MES-SIAH.
MESSIAH.
KNOCK IT OFF, YOU PAINS IN THE ASS.
THE SAVIOR OF THE WORLD
ISN'T THAT HOT, MIYAMURA?
THE OUTFIT.
YES, AS I KEEP SAYING, I'M ROASTING.
HEY, IT'S YASUDA.
HA HA HA!
A LITTLE TIRED OF HEARING THAT ONE, HUH?
WHY ARE YOU HERE, SENSEI?
THE GIRLS WENT HOME, SO I'M BORED.
HAAAH... IT'S ALL GUYS.
I THOUGHT THAT WAS PROBABLY IT.
YASUDA-SENSEI!!!
GEH!
TERAJIMA-SENSEI.
HA (GASP)
I ASKED YOU TO SUPERVISE THE BOYS' SUPPLE-MENTAL CLASS!!
ARE YOU AN IDIOT!?
YOU'RE OUTSIDE!!
KUWA (ROAR)
GYAAASU (SHRIEK)
WELL... I'M ON THE IDIOT SPECTRUM.
HE SAID HE WAS SMART FOUR DAYS AGO.

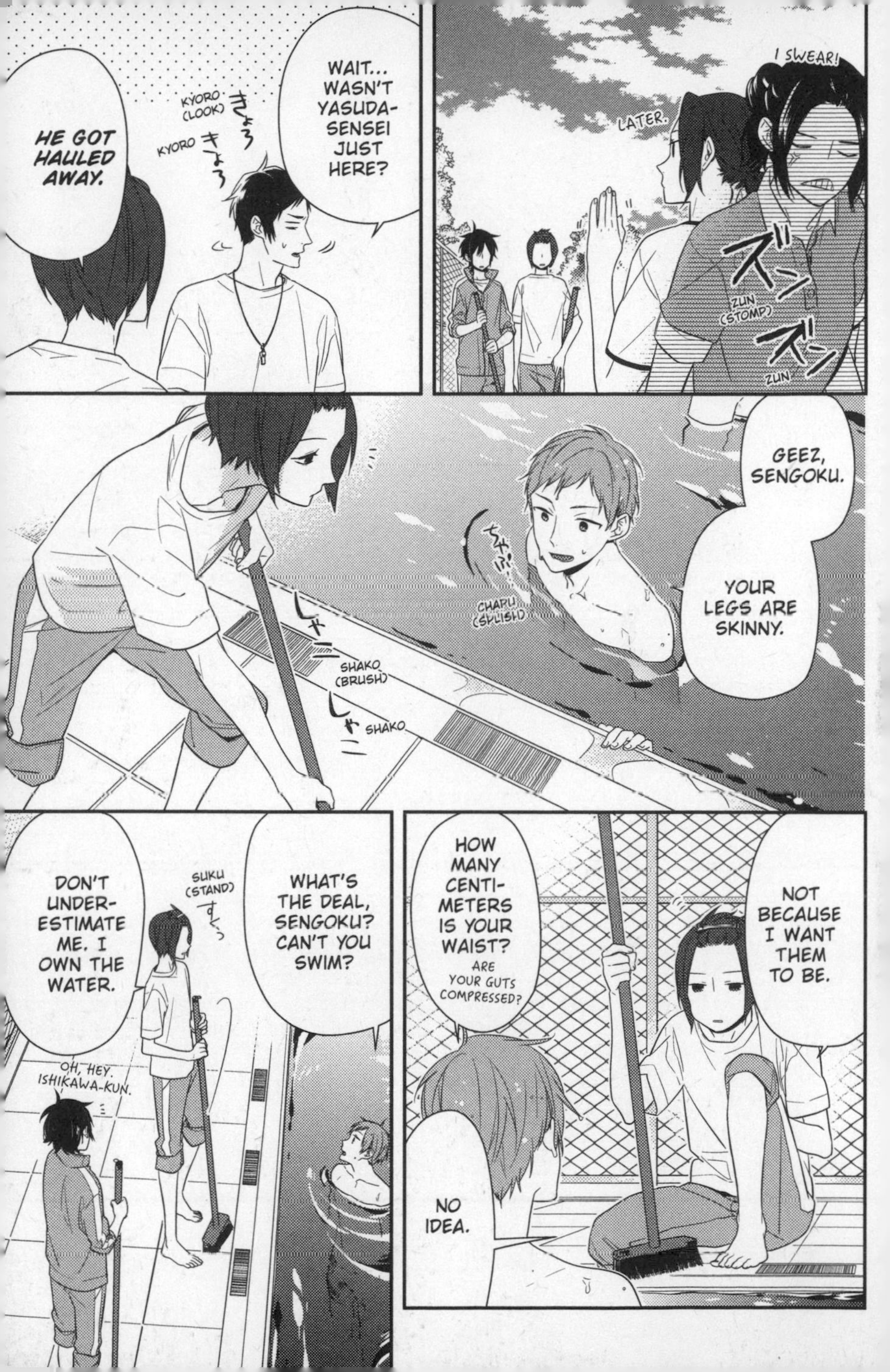
I SWEAR!
LATER.
ズン
ZUN (STOMP)
ズン
ZUN
WAIT... WASN'T YASUDA-SENSEI JUST HERE?
きょろ
KYORO (LOOK)
きょろ
KYORO
HE GOT HAULED AWAY.
GEEZ, SENGOKU.
YOUR LEGS ARE SKINNY.
ちゃぷ
CHAPU (SPLISH)
しゃこ
SHAKO (BRUSH)
しゃこ
SHAKO
NOT BECAUSE I WANT THEM TO BE.
HOW MANY CENTIMETERS IS YOUR WAIST? ARE YOUR GUTS COMPRESSED?
NO IDEA.
WHAT'S THE DEAL, SENGOKU? CAN'T YOU SWIM?
すっ
SUKU (STAND)
DON'T UNDERESTIMATE ME. I OWN THE WATER.
OH, HEY. ISHIKAWA-KUN.

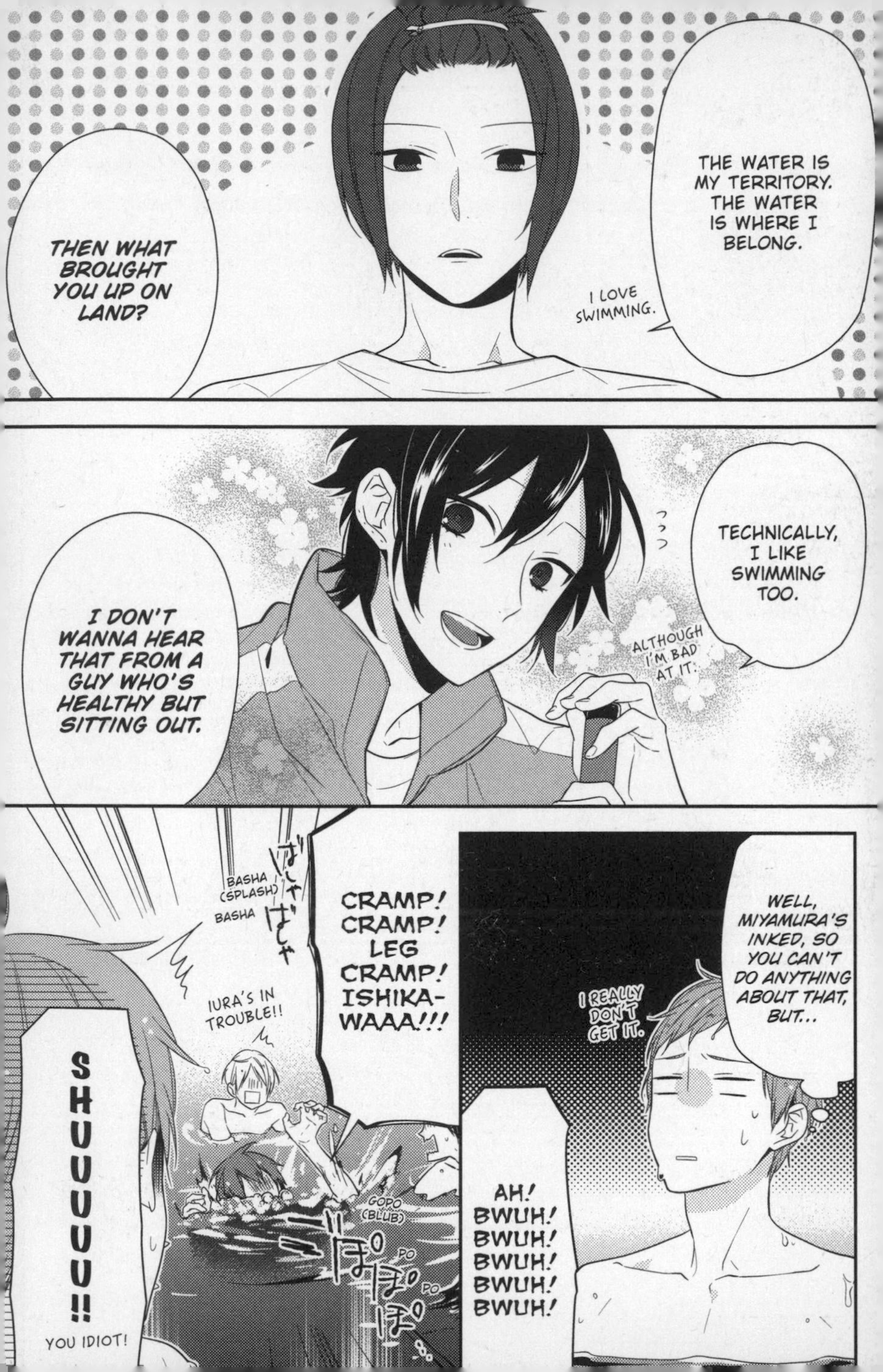
THE WATER IS MY TERRITORY. THE WATER IS WHERE I BELONG.
I LOVE SWIMMING.
THEN WHAT BROUGHT YOU UP ON LAND?
TECHNICALLY, I LIKE SWIMMING TOO.
ALTHOUGH I'M BAD AT IT.
I DON'T WANNA HEAR THAT FROM A GUY WHO'S HEALTHY BUT SITTING OUT.
WELL, MIYAMURA'S INKED, SO YOU CAN'T DO ANYTHING ABOUT THAT, BUT...
I REALLY DON'T GET IT.
AH! BWUH! BWUH! BWUH! BWUH! BWUH!
CRAMP! CRAMP! LEG CRAMP! ISHIKA-WAAA!!!
BASHA (SPLASH)
BASHA
IURA'S IN TROUBLE!!
GOPO (BLUB)
PO
PO
SHUUUUUU!!
YOU IDIOT!

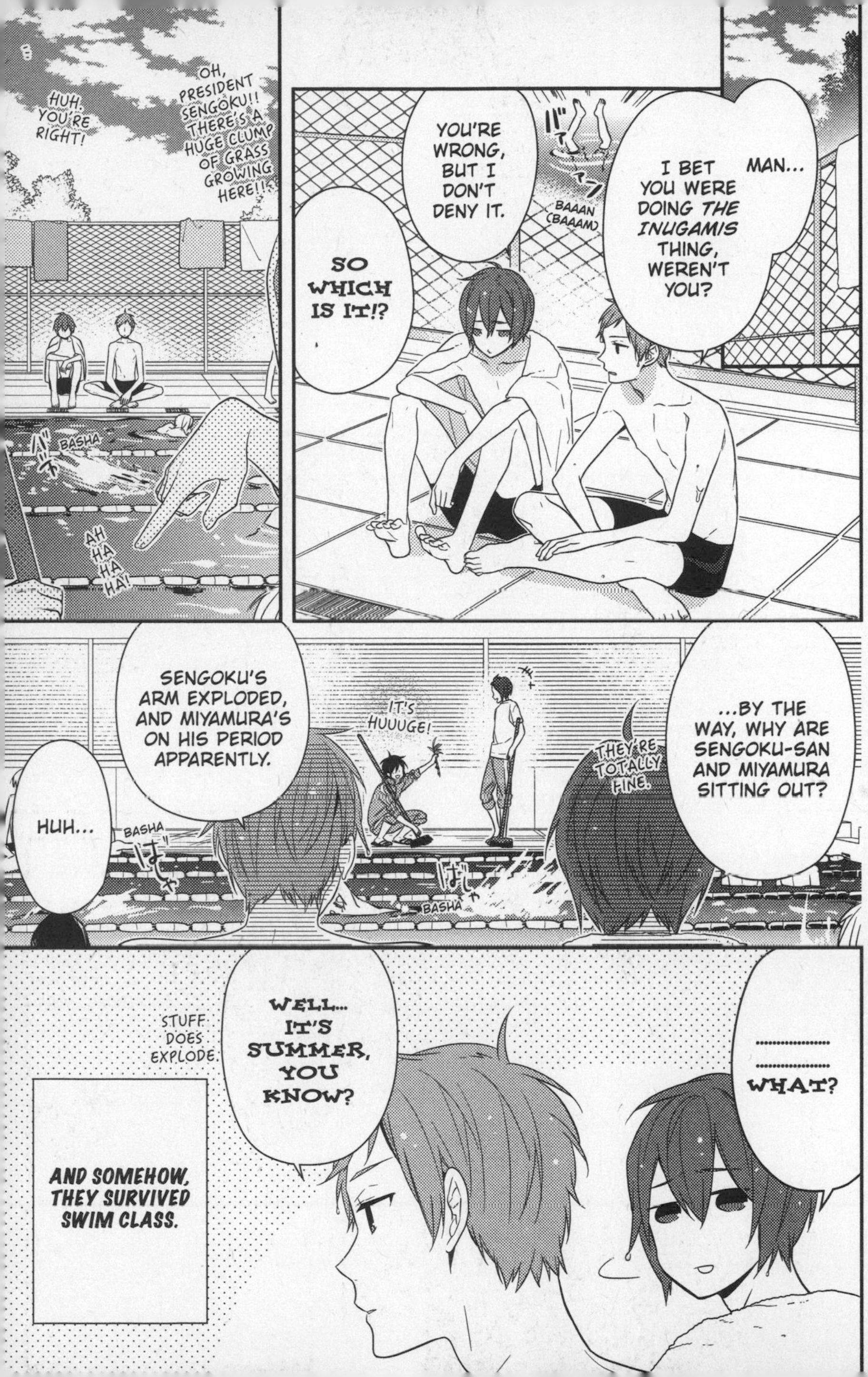
MAN...
I BET YOU WERE DOING *THE INUGAMIS* THING, WEREN'T YOU?
BAAAN (BAAAM)
YOU'RE WRONG, BUT I DON'T DENY IT.
SO WHICH IS IT!?
OH, PRESIDENT SENGOKU!! THERE'S A HUGE CLUMP OF GRASS GROWING HERE!!
HUH. YOU'RE RIGHT!
BASHA
AH HA HA HA!
...BY THE WAY, WHY ARE SENGOKU-SAN AND MIYAMURA SITTING OUT?
THEY'RE TOTALLY FINE.
IT'S HUUUGE!
SENGOKU'S ARM EXPLODED, AND MIYAMURA'S ON HIS PERIOD APPARENTLY.
BASHA
BASHA
HUH...
.... WHAT?
WELL... IT'S SUMMER, YOU KNOW?
STUFF DOES EXPLODE.
AND SOMEHOW, THEY SURVIVED SWIM CLASS.

HORIMIYA

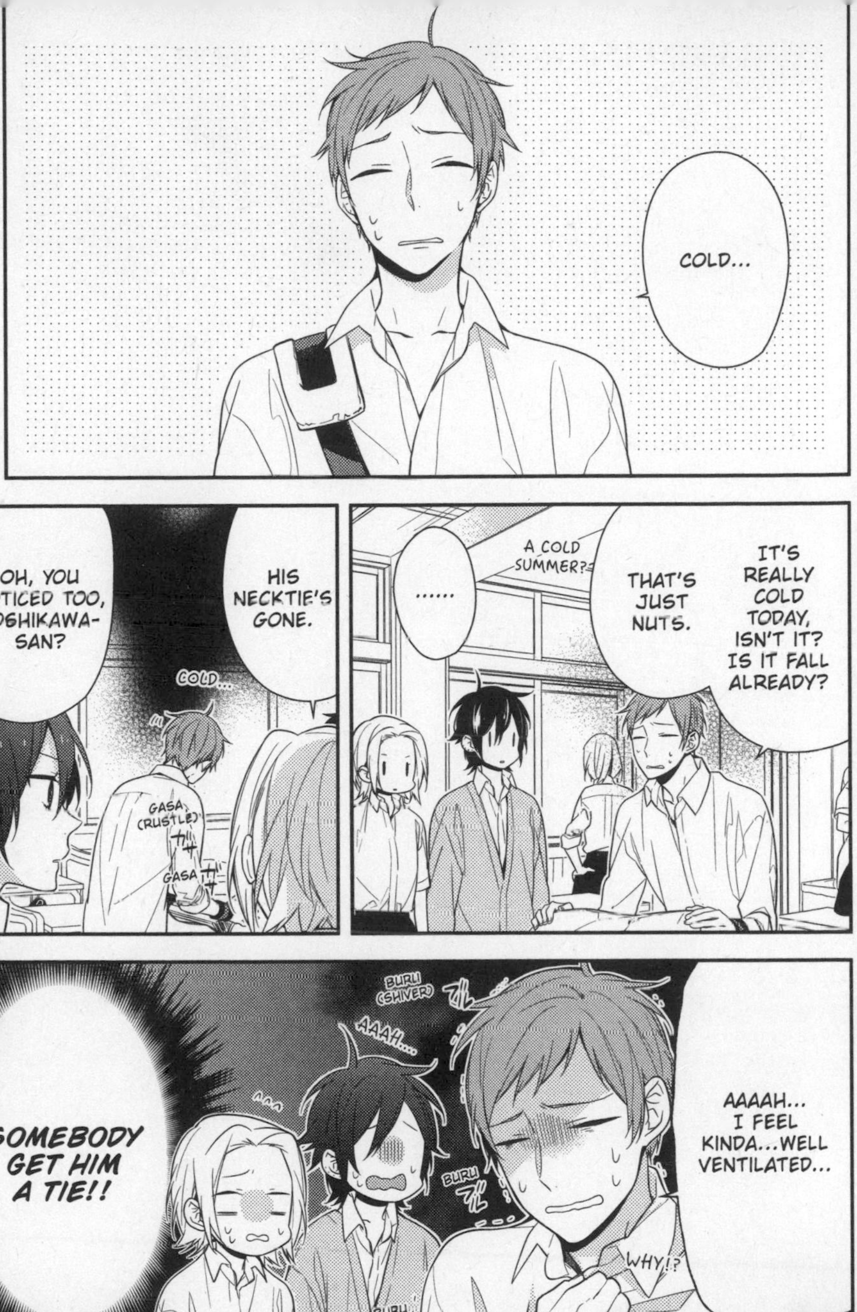
COLD...
IT'S REALLY COLD TODAY, ISN'T IT? IS IT FALL ALREADY?
THAT'S JUST NUTS.
A COLD SUMMER?
......
HIS NECKTIE'S GONE.
OH, YOU NOTICED TOO, YOSHIKAWA-SAN?
COLD...
GASA (RUSTLE)
GASA
AAAAH... I FEEL KINDA...WELL VENTILATED...
WHY!?
BURU (SHIVER)
AAAH...
BURU
BURU
SOMEBODY GET HIM A TIE!!

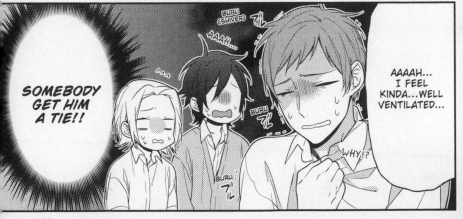

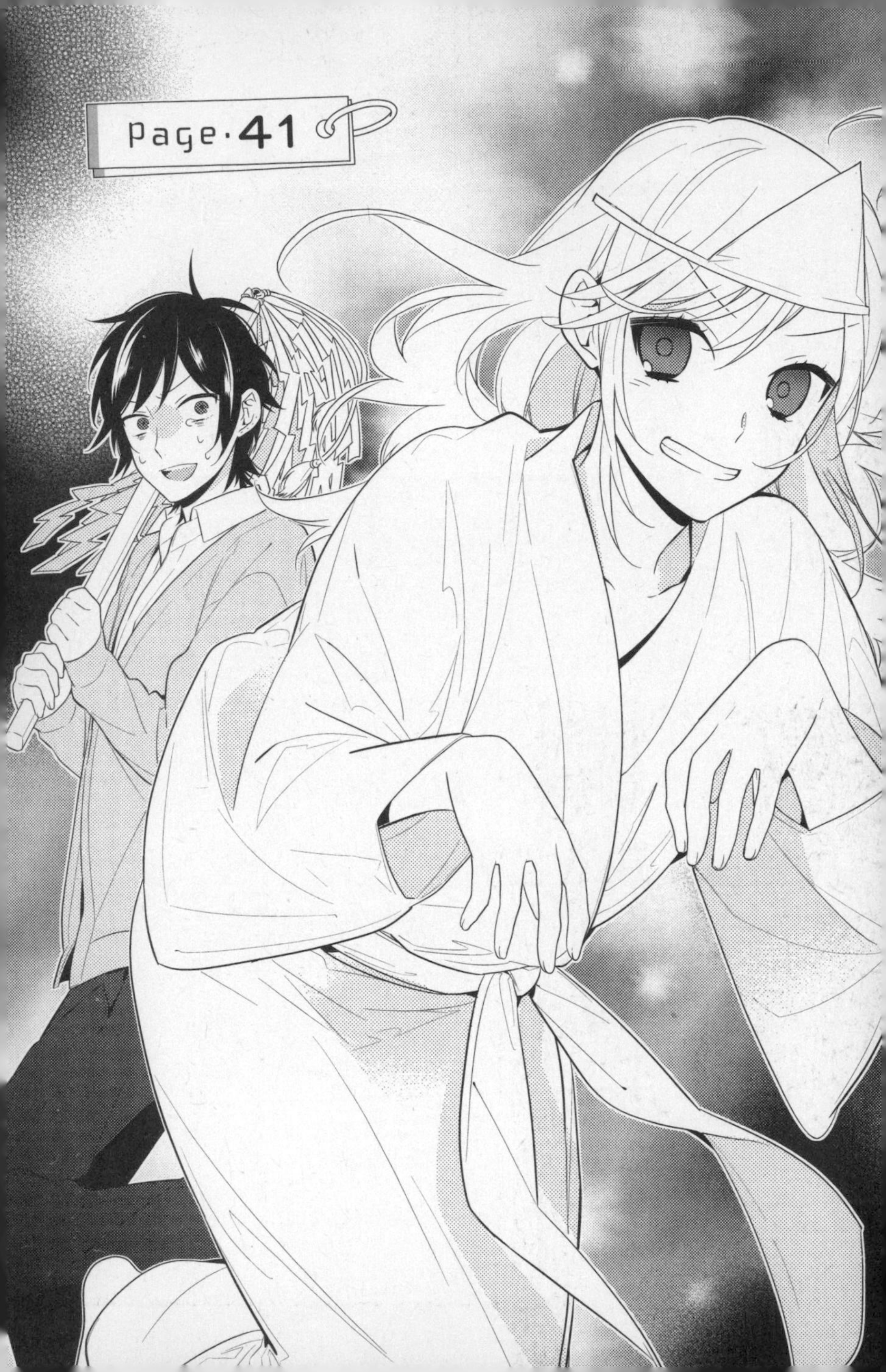
Page·41

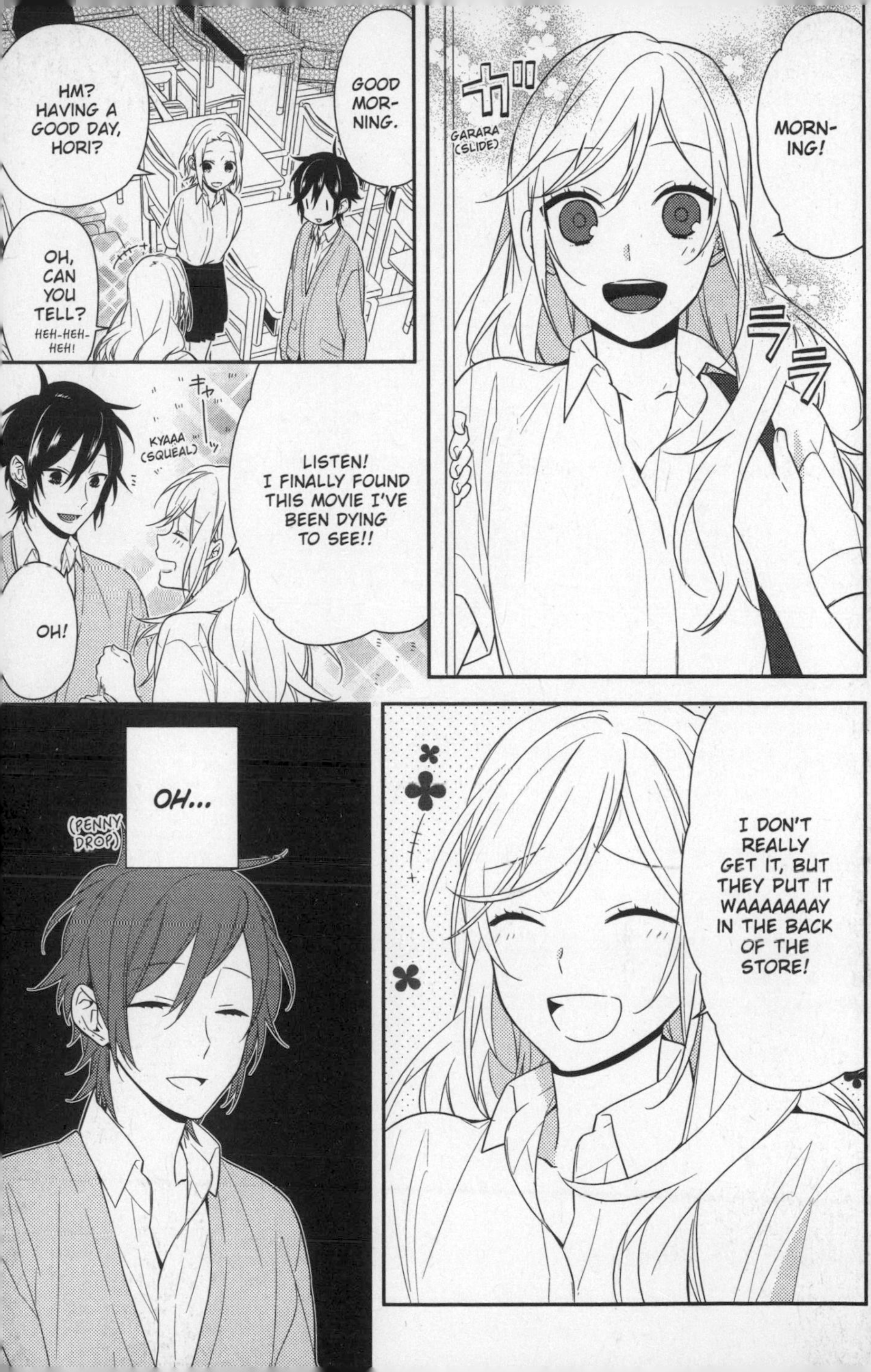
MORNING!
GARARA (SLIDE)
GOOD MORNING.
HM? HAVING A GOOD DAY, HORI?
OH, CAN YOU TELL? HEH-HEH-HEH!
KYAAA (SQUEAL)
LISTEN! I FINALLY FOUND THIS MOVIE I'VE BEEN DYING TO SEE!!
OH!
I DON'T REALLY GET IT, BUT THEY PUT IT WAAAAAAAY IN THE BACK OF THE STORE!
OH...
(PENNY DROP)

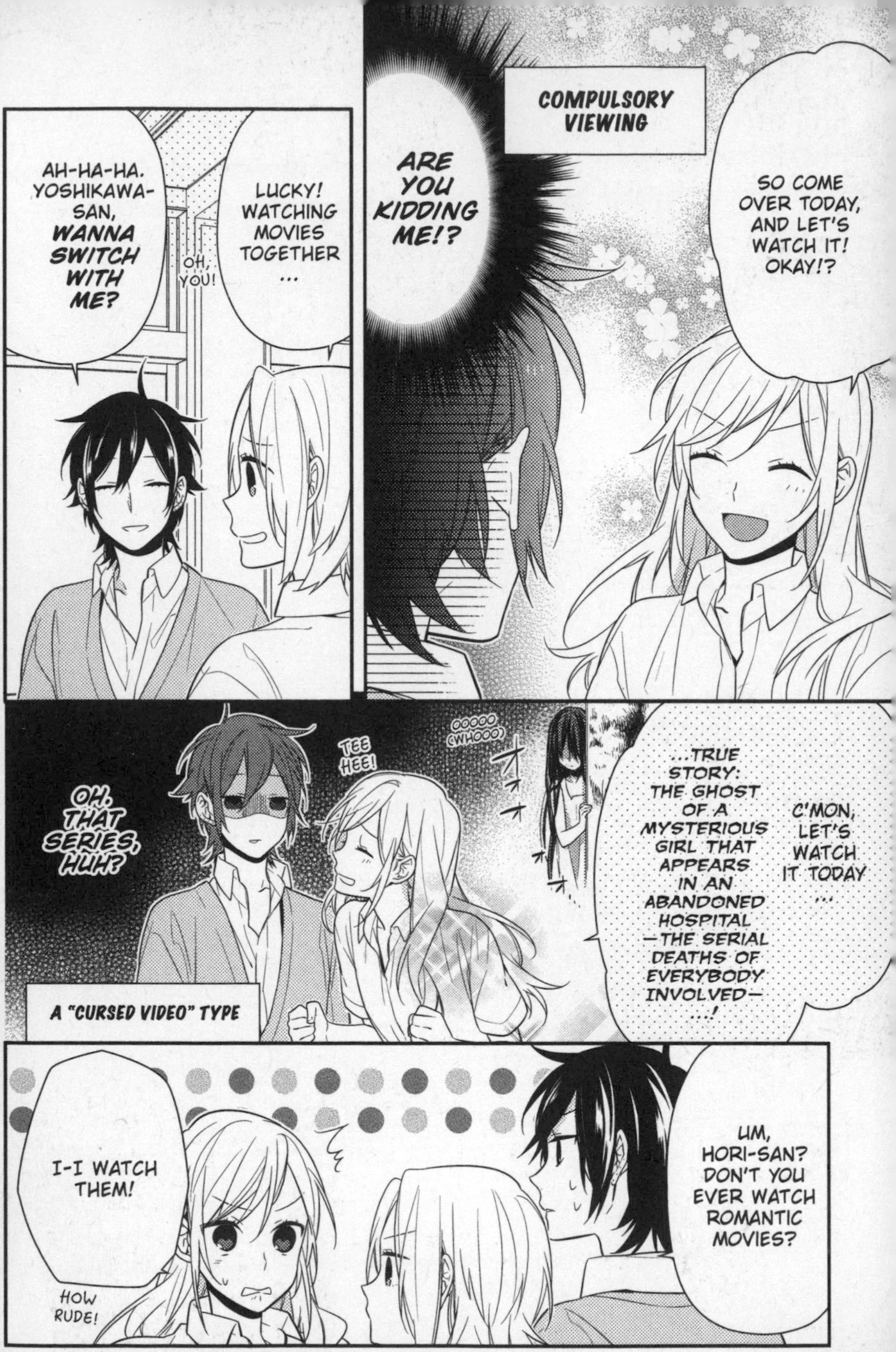
COMPULSORY VIEWING
SO COME OVER TODAY, AND LET'S WATCH IT! OKAY!?
ARE YOU KIDDING ME!?
LUCKY! WATCHING MOVIES TOGETHER ...
OH, YOU!
AH-HA-HA. YOSHIKAWA-SAN, WANNA SWITCH WITH ME?
C'MON, LET'S WATCH IT TODAY ...
...TRUE STORY: THE GHOST OF A MYSTERIOUS GIRL THAT APPEARS IN AN ABANDONED HOSPITAL —THE SERIAL DEATHS OF EVERYBODY INVOLVED— ...!
OOOOO (WHOOO)
TEE HEE!
OH. THAT SERIES, HUH?
A "CURSED VIDEO" TYPE
UM, HORI-SAN? DON'T YOU EVER WATCH ROMANTIC MOVIES?
I-I WATCH THEM!
HOW RUDE!

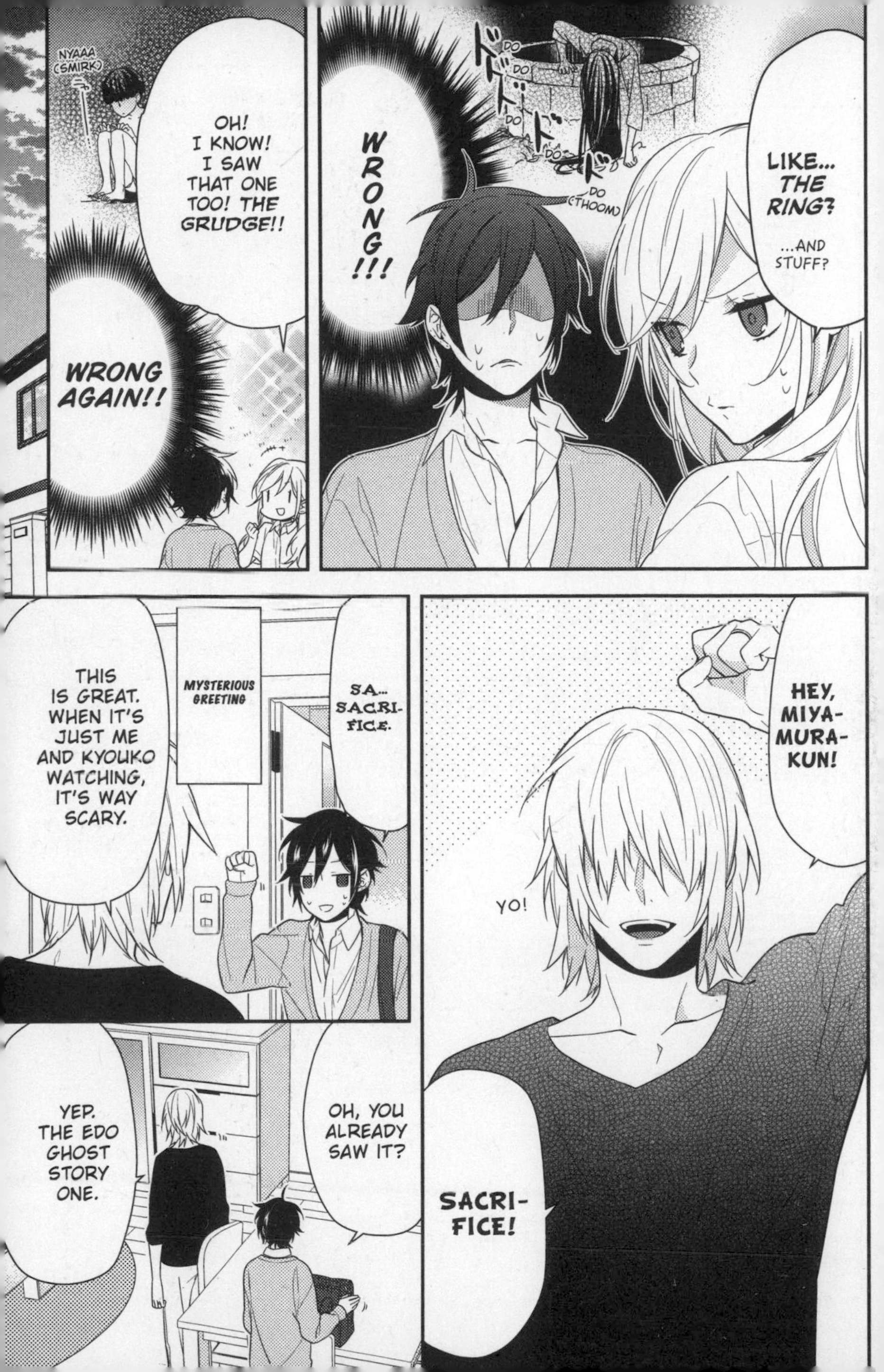
LIKE... THE RING?
...AND STUFF?
DO DO DO DO DO DO (THOOM)
WRONG!!!
NYAAA (SMIRK)
OH! I KNOW! I SAW THAT ONE TOO! THE GRUDGE!!
WRONG AGAIN!!
HEY, MIYAMURA-KUN!
YO!
SACRIFICE!
SA... SACRIFICE.
MYSTERIOUS GREETING
THIS IS GREAT. WHEN IT'S JUST ME AND KYOUKO WATCHING, IT'S WAY SCARY.
OH, YOU ALREADY SAW IT?
YEP. THE EDO GHOST STORY ONE.

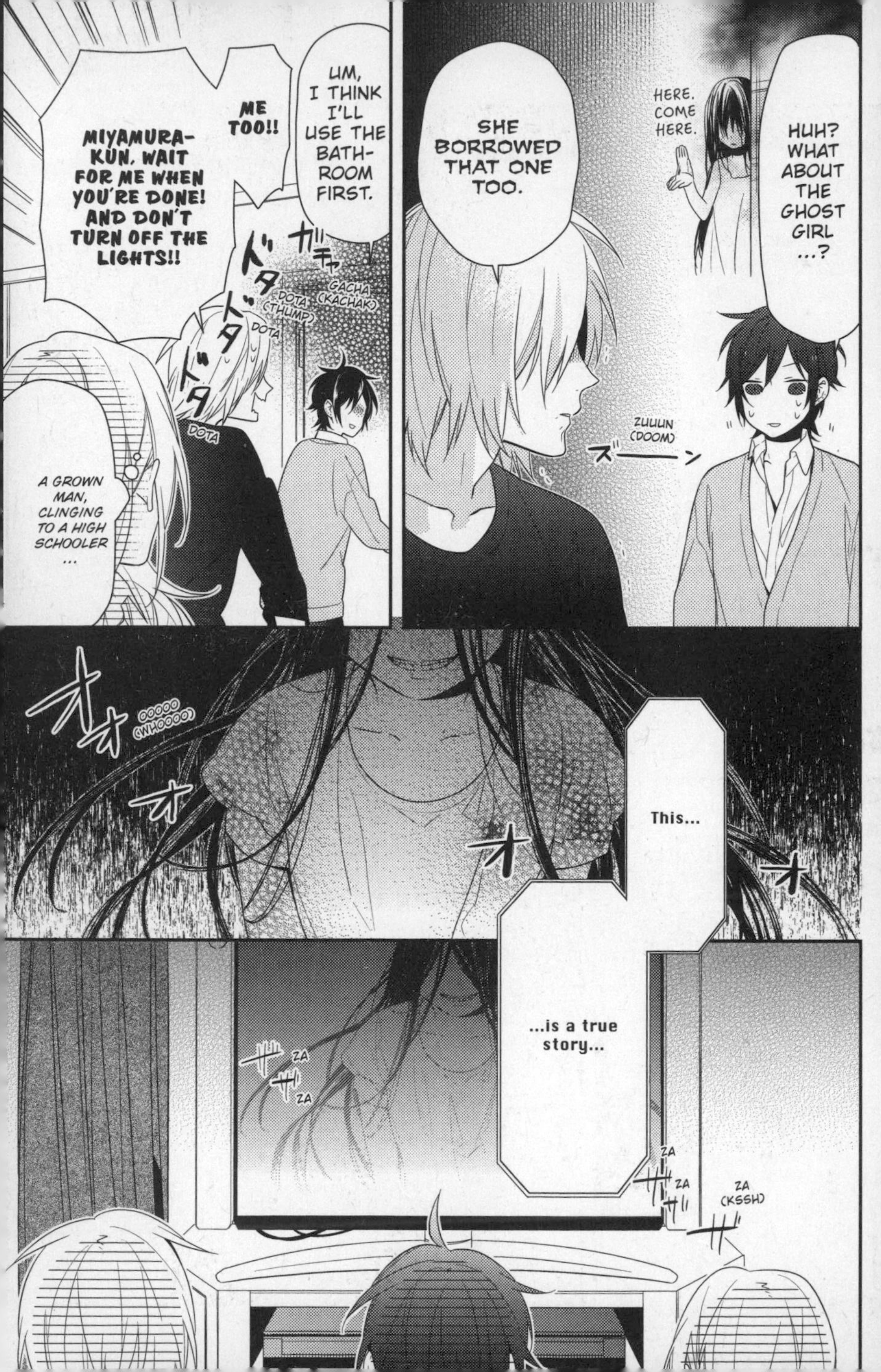
HUH? WHAT ABOUT THE GHOST GIRL ...?
HERE. COME HERE.
SHE BORROWED THAT ONE TOO.
ZUUUN (DOOM)
UM, I THINK I'LL USE THE BATH-ROOM FIRST.
GACHA (KACHAK)
ME TOO!!
DOTA (THUMP)
DOTA
DOTA
MIYAMURA-KUN, WAIT FOR ME WHEN YOU'RE DONE! AND DON'T TURN OFF THE LIGHTS!!
A GROWN MAN, CLINGING TO A HIGH SCHOOLER ...
OOOOO (WHOOOO)
This...
...is a true story...
ZA
ZA
ZA
ZA
ZA (KSSH)
ZA
ZA

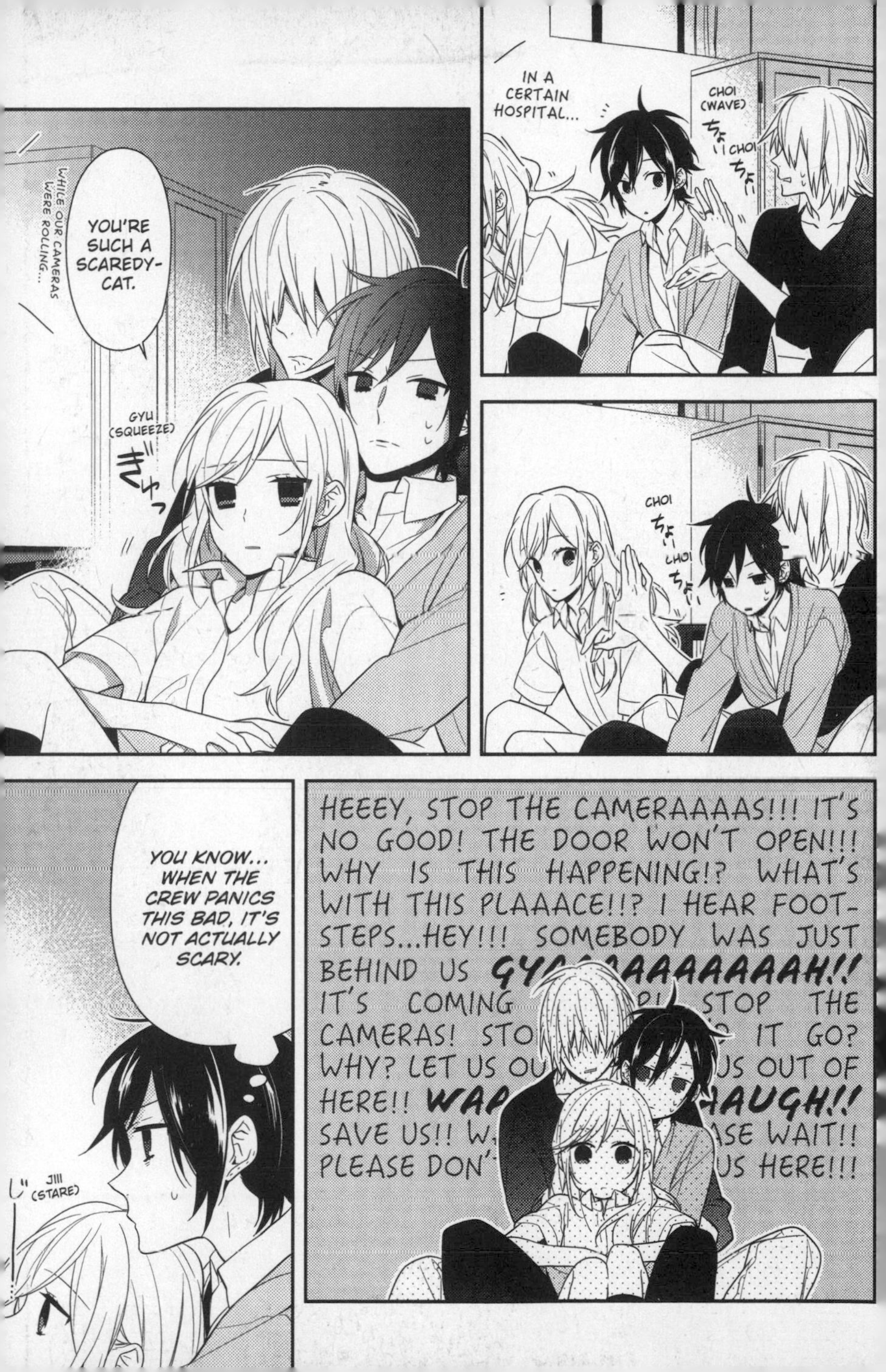
IN A CERTAIN HOSPITAL...
CHOI (WAVE)
ちょい
CHOI
ちょい
CHOI
ちょい
CHOI
ちょい
YOU'RE SUCH A SCAREDY-CAT.
WHILE OUR CAMERAS WERE ROLLING...
GYU (SQUEEZE)
ぎゅっ
HEEEY, STOP THE CAMERAAAAS!!! IT'S NO GOOD! THE DOOR WON'T OPEN!!! WHY IS THIS HAPPENING!? WHAT'S WITH THIS PLAAACE!!? I HEAR FOOT-STEPS...HEY!!! SOMEBODY WAS JUST BEHIND US GYA AAAAAAAAH!! IT'S COMING STOP THE CAMERAS! STO IT GO? WHY? LET US OU US OUT OF HERE!! WA HAUGH!! SAVE US!! W. ASE WAIT!! PLEASE DON' US HERE!!!
YOU KNOW... WHEN THE CREW PANICS THIS BAD, IT'S NOT ACTUALLY SCARY.
JIII (STARE)
じ

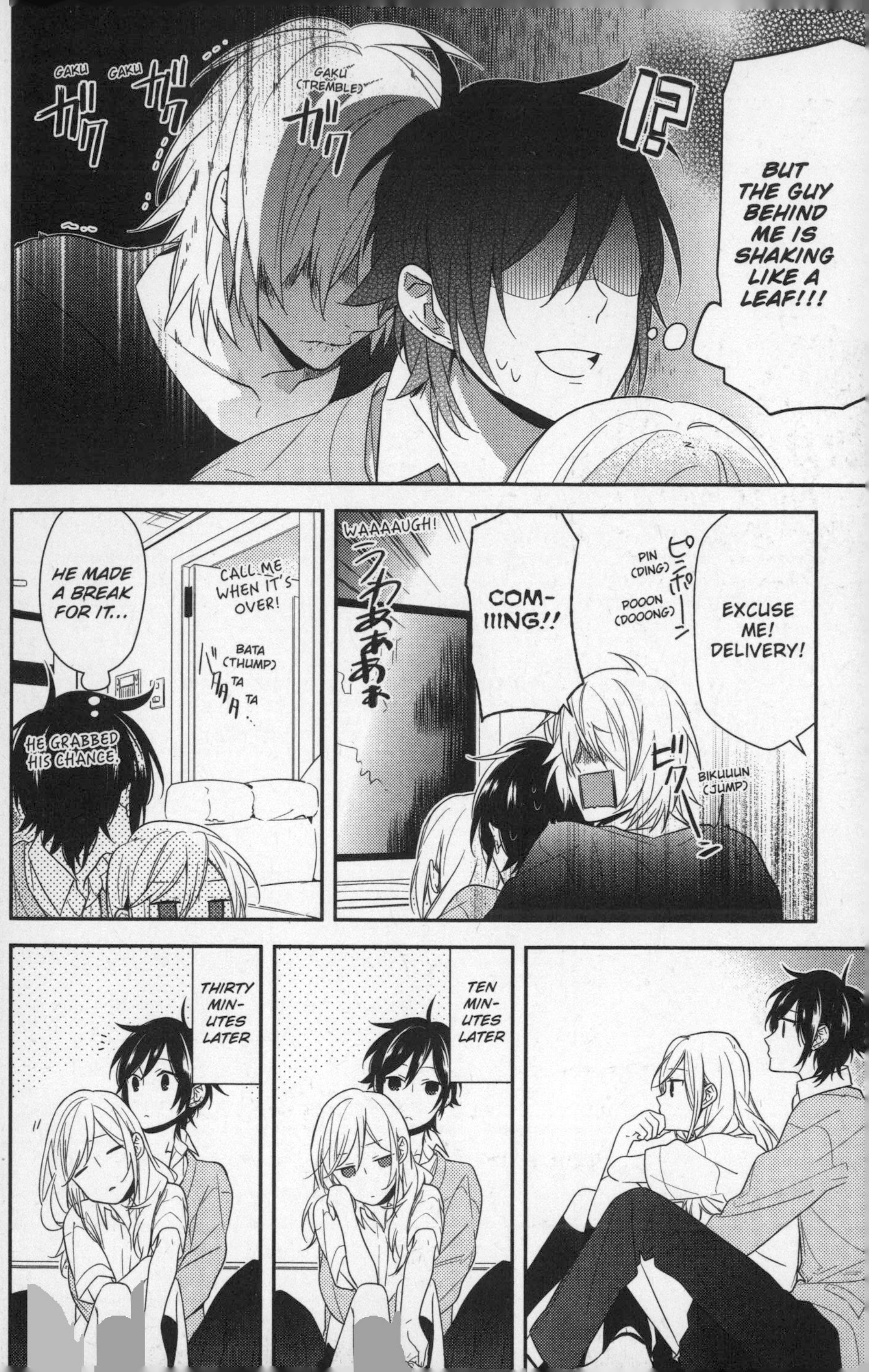
BUT THE GUY BEHIND ME IS SHAKING LIKE A LEAF!!!
!?
GAKU (TREMBLE)
GAKU GAKU
EXCUSE ME! DELIVERY!
PIN (DING) POOON (DOOONG)
COM-IIING!!
WAAAAUGH!
BIKUUUN (JUMP)
CALL ME WHEN IT'S OVER!
BATA (THUMP) TA TA
HE MADE A BREAK FOR IT...
HE GRABBED HIS CHANCE.
TEN MIN-UTES LATER
THIRTY MIN-UTES LATER

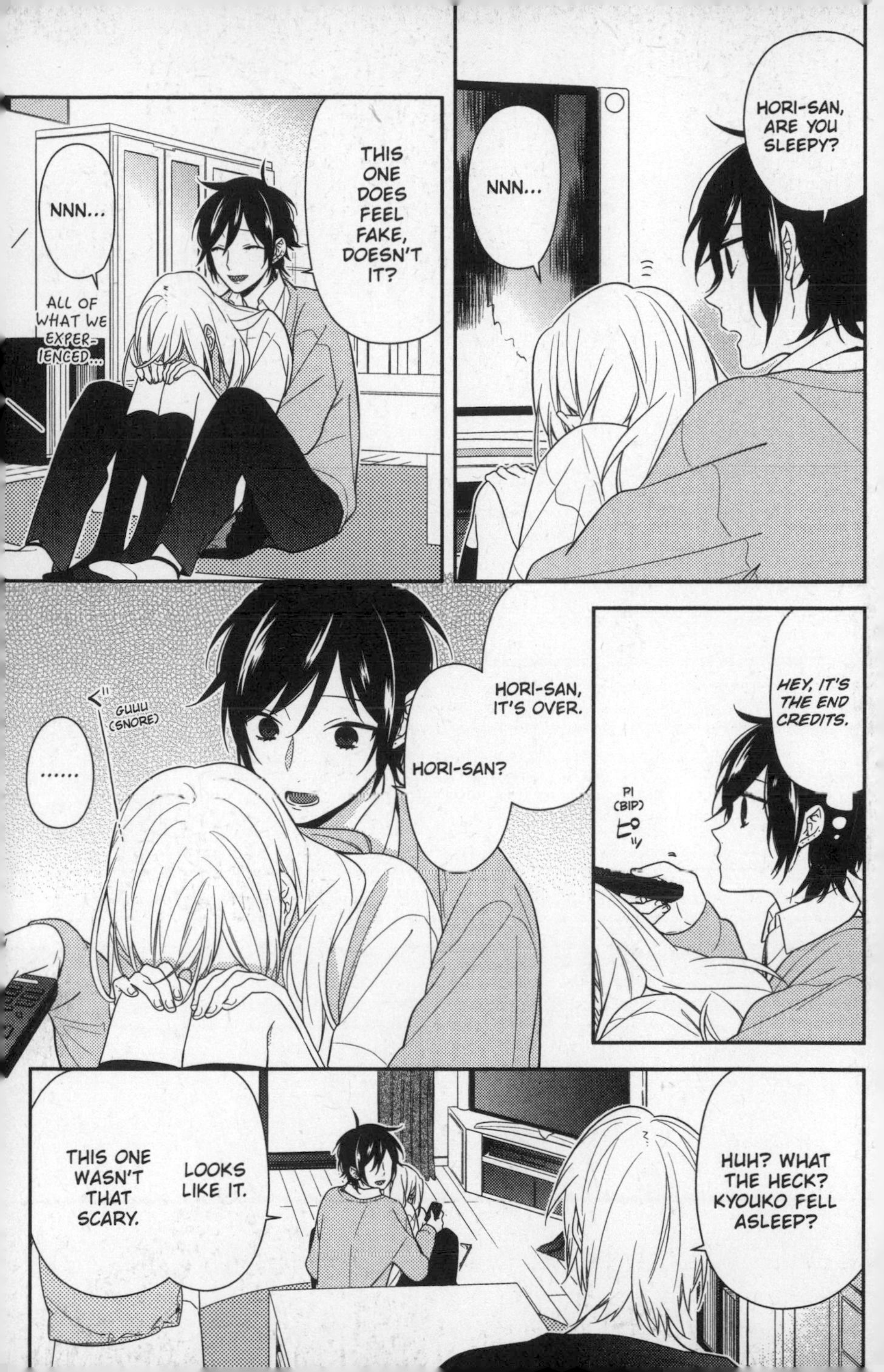
HORI-SAN, ARE YOU SLEEPY?
NNN...
THIS ONE DOES FEEL FAKE, DOESN'T IT?
NNN...
ALL OF WHAT WE EXPERIENCED...
HEY, IT'S THE END CREDITS.
PI (BIP)
HORI-SAN, IT'S OVER.
HORI-SAN?
......
GUUU (SNORE)
HUH? WHAT THE HECK? KYOUKO FELL ASLEEP?
LOOKS LIKE IT.
THIS ONE WASN'T THAT SCARY.

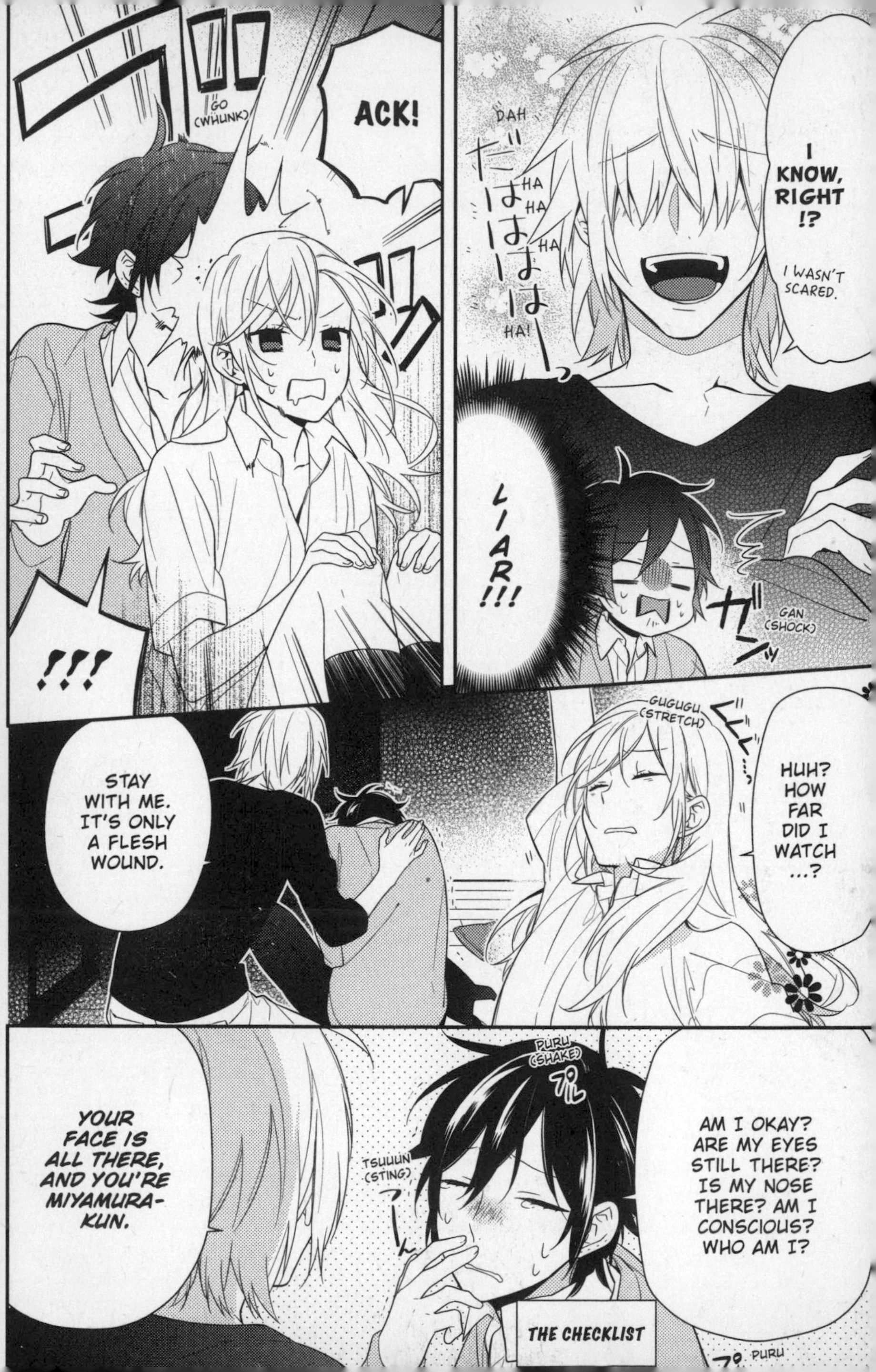

DAH HA HA HA HA!
I KNOW, RIGHT!?
I WASN'T SCARED.
LIAR!!!
GAN (SHOCK)
GO (WHUNK)
ACK!
!!!
GUGUGU (STRETCH)
HUH? HOW FAR DID I WATCH...?
STAY WITH ME. IT'S ONLY A FLESH WOUND.
PURU (SHAKE)
AM I OKAY? ARE MY EYES STILL THERE? IS MY NOSE THERE? AM I CONSCIOUS? WHO AM I?
TSUUUN (STING)
YOUR FACE IS ALL THERE, AND YOU'RE MIYAMURA-KUN.
THE CHECKLIST
PURU

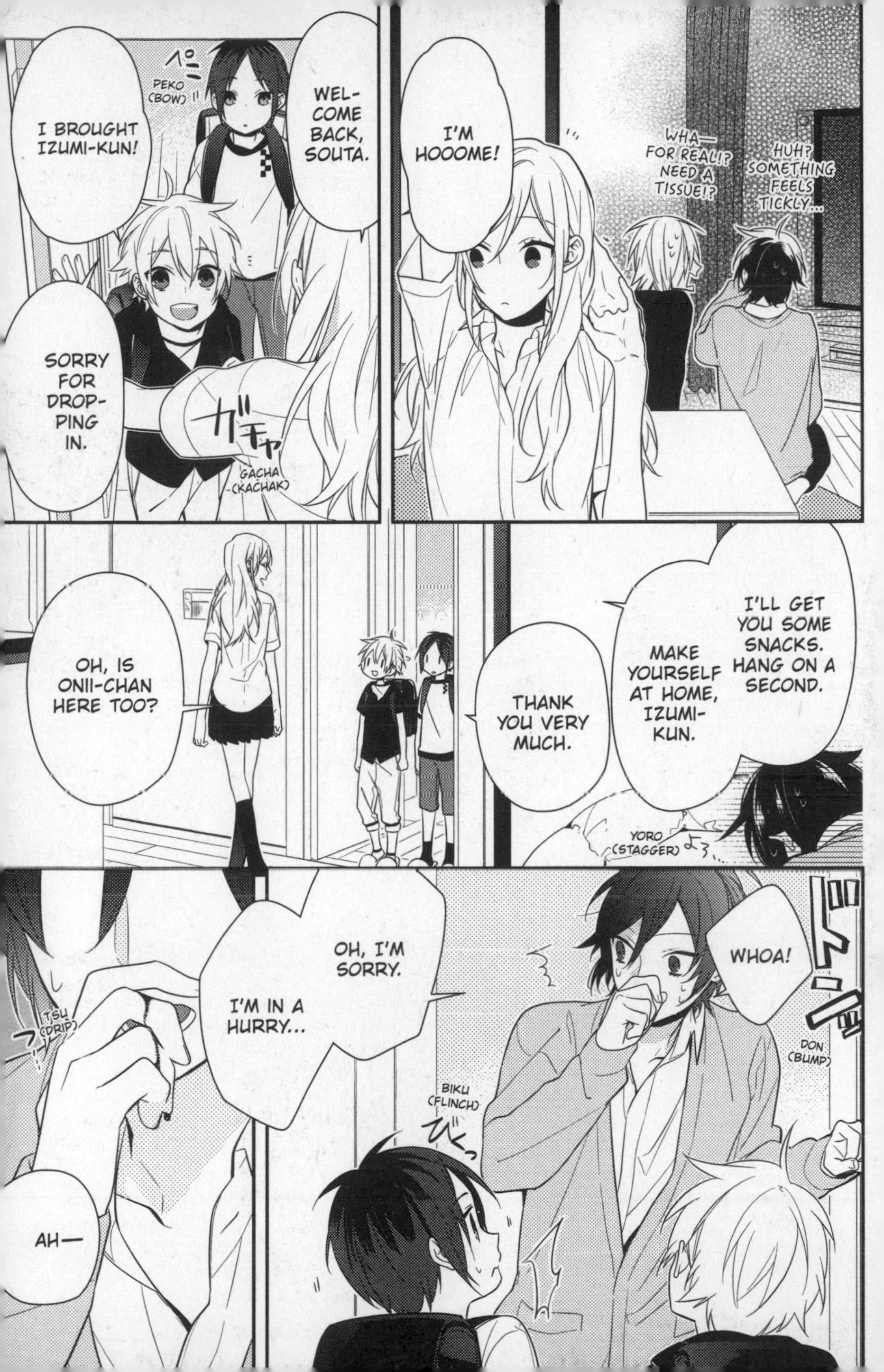
HUH? SOMETHING FEELS TICKLY...
WHA— FOR REAL!? NEED A TISSUE!?
I'M HOOOME!
WEL-COME BACK, SOUTA.
PEKO (BOW)
I BROUGHT IZUMI-KUN!
SORRY FOR DROP-PING IN.
GACHA (KACHAK)
I'LL GET YOU SOME SNACKS. HANG ON A SECOND.
MAKE YOURSELF AT HOME, IZUMI-KUN.
THANK YOU VERY MUCH.
YORO (STAGGER)
OH, IS ONII-CHAN HERE TOO?
WHOA!
DON (BUMP)
OH, I'M SORRY.
I'M IN A HURRY...
BIKU (FLINCH)
TSU (DRIP)
AH—

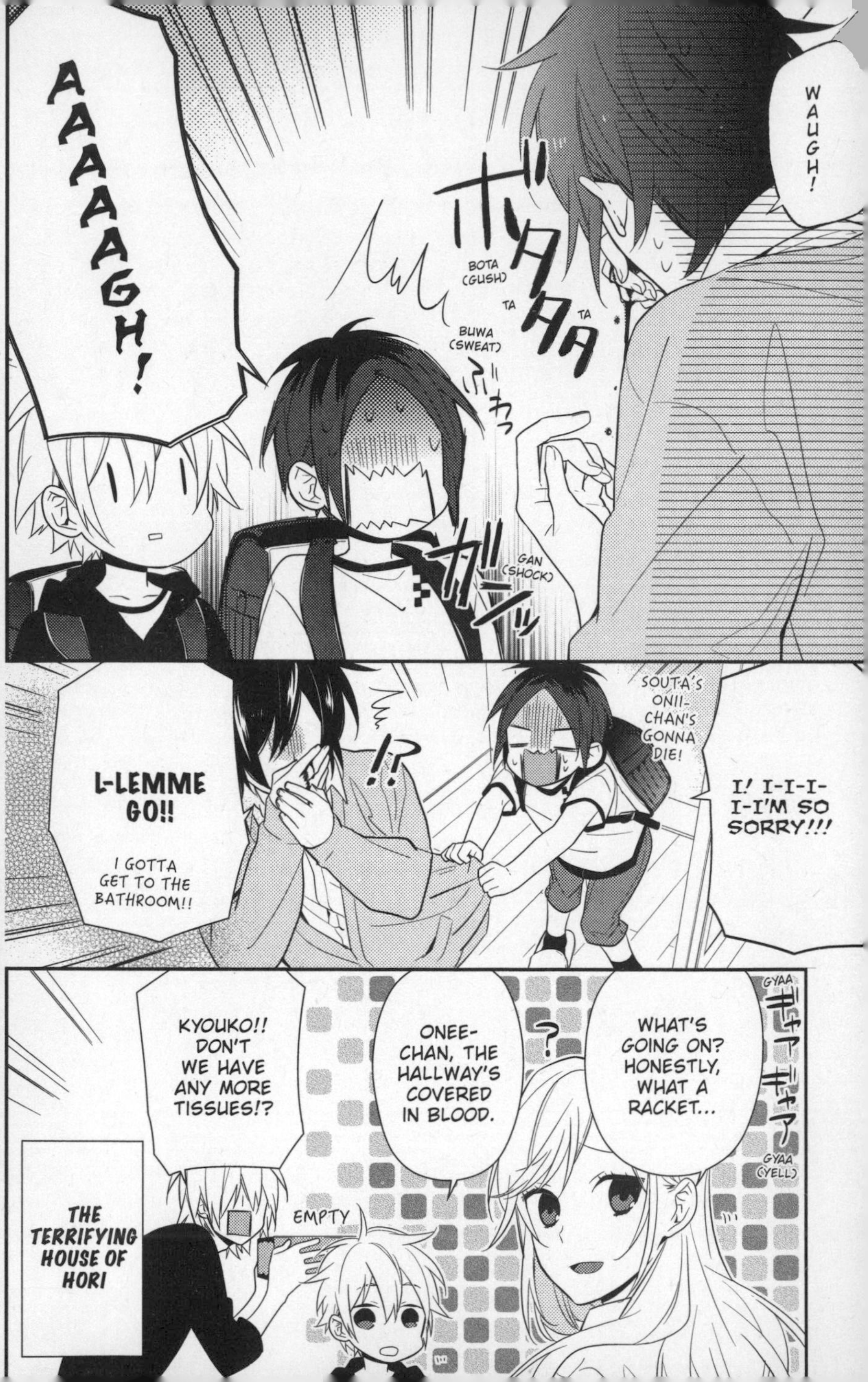
WAUGH!
ボタタタ
BOTA (GUSH)
TA
TA
BUWA (SWEAT)
ぶわっ
AAAAAGH!
ガーン
GAN (SHOCK)
SOUTA'S ONII-CHAN'S GONNA DIE!
I! I-I-I-I-I'M SO SORRY!!!
!?
L-LEMME GO!!
I GOTTA GET TO THE BATHROOM!!
GYAA
ギャア
ギャア
GYAA (YELL)
WHAT'S GOING ON? HONESTLY, WHAT A RACKET...
?
ONEE-CHAN, THE HALLWAY'S COVERED IN BLOOD.
KYOUKO!! DON'T WE HAVE ANY MORE TISSUES!?
EMPTY
THE TERRIFYING HOUSE OF HORI

HORIMIYA

HORIMIYA

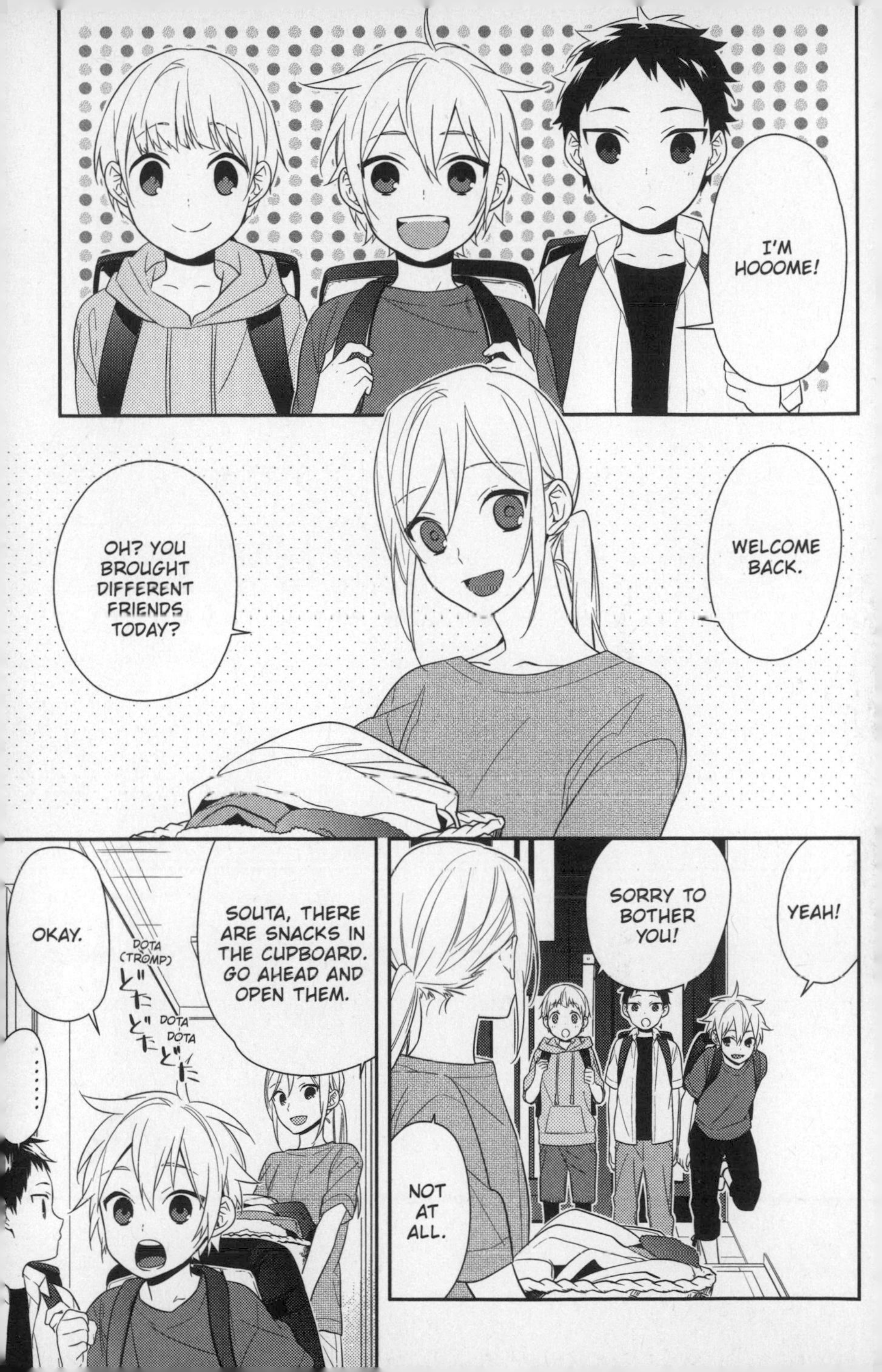
I'M HOOOME!
WELCOME BACK.
OH? YOU BROUGHT DIFFERENT FRIENDS TODAY?
YEAH!
SORRY TO BOTHER YOU!
NOT AT ALL.
SOUTA, THERE ARE SNACKS IN THE CUPBOARD. GO AHEAD AND OPEN THEM.
DOTA (TROMP)
どた
どた どた
DOTA DOTA
OKAY.
......

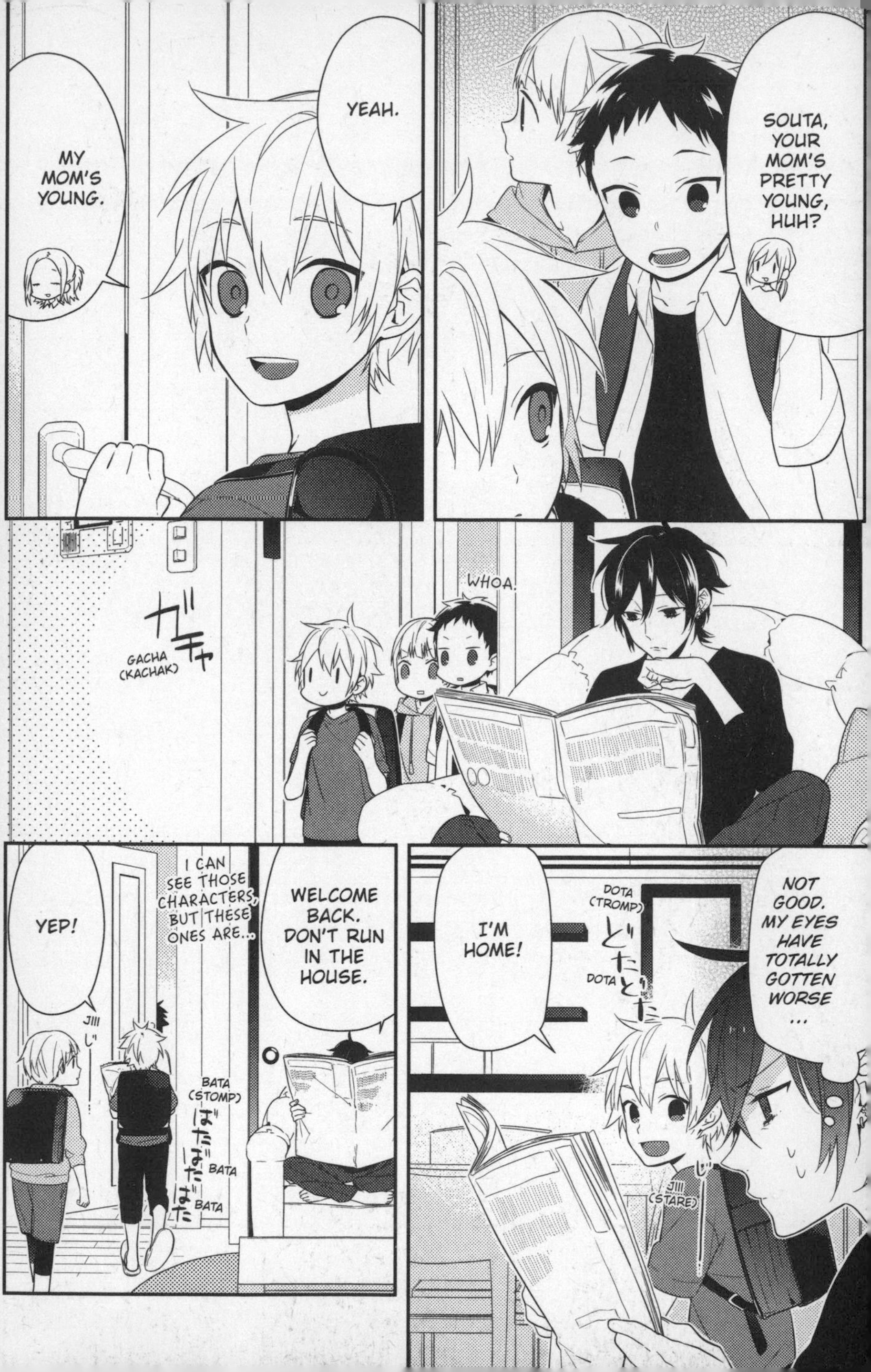
SOUTA, YOUR MOM'S PRETTY YOUNG, HUH?
YEAH.
MY MOM'S YOUNG.
WHOA!
ガチャ
GACHA (KACHAK)
NOT GOOD. MY EYES HAVE TOTALLY GOTTEN WORSE ...
DOTA (TROMP) どた
DOTA どた
I'M HOME!
じ
JIII (STARE)
WELCOME BACK. DON'T RUN IN THE HOUSE.
I CAN SEE THOSE CHARACTERS, BUT THESE ONES ARE...
YEP!
JIII じ
BATA (STOMP) ばた
BATA ばた
BATA

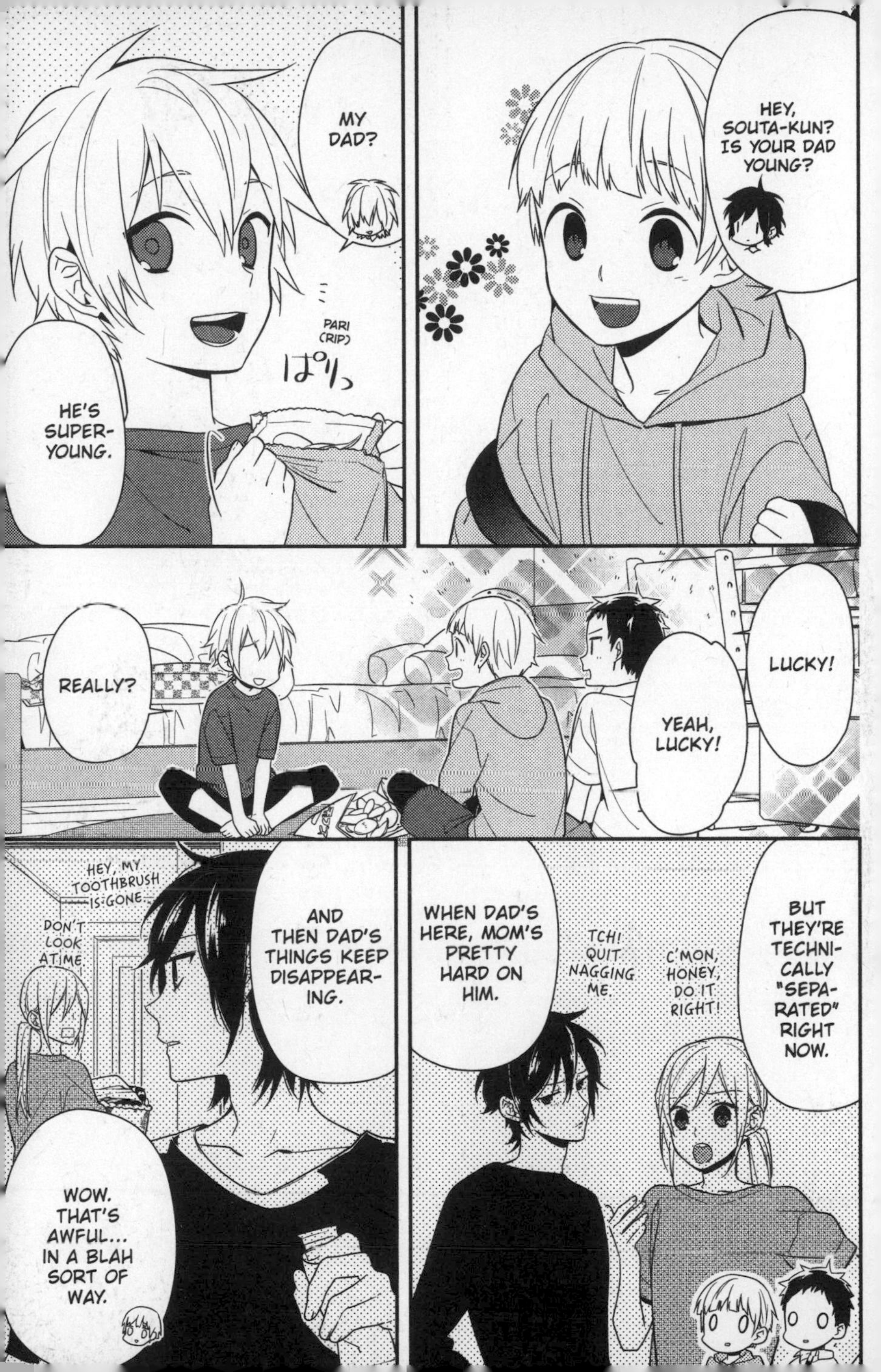
HEY, SOUTA-KUN? IS YOUR DAD YOUNG?
MY DAD?
PARI (RIP)
ぱりっ
HE'S SUPER-YOUNG.
LUCKY!
YEAH, LUCKY!
REALLY?
BUT THEY'RE TECHNICALLY "SEPARATED" RIGHT NOW.
C'MON, HONEY, DO IT RIGHT!
TCH! QUIT NAGGING ME.
WHEN DAD'S HERE, MOM'S PRETTY HARD ON HIM.
AND THEN DAD'S THINGS KEEP DISAPPEARING.
HEY, MY TOOTHBRUSH IS GONE...
DON'T LOOK AT ME.
WOW. THAT'S AWFUL... IN A BLAH SORT OF WAY.

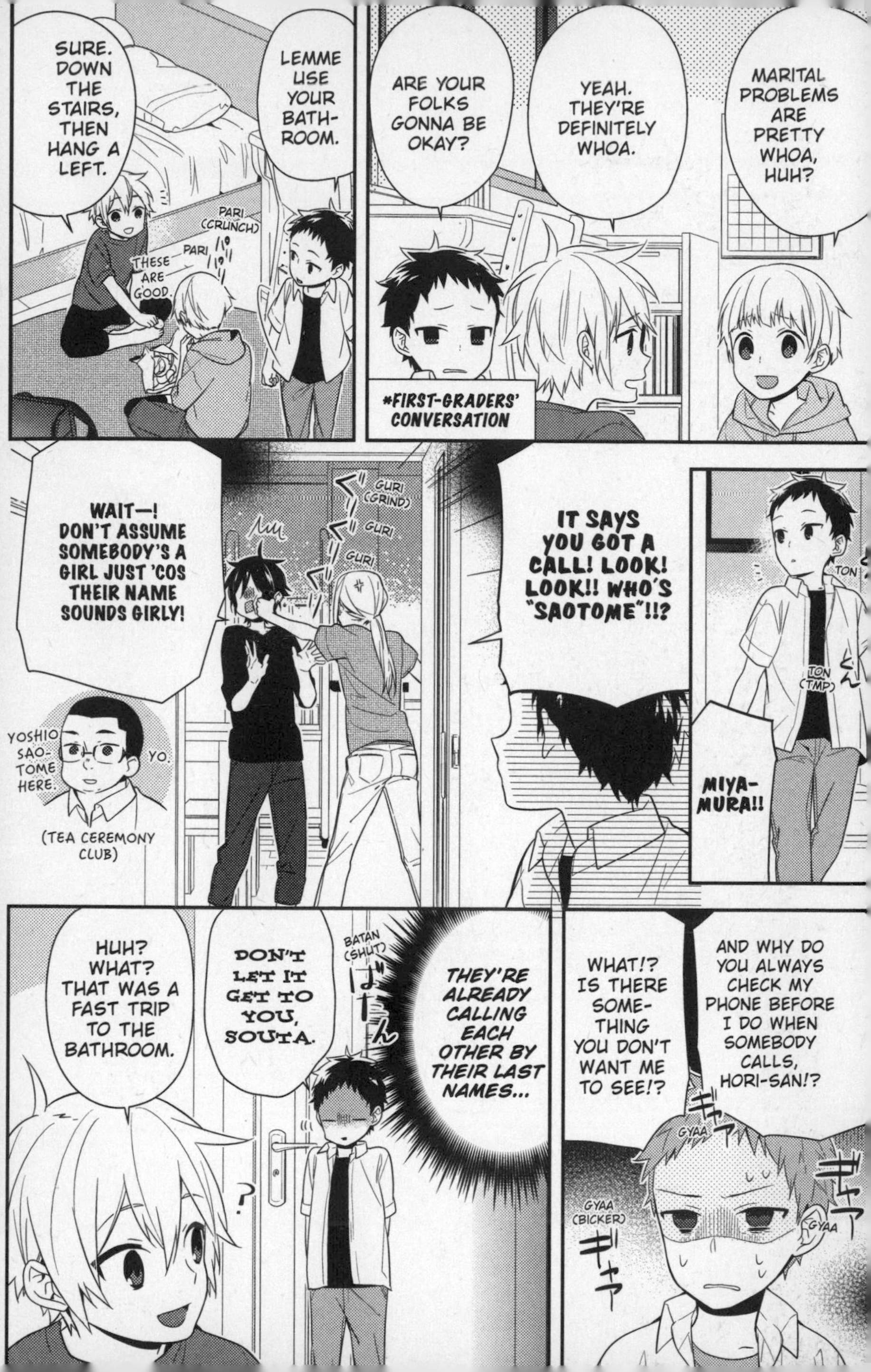
MARITAL PROBLEMS ARE PRETTY WHOA, HUH?
YEAH. THEY'RE DEFINITELY WHOA.
ARE YOUR FOLKS GONNA BE OKAY?
#FIRST-GRADERS' CONVERSATION
LEMME USE YOUR BATH-ROOM.
SURE. DOWN THE STAIRS, THEN HANG A LEFT.
PARI (CRUNCH)
PARI
THESE ARE GOOD.
TON
TON (TMP)
MIYA-MURA!!
IT SAYS YOU GOT A CALL! LOOK! LOOK!! WHO'S "SAOTOME"!!?
GURI (GRIND)
GURI
GURI
WAIT—! DON'T ASSUME SOMEBODY'S A GIRL JUST 'COS THEIR NAME SOUNDS GIRLY!
YOSHIO SAO-TOME HERE.
YO.
(TEA CEREMONY CLUB)
AND WHY DO YOU ALWAYS CHECK MY PHONE BEFORE I DO WHEN SOMEBODY CALLS, HORI-SAN!?
WHAT!? IS THERE SOME-THING YOU DON'T WANT ME TO SEE!?
GYAA
GYAA
GYAA (BICKER)
THEY'RE ALREADY CALLING EACH OTHER BY THEIR LAST NAMES...
BATAN (SHUT)
DON'T LET IT GET TO YOU, SOUTA.
HUH? WHAT? THAT WAS A FAST TRIP TO THE BATHROOM.
?

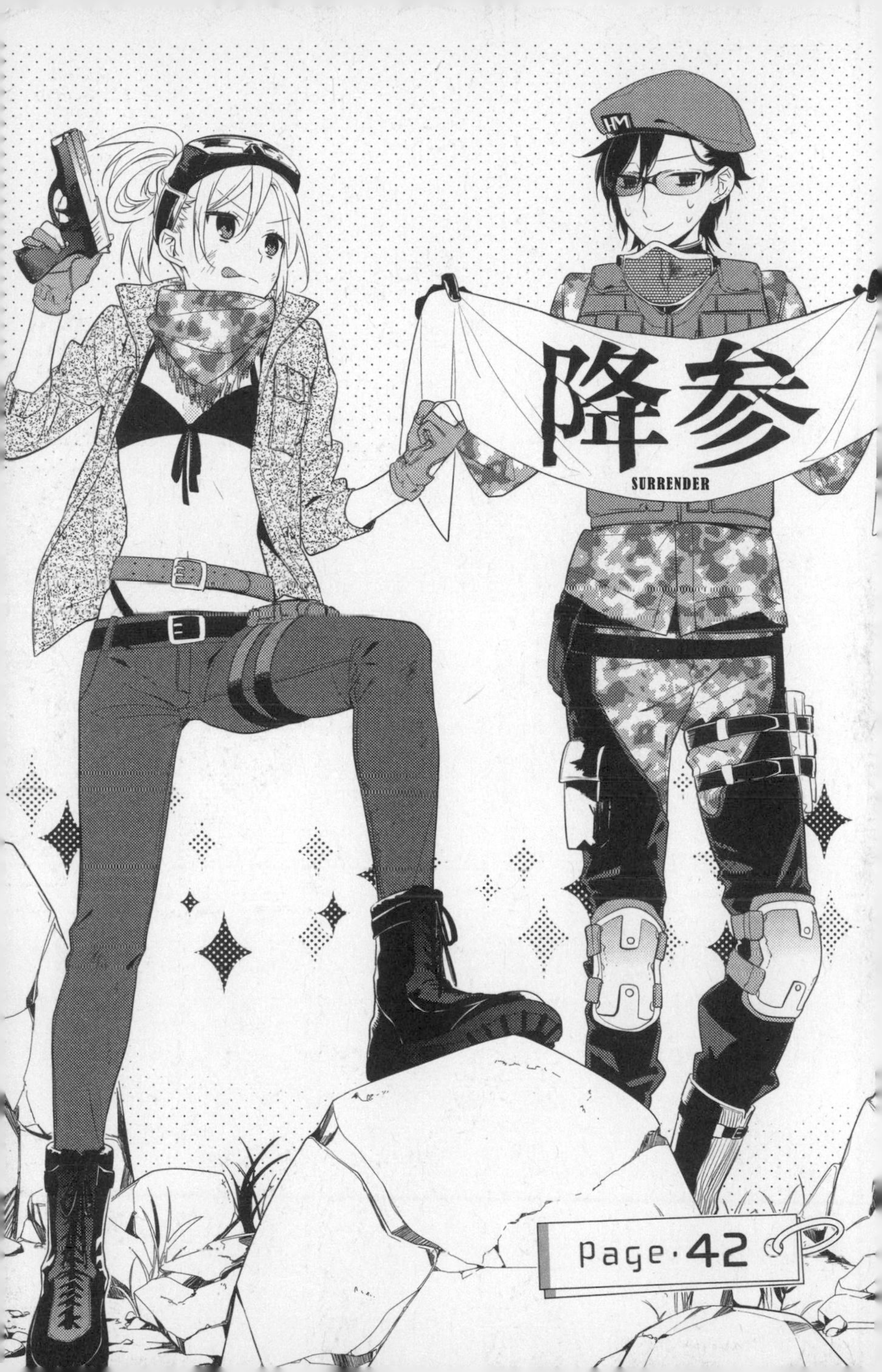
降参
SURRENDER
page.42

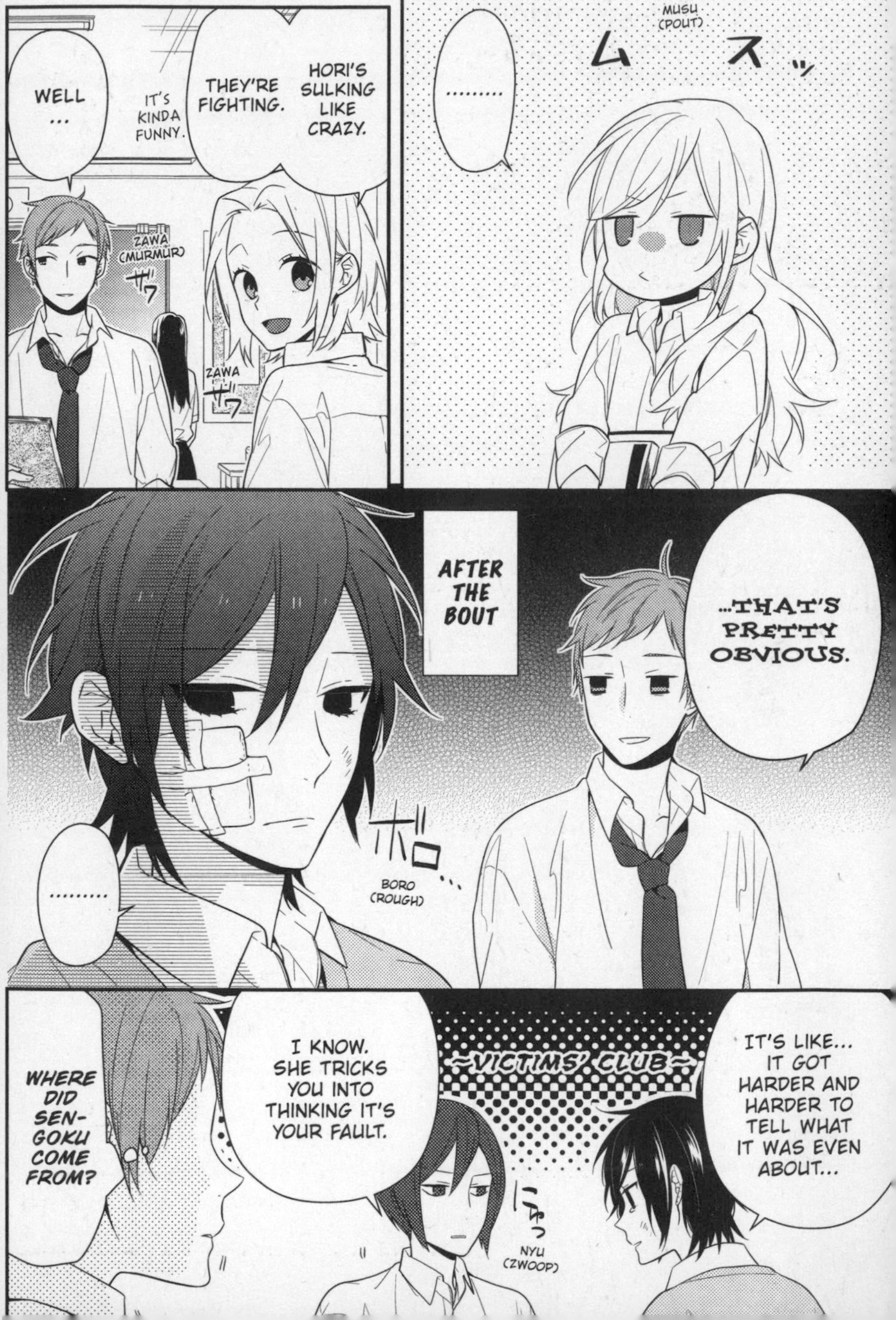
MUSU (POUT)
ムスッ
....
HORI'S SULKING LIKE CRAZY.
THEY'RE FIGHTING.
IT'S KINDA FUNNY.
WELL ...
ZAWA (MURMUR)
ザワ
ZAWA
ザワ
...THAT'S PRETTY OBVIOUS.
AFTER THE BOUT
BORO (ROUGH)
ボロ…
....
IT'S LIKE... IT GOT HARDER AND HARDER TO TELL WHAT IT WAS EVEN ABOUT...
~VICTIMS' CLUB~
I KNOW. SHE TRICKS YOU INTO THINKING IT'S YOUR FAULT.
NYU (ZWOOP)
にゅっ
WHERE DID SEN-GOKU COME FROM?

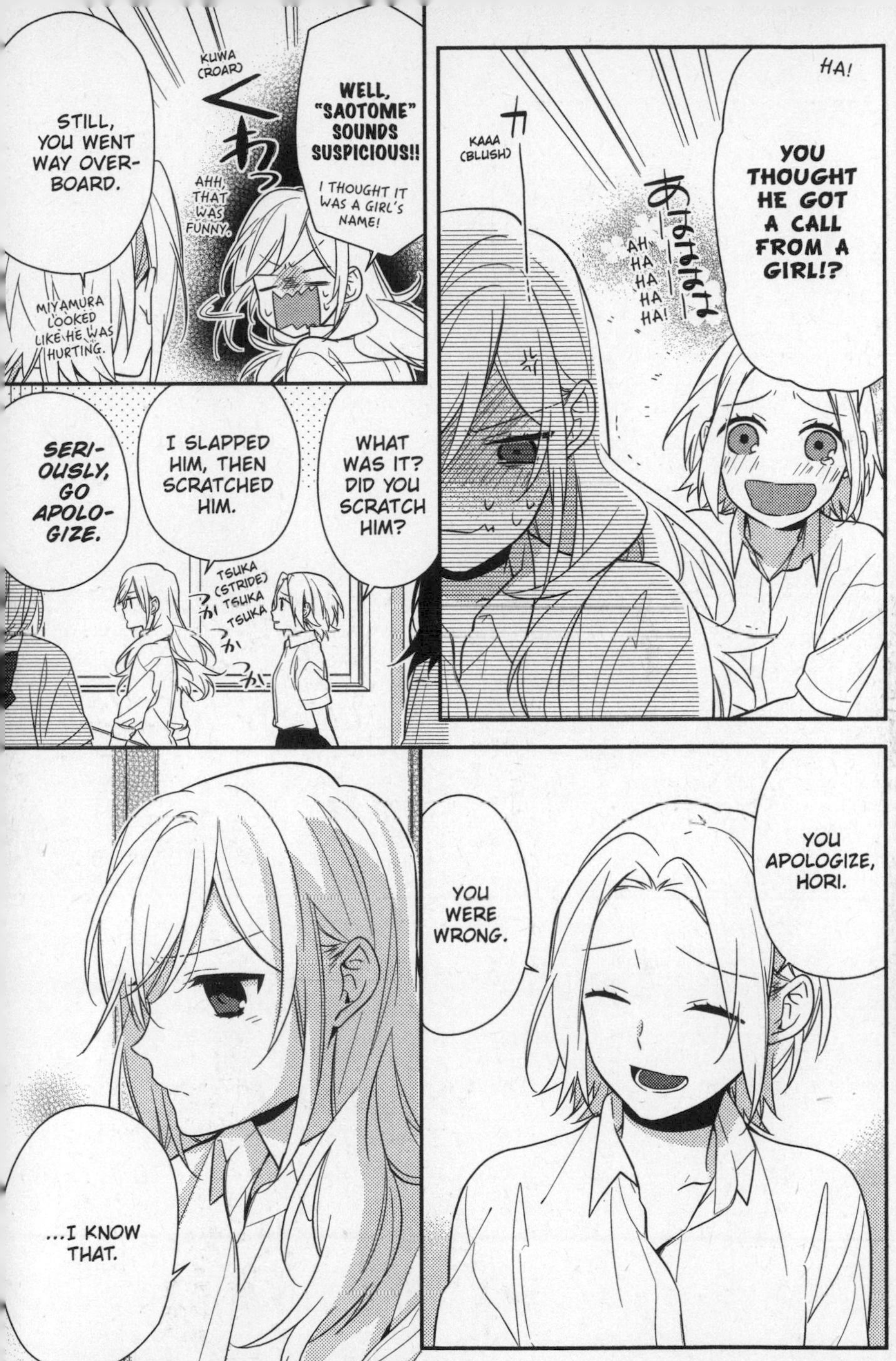
HA!
YOU THOUGHT HE GOT A CALL FROM A GIRL!?
AH HA HA HA HA!
あはははは
KAAA (BLUSH)
カ
WELL, "SAOTOME" SOUNDS SUSPICIOUS!!
I THOUGHT IT WAS A GIRL'S NAME!
KUWA (ROAR)
くわっ
AHH, THAT WAS FUNNY.
STILL, YOU WENT WAY OVER-BOARD.
MIYAMURA LOOKED LIKE HE WAS HURTING.
WHAT WAS IT? DID YOU SCRATCH HIM?
I SLAPPED HIM, THEN SCRATCHED HIM.
TSUKA (STRIDE) TSUKA TSUKA
SERI-OUSLY, GO APOLO-GIZE.
YOU APOLOGIZE, HORI.
YOU WERE WRONG.
...I KNOW THAT.

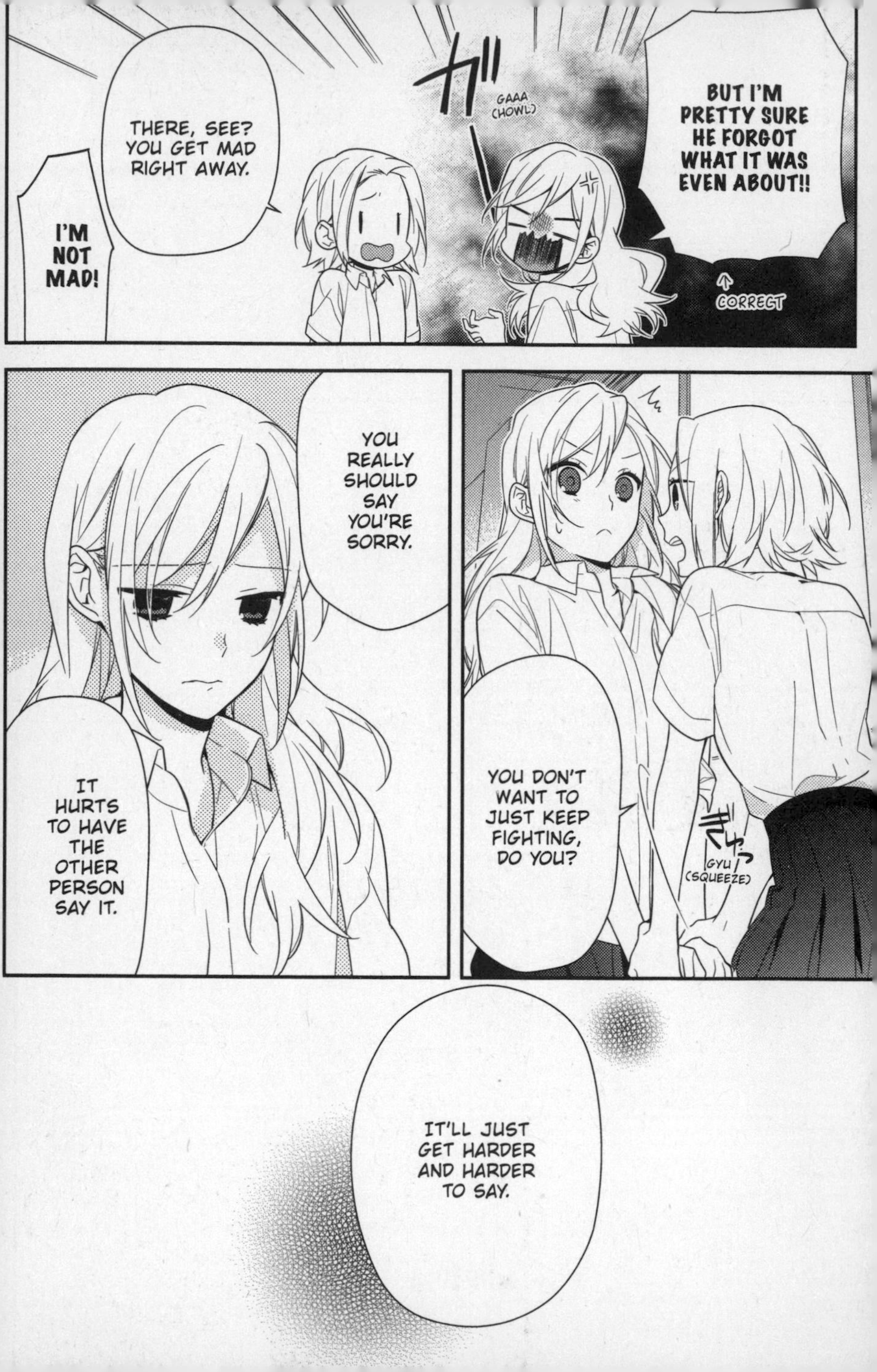
BUT I'M PRETTY SURE HE FORGOT WHAT IT WAS EVEN ABOUT!!
↑ CORRECT
GAAA (HOWL)
THERE, SEE? YOU GET MAD RIGHT AWAY.
I'M NOT MAD!
YOU DON'T WANT TO JUST KEEP FIGHTING, DO YOU?
GYU (SQUEEZE)
YOU REALLY SHOULD SAY YOU'RE SORRY.
IT HURTS TO HAVE THE OTHER PERSON SAY IT.
IT'LL JUST GET HARDER AND HARDER TO SAY.

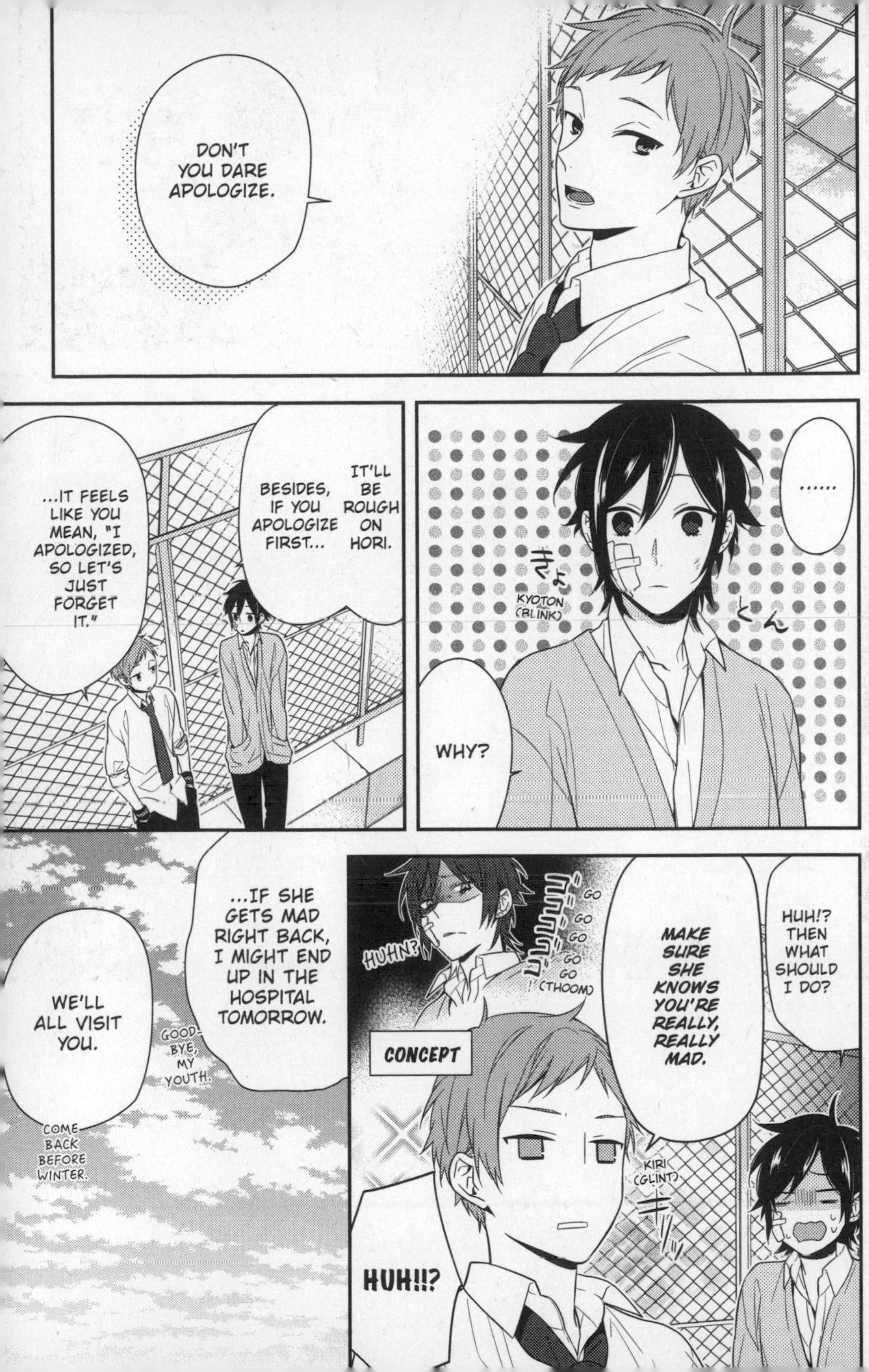
DON'T YOU DARE APOLOGIZE.
......
きょ
KYOTON (BLINK)
とん
WHY?
BESIDES, IF YOU APOLOGIZE FIRST... IT'LL BE ROUGH ON HORI.
...IT FEELS LIKE YOU MEAN, "I APOLOGIZED, SO LET'S JUST FORGET IT."
HUH!? THEN WHAT SHOULD I DO?
MAKE SURE SHE KNOWS YOU'RE REALLY, REALLY MAD.
HUHN?
GO GO GO GO GO (THOOM)
CONCEPT
KIRI (GLINT)
HUH!!?
...IF SHE GETS MAD RIGHT BACK, I MIGHT END UP IN THE HOSPITAL TOMORROW.
GOOD-BYE, MY YOUTH.
WE'LL ALL VISIT YOU.
COME BACK BEFORE WINTER.

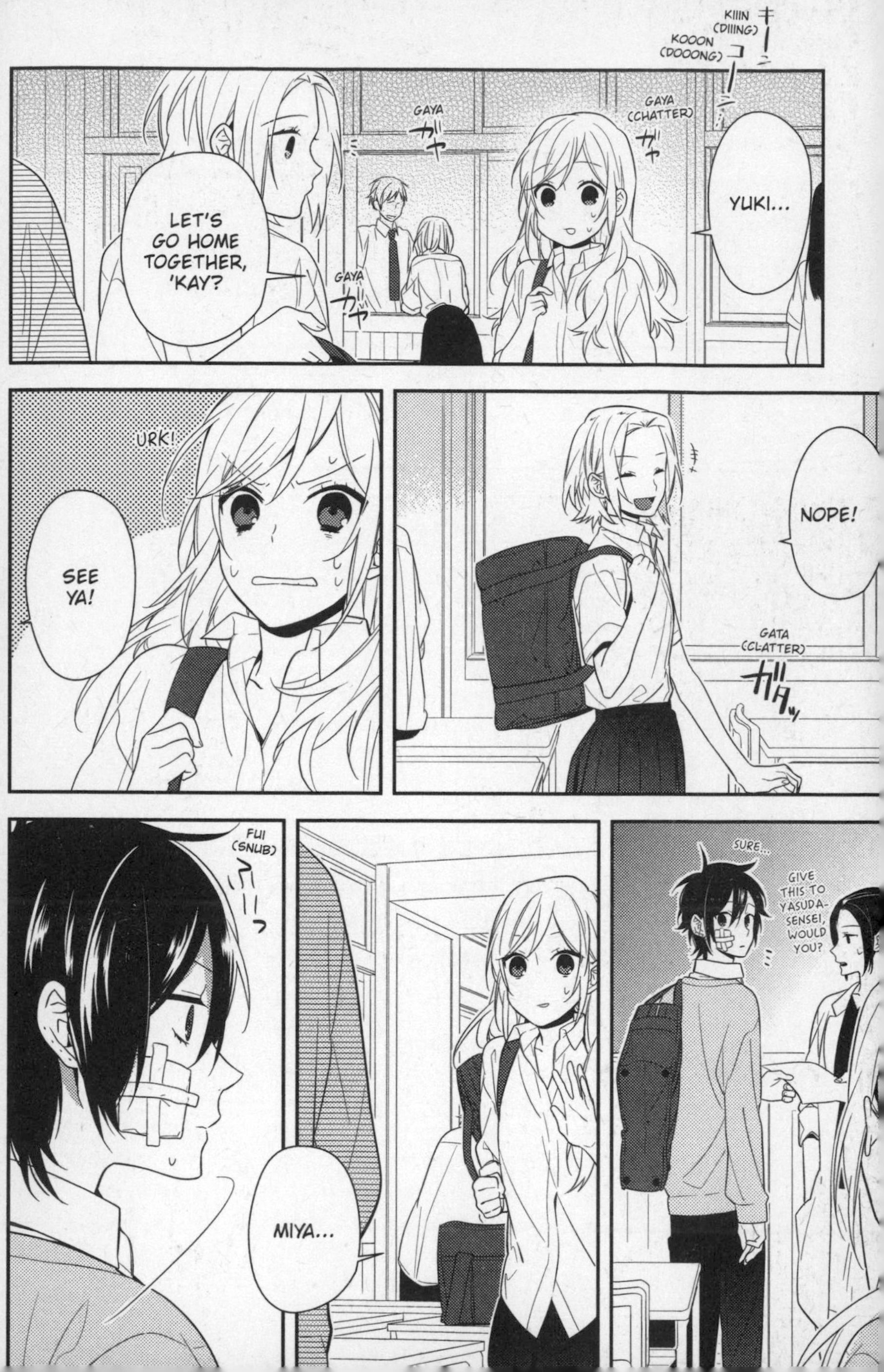
KIIN (DIIING)
KOOON (DOOONG)
YUKI...
GAYA (CHATTER)
GAYA
LET'S GO HOME TOGETHER, 'KAY?
GAYA
NOPE!
GATA (CLATTER)
URK!
SEE YA!
GIVE THIS TO YASUDA-SENSEI, WOULD YOU?
SURE...
FUI (SNUB)
MIYA...

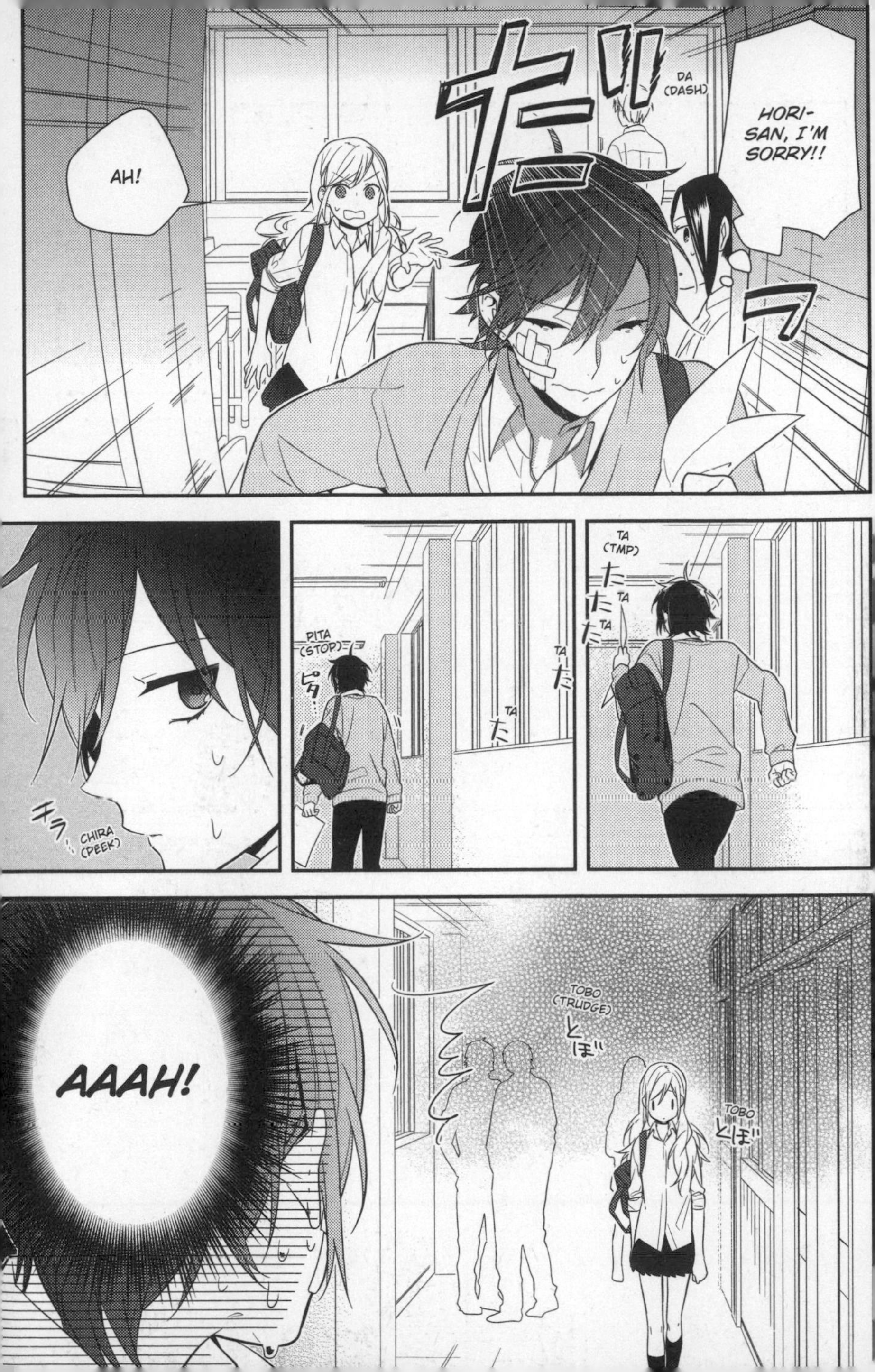
HORI-SAN, I'M SORRY!!
たッ
DA (DASH)
AH!
TA (TMP)
たたた
TA
TA
TA
だ
TA
た
PITA (STOP)
ピタ
チラ
CHIRA (PEEK)
TOBO (TRUDGE)
とぼ
TOBO
とぼ
AAAH!

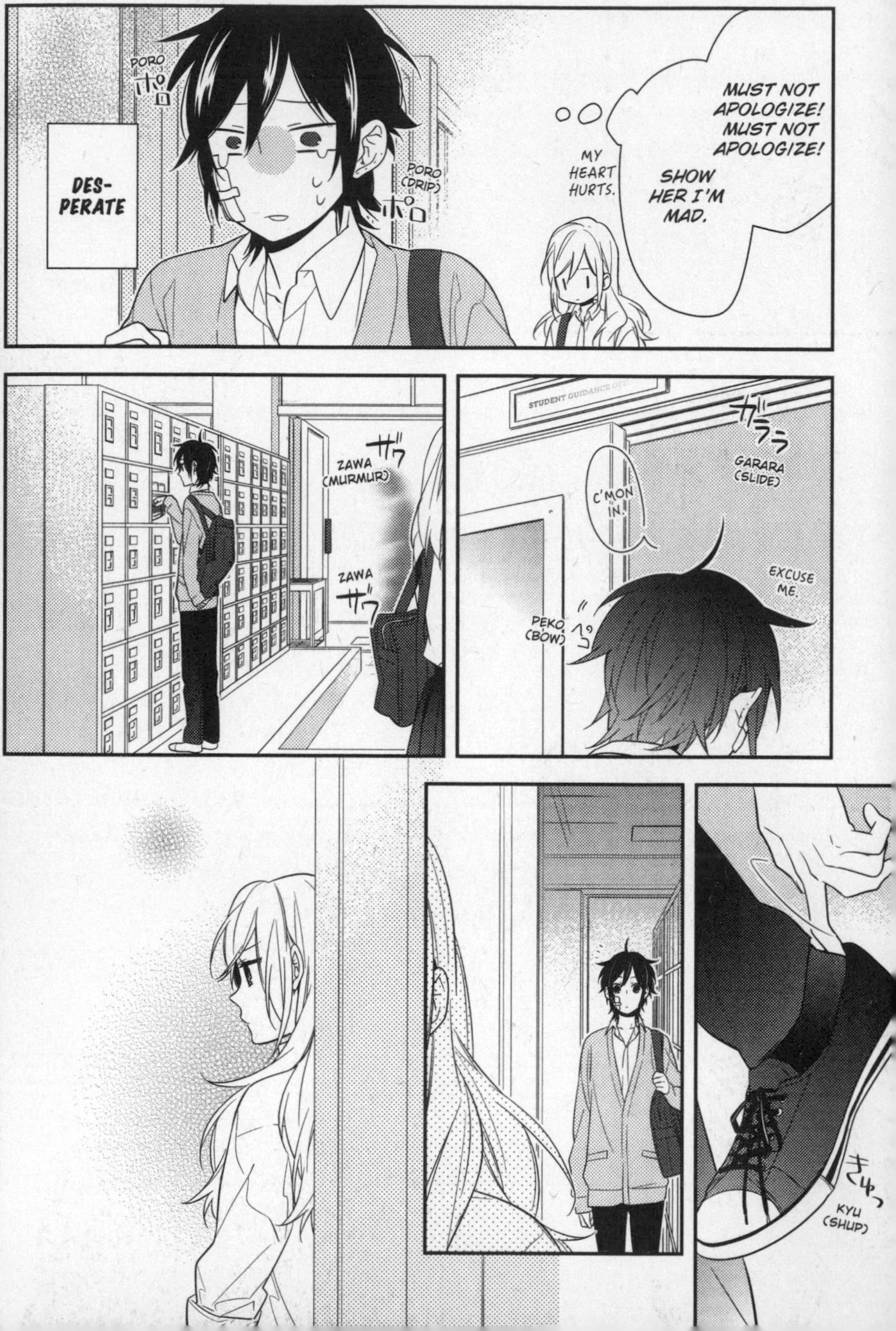
MUST NOT APOLOGIZE! MUST NOT APOLOGIZE!
SHOW HER I'M MAD.
MY HEART HURTS.
PORO (DRIP)
ポロ
PORO
ポロ
DES-PERATE
ガララ
GARARA (SLIDE)
C'MON IN.
EXCUSE ME.
PEKO (BOW)
ペコ
ザワ
ZAWA (MURMUR)
ZAWA
ザワ
きゅっ
KYU (SHUP)

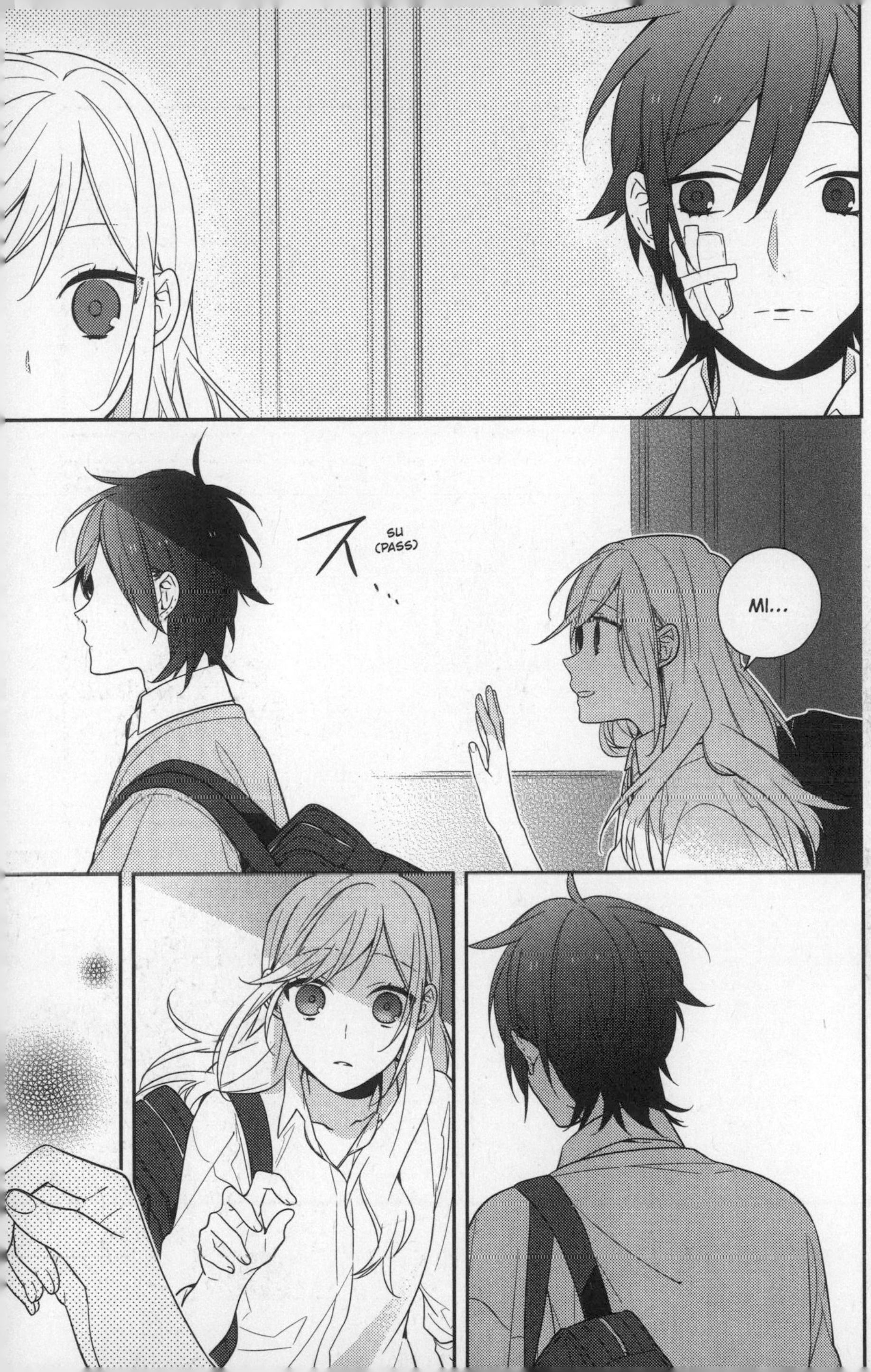
ス
SU
(PASS)
MI...

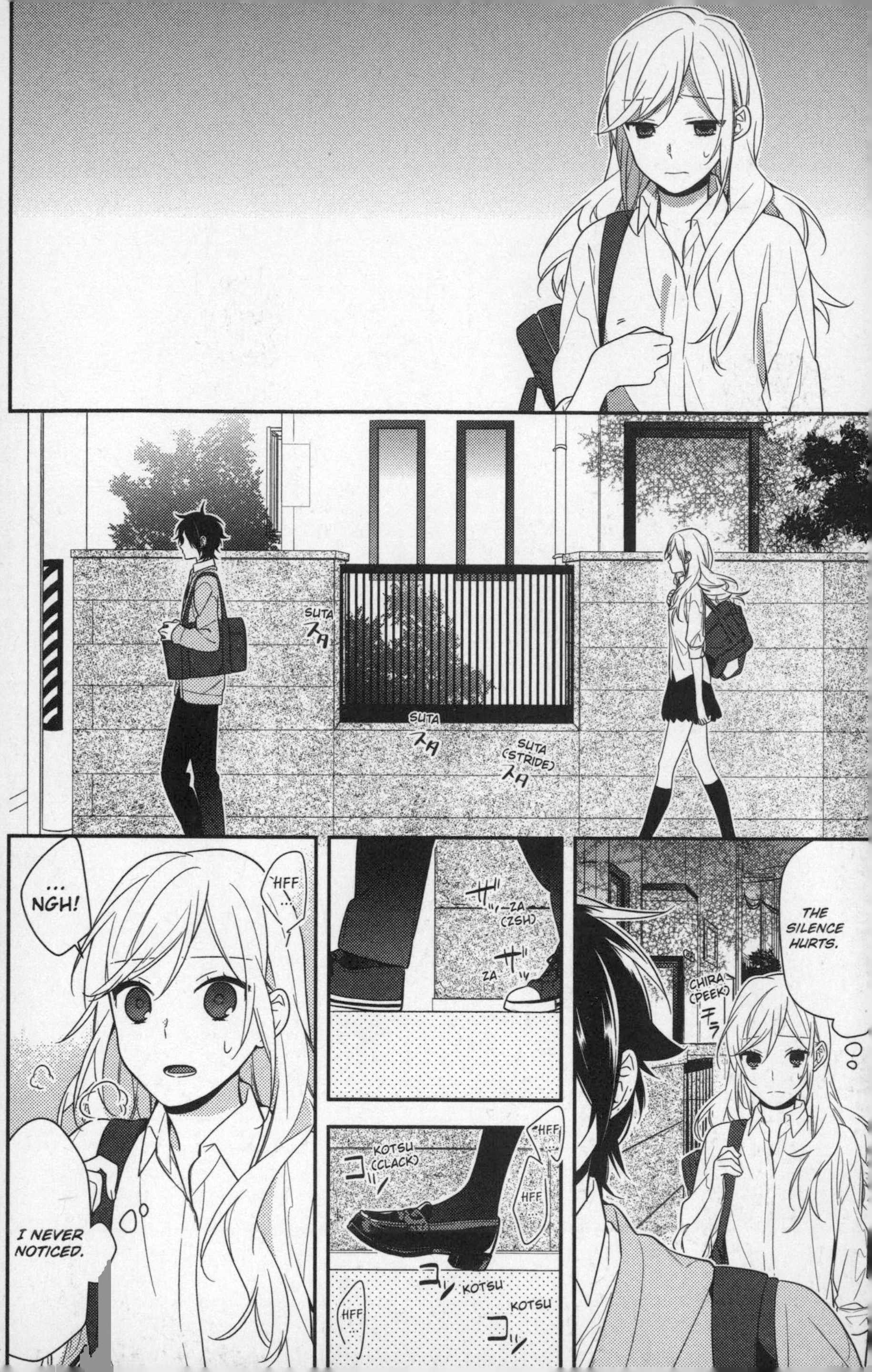
SUTA (STRIDE) スタ
SUTA スタ
SUTA スタ
THE SILENCE HURTS.
CHIRA (PEEK) チラ
ZA (ZSH) ザッ
ZA ザッ
HFF ... HFF
KOTSU (CLACK) コツ
KOTSU コツ
KOTSU コツ
HFF
... NGH!
HFF ...
I NEVER NOTICED.

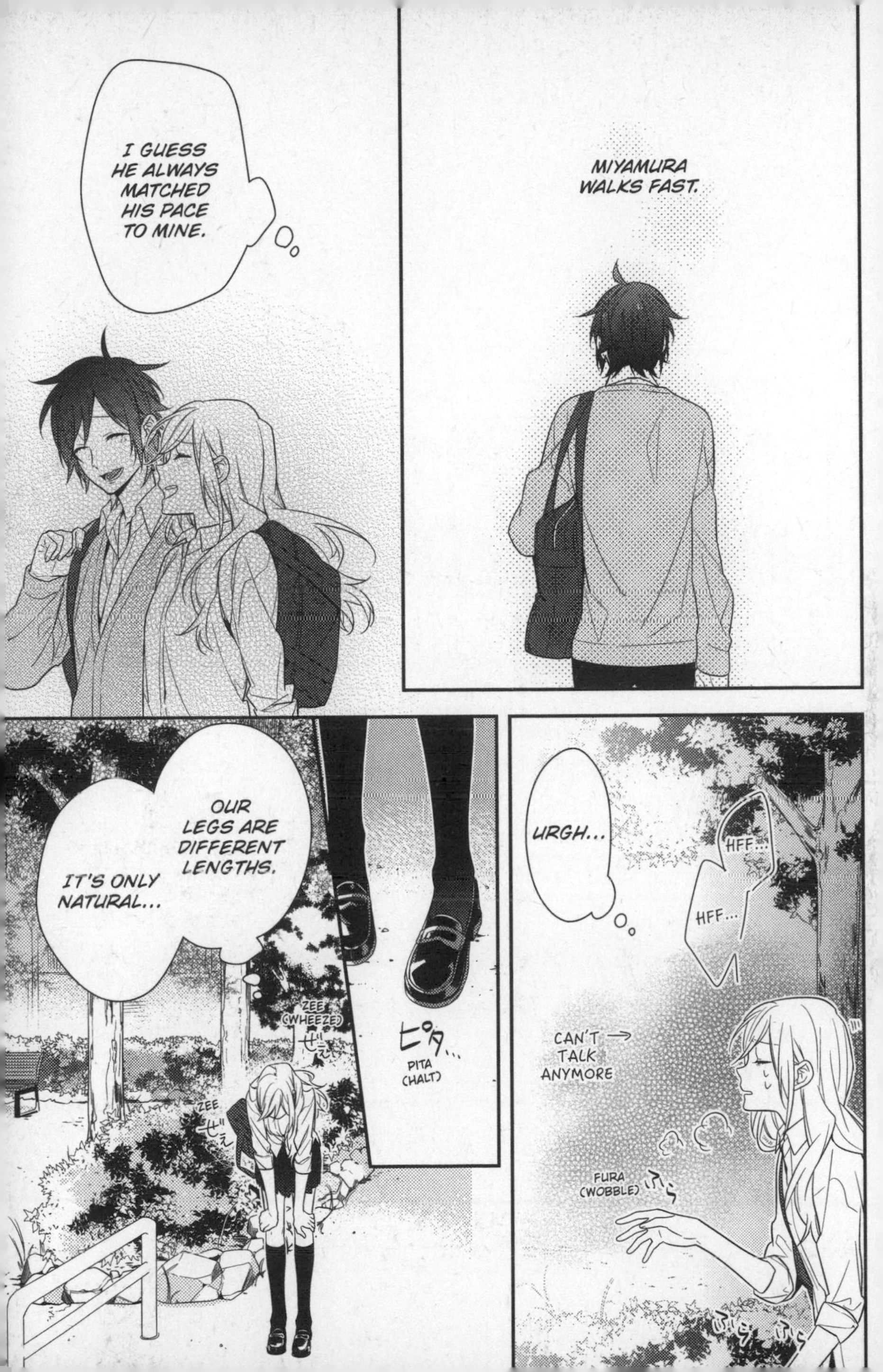
MIYAMURA WALKS FAST.
I GUESS HE ALWAYS MATCHED HIS PACE TO MINE.
URGH...
HFF...
HFF...
CAN'T TALK ANYMORE →
FURA (WOBBLE) ふら
ふら ふら
ピタ…
PITA (HALT)
OUR LEGS ARE DIFFERENT LENGTHS.
IT'S ONLY NATURAL...
ZEE (WHEEZE) ぜぇ
ZEE ぜぇ

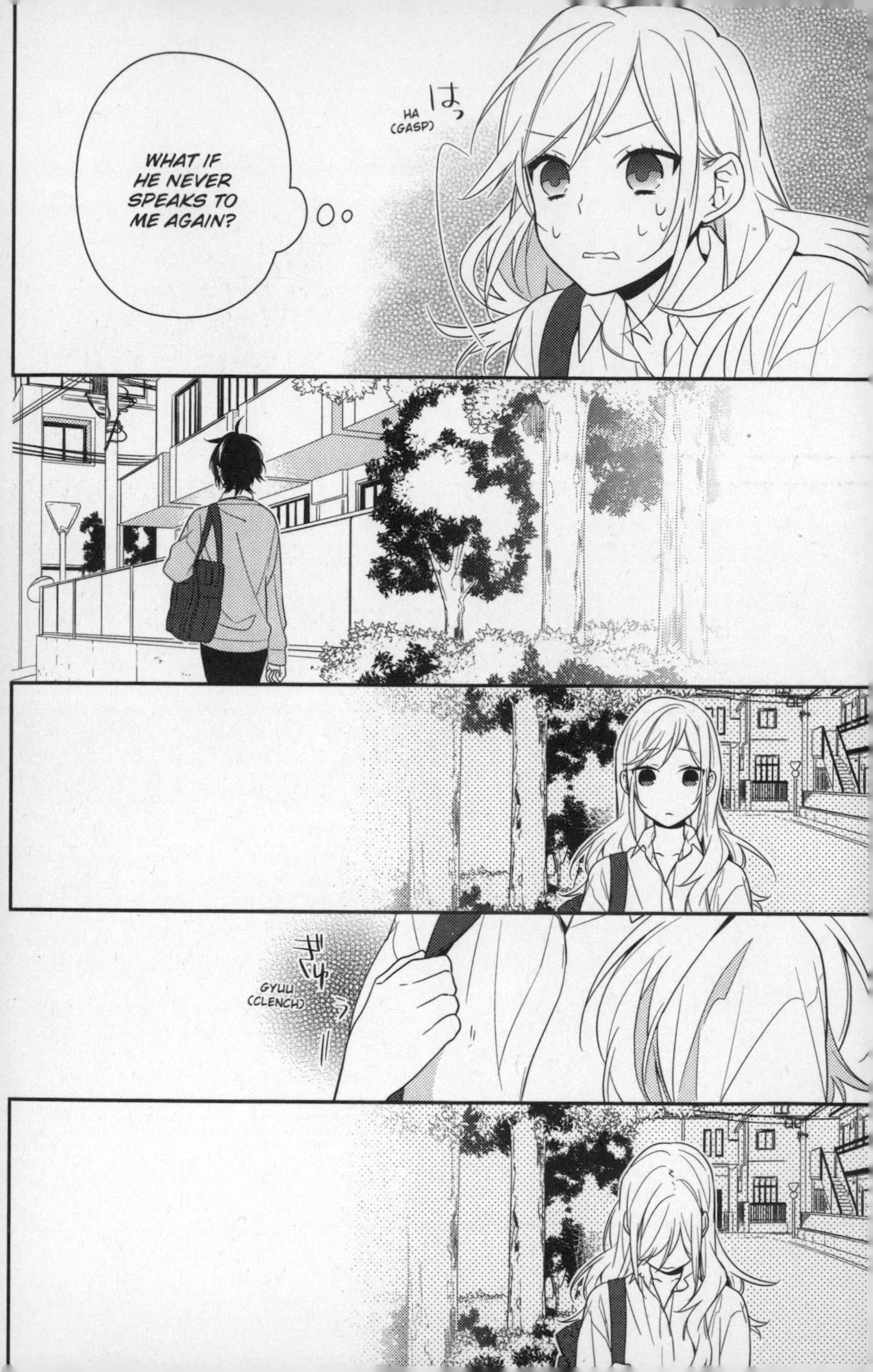
はっ
HA (GASP)
WHAT IF HE NEVER SPEAKS TO ME AGAIN?
ぎゅっ
GYUU (CLENCH)

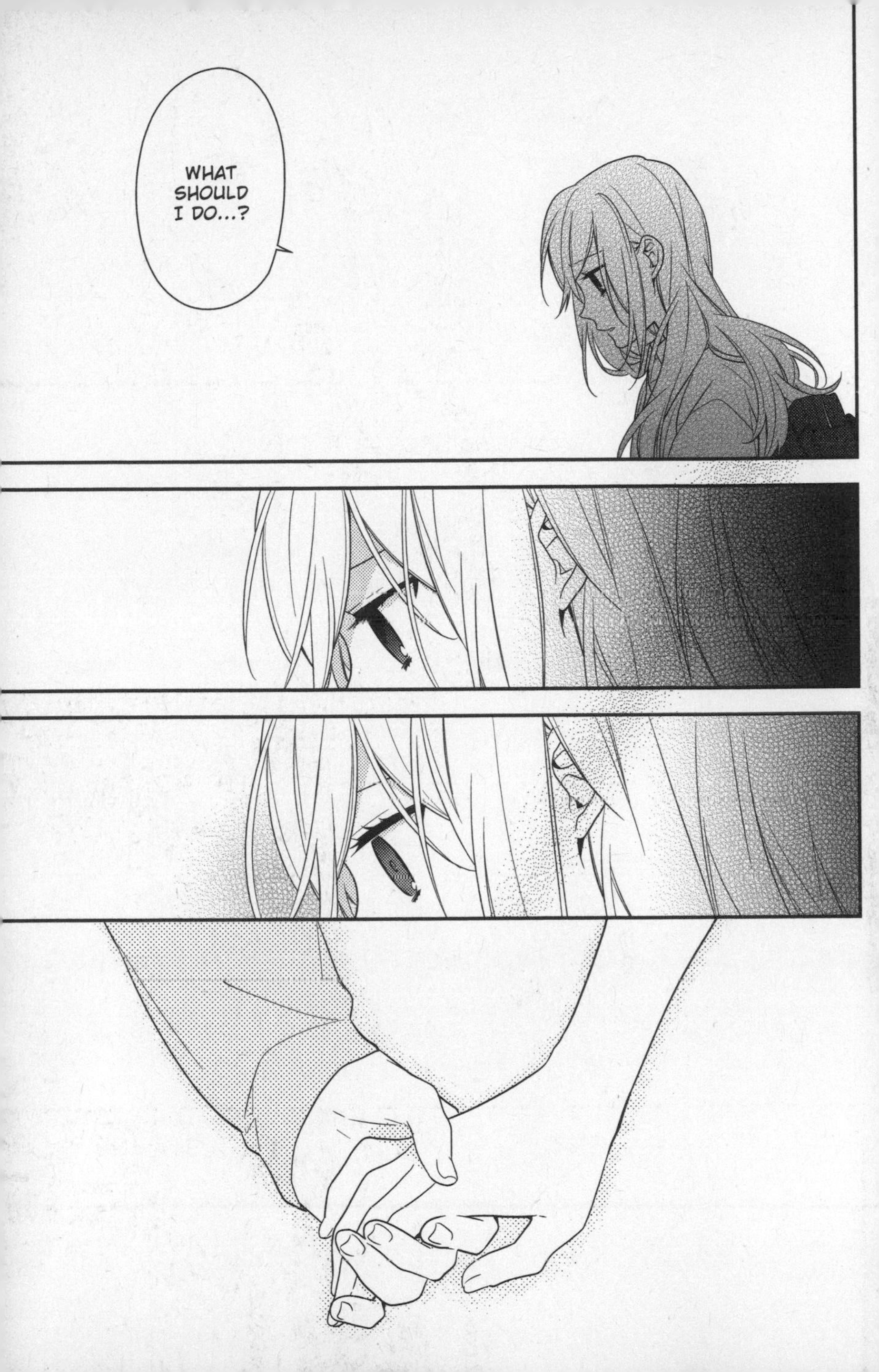
WHAT SHOULD I DO...?

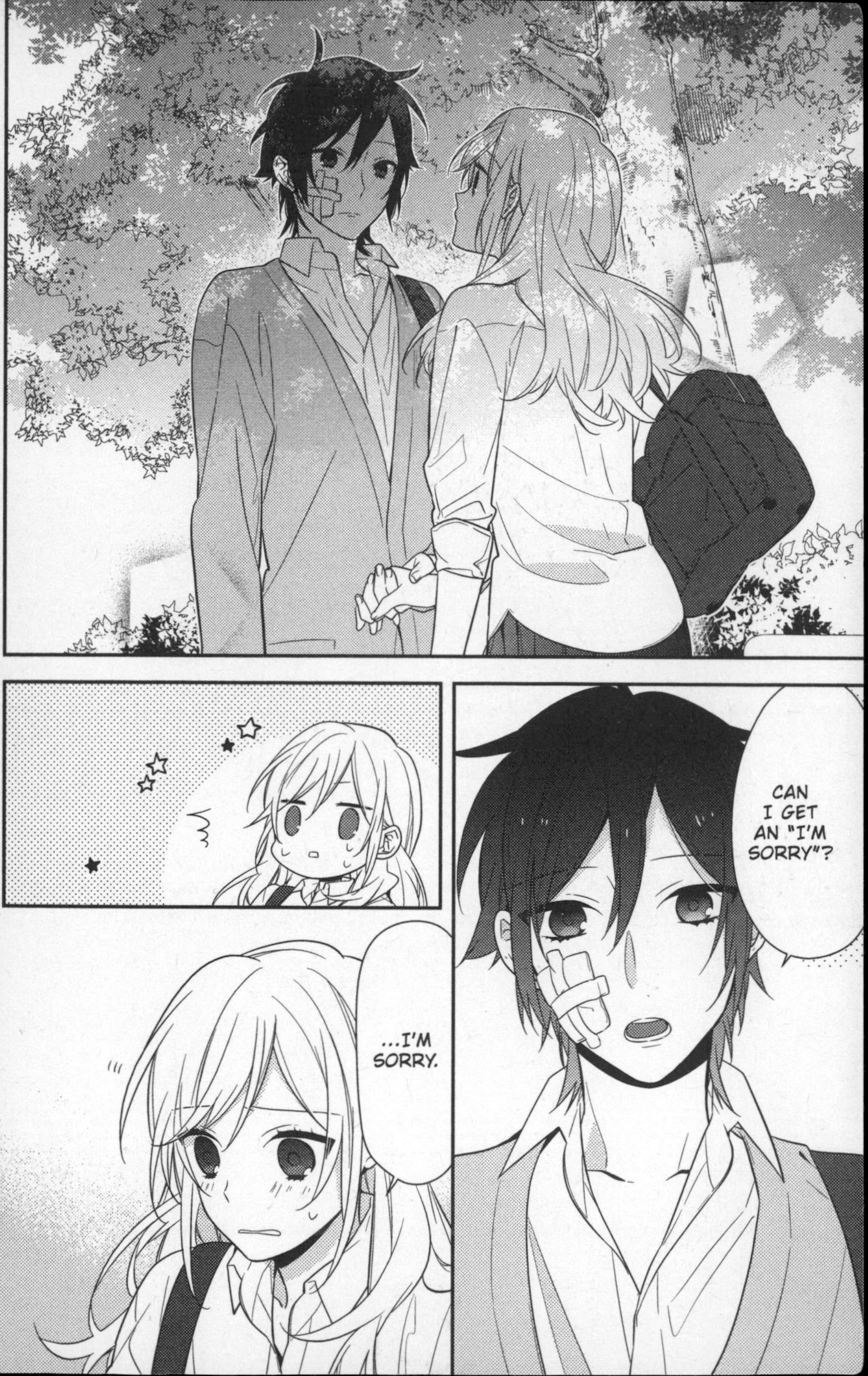
CAN I GET AN "I'M SORRY"?
...I'M SORRY.

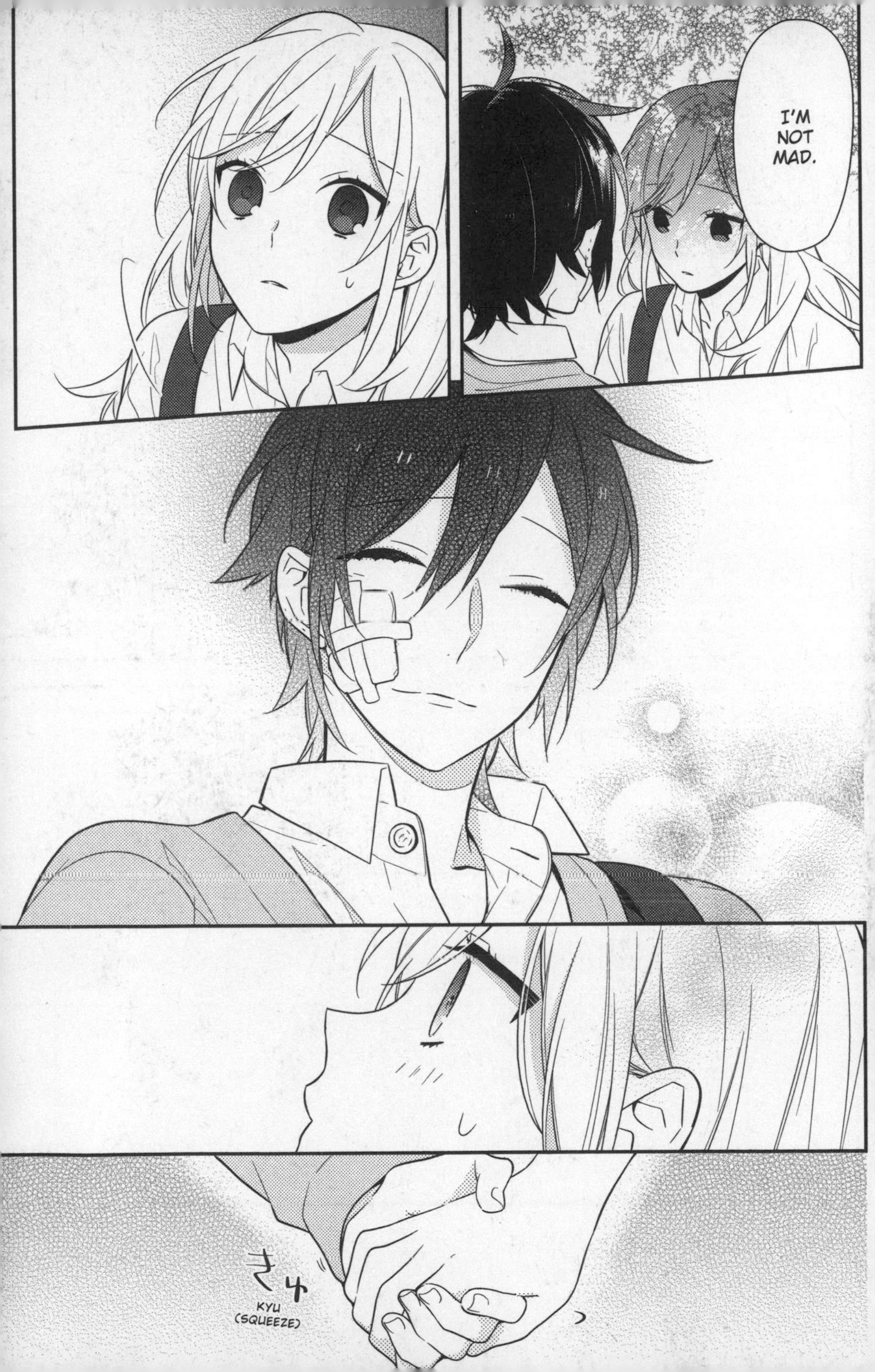
I'M NOT MAD.
きゅ
KYU (SQUEEZE)

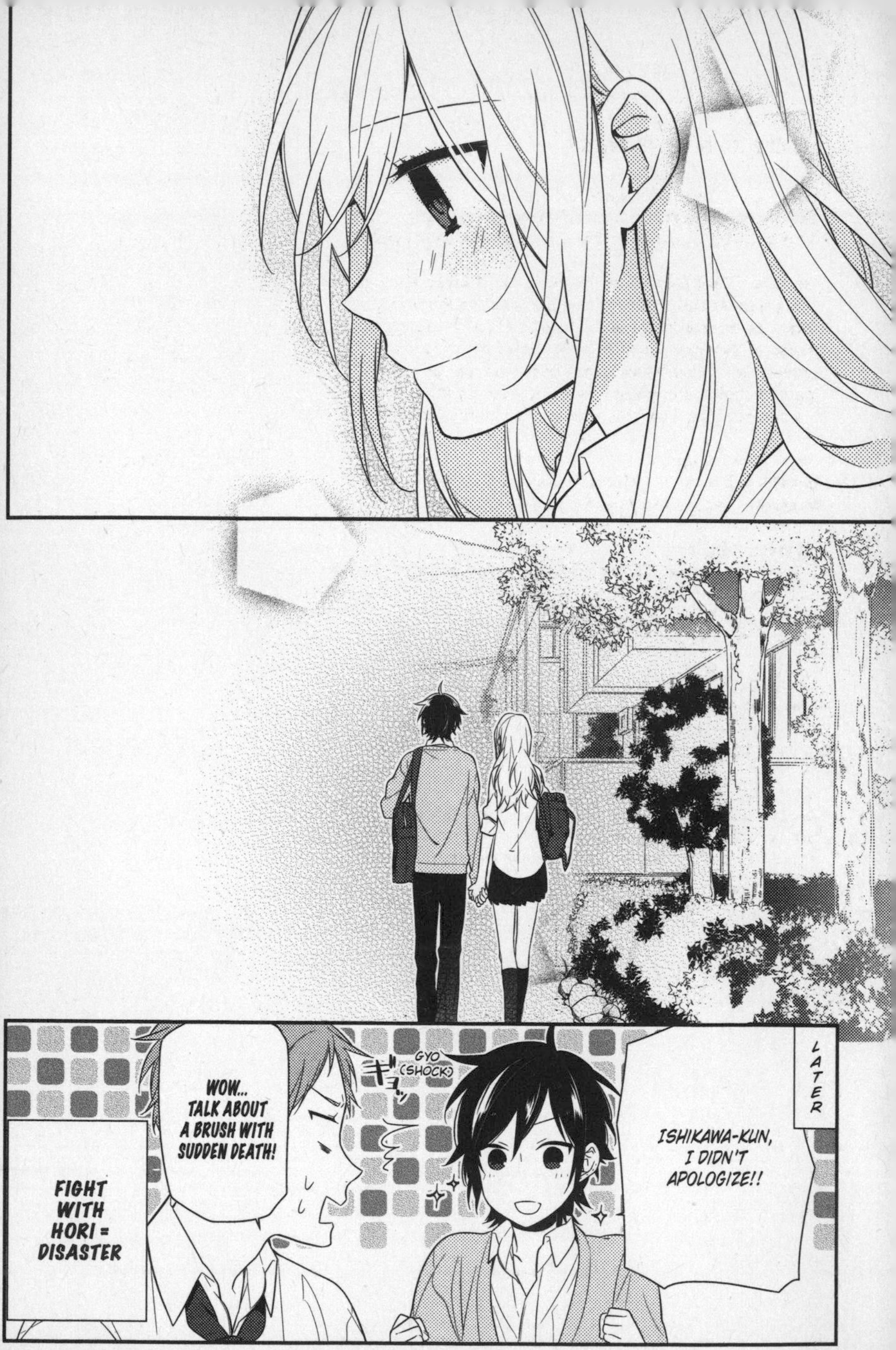
LATER
ISHIKAWA-KUN, I DIDN'T APOLOGIZE!!
GYO (SHOCK)
WOW... TALK ABOUT A BRUSH WITH SUDDEN DEATH!
FIGHT WITH HORI = DISASTER

Translation Notes

Page 25 – Sakura-colored cookies
Sakura is the Japanese word for "cherry tree." It is also used to refer to the blossoms of the tree, which are a pale pink.

Page 60 – *Dead Ghost Guardian ~The Third Nightmare~*
The Japanese title, *Haigorei*, is a pun because the first character means "deserted," "abandoned," or "dead." Typically, *haigorei* is written with different kanji and refers to a ghost that's always at someone's back, a sort of unlicensed guardian spirit. The ghost may think they're protecting the person, but they generally end up causing big problems.

Page 132 – *Youkai*
This term is a catch-all for supernatural creatures that often have ties to Japanese folklore.

Page 135 – *Kappa*
A *kappa* is a vaguely human-looking water spirit from Japanese folklore. It is usually depicted with greenish skin, a beak, a shell, and a water-filled plate or cavity on top of its head. *Kappa* are said to have a lusty attitude toward women.

Page 139 – *The Inugamis* thing
The Inugamis is a famous Japanese film from 1976 that was remade in 2006. In this thriller, one of the murder victims is discovered in a lake with his legs sticking up in the air.

Page 161 – Saotome
Saotome as a common noun means "young maiden" and is used to refer to the women who would traditionally plant the rice in the paddies during rice-planting seasons in Japan.

Page 176 – *Niboshi*
Niboshi are small, whole dried sardines.

To Be Continued...

BONUS MANGA: MYAMURA ⑤

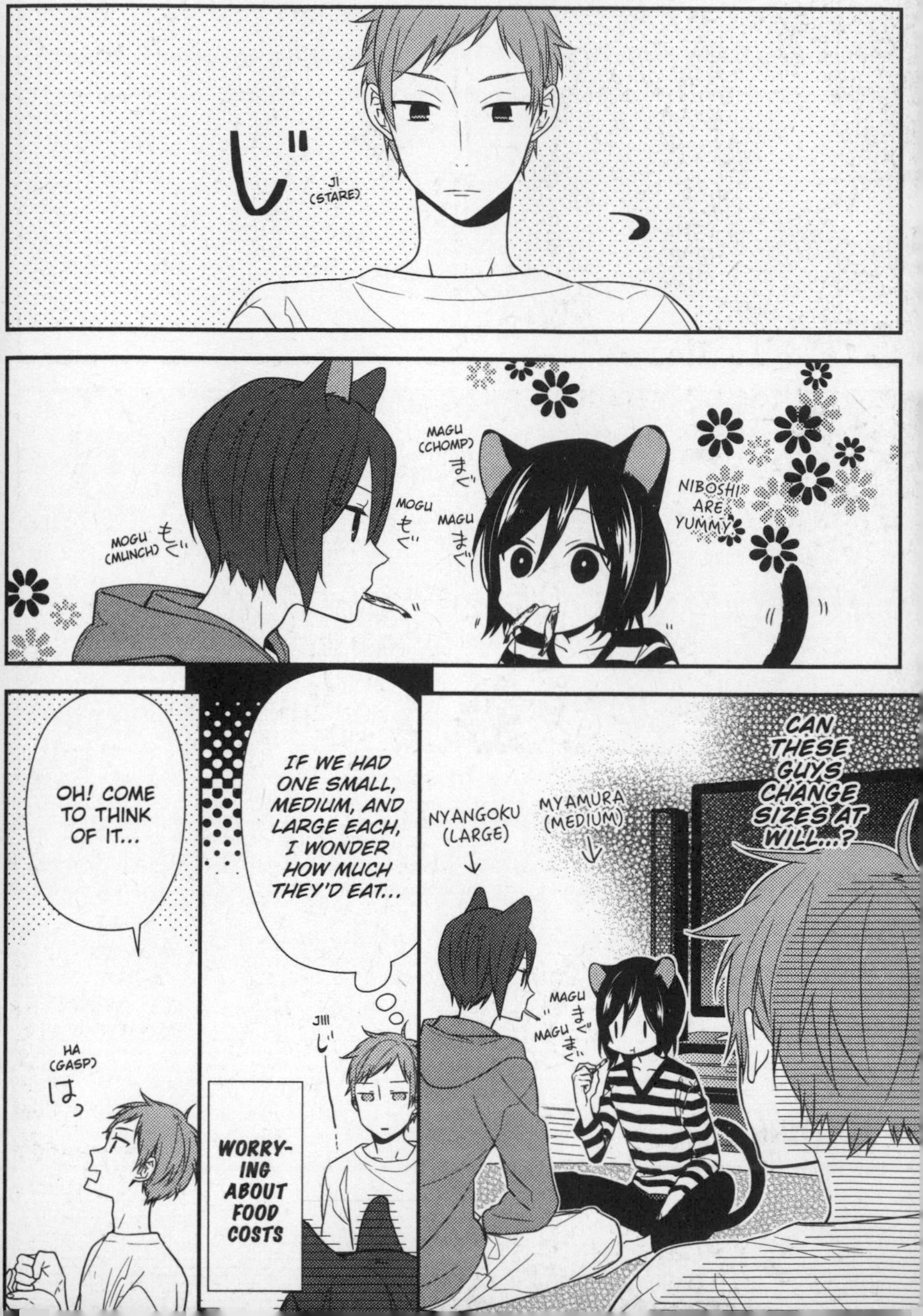

じ
JI (STARE)
NIBOSHI ARE YUMMY
MAGU (CHOMP) まぐ
MAGU まぐ
MOGU もぐ
MOGU (MUNCH) もぐ
CAN THESE GUYS CHANGE SIZES AT WILL...?
MYAMURA (MEDIUM)
NYANGOKU (LARGE)
MAGU まぐ
MAGU まぐ
IF WE HAD ONE SMALL, MEDIUM, AND LARGE EACH, I WONDER HOW MUCH THEY'D EAT...
JIII じ
WORRYING ABOUT FOOD COSTS
OH! COME TO THINK OF IT...
HA (GASP) はっ

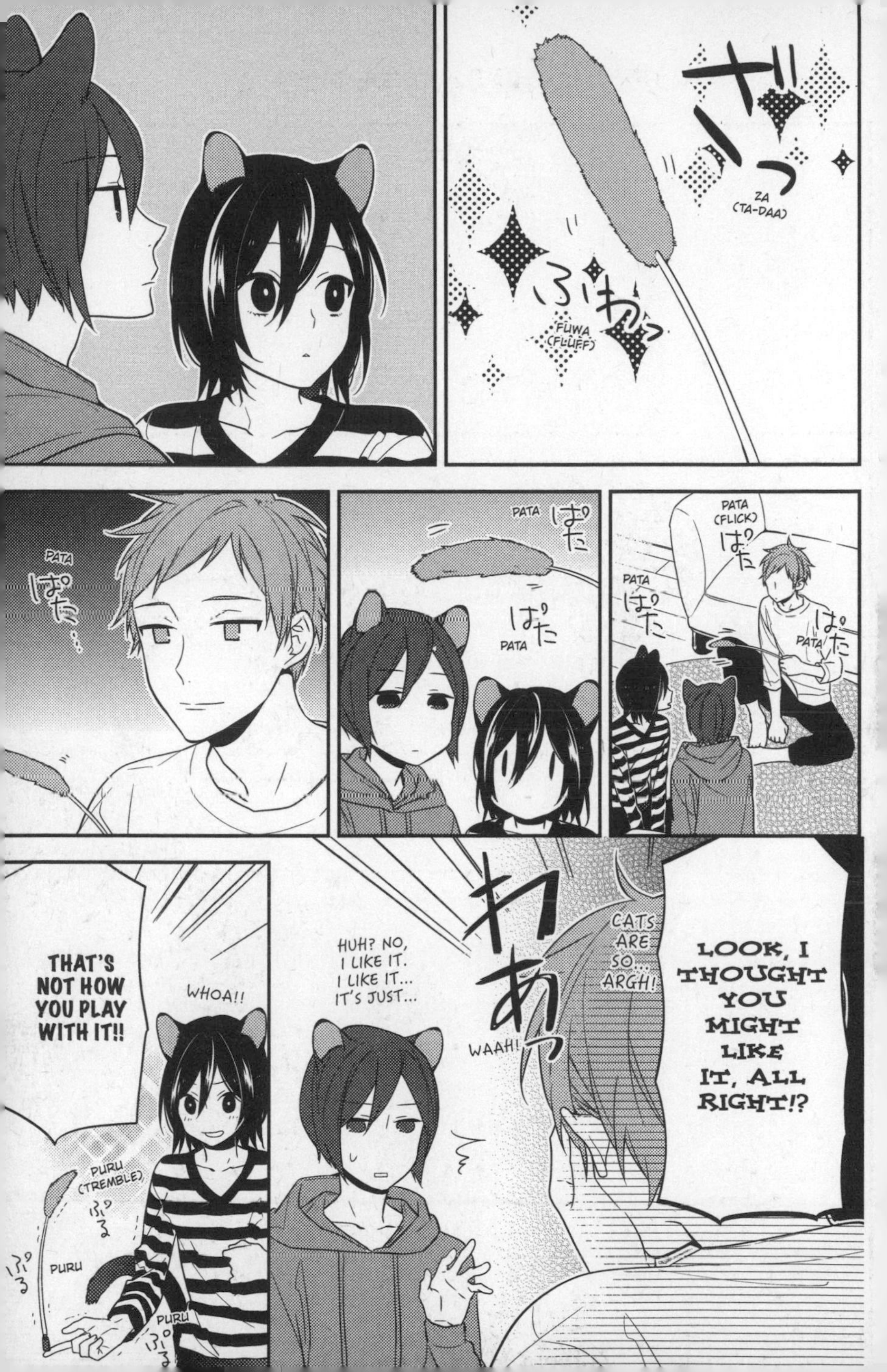
ざっ
ZA (TA-DAA)
ふわっ
FUWA (FLUFF)
PATA (FLICK)
ぱた
PATA
ぱた
PATA
ぱた
PATA
ぱた
ぱた
PATA
PATA
ぱた…
LOOK, I THOUGHT YOU MIGHT LIKE IT, ALL RIGHT!?
CATS ARE SO... ARGH!
わあっ
WAAH!
HUH? NO, I LIKE IT. I LIKE IT... IT'S JUST...
WHOA!!
THAT'S NOT HOW YOU PLAY WITH IT!!
PURU (TREMBLE)
ぷる
PURU
ぷる
PURU
ぷる

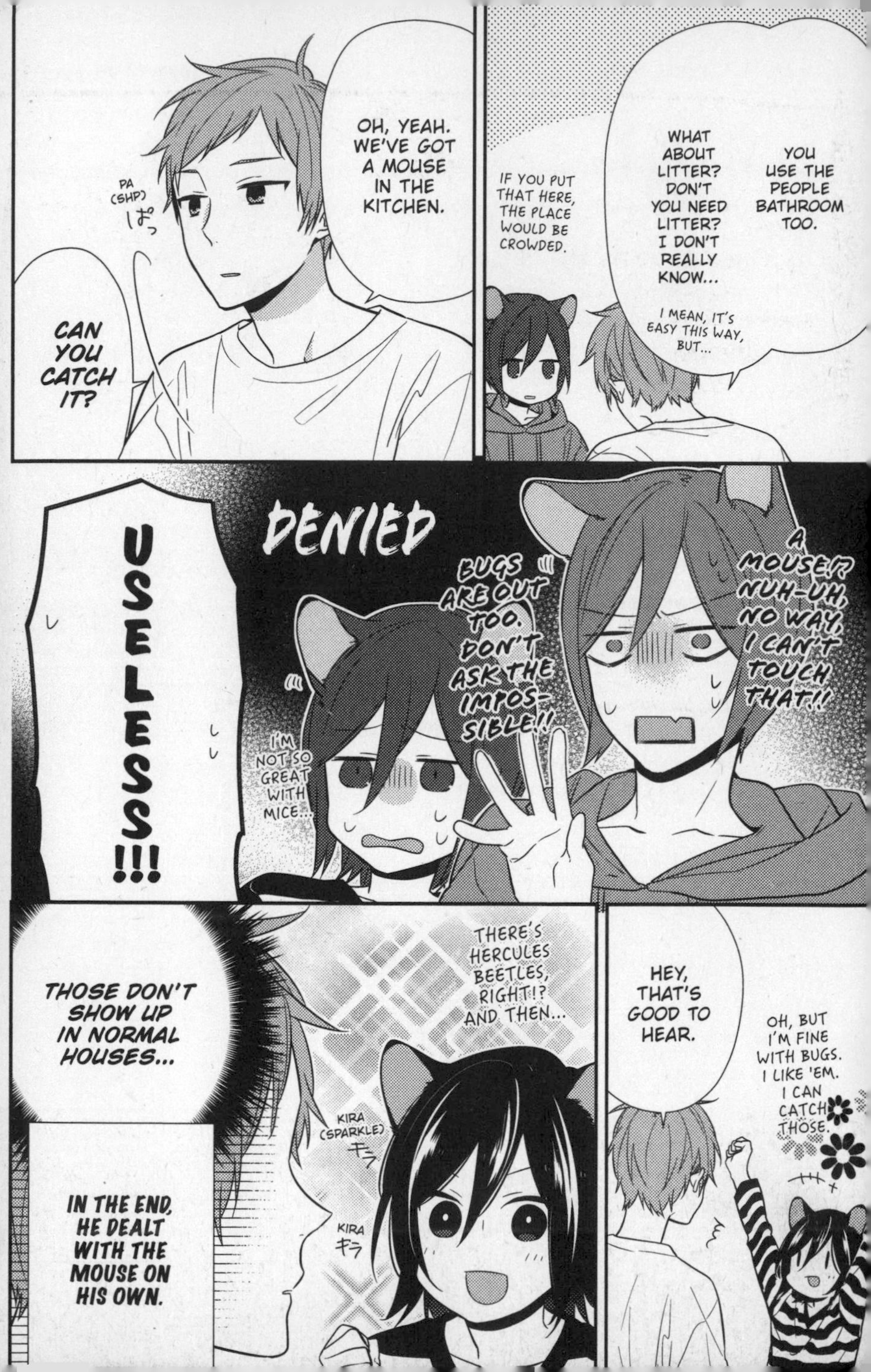
YOU USE THE PEOPLE BATHROOM TOO.
WHAT ABOUT LITTER? DON'T YOU NEED LITTER? I DON'T REALLY KNOW...
I MEAN, IT'S EASY THIS WAY, BUT...
IF YOU PUT THAT HERE, THE PLACE WOULD BE CROWDED.
OH, YEAH. WE'VE GOT A MOUSE IN THE KITCHEN.
PA (SHP) ぱっ
CAN YOU CATCH IT?
A MOUSE!? NUH-UH, NO WAY, I CAN'T TOUCH THAT!!
BUGS ARE OUT TOO. DON'T ASK THE IMPOSSIBLE!!
DENIED
I'M NOT SO GREAT WITH MICE...
USELESS!!!
HEY, THAT'S GOOD TO HEAR.
OH, BUT I'M FINE WITH BUGS. I LIKE 'EM. I CAN CATCH THOSE.
THERE'S HERCULES BEETLES, RIGHT!? AND THEN...
KIRA (SPARKLE) キラ
KIRA キラ
THOSE DON'T SHOW UP IN NORMAL HOUSES...
IN THE END, HE DEALT WITH THE MOUSE ON HIS OWN.

☆STAFF☆

☆ ORIGINAL WORKS ☆
HERO-sama
"HORI-SAN AND MIYAMURA-KUN"

☆ ASSISTANT WORKS ☆
Yossan

☆ EDITOR ☆
Ishikawa-sama

You have my eternal thanks...!!

☆SPECIAL THANKs

To my family, my friends, the editorial department, everyone involved with this story, and everyone who picked up this book— Thank you!!

AFTERWORD.

Safe!? Out!? My heart was pounding as I drew. I thought it would jump right out of my mouth. I'm just glad I didn't barf. I kept thinking, "I hope I get to put in the relationships between the kids around Hori-san and Miyamura-kun, not just theirs..." I hope you'll continue to follow Hori-san and the rest through their youth. Thank you for reading this bit too!!

HORIMIYA VOLUME 7 IS OUT IN APRIL 2017!!

HERO × Daisuke Hagiwara

Translation: Taylor Engel
Lettering: Alexis Eckerman

HORIMIYA vol. 6
© HERO • OOZ
© 2014 Daisuke Hagiwara / SQUARE ENIX CO., LTD. First published in Japan in 2014 by SQUARE ENIX CO., LTD. English translation rights arranged with SQUARE ENIX CO., LTD. and Yen Press, LLC through Tuttle-Mori Agency, Inc.

English translation © 2017 by SQUARE ENIX CO., LTD.

Yen Press
1290 Avenue of the Americas
New York, NY 10104

Visit us at yenpress.com • facebook.com/yenpress •
twitter.com/yenpress • yenpress.tumblr.com •
instagram.com/yenpress

First Yen Press Edition: January 2017

Yen Press is an imprint of Yen Press, LLC.
The Yen Press name and logo are trademarks
of Yen Press, LLC.

The publisher is not responsible for websites
(or their content) that are not owned by the
publisher.

Library of Congress Control Number:
2015960115

ISBNs: 978-0-316-27013-7 (paperback)
978-0-316-35673-2 (ebook)

10 9 8 7 6 5 4

WOR

Printed in the United States of America